Tort

BUTTERWORTHS CORE TEXT SERIES

Tort

Steve Hedley MA, LLB
Fellow in Law, Christ's College, Cambridge

Butterworths
London, Edinburgh, Dublin
1998

United Kingdom	Butterworths, a Division of Reed Elsevier (UK) Ltd, Halsbury House, 35 Chancery Lane, LONDON WC2A 1EL and 4 Hill Street, EDINBURGH EH2 3JZ
Australia	Butterworths, a Division of Reed International Books Australia Pty Ltd, CHATSWOOD, New South Wales
Canada	Butterworths Canada Ltd, MARKHAM, Ontario
Hong Kong	Butterworths Asia (Hong Kong), HONG KONG
India	Butterworths India, NEW DELHI
Ireland	Butterworth (Ireland) Ltd, DUBLIN
Malaysia	Malayan Law Journal Sdn Bhd, KUALA LUMPUR
New Zealand	Butterworths of New Zealand Ltd, WELLINGTON
Singapore	Butterworths Asia, SINGAPORE
South Africa	Butterworths Publishers (Pty) Ltd, DURBAN
USA	Lexis Law Publishing, CHARLOTTESVILLE, Virginia

© Reed Elsevier (UK) Ltd 1998

A CIP Catalogue record for this book is available from the British Library.

ISBN 0 406 03314 5

Printed and bound by Mackays of Chatham plc, Chatham, Kent

Visit us at our website: http://www.butterworths.co.uk

Preface

I have attempted in this book to provide a brief summary of the principles of Tort, with proper attention also to the policy basis of the law. Inevitably, I have simplified somewhat; a book of this size cannot be a substitute for a full treatise. Nonetheless, I hope that it will be of some use to students of the area. Overall, I have done my best not simply to state what the law is, but to give some sense of *why* it is, and what its significance is.

I have attempted to state the law as at 1 January 1998, though a small amount of later case material is included.

Two people deserve particular thanks for help and encouragement in the production of this book. Nicky Padfield had the original idea for this series, and has given support and assistance throughout; the simple truth is that this book would not have been written but for her, and for this I am grateful. Thanks are also due to Lynette Costello, for different but equally compelling reasons.

This book is dedicated to the memory of my grandfather, Wilfrid Joyce.

Steve Hedley
30 April 1998

Contents

→ CONTENTS ←

Table of statutes

References in the right hand column are to paragraph number. Where a paragraph number is in **bold** this indicates that the Statute is set out in part or in full.

List of cases

Cases are listed under the name of the accused whenever the usual method of citation would cause them to be preceded by the abbreviation 'R v' signifying that the prosecution was undertaken by the Crown.

CHAPTER ONE

What is tort?

SUMMARY
The law of tort provides remedies in a wide variety of situations. Overall it has a rather tangled appearance. But there is some underlying order. This chapter tries to explain some of that order. It also reviews the main functions of the law of tort. These include deterring unsafe behaviour, giving a just response to wrongdoing, and spreading the cost of accidents broadly. The chapter then introduces two major institutions within the law of tort: the tort of negligence and the role played by statute law.

Introduction

Tort: part of the law of civil wrongs

1.1 Where P sues D for a tort, P is complaining of a wrong suffered at D's hands. The remedy P is claiming is usually a money payment. So proceedings in tort are different from criminal proceedings: in a criminal court, typically, it is not the *victim* of the wrong who starts the proceedings, but some official prosecutor. The remedy will also be different. A criminal court *may* decide that D should pay a sum of money, but if it does, the money will usually be forfeited to the state, rather than to P. (For this reason, some say that tort is about *compensating* P, whereas the criminal law is about *punishing* D. But as you will see, this begs various questions about what 'punishment' means; we will soon return to this issue.) This is the most basic defining feature of tort. It is a civil, not a criminal, action. The claim is pursued in a civil court, and civil procedure is very different from criminal procedure. The initiative in beginning the action, and many decisions as to the conduct of the action, lie with P; whereas in criminal proceedings, P's role is at most that of a mere witness.

(It is not *quite* that simple. Criminal courts can sometimes award compensation to the victims of crime – about 100,000 compensation orders are made in any one year. And in theory, though only very rarely in practice, the victim of a crime may prosecute, rather than leaving it up to officials. But as a broad picture this is substantially accurate. Very often, civil and criminal proceedings are taken over the same wrong.)

Tort is not the whole of the law of civil wrongs

1.2   The remedies available in tort are only part of the large array of remedies available in different situations. Tort represents a diverse and (at first sight) almost random selection of this wider whole. P's complaint may be that D injured P's reputation ('defamation': **8.1**). Or P may be complaining about trespass to P's land (**7.2**), or interference with P's enjoyment of it ('nuisance': **7.5**). A wide variety of careless behaviour threatening P's interests is caught by the tort of 'negligence' (**1.22**). And D may be liable for some source of danger over which D has or ought to have some control, such as D's animals (**7.44**). Or D may be held responsible for the acts of others, particularly D's own employees (**9.2**).

Tort is, then, a radically miscellaneous subject. Can we impose some sort of order on this jumble?

Q.   Are there common themes running through all the various torts?

A.   Yes, and they are sufficiently coherent to give an overall picture of the way tort works. But these themes cannot be pushed too far, and certainly cannot be used to resolve problems in concrete situations.

A whole view of tort

Types of misconduct

1.3   In all tort cases, P is making some sort of complaint about misconduct, either D's misconduct or misconduct for which D is responsible in law. But the type of misconduct varies. In some situations, D must have had an *intention* to harm P before liability can be established. In others, it is enough if D was *negligent* (roughly, careless). In others still, D is subject to *strict liability*, which means that the criterion for liability is harsher than negligence. (Some writers use 'strict liability' to mean that the standard by which D is judged is harsher than 'negligence' but still recognisably a fault criterion, and 'absolute liability' to refer to standards which have nothing to do with fault. But this distinction is very hard to apply in practice.)

So there is a range of different types of wrongdoing, and which type is relevant must depend on the context. However, it is also important to remember that these various types of fault represent a smooth continuum, rather than entirely separate entities.

- 'Intention' is defined differently in different contexts. So a mugger who injures his victims would unquestionably be said to 'intend' harm for the purposes of the tort of battery (2.1). But it is more difficult to say whether an entrepreneur who sets out to ruin a competitor 'intends' harm to that competitor for the purposes of the economic torts – even though the loss is equally deliberate (6.18).

- The courts sometimes talk of a requirement of 'malice' in relation to some torts. This sometimes means the same as intent to harm, but sometimes something narrower, such as personal spite against the victim, and sometimes something broader (see 8.30). In legal contexts, it is wise never to use the word 'malice' unless you can say precisely what you mean by the expression.

- 'Negligence' is a useful word, and means roughly that D has been clumsy in such a way as to threaten P's legitimate interests. But it is a word to be used carefully, for it runs together two different questions: whether D needs to look out for P's interests *at all* and, if so, *how* careful D must be. The first question is often rephrased as asking whether D owes P a *duty of care*, and the second as to the *standard of care* required (1.32). It often happens that D owes a similar duty to P1 and P2, but the standard is quite different. For example, if D conducts dangerous activities on his or her premises and injures P as a result, the level of duty depends on whether P was on the premises or off, and if on, whether P was a trespasser or a lawful visitor.

- 'Strict liability' can arise in a variety of circumstances, each with their own peculiarities. It is, however, very rare indeed to find an example of strict liability which has no element of 'negligence' in it somewhere.

3

For example, liability for defective products is in theory strict, but a manufacturer is often able to escape liability by proving that all due care was taken (**4.2**).

This classification by type of wrongdoing has its uses, particularly in emphasising the range of different types of conduct with which we are concerned. But in itself it only begins to unlock the secrets of the area.

Types of injury

1.4 Can we get any further by asking about the injury to P? The injury can take many forms: injury to or interference with P's property or P's body; injury to P's economic interests; or injury to P's reputation. This is a useful approach, though following it through brings to the fore the patchwork nature of tort and how little some parts of it have in common with others:

- *Interests in land* are well protected by the law of tort, whether against deliberate intrusions ('trespass': **7.2**), careless damage ('negligence': **5.1**) or interference with P's right to enjoy it ('nuisance': **7.11**). The law of real property is of course a distinct subject in itself, and very often it is purely arbitrary which doctrines are treated as part of tort and which as part of property.

- *Interests in other forms of property* are protected up to a point by the law of tort. So deliberate taking of tangible property is caught by the tort of conversion, and careless damage by the tort of negligence (**5.1**). But the law of tort has far more to say on some forms of property than others. It has next to nothing to say on (for example) shares or financial assets. This makes little twentieth-century sense, given the importance of these financial assets; the reasons are historical.

- *P's interest in his or her own bodily integrity* is well protected by the law of tort, and accounts for the overwhelming majority of actions actually brought. P is protected from deliberate injury by the torts of assault and battery (**2.1**), from careless injury by the tort of negligence (**3.1**), and from many other dangers by the tort of breach of statutory duty (**1.42**). But this system of liability makes little sense on its own. It can only be properly assessed in the context of health and safety law, pensions and social security law, and the various ways in which tort liability in this area has been encouraged. The explosion of liability in this area, so surprising in historical terms, was no accident, but a deliberate object of official policy (**3.14**).

• *Economic interests*, by contrast, are only patchily protected by tort law. The protection, such as it is, is against either deliberate harm (**6.1**) or negligent harm (**5.1**). This is a confused and rapidly developing area.

• *Reputation* is protected by tort through 'defamation' (**8.1**). This is one of the more ancient torts, and the manner in which it protects reputation, and the associated costs, ensures that it is a matter of repeated and bitter controversy (**8.43**).

Combining the approaches

1.5   These approaches to tort may be combined in a single diagram, giving a map of most of tort (see Figure 1 on p 6).

How useful is such a diagram? That rather depends what problem you are trying to solve. As a way of seeing, roughly, what sort of topics tort covers, then it has its uses. Again, if you are trying to answer a practical problem in tort, you can use it to work out, roughly, which area of tort law you should be considering. But it would be hopeless as, say, a guide to how the courts or Parliament are likely to develop the law in the future. If, for example, a right to privacy were introduced, with breach of privacy being a new tort (see **2.16**), where would *that* fit? It would have elements of protection of property, also of reputation, also of protection of bodily integrity. Or again, it is clear that the tort of negligence extends across many of the different boxes of the diagram. So when is it appropriate to speak of 'negligence' as a single entity, and when is it best to divide it up by context? You should be in a position to answer that question for yourself by the end of your tort course, but there is no very neat answer that can be given at the beginning.

Does tort form a unity?

1.6   As the various torts are all so very different, so much so that it requires considerable mental effort to see any kind of overall pattern at all, why is tort regarded as a subject at all? Certainly the fact that the

	INTENTION TO HARM (OR 'MALICE')	LACK OF CARE	STRICT LIABILITY
LAND	Trespass to land (7.2)	Negligence /nuisance (7.11)	*Rylands v Fletcher* and liability for fire (7.34)
CHATTELS	Trespass to goods	Negligence (5.1)	Specific statutes eg Animals Act 1971 (7.44)
BODILY SAFETY AND SECURITY	Assault and battery (2.1), false imprisonment (2.11)	Negligence (3.1, 4.1)	'Breach of statutory duty' (1.42)
ECONOMIC INTERESTS GENERALLY	Economic torts (6.1)	Negligence (5.1)	Specific statutes eg Financial Services Act 1986
REPUTATION	Defamation in cases of qualified privilege (8.30), malicious falsehood (8.42)	'Unintentional defamation' (8.25), Negligence (8.42)	Defamation (8.1)

professional bodies require entrants to study 'tort', and the general conservatism that make lawyers stick with the concepts they are familiar with, do much to maintain 'tort' as it is. But is that all? If a cynic were to say that 'tort' only exists because examination regulations say that it does, would this be right? There is, after all, no such creature as a 'tort practitioner'. There are general civil practitioners and there are personal injury specialists, and many others who use particular torts on a regular basis. But 'tort' itself seems to make little sense in legal professional terms. Does it make sense in teaching terms, or theoretical terms?

The idea that there is a coherent law of tort, based on a single principle of liability for loss wrongfully caused, was first taken seriously in academic writings in the inter-War period, especially by Winfield's *Tort* (1937). This text did much to promote the ideas that tort (not 'torts') was a real subject, rather than a mixture of legal odds and ends. Winfield's view was controversial, and even he does not seem to have thought that tort approached the internal rigour achieved by the law of contract. But by building models into which all the case law fitted, but which was never meant to include much statute, the eventual obsolescence of his scheme was assured. To ignore statute today is to confine yourself to marginalia.

Much that has happened since 1960 has complicated Winfield's neat picture of a unified law of tort. The growth of the tort of negligence, very much along the unitary lines which Winfield envisaged, has come to dominate the textbooks and (by its sheer bulk and practical importance) to force the other torts into relative obscurity. The student's study of negligence alone now accounts for easily half of the tort course, and whatever may be said of the other torts' internal coherence, the tort of negligence is at least fairly easy to treat systematically. Further, the courts are beginning to come to terms with the relationship between statute and tort, and this too brings in a unifying element. All in all, the cause of tort as a tolerably coherent discipline is stronger today that it has been for the past 50 years.

In any event, while tort up to a point consists of odds and ends, they are for the most part *useful* odds and ends. This is no backwater of the law. Tort, then, seems in no immediate danger of extinction, its ramshackle nature notwithstanding.

How uncertain is tort?

1.7 It is easy to imagine the frustration of many students with tort, on finding many seemingly fundamental questions answered with a 'Don't know', or given different answers by different writers. But this must be kept in perspective. Many questions in the law of tort have not received a firm answer precisely because they are *un*important. The question of whether breach of confidence is 'really' a tort, for example, hardly matters to practitioners; so long as the subject is written up in some readily-accessible text, it hardly matters whether that text has 'tort' on its spine, or not. There is a certain amount of looseness in the law – given the wide variety of situations it applies to, this can hardly be avoided. But there is sufficient practical certainty for practitioners to settle nearly all cases by agreement, only a tiny proportion being sent to trial for a judge to decide on. There are certainly some areas of fundamental obscurity and hideous complexity – recovery of purely economic losses (**5.27**) being the most obvious example – but that very obscurity reflects the rarity of such cases. Marginality breeds doubt. So while student confusion at many aspects of tort is understandable, it does not point to a legal system in chaos. At most, it indicates that academic concerns are not always identical with professional concerns – which should not surprise or worry anyone. Many view the loose and open-ended nature of tort as a strength rather than a weakness: it permits the law to adapt to new needs without excessive strain. At least by the end of your course, and possibly before, I imagine that you will have a view on whether this is plausible or not!

Overlap with other heads of civil liability

1.8 This book has no systematic treatment of the other heads of liability which run parallel with tort, but there will be many references to them throughout. It was at one time thought that tort could be rigorously separated from *breach of contract*, but while academics are still divided on how far it is still possible to do so, a complete division is hard to maintain. Indeed, the impossibility of doing so absolutely is almost a cliché in modern legal writing. Tort has traditionally been wary of imposing a duty in areas where contract usually governs, but this tradition appears to be on its last legs; it will later be necessary to ask whether there is any life left in it at all (**5.45**). What of other areas of the civil law? The only cast-iron distinction that can be made between tortious duties of care and *fiduciary duties* is a historical one: before 1875, these duties were applied by quite different courts, applying very different principles. Over a century on, however, it may perhaps make sense to amalgamate the two (**5.43**). The difference between tort and *restitution* is rather more obvious, but even there there is a certain area of overlap (**10.10, 10.20**). Some writers would amalgamate all these various heads of liability, including tort, into a single unitary '*law of obligations*', though it has to be said that this monster unit would be a little inconvenient for teaching purposes. This book, then, will consider tort alone: but there will be constant references to tort's neighbours.

Fundamentals of the law of tort

How is tort paid for?

1.9 It is said that in some Victorian households, piano legs were covered in drapes, as they otherwise seemed too indecently suggestive. Until very recently, a similar reticence hung about the financing of tort. Issues such as insurance and funding of tort actions were rarely discussed publicly, either in the law reports or in academic articles. Academics and judges pretended that the law of tort floated freely, with no need for support. This was always nonsense, of course, and is today acknowledged as such. It is obvious that running the tort system involves substantial costs. Further, the law itself is profoundly influenced by the way those costs are distributed. And arguments about how these costs should be distributed cannot be separated from arguments over what the law should be. It is no longer possible to have an adequate knowledge of tort law, then, without some understanding of what tort is for and how the cost of the system is met.

The need for a substantial defendant

1.10 There is usually little point in securing a legal judgment against D unless D has the means to meet it. Yet whether P's injuries were inflicted by someone rich or someone poor will often be a matter of chance. P may often get help from the doctrine of *vicarious liability*, under which D's employer may be liable for torts which D committed in the course of D's employment (**9.2**), so the real defendant in that case may be a substantial company. Or again, P may find that D has taken out liability insurance, that is, D has paid premiums to an insurance company, so that the insurers will themselves fight any action brought against D, and pay the damages if they lose.

It might be asked why anyone would ever take out liability insurance, given that without it the prospect of legal action may be remote. The answer is partly that many people insure against remote risks; also that liability insurance sometimes comes as an incidental part of a wider package (as part of a mortgage arrangement, for example); and finally (most importantly in practice) because the law often *requires* D to have such insurance. So both in the case of drivers (**4.12**) and employers (**4.32**), the law insists not only that those who create dangers must be responsible for them in tort, but also that they pay premiums to ensure that they can meet those liabilities if they materialise.

Consider every possible plaintiff and defendant In many tort exam problems, it may seem that D either is unlikely to have money, or P is unlikely to sue him. You might find yourself saying, for example, 'Surely a two-year old child wouldn't sue her own parents? And anyway, how would she instruct a solicitor?' This shows commendable attention to practicalities, but the examiner is testing your knowledge of *tort*, not of the legal system generally. Perhaps the parents are insured. Perhaps they have just won the lottery. Perhaps demonstrating that they are liable is a step on the way to showing that *someone else* is liable. And it most certainly *is* possible for a two-year old to start a tort action, though for the detail you should study civil procedure as well as tort. Besides, P may be a good deal older by the time the proceedings are started (eg *Surtees v Kingston-on-Thames Borough Council* (1991)). As a general rule *assume that any individual named in a tort problem can sue and be sued, however implausible it may seem to you now.*

The need for a plaintiff

1.11 It cannot be assumed that every potential plaintiff is aware of the possibility of legal action, or that they would want to sue if they knew they could. An authoritative survey of people involved in accidents found that only 14% went so far as to consult a solicitor. Very often P has access to alternative remedies or benefits, such as insurance, that lessen the incentive to sue. The costs of litigation are unpredictable, and can be quite large, thus deterring possible plaintiffs. Civil legal aid makes the legal system accessible to many, but is a victim of its own success. The high take-up rate has increased the cost to government, which has responded by reducing availability. A plaintiff not already down to benefit levels is unlikely today to gain much support from the legal aid fund, and abolition of the entire system of civil legal aid is currently being mooted. Some plaintiffs have a private entitlement to legal advice: for example, many trade unions offer free legal advice as one benefit to their members, and some forms of insurance carry similar benefits. But for many, legal action remains either unavailable or uncongenial. It remains to be seen what impact the new conditional fee ('no win, no fee') arrangements will have on accessibility of remedies.

The purposes of tort

1.12 Not everyone is agreed on the precise purpose of tort law, or indeed that every part of it *does* serve a useful purpose. But there seems to be virtual unanimity on the sorts of objects such a system must serve if it is to be useful – though terminology and emphasis vary considerably. First, the fact that injured people can sue can *deter* people from harming one another in the first place. Second, it can serve as a *fair and just response* to the infliction of harm: justice may demand that if D injures P, then D should pay compensation to P. Third, it can provide a means of *loss-spreading*: regardless of the rights and wrongs of the injury, tort might provide a conduit for distributing P's loss over the entire community, rather than making P bear the whole. From this third point of view, the objectives of the tort system are not so very different from those of (say) pensions law or social security law.

It should be clear now why I hesitated above (1.1) to distinguish tort from crime by saying that the law *punishes* crimes, whereas it *compensates for* torts. The objects of the law of tort are not so very different from those of the criminal law, and handing D a large bill as a result of D's own wrongful behaviour *is* a punishment in one sense, whatever else it may be. But there is always controversy over what the objects of tort should be and over how closely the actual law complies with them. Moreover, the three broad goals (deterrence, just response, loss-spreading) are not always compatible with one another. It would be very much a mistake to assume that there is unanimity on these questions – or even that most of the contributors to the debate are clear in their own minds what they want from the law.

Deterrence

General considerations

1.13   It is obvious that tort often has a deterrent effect. It is not merely that individual awards make defendants anxious not to repeat the experience. It is also that a general awareness that awards are possible encourages care to avoid injuring potential plaintiffs. Awareness amongst publishers of defamation law (**8.1**), and amongst unions of the economic torts (**6.1**) is high and, up to a point, this is true of occupiers of premises, and employers, in respect of the law of negligence (**4.15**, **4.32**). But arguments as to the size of the deterrent effect, or as to whether it is too small or too great, quickly run into impossible questions of quantification. Does the law on employers' liability really make employers more careful, or is the legal system too slow and too random to drive home the connection between employer carelessness and awards against them? Does the law over-deter surgeons, leading to 'defensive medicine', or is 'defensive medicine' a myth? There are no simple or uncontroversial answers to these questions.

Attention to context

1.14   There are a number of questions we need to ask before we can hope to determine how great the deterrent effect of tort is in any one situation:

- *Is it clear what D is being deterred from?*   For example, is the tort of negligence's general command to be 'reasonably careful' sufficiently definite? Or should it be more specific?

- *Are victims of D's actions able and willing to sue?*   Or can the major perpetrators only be caught by establishing a central agency to conduct prosecutions where necessary? Clearly, a system of deterrence based on tort alone is biased towards the interests of the rich and knowledgeable, who are best able to set the law of tort in motion.

- *Does D carry liability insurance?*   In this respect, the 'deterrence' object is straightforwardly opposed to the 'loss-spreading' objective: D may be powerfully deterred by the prospect of a liability greater than D's assets, but if that liability materialises then D will be unable to compensate P fully. Of course, D's insurer may in some cases pressure D to act more carefully, but this effect is in most situations rather a weak one.

The law-and-economics approach

1.15 The deterrence approach is pushed to its greatest level of sophistication by the proponents of law-and-economics. They assume that economic actors themselves weigh up the costs and benefits of their possible actions and choose the course of action which brings the maximum aggregate benefit. The lawyer-economists argue that it is unnecessary for the law to do so as well. Rather, the law should make sure that the full costs and benefits to society are reflected in the decisions of certain crucial economic actors. We cannot, for example, turn manufacturers into altruists, but by ensuring that the costs resulting from unsafe products fall on them, we give them an incentive in that direction.

Absolute safety is not the lawyer-economists' aim. Rather, they aim for *efficiency* in spending on safety. That is, if spending £1 more on safety would produce more than £1 in benefits for society, then the law should give incentives to spend that £1, but not if the benefits would be less. A full survey of the various different approaches within law-and-economics would take far more space than is available here, and there are many different views. Like the language of tort, the language of law-and-economics is a medium for arguing, not a determinate set of clear prescriptions.

Criticisms of the law-and-economics approach

1.16 Criticisms of the law-and-economics approach have been many, some attempting to modify it, others to dismiss it outright. The assumption that economic actors are motivated solely by a wish to boost their wealth (even if including their 'psychic wealth', however defined), is at best a loose approximation to reality. There is much debate about how useful an approximation it is. It is hard to put a value on human health and safety; arguments over this are necessarily imprecise, and may be incapable of practical resolution. The viability of tort as a means for bringing all societal costs to bear on those who create them must be doubted, given the many barriers between a plaintiff and a court which can adjudicate the issue.

In any event, the incentive so created is an incentive to reduce the costs involved in litigation, and so involves an incentive to hide information and to delay and frustrate awards.

Do we really *want* to encourage cost-benefit calculations by potential defendants? In one notorious US case, employees of the Ford Motor Corporation noticed a fundamental design defect in their new 'Pinto' model: due to the placing of the fuel tank, when rear-ended this car would have a high propensity to explode. Calculating that the total cost of a re-design would exceed their total legal costs if sued over the inevitable deaths, they deliberately left the design untouched (*Ford Motor Co v Durrill* (1986)). This was thought disgraceful behaviour by the Texas court, meriting an award of punitive damages. Yet is this not precisely the sort of calculation the lawyer-economists seek to encourage? We can hardly complain merely that a decision on the costs and benefits of safety was actually made. Someone had to make it. If the corporation's assessment of the costs was wrong, that may only emphasise what a feeble reed the economists' assumption of economic rationality is. Right or wrong, the economic approach to law certainly brings to the fore some awkward questions.

Tort as a just response to wrongdoing

1.17   On this view, D must compensate P because that is what justice demands. This is the traditional justification of tort. While it is often side-lined in academic discussions, it is probably what the courts think they are doing most of the time, and certainly what the press think they ought to be doing. Yet many features of tort jar with this conception:

- *Tort ignores many factors crucial to a moral view of whether D should compensate P.* A notable example is in respect of partial liability: generally speaking D is either liable or not, with only the occasional concessions to degrees of fault (see **9.26, 11.17**). D's ability to pay is similarly irrelevant.

- *Assessment of damages does not depend on moral fault.* D tortiously injures P1 and P2, in both cases severely. P1 is a retired 70-year old, P2 an employed 30-year old with excellent promotion prospects. Morally, P1's case against D is no different from P2's. Yet P2's damages will almost certainly dwarf P1's, because P2's loss of income will be higher, and P2 will also need medical care for more years than P1. Does this disparity accord with morality? Not everyone thinks so.

- *Some of the duties imposed by tort are in fact **impossible** to comply with* – and this is so not merely in the case of the stricter forms of liability (eg **4.2**), but even sometimes in the tort of negligence (eg **3.9**). Can we really say that D is guilty of 'wrongdoing' when D could not in fact have done anything else? Some cases can be explained by a more sophisticated conception of wrongdoing – perhaps the 'wrongdoing' consisted of D's placing himself in a position where he or she would inevitably harm someone. But such refinements can take us very far indeed from any recognisable form of morality.

- *The identity of the defendant.* Having brought its vast resources and sophistication to bear on the question whether D was morally to blame, the law of tort then proceeds to impose liability on ... someone else, usually. It is rarely that the person actually at fault pays the bill. Either the liability is paid for by insurance, or by someone responsible for D under the doctrine of vicarious liability. Again, this is not *impossible* to justify in moral terms, but the arguments necessary to do so open up wide vistas of moral argument, without a conclusion in sight.

So an explanation of tort in terms of morality explains little in itself. No doubt we should correct a tort system which actively does injustice; but it is another question how much tort is improved by reflections on the meaning of justice. Moreover, on no view can tort be more than a small part of the law's response to injustice. Whatever it does only reveals its true significance when seen in the light of what else the law does in that area.

Tort as a device for loss-spreading

1.18 This final purpose seeks to ignore the precise cause of P's loss and to focus more on P's need which has resulted. The philosophy is that the moral rights and wrongs of D's infliction of the loss are beside the point – either way, P has suffered a loss which demands compensation of some kind – or that any retribution for D's wrong can be better dealt with by the criminal law. The person or organisation made to bear liability will therefore be the one best suited to pass on the loss to the wider community. Liability for defective products, for example, might be placed with the manu-facturers (**4.2**), who can increase their prices if the losses prove great.

This approach is plainly of more help in some areas than others. It would be vacuous in relation to (say) nuisance, where the 'harm' for which P seeks a remedy is P's loss of the right to use land when D uses land as D wishes. Generally, in relation to property, there are immense practical difficulties in the way of anything which would amount to a centrally-organised insurance scheme. In relation to personal injury, the idea has more to be said for it. But it has to be said that, considered as a system of insurance, tort is exceedingly inefficient. In the order of 50% of the sums circulating in the tort system end up paying for lawyers' fees and other overheads, as contrasted with perhaps 10%-15% in insurance schemes proper. If the law of tort is a loss-spreading device, it is an expensive and inefficient one.

Tort at war with itself

1.19 It will be obvious that no one policy objective explains the whole of tort. Consider the way the law of tort deals with road accidents (**4.12**). This has elements of a 'just response' solution: drivers are made liable for their negligence. However, it is, as we shall see, a fairly strange version of negligence: even learner drivers are considered to be 'negligent' for not having a depth of experience they never held themselves out as having acquired (**4.14**). There are elements of deterrence, too, but they are very indirect: the more dangerous drivers may perhaps have to pay higher premiums, the safer drivers may perhaps win a 'no-claims bonus'. But these seem feeble spurs indeed to safer driving. There are also aspects of loss-spreading: all drivers are compelled to contribute, via their insurance premiums, to a system of compensation for all victims of poor driving. But if that is the rationale of the system, do we really need the time-consuming and expensive enquiry into the cause of the accident? What purpose does it serve, from a loss-spreading point of view?

'The floodgates of litigation'

1.20 Up to a point, then, we can debate what purpose tort should rationally serve and how its rules might be modified to achieve useful ends. But most of the important decisions in tort cases are made by individual lawyers and their clients, with their own purposes in mind, and these decisions are hard to predict in advance, either individually or wholesale. It is common, for example, to argue for or against suggested changes on the ground that they will reduce or increase the amount of litigation. But such claims are very hard to substantiate, even in retrospect. No-one really knows, for example, how much effect on the legal system the new system of 'conditional fees' will have. How broadly will the government permit the use of 'conditional fees', and on what terms? Within the constraints set by government, by the Bar and by insurers, what terms will solicitors be able to offer potential clients? How many of those clients will find those terms preferable to their other alternatives? And if more litigation *does* result, what will be the effect of *that* – on government, on lawyers, on insurers? It is a mistake to assume that the tort system is rationally planned and systematically ordered. Many individuals, with vastly differing motives, each have an influence on it.

The role of the higher courts

1.21 Fashions and styles of judicial action change with bewildering rapidity. It is trite to say that the courts are only subordinate policy-makers and should have respect for Parliament's superior authority. Some deduce from this that the courts should do as little as possible that is innovative, leaving all major changes to Parliament's initiative. Others conclude the reverse, reasoning that *because* Parliament can put the judges right if they err, the courts should be bold where it seems that the law is improved by doing so. Willingness to refer to policy varies from time to time and from judge to judge. At the time of writing, the judges are pretty willing, by the standards of earlier decades, to innovate. Yet they still pay respect to Parliamentary policy. Respect for Parliament means checking that the innovation gels with whatever else Parliament has done in the area; it does *not* mean waiting for Parliament's explicit permission before doing anything at all. As for Parliament itself, reform of tort law is a highly technical matter, which does not usually arouse great passions, or command much Parliamentary time.

Negligence: an introduction

Preliminary

1.22 Much of this book is concerned with variations on the tort of negligence. How coherent is the tort of negligence? The tort of negligence covers a wide variety of situations. It is (perhaps inevitably) somewhat uneven as a result. But there is certainly a unitary *terminology*, and certain problems which crop up again and again in different contexts.

In general, if P wishes to establish negligence against D, P must demonstrate the following: *(i)* that D owed P a duty of care; *(ii)* that D broke this duty; and *(iii)* that this breach of duty caused loss to P. Further, *(iv)* there are various possible defences open to D. At this stage, I give a brief description of the law in general. The function of the following paragraphs is not so much to tell you what the law is, as to teach you the language you will need before you can understand an explanation of what the law is. The details of the law will appear in later chapters.

Vagueness A common complaint about texts on the tort of negligence is that the terminology used is too vague. One answer is that the texts are at least telling it like it is. The law *is* vague, and more precise renditions would be misleading. Indeed, the startling growth of the tort over the last few decades would have been difficult if the courts had been made to express themselves in a more limited and precise way. But it is *also* true that knowledge of how the law of negligence impacts on a particular situation involves not only general concepts, but also the case law for that particular area. This chapter should therefore be treated as introductory, before we come on to how the law applies in particular situations.

Duty

Basic concepts

1.23 The most famous statement about duty was made by Lord Atkin. This was in a case where P was seeking to show that D, the manufacturer of a soft drink, owed her a duty to make the drink reasonably safe. The drink had been bought for her by a friend in a restaurant. On pouring out the drink, her nostrils had been assaulted by a decaying snail in the drink bottle and (she alleged) she became ill as a result. In finding that a duty was owed, Lord Atkin said the following:

> The [Biblical] rule that you are to love your neighbour becomes in law, you must not injure your neighbour; and the lawyer's question, 'Who is my neighbour?' receives a restricted reply. You must take reasonable care

to avoid acts or omissions which you can reasonably foresee would be likely to injure your neighbour. Who then, in law, is my neighbour? The answer seems to be – persons who are so closely and directly affected by my act that I ought reasonably to have them in contemplation as being so affected when I am directing my mind to the acts or omissions which are called in question. (*Donoghue v Stevenson* [1932] AC 562, 580, Lord Atkin)

This is one of the most quoted passages of the whole law of tort. Its influence is not diminished because the facts of the case are obscure and unusual and the result overtaken by legislation (**4.2**). The idea that a duty is owed to those in D's 'reasonable contemplation' is a powerful one. Nonetheless, it has to be said immediately that the whole of the tort of negligence cannot be reduced to this one judicial *bon mot*. This is for a number of reasons:

- In any common situation, there will usually be far more precise rules, and the 'neighbour' principle is of no real help. It would be a mistake to cite the 'neighbour' *dictum* to support such settled duties as (for example) that owed by one road-user to another. It is only on novel questions that Atkin's *dictum* comes into its own.

- On no view did Atkin mention every relevant matter for determining a negligence claim. Some suggest that it is a strongly suggestive principle: that once P has shown that the 'neighbour' criterion is satisfied, it is for D to suggest reasons why it should not be applied (eg *Anns v London Borough of Merton* [1978] AC 728, 751-752; this is sometimes called Wilberforce's 'two-stage' test). Yet even this is far too enthusiastic an approach for others. Reasonable foresight is a necessary part of the test, but not nearly enough in itself (*Yuen Kun-Yeu v A-G for Hong Kong* [1987] 2 All ER 705, 710, Lord Keith). Others still deny that any general principle can resolve individual cases (*Caparo Industries plc v Dickman* [1990] 2 AC 605, 618, Lord Bridge). The differences here are really only differences of emphasis, but they are none the less profound for that.

- Negligence is not the whole of the law of tort. For example, if D openly vilifies P, very often D will foresee that P will come to harm through injury to reputation. Yet we would expect most such cases to be dealt with through the tort of defamation, not negligence. To what extent negligence will be allowed to intrude into other areas of law, be it other torts or entirely distinct areas, is often a controversial question. In *Donoghue v Stevenson*, the argument against liability (which convinced several judges), was precisely that P's claim intruded too much into the sphere of contract. It is never enough in those circumstances to stress that D and P are 'neighbours'; much more is required.

- 'Reasonable contemplation' is really a question of values rather than a factual question. There is no such individual as 'the reasonable person', and no one pretends otherwise. Atkin's *dictum* is not so much about what the courts will do, as the language they use in justifying what they do.

The type of loss

1.24 Atkin's neighbour *dictum* does not seem to distinguish between the various different types of loss P might suffer at D's hands. Yet the law of negligence undoubtedly does distinguish. For example, if it was foreseeable that Donoghue's health would suffer through the unwanted intrusion of a snail from Stevenson's factory, then surely it was equally or more foreseeable that she would lose a perfectly good ginger beer from it. So she might claim that, but for Stevenson's behaviour, she would have received good and wholesome ginger beer, whereas as it was she got a nauseous mess. Yet a claim for the cost of a replacement ginger beer would almost certainly fail. Most negligence claims are either for *personal injury* or for *damage to property*. A claim for a *pure economic loss* – that is, an economic loss other than personal injury or property damage – only rarely succeeds (**5.7**). Other forms of loss may simply not be recognised at all; for example, P cannot usually recover for grief or mental distress caused by D (though see **3.18**, **10.58**).

'Proximity' and 'remoteness'

1.25 Sometimes duty is discussed in terms of 'proximity'. This is a metaphor, but a simple one. If D wields an axe or some other dangerous tool, the people who are potentially in danger are those who are close by ('proximate'). People who are a long way away ('remote') are not in danger. So if a duty is owed by D, it is to people who are 'proximate' and not to those who are 'remote'. However, the case of the axe is a special case. The danger posed to Donoghue was nothing to do with her being *physically* proximate to Stevenson's factory; what put her in danger was, first, her taste for ginger beer and, second, Stevenson's opaque bottles, which prevented inspection of the ginger beer before it reached her. These factors put her in *causal* proximity to Stevenson. The physical distance between them was irrelevant. 'Proximity' is therefore a rather ambiguous term. It can mean closeness ('physical proximity'). It can mean causal closeness ('causal proximity'). Or it simply denotes legal duty: asking whether there is 'proximity' between P and D might simply be a way of asking whether D owes P a duty ('legal proximity'). Statements about 'proximity' can therefore usually be resolved into statements about foresight, or duty, or both. If 'proximity' means anything else, that additional sense seems hard to define and is therefore best avoided.

No liability for omissions?

1.26   Atkin's 'neighbour' *dictum* includes not simply acts of D which might injure P, but also omissions. Yet other authorities are keen to insist that there is no general liability for omissions: if D sees P drowning, D is usually under no legal duty to help P, however easy it would be to do so. Which view is right? There is truth in both viewpoints. It is certainly true that *once a duty has been established*, it makes no difference whether D breaks it by acts or by omissions. If D drives carelessly and injures P, it makes no difference whether D's mistake was over-enthusiasm with the accelerator, or reluctance to use the brake. Both negligent acts and negligent omissions attract liability. But if P is still seeking to establish that D owes a duty, D is usually in a strong position if D's activities do not in themselves pose a danger to P and P is complaining that D did not *prevent someone or something else* from harming P. A strong case is needed if P is to hold D responsible for another's misbehaviour. P can usually establish a positive duty to act only for very specific reasons, such as:

*   D controls premises, the condition of which endangers P (**4.15**);

*   P is a child and D has undertaken responsibility for P's safety (eg *Carmarthenshire County Council v Lewis* (1955));

*   An animal over which D had control, or ought to have had control, endangers P (**7.44**);

*   D creates a situation on the road where others are likely to come to harm (eg *Haley v London Electricity Board* (1965));

- D has promised P that D will take due care.

There will be much more to say about this below, but it will have to be said in individual contexts. In some contexts the judges do indeed say that there is no liability for omissions. In a spate of recent cases on the liability of fire services, the courts have said precisely that. Fire services are liable if they increased the risk of fire by turning off a sprinkler system (*Capital and Counties plc v Hampshire County Council* (1997)). But they are not liable for omissions, such as failing to spot smouldering debris (*John Munroe (Acrylics) Ltd v London Fire and Civil Defence Authority* (1997)) or failing to maintain fire hydrants (*Church of Jesus Christ of Latter Day Saints (GB) v West Yorkshire Fire and Civil Defence Authority* (1997)). In other contexts, the courts say that if D had (or should have had) control over some dangerous thing, then D has a positive duty to prevent it doing harm to P (**3.4**). In yet others, the courts say that if statute imposes a positive duty on D, then P may sue in negligence for breach of it (**1.41**). And in yet others they say that D will be under a positive duty to act if D promised to act responsibly: D is only under a duty because D has positively assumed that duty (**5.37**). So, overall, the position is very mixed. The courts are frequently cautious in imposing liability on those who have not done any positive wrongful act, but in some situations this is not an overriding consideration. (Some judges express this truth by saying that D is not liable for 'pure' omissions, but that a breach of a pre-existing legal duty on D prevents D from saying that the omission is 'pure'.)

No liability for others?

1.27 *Introduction* It is very often said that D is responsible only for what D has done and not for what others do. There is a kernel of truth in this, but it is a very small part of the truth. The doctrine of vicarious liability and other related notions (**9.1**) often make D liable for the wrongdoing of others. And where both D and some other party share responsibility for P's injury, P may sue either of those responsible. It is no answer to P's action against D that P *could* have sued someone else – although sometimes D may be able to claim contributions from the other guilty parties (**9.26**).

The kernel of truth in the 'no liability for others' rule is this: if all that D has done is to create a dangerous situation, and P is then hurt by deliberate human conduct, then there is a certain reluctance (to put it no higher) to hold D liable. This reluctance sometimes manifests itself through a denial of duty, and sometimes through the idea that the loss is 'too remote'. But it would be misleading to suggest that there is a blanket denial of liability whenever the conduct of others than D has intervened. Some examples may help.

1.28 *P's own conduct* It is a rare case where P successfully sues D for an injury which P did to himself or herself. It will usually involve a demonstration that P was incapable of looking after himself or herself, and some particular reason why D was under a duty to guard P. Typically P will be a child and D an adult with a duty to care for P. But action has occasionally succeeded even where P is an adult.

> *Kirkham v Greater Manchester Chief Constable* (1990) Kirkham, a depressed alcoholic with suicidal tendencies, committed suicide while being held on remand for criminal damage. The arresting officer had not passed on a warning of his dangerous condition, with the result that no special precautions had been taken and he was treated as an ordinary prisoner. It was held that the police were liable to Kirkham's widow for this failure.

A class of case where even fully responsible adults can recover is where P is a rescuer, who suffers injuries while rescuing others from a source of danger for which D is responsible. The courts tend to assume that 'danger invites rescue' and that it is no answer to P's claim that P could very easily have avoided the injury (**3.31**).

1.29 *Conduct of third parties* The courts have always been exceedingly reluctant to hold D liable for the bad behaviour of others, no matter how foreseeable. A highly significant ruling, which broke with this stance, was the path-breaking case of *Home Office v Dorset Yacht Co* (1970). Here, prisoners escaping from borstal destroyed P's property and P sued the Home Office, on the ground that but for their negligence there would have been no escape and no injury to P's interests. A majority of the House of Lords was prepared to find that P could sue. But it was made clear that liability was restricted to incidents which took place near the borstal itself; and later cases have not been eager to extend liability.

> *Smith v Littlewoods Organisation* (1987) Littlewoods bought a disused cinema, intending to redevelop the site as a supermarket. Vandals

broke into the site and started a fire, which spread to neighbouring properties, including Smith's. Held: Smith could not sue Littlewoods for failing to prevent this injury.

However, while the Lords in *Smith v Littlewoods* gave different reasons, all were clear that there was no absolute ban on liability and that D might sometimes come under a duty to guard against injury to P from third parties. For example, Lord Goff suggested that the case might have been different if Littlewoods had knowledge (or even *means* of knowledge) of the threat, or if they had created some unusual source of danger to others ([1987] AC 278).

No liability for statements?

1.30 It is simply untrue that there is no liability in negligence for misstatements, despite many *dicta* to the contrary. Words can and do cause a great deal of harm, and there is no particular reason why the courts should look on this harm with indifference. Moreover, it is often hard to draw the line between statements and acts. Nonetheless, it is understandable that liability for statements is restricted, for two reasons. First, in most cases the loss that is caused is a purely economic loss – and, as we shall see, the courts tend to take a restrictive attitude to losses of that sort (**5.7**). Second, where P suffers loss by relying on D's statement, we run into the courts' reluctance to make D liable for P's independent actions (**1.26**). So if D gives P bad investment advice, on which P relies and suffers loss, the courts are likely to say that investment is a risky business anyway, and P should carry the loss resulting from P's own investment decisions. So if P's case is that P suffered loss in relying on D's advice, P must be prepared for a rough ride from the courts and must be ready to meet the argument that P should take full responsibility for his or her own decisions.

Is 'duty' a necessary concept?

1.31 Not all writers in this area agree that it is useful to talk of 'duties of care' at all. After all, a 'duty of care' has no legal consequences until it is broken and it seems a fiction to say that a duty hangs over D's relations with others, waiting to turn into some type of legal liability. On this view, a judge who says that D owed P no duty at all must mean something like 'D is not liable here, nor would D ever be liable on facts like these'; and a judge who says that D owed P a duty but had not broken it must mean 'D is not liable here, but might have been if the facts had been slightly different'. Nonetheless, 'duty' is a common enough notion, and not everyone agrees it is dispensable in this context. There is no fiction involved in advising potential defendants before the event that they need to take care to avoid liability; nor is there anything unreal about the insurance policies many defendants take out against this risk. It is *also* true, however, that the courts sometimes find 'duties' after the fact, where one would hardly have suspected their existence before it.

Breach of duty

Introduction

1.32   Assuming that a duty is established, the next question is whether D has broken it. In other words, has D failed to come up to the standard required by the law for fulfilment of the duty and is in that sense at fault. Perfection is not required, only reasonable behaviour. It is commonly said that the standard of care required is an 'objective' one; and this is certainly true in one sense. The question is whether the *court* considers that D was at fault, not whether D personally considered his or her behaviour reasonable. But there are other notions buried in this idea of an 'objective' standard, and there will be more to say on this below (**3.9**).

Particularity of D's situation

1.33   The enquiry is into the reasonableness of D's behaviour in the particular circumstances in which D was placed. Accordingly, the court may be required to conduct an elaborate investigation into those precise circumstances. So one effect of this is that while past precedents have considerable value as containing general principles, there will always be *some* differences between any two cases, and there is usually little to be gained from discussions of differences and similarities. Individual cases should therefore not be treated as laying down precise rules for the level of duty in concrete situations, even if they purport to. A judge who has adhered to proper general principles will not be reversed on appeal simply for failure to follow apparently similar cases (*Qualcast (Wolverhampton) v Haynes* (1959)). A potential defendant who wishes to be told precisely what he or she must do to avoid the possibility of liability in the future is unlikely to receive a satisfactory answer.

Burden of proof

1.34 It is for P to prove that D broke the duty of care. The standard of proof is that of the balance of probabilities. That is, P must show that it is more likely than not that D was in breach. However, there is no rule that P must demonstrate *how* the accident happened, so long as P satisfies the burden of proof. Accordingly, P can sometimes argue that 'the facts speak for themselves' ('*res ipsa loquitur*'). This argument is that a mere recital of the facts so strongly suggests negligence that it is for D to suggest some alternative explanation. For example, if P is admitted to D's hospital for ingrown toenails but is discharged with an amputated arm, the court will probably hold that (practically if not technically) the burden of proof has shifted to D. And if P is hurt by a machine which was wholly under D's control, again it would be for D to explain what went wrong (eg *Scott v London and St Katherine Docks Co* (1865)). However, the maxim *res ipsa loquitur* has never developed into a doctrine of law, unlike the experience of other jurisdictions: it is an example of the application of normal principle, not an exception to it.

Relevant factors

1.35 Various factors are consistently mentioned as relevant to the question of whether D was in breach of duty:

- *Size of the risk and size of the threatened harm*   The greater the risk of injury to P, the more likely is the court to find D's conduct to be a breach of duty. Similarly, the greater the possible harm to P (and to others) from D's behaviour, the greater the chances of establishing liability.

- *Cost and practicability of precautions*   Even if the risk was obvious and preventable, D may argue that it was nonetheless unreasonable to expect D to avoid it. This may be on grounds of cost or other practical considerations. So a factory owner whose factory is in a dangerous condition due to flooding, is not necessarily bound to shut it down until it is safe again (*Latimer v AEC Ltd* (1953)).

- *Utility of D's behaviour*   There is no blanket defence of public benefit. Nonetheless, the value to society of D's activities is a factor in determining their reasonableness. So those who needlessly pollute public waterways are liable for quite unlikely results of it (*Overseas*

Tankship (UK) v Miller SS Co Pty, The Wagon Mound (No 2) (1967)). But those who play cricket are not liable for unlikely, though entirely foreseeable, results of their activities (*Bolton v Stone* (1951)). And those engaged in valuable contributions to the war-time economy can neglect even quite sizeable risks (*Daborn v Bath Tramways Motor Co* (1946)).

*   *General practice*   Again, there is no defence of common practice, and the courts have on occasion even ruled that the *universal* practice of particular professions is negligent (eg *Edward Wong Finance Co v Johnson Stokes & Master* (1984)). Nonetheless, it is relevant to enquire whether P is demanding a common precaution, or an exceptional one.

It was once suggested that the test for breach of duty can be expressed in mathematical terms: D will be found negligent if and only if (cost of precautions) is greater than (probability of loss) multiplied by (extent of loss). This is the so-called 'Learned Hand' formula, named after its inventor: see *United States v Carroll Towing Co* (1947), Learned Hand J. So put, this test is misleadingly precise, even in a case where the factors mentioned can be precisely quantified, and it is unduly narrow in ignoring other relevant facts. Nonetheless, it is a good general indicator, in cases where it can be applied.

Very small risks

1.36   The smaller the risk, the less likely D is to be held responsible for it. And so if the risk is very small indeed, it is most unlikely that D will be held liable. There are, however, two quite separate arguments D can make in that situation, which need to be carefully distinguished. First, D might argue that a particular risk appeared to be so small that it was in fact quite imperceptible: it would not have occurred to a reasonable person that that sort of accident might happen, and so the accident was unforeseeable. Second, D might concede that the risk was perceptible, but might argue that reasonable people would decide it was not worth the effort of eliminating it. So it is not that reasonable people would not realise the risk, but that, having realised it, they would see no point in doing anything about it. Either argument defeats P's claim if the court accepts it, but different evidence is appropriate in respect of each. The first is simply a matter of showing that the event was extremely unlikely, and so reasonable people would have dismissed the possibility as absurd.

The second involves a much broader enquiry, for D's argument is that there was nothing reasonable that could be done about the risk – usually on the ground that any effective precautions would have been too costly. The appeal is not simply to the smallness of the risk, but also to the cost of precautions.

> *Bolton v Stone* (1951)   A cricket ball was hit for six out of Stone's ground. It flew over 100 yards and hit Bolton, who was standing in the street just outside her house. Balls had been driven out of the ground on average about once every five years. Held: no negligence was established.

> *Overseas Tankship (UK) v Miller SS Co Pty Ltd, The Wagon Mound (No 2)*(1967)   Furnace oil was spilled in Sydney Harbour from Miller's ship. The flash point of the oil was very high, so reasonable engineers would have considered a fire possible but highly unlikely. However, a fire started in consequence of welding operations carried on by the wharf owner. Held: Miller was liable to the owners of ships damaged by the fire.

It is very hard to distinguish these cases from one another merely on grounds of the apparent degree of risk. In both cases the risk was very small. In neither case did the court make an attempt to estimate it numerically. *Bolton* involved personal injury and *The Wagon Mound* property damage; but that only intensifies the puzzle, because the courts usually treat personal injury more generously than property damage. The difference between the cases emerges more clearly when we consider cost of precautions. In *Bolton*, the risk could only have been avoided either by building some (very high and very expense) extra netting, or by ceasing altogether to play cricket at the ground. Whereas in *The Wagon Mound*, not only would it have been very easy to avoid spilling the oil, it would even have saved Miller money, as the furnace oil was far from worthless. A deeper difference between the cases lies in the value of the activity pursued by D. Deliberate pollution of harbours is an activity with rather obvious social costs, and no obvious benefits; whereas cricket, whatever one thinks of it, is at worst neutral on that score. Of course, if the risk of harm increases, even cricket may attract liability: so in a case where about eight or nine balls a years flew out of D's ground, liability was established for damage caused (*Miller v Jackson* (1977) (**7.16**)).

The 'objectivity' of the test

1.37 It is often stressed that the test of negligence is an 'objective' one. One of the things this entails is that D's own view of the reasonableness of his or her conduct is irrelevant. But it also seems to entail that the court should ignore certain characteristics of D, and of the situation D is in:

- D cannot always plead his or her own personal characteristics. Certainly D cannot plead an impulsive or careless disposition. It seems (though there is no direct English authority) that D can demand to be judged by the standard of a reasonable person of D's own age, at least if D is under 18. It has been held that a driver who suffered a stroke at the wheel was still 'objectively' guilty of negligence if he collided with another car, although the court suggested that matters might be different if the stroke had rendered him unconscious (*Roberts v Ramsbottom* (1980) (**4.14**)).

- If D is performing a task requiring some special skill, D cannot usually plead amateur status or lack of experience. But the precise level of skill demanded is unclear. It appears that DIY enthusiasts, whose creations endanger their house guests, must reach a certain level of competence, though it need not be that of a paid professional (*Wells v Cooper* (1958)). It is sometimes suggested that the governing principle is that D must display any skills which D has given others the impression that D has (sometimes called the 'holding-out' principle). But this cannot explain all the cases – in particular, why a learner driver is expected to show all the skill of a reasonably experienced driver no matter how prominently the 'L' plates are displayed (*Nettleship v Weston* (1971) (**4.14**)). It seems that a defendant who has *better* skills than most professionals is required to use those higher skills properly, and cannot plead mere average competence (*Ashcroft v Mersey Regional Health Authority* (1983)).

- While D can certainly plead the cost of precautions, it appears that D cannot usually plead poverty, or that he or she personally cannot afford the suggested precautions. The amount that better precautions would cost is relevant (**1.35**), but whether D had that much cash to spare is not. The distinction is a subtle one, however, and in one context at least it has been ignored: see *Leakey v National Trust* (1980) (liability of owner of land for hazards naturally arising – **7.23**) (see also **4.28** for another possible exception). It has also been suggested that where D is a government department, D's level of funding may be relevant to the level of duty (see *Knight v Home Office* (1990)), but the limits of this are quite unclear.

The law here is confused. These ideas make major inroads into the principle that D must personally be at fault, without always explaining why this should be. Some at least of the cases are explicable, if not always defensible, by noting the judicial generosity to those injured in car accidents (on which see below, **4.12**). And others are defensible on the ground that D may bear some responsibility for getting into a situation he or she was incapable of handling. It is frequently unclear, however, what policy is served by holding D to a standard which D cannot possibly meet.

Quantification of loss, and defences

1.38 Assuming that P has managed to establish both the existence of duty and its breach, a few hurdles yet remain, which are dealt with below as they are common to most torts. P must demonstrate that a loss has been suffered and must quantify it (**10.18**); must show that there is a sufficient causal link between D's conduct and the loss P suffers (**10.21**); and must show that the loss is not too 'remote' – roughly, that it was not too freakish a consequence of D's conduct (**10.28**). There are also various defences which may go to reduce or eliminate P's claim (**11.1**).

Conclusion: negligence as personal fault

1.39 In summary, then, any brief description of the law of negligence is likely to give the impression that it is an enquiry into whether D is personally at fault for P's loss. Yet there are several factors at work which look a little odd from that perspective. The level of fault is often high, sometimes inhumanly so. The courts' commitment to examining each case on its merits, after the event, is quite incompatible with laying down firm rules in advance. And despite the apparently stern message of personal responsibility the law embodies, in most cases no-one supposes that D will personally bear the loss. Rather, it is borne by D's insurer, or D's employer. It seems futile to debate whether negligence 'really' involves an enquiry into fault, or whether this enquiry is a sham; rather, the tort confronts a wildly diverse array of circumstances and pursues a variety of policies in relation to each.

Tort and statute

Introduction

1.40 The growth of tort over the past century is truly remarkable. But it is dwarfed by the growth of statute law over the same period. Many statutes modify tort liability, whether by expanding it or contracting it. Today, it makes no great sense to discriminate between 'common law torts' and 'statutory torts', because most torts are influenced by both. However, there are two recurrent problems. They concern the case where a statute places D under an obligation, but fails to spell out whether D can be sued for breach of that obligation by those affected. First, when is a breach of statute sufficient in itself to amount to a tort? And second, can the statute be invoked in the context of an action for negligence?

Tortious consequences of statutory duties

1.41 There are three main ways in which the infringement of a statute may result in action in tort, and it is important to keep them distinct. First, there are some torts where it is necessary for P to show that D's conduct was in some sense 'unlawful', and breach of a statute may supply this missing element (**6.27**). Second, there is a distinct tort of breach of statutory duty, under which those who suffer from D's breach of statute may sometimes recover damages (**1.42**). And third, a statutory duty may form part of a case that D was under a duty in the tort of negligence to look after P's interests (**1.49**). These torts are all distinct from one another.

It has frequently been suggested that this arrangement of the law is over-elaborate, especially since all three of the torts concerned are rather obscure and uncertain in their application. Nonetheless the courts have to date resisted attempts to amalgamate them into a single entity.

Chipchase v British Titan Products Co (1956)   Chipchase was injured at work when he fell from a ledge six feet from the ground. If the ledge had been six inches higher, his employers would have been in breach of statutory obligations as to safe working conditions. Chipchase argued that facts so close to being in breach of safety regulations constituted evidence of negligence. Held: there was no evidence of negligence.

It is possible for the same facts to give rise to action under more than one of the torts. In some contexts (and particularly that of industrial accidents) it is common for P to combine action for negligence with action for breach of statutory duty (**4.32**).

The tort of breach of statutory duty

Introduction: an antique doctrine

1.42 The tort of breach of statutory duty consists of breaking the provisions of a statute, in such a way as to cause loss to P. While not as ancient as some torts – it is barely a century and a half old – nonetheless it is showing its age. Methods of statutory drafting have altered considerably over that time, yet this has not made much difference to the doctrine. In practice, the tort is little used, because the judges have consistently refused to find it applicable to most statutes. The major area where it applies is industrial safety legislation. Here, infringements of the law not only lead to criminal penalties, but also to private action in tort by injured workers. However, the doctrine has never, in theory, been confined to that situation, and it makes occasional appearances outside it (eg **1.44**).

'Parliamentary intention'

1.43 The orthodox view is that no action lies for breach of statutory duty unless Parliament intended that it should. The statute must therefore be scanned in detail for indications of intention on the matter. This enquiry might have had some purpose when the doctrine was in its infancy, in the early Victorian period. Given the modern style of drafting statutes, however, it seems futile. If Parliament had intended action to lie, in modern circumstances we would expect the statute to say so expressly: and this is very frequently the conclusion to which the courts come in individual cases. Very occasionally, statutes state expressly that no action lies (eg Health and Safety at Work etc Act 1974, s 47(1)). In general, however, statutes contain no indication either way. So there is a farcical evasion of responsibility, under which Parliament leaves the matter to the courts, who themselves pretend to defer to 'Parliament's intention'. A Law Commission Proposal for a statutory presumption of liability (*The Interpretation of Statutes* Law Com 21, 1969) found no favour in Parliament and has never been acted on.

'Parliament's intention' is here largely fictitious. The real question is therefore what the courts do under cover of interpreting Parliament's intention. Unfortunately, this is very unclear. In practice, the courts rely on a few general presumptions about what Parliament is likely to have meant. The House of Lords (eg *Lonrho Ltd v Shell Petroleum Co Ltd (No 2)(1982)* has approved the use of these presumptions, which I now describe.

Legislation meant to protect specific groups

1.44   There is a presumption that a statute intended to protect a specific group of people gives a right to those people to sue.

> *Monk v Warbey (1935)*   Warbey lent his car to a friend, without arranging for third party insurance. Monk was injured by the friend's poor driving. Monk successfully sued Warbey for failing to arrange for insurance to ensure compensation in these circumstances.

Conversely, D may defeat an action by pointing out that P is not a member of the class meant to be protected.

> *Cutler v Wandsworth Stadium (1949)*   Cutler, a bookmaker, argued that Wandsworth Stadium had caused him loss of business by failing to make space available for him, contrary to the Betting and Lotteries Act 1934. Held: that Act was passed to benefit Cutler's potential customers rather than Cutler himself, and accordingly no action lay.

The presumption has been criticised, most famously by Atkin LJ. He pointed out that it is odd that a duty owed to everyone is not thought to merit legal action, whereas a duty to a narrow class is (*Phillips v Britannia Hygienic Laundry Co* [1923] 2 KB 832, 841). The criterion is often difficult to apply. Nonetheless, the presumption is well established, though judges differ in how much weight they give to it. There will also often be scope for argument over the precise purpose of legislation. So, for example, while *one* purpose of the prison rules on segregation of prisoners was to protect especially vulnerable prisoners, it was not their *only* purpose, and accordingly no action lay by a prisoner under them (*R v Deputy Governor of Parkhurst Prison, ex p Hague* (1992)). Or again, homeless persons legislation has recently been held to be for the public benefit generally, rather than particularly for the benefit of homeless persons (*O'Rourke v Camden London Borough Council* (1997)). As the latter case shows, the presumption is of only limited use today.

The type of loss

1.45 Where P suffers loss as a result of D's breach of statutory duty, D has a defence if P's loss was of a different sort from that which the statute was meant to prevent.

> *Gorris v Scott* (1874)   Sheep belonging to Gorris were lost overboard, which Gorris argued was the result of Scott's breach of provisions of the Contagious Diseases (Animals) Act 1869. Held: as the purpose of that Act was to safeguard public health rather than to prevent damage to property, Gorris's claim was outside the statute.

This apparently straightforward rule allows for many differences in approach. It has sometimes been used with nit-picking exactness.

> *Nicholls v F Austin (Leyton) Ltd* (1946)   Nicholls was injured when the circular saw he was using threw out a sharp piece of wood. This would not have happened if his employers had fenced the saw, as statute required. Held: the object of the fencing obligation was to keep workers' fingers out, not the machine itself in, so Nicholls's claim under the statute was not admissible.

Adequacy of other remedies

1.46 All agree that it is highly relevant what other remedies are available. But there are important differences of emphasis. Some judges say that if the statute provides its own remedy, then it is not for the courts to add others. If right, that would effectively mean that the doctrine should *never* apply, except in the rare case where Parliament specifies a duty but says nothing about the consequences of failure to carry it out (as in *Dawson & Co v Bingley UDC* (1911)). This approach would mean that the tort of breach of statutory duty would hardly ever apply in modern conditions. Another approach is more lenient: an apparently complete code of enforcement is taken only as a strong indication that additional remedies are not called for.

X v Bedfordshire County Council (1995)   Children who claimed to have suffered injury as a result of breaches of the Children Act 1989 by their local authority, sued the authority. Held: in the light of the elaborate range of remedies available under that Act, it was inconceivable that Parliament intended an additional right of action for breach of statutory duty .

A subtly different approach is to look at P's legal rights and remedies in the round and to ask whether other statutory or common law remedies are adequate, or whether justice demands a remedy for breach of the statute.

McCall v Abelesz (1976)   McCall, the tenant of property, sued his landlord, for breach of the duty not to harass tenants in Rent Act 1965, s 30. Held: McCall and others in his position had adequate common law remedies for breach of contract and for trespass, and the action for breach of statutory duty did not lie.

Whatever we may make of individual decisions, there is a lot to be said for this approach generally. It allows the court to argue openly about whether liability should be imposed, in the light of the provision the law makes in that area generally. However, there can be no pretence that all the case law is reconcilable with it.

If in doubt, refuse to find liability?

1.47   It is tempting today, in the light of frequent refusals to find liability, to postulate a final presumption: that unless there is strong reason to the contrary, either in the form of earlier cases favouring liability or indications in the statute itself, liability will be refused. It is always open to Parliament to impose liability expressly, and if it has not done so it is usually hopeless to argue that it nonetheless intended so to do. The tort is considered by many to be a historical relic and there is little enthusiasm for extending it.

No defence of due diligence

1.48   If liability is found, there is no defence of due diligence or lack of care. Of course, a statutory duty may be expressed as a duty to take due care, or words may be used which have a similar effect, such as by providing a defence where it is 'impracticable' to act in a safe way (Mines and Quarries Act 1954, s 157). But there is no presumption that common law negligence is the standard imposed by any regulatory act. If a breach is established, it is no defence that compliance is difficult – or even that it is impossible.

John Summers & Sons v Frost (1955)   Frost was injured as a result of his employers' not having securely fenced the machine on which he was working. The employers argued that the machine could not be used if it were fenced as the Act required. Held: the employers were nonetheless liable for breach of statutory duty.

Statutory powers and negligence

Introduction

1.49   Where D is a public authority with statutory powers, P may claim that those powers should not be used in ways which injure P. So P may sue in negligence, alleging misuse of D's statutory powers. It was at one time thought that a statutory power could not be the foundation of an action in negligence. It was said that there was a world of difference between a statutory *duty*, which was mandatory, and a statutory *power*, which was not. Most famously in *East Suffolk Rivers Catchment Board v Kent* (1941), where a statutory body ineptly failed to prevent flooding to P's land, it was thought crucial that the body was under no duty to act. And so a majority of the House of Lords considered that no action lay for their failure to do the work to a satisfactory standard.

However, that approach was disapproved in *Home Office v Dorset Yacht Co* (1970). That case involved mismanagement of a borstal, so that some of the inmates escaped and destroyed P's property. Liability was established. The distinction between the authority's powers and its duties was not thought particularly helpful. It was suggested that the true distinction was between *policy decisions*, which could not be questioned in an action for negligence, and merely *operational decisions*, which could. But this distinction has in its turn been subjected to criticism, and is in any event a very hard line to draw.

The policy/operation distinction

1.50   It is clear that this distinction is no magic key to the area: it 'does not provide a touchstone of liability' (*Rowling v Takaro Properties Ltd* [1988]

I All ER 163, 172, Lord Keith). It is still, however, of some importance. There is a great difference between suggesting that a mistake was made in matters of policy formation, on the one hand, and suggesting that there was incompetence in carrying out a settled policy, the merits of which are not in issue on the other. In the former case, opinions can reasonably differ, and democracy requires judges to leave certain decisions to other public officials, whereas there is no democratic mandate for everyday incompetence. The policy/operation distinction is therefore of considerable utility. It is frequently deployed to justify the court's keeping out of high-level decisions, while leaving the door open for complaints on day-to-day matters (eg *Barrett v Enfield London Borough Council* (1997)). It is another question, however, whether individual administrative decisions can be mechanically classified as 'policy' or 'operational' decisions, or whether a finding that a decision is a 'policy' matter precludes legal challenge entirely.

D's action must be ultra vires

1.51 P must demonstrate that the decision of which P complains was beyond the scope of the powers conferred on D ('*ultra vires*'). If this is not so, then the defendant authority has done only what Parliament told it to do, and no legal action lies. The precise limits of the *ultra vires* principle are beyond the scope of this book. In brief, there are a number of grounds on which it can be argued that a power has been improperly exercised. They include exceeding the precise terms of the power itself, bias, irrationality, and attention to irrelevant considerations. The usual remedies for *ultra vires* conduct are public law remedies to quash the decision, or to force the relevant officials to take it again. Much of the reluctance of the courts to extend the tort of negligence into this area results from a wish not to subvert those public law remedies.

Must the issue be justiciable?

1.52 Some judges suggest that even if the challenged decision was *ultra vires*, in certain circumstances the courts will not intervene, on the ground that the matter is not one for a court of law to involve itself in. The issue is said not to be 'justiciable', that is, not suitable for resolution in a law court. This concept seems unnecessary, however. In many cases this is just the policy/operation distinction again: policy issues are usually unsuitable for courts, operational matters are not. Most of the other cases seem to involve causation. It is one thing to show that D's decision not to grant P some benefit is *ultra vires*. It is quite another to show that D had no lawful alternative but to grant it to P – to show, in other words, that *any* decision to refuse P the benefit would have been *ultra vires*. Yet if P cannot show the latter (or at least that a decision within D's powers would *probably* have been in P's favour), then it is unclear how D's behaviour has caused any loss to P. So a court might agree that D's reasons for failing to help P were wrong, without necessarily agreeing that D's only lawful alternative was to help P.

Consistency with Parliamentary intention

1.53 The courts will consider the statute itself and will not find liability if that would conflict with the policy embodied in the statute. So if the statute provides its own regime of rights and procedures for challenging decisions made under it, the courts will avoid creating additional rights under the tort of negligence (eg *Jones v Department of Employment* (1989), social security tribunals; *M v Newham London Borough Council* (1995), the Children Act 1989). Or again, the courts may refuse to allow P an action on the ground that P was not the sort of person the Act was meant to benefit (*Caparo Industries plc v Dickman* (1990)).

It is currently an open question whether P must go further, and demonstrate some positive indication that Parliament intended action in negligence to lie. In *X v Bedfordshire County Council* (1995) the Lords were prepared to find that powers to provide for special educational needs could be made the basis of action by those whose needs were unmet, even though there was no indication that Parliament had intended this. Yet in *Stovin v Wise* (1996) a differently-constituted House of Lords held, by a majority, that no action lay for motorists injured by negligent exercise of powers to improve highways, seemingly on the ground that there was no reason to suppose that Parliament intended an action to lie. The former view seems preferable; the latter seems to demand an answer to the unanswerable question of what Parliament meant, whereas the former enquiry – whether the imposition of liability sabotages what Parliament expressly provided – seems at least in principle capable of sensible answer.

Further Reading

Relevant sections of tort reference books may be supplemented with:

Convery 'Public or Private? Duty of care in a statutory framework: *Stovin v Wise* in the House of Lords' (1997) 60 MLR 559.

Self-test questions

1. Given that having a liability insurance policy greatly increases the chances of being sued, why does any rational person ever take one out (**1.10**)?

2. Is it true that there is no liability in negligence for:

(a) omissions (**1.26**)?

(b) statements (**1.30**)?

(c) policy decisions of a public authority (**1.50**)?

3. What interests are protected by the law of tort (**1.4**)?

4. How accurate is Atkin's 'neighbour' *dictum* as a statement of the modern law of negligence (**1.23**)?

5. Would it be more accurate to call this subject 'tort' or 'torts' (**1.6**)?

6. Is there a defence of public benefit in negligence (**1.35**)?

7. How effective is tort as a method of deterring harmful behaviour (**1.13–1.16**)?

CHAPTER TWO

Deliberate harm to the person

SUMMARY
Certain types of harm to P are tortious if they are deliberate:

- **Assault**

- **Battery**

- **False imprisonment**

- **Unlawful harassment**

- **Invasion of privacy (possibly)**

Tort here plays second fiddle to the criminal law. But it has an important role where substantial compensation is demanded. It may also be useful if the victim wants to retain control of the conduct of proceedings, rather than appearing as a mere witness.

Assault and battery

Terminology

2.1   If D deliberately inflicts force on P, D has committed the tort of *battery*, unless D has some defence. To threaten immediate force constitutes the tort of *assault*. Both torts are actionable without proof that any financial loss resulted from D's activities ('actionable without proof of special damage'). There can be assault without battery (eg D threatens to hit P but does not), and battery without assault (eg D creeps up behind P and hits her). The distinction between the two torts is clear enough in theory, but is in many situations unimportant. In practice it is common, if not entirely accurate, to refer to instances of assault and of battery as 'assault'.

Deliberate, not negligent, harm

2.2   Assault and battery are different species of the tort of trespass to the person. (The third species, false imprisonment, is dealt with below: **2.11**) Whatever may have been the position historically, it is now clear that merely careless harm is actionable only if negligence is proved.

> *Fowler v Lanning* (1959)   While on a hunting expedition, Fowler was injured by a bullet from Lanning's gun. Fowler argued that Lanning was guilty of trespass to the person, unless he could prove that it was a non-negligent accident. Held: Lanning would be liable if intent to wound or negligence could be shown, but in either case the burden of proof was on Fowler.

Where D negligently inflicts force on P, it is not entirely clear whether P may sue in battery, or whether P must sue in negligence. It makes little practical difference. Either way, it is P who has the burden of proof. Yet, given that there is no action in negligence without proof of special damage, it would be rash to say that it will *never* matter which tort P uses.

Assault: definition

2.3   D commits assault if D causes P to fear immediate personal violence from D. There are various defences available (**11.1**). The threat to P must be immediate: mere hostility is not enough, unless P apprehends violence then and there.

> *Tuberville v Savage* (1669)   In the course of a furious argument, Tuberville put his hand on his sword and said to Savage 'If it were not assize time, I would not take such language from you'. Held: this did not amount to an assault.

Tuberville v Savage was at one time thought to mean that words alone cannot constitute an assault. But that is not what the report says and would be a strange rule – why shouldn't D's words be an indication of whether D is likely to be violent? In any event it does not explain the decision, as Tuberville had used a gesture to his sword as well as threatening words. And it is certainly not true that there can be no assault if D makes qualifications to his hostile intent.

Read v Coker (1853)   Coker demanded that Read leave the premises where he was, saying that he would break Read's neck if he did not go. Held: this constituted assault against Read.

P's fear of violence must be reasonable. There is no liability for assault if D makes a threat which P knows D cannot carry out, or where D points a gun at P which P knows is not loaded.

Thomas v National Union of Mineworkers (South Wales Area) [1985] 2 All ER 1, 20, Scott J   Mineworkers were bused into work, passing through considerable numbers of pickets urging a strike and making violent threats and gestures. Held: this could not be assault, as there was no way in which the pickets could reach those in the bus.

Battery: definition

2.4   D is liable for battery if D inflicts force on P. There are various defences available (11.1). The degree of force does not matter: 'the least touching of another in anger is a battery' (*Cole v Turner* (1704)); and so, presumably, an unwelcome kiss is a battery as well, though there is no authority on the point. The force can be transmitted indirectly, as for example where:

- Horn threw a bucket of boiling water over Pursell (*Pursell v Horn* (1838)).

- Reeve deliberately drove his gig at a carriage, which overturned; Hopper, inside, was hurt (*Hopper v Reeve* (1817)).

- Burford hit Dodwell's horse, which ran off and threw Dodwell down (*Dodwell v Burford* (1670)).

- Fagan accidentally drove his car onto a policeman's foot. He then refused to reverse, and switched the engine off. Held: Fagan was guilty of assault on a constable contrary to Police Act 1964, s 51 (*Fagan v Metropolitan Police Comr* (1969)).

(*Fagan* was a criminal case, and there is a closely-reasoned dissent by Bridge J; it is therefore a weak authority and it is uncertain whether it is correct as to the tort of battery.)

43

Assault and battery: the mental element

2.5   It is usually stated that intention on D's part is necessary if P's action is to succeed. This is broadly true, but certain qualifications must be made. First, there is clear criminal law authority that 'subjective recklessness' (conscious risk-taking) is sufficient. So D is guilty of battery if he kicks out at random and happens to connect with P (*R v Venna* (1976)). Presumably this is true of the tort of assault as well. Second, if D intended to batter *someone*, it seems not to matter if he accidentally hits P, rather than the person he intended to hit. Third, one modern case casts considerable doubt on the whole matter, by suggesting an additional requirement of 'hostile intent'.

> *Wilson v Pringle* (1986)   Wilson and Pringle were both schoolboys. Pringle kicked Wilson, causing him to fall over and injure himself. Was there any possible defence to an action of battery? Held: the kicking was intentional and it was no defence that the consequential injury was not; however, Wilson must also prove that Pringle acted with hostility, and there was a triable issue whether that was so.

This suggested additional element of 'hostility' is vague, particularly as the court insisted that it did not mean malevolence or ill-will. The meaning is unclear. If there is such a requirement, it is likely to lead to confusion in sexual harassment cases, where D and P are likely to disagree on whether D's behaviour can be styled 'hostile'. The notion was disapproved by Lord Goff in *Re F* (1990), though he added that D's behaviour would not constitute battery where it was merely 'physical contact which is generally acceptable in the ordinary conduct of everyday life' ([1990] 2 AC 73).

Impact of the criminal law

2.6   Both assault and battery are crimes as well as torts. Under Powers of Criminal Courts Act 1973, ss 35-38 (as amended), a court which has just convicted D may order D to pay compensation to P for personal injuries or property damage. However, these powers are limited, and in deciding whether to make an order the court must take into account D's ability to pay – which would be an irrelevant matter if P were suing D in a civil court. In practice, the powers are little used for victims of personal injury, though much used in cases of property damage.

Under the Criminal Injuries Compensation Scheme, the victims of violent crimes may recover benefits from public funds. Under the original scheme, as established in 1964, these benefits were the same as would have been available against the criminal in tort, had the criminal been able to pay. However, these benefits have now been reduced, and under the Criminal Injuries Compensation Act 1995 the victims of crimes receive sums set by a fixed statutory tariff, which is unrelated to tort damages. The total paid out under the scheme is currently running at about £200m annually.

Harassment and other deliberate harm

Beyond assault and battery

2.7 It has long been recognised that D should be responsible for deliberate physical harm to P, even where it would be difficult to describe D's conduct as battery.

> *Wilkinson v Downton* (1897)   As a practical joke, Downton told Wilkinson that her husband had been injured in a road accident and was in hospital. Wilkinson suffered nervous shock and was sick for some weeks before she recovered. Held: she could sue Downton for the consequences of his unlawful and unjustifiable conduct, even though there was no evidence that he intended her illness.

The case is a strong one, particularly as it was decided before general tortious recovery for nervous shock (**3.18**) was recognised in law. The result has been confirmed by the court of appeal in *Janvier v Sweeney* (1919). Nonetheless it is unhelpful as a general precedent, because P may not be able to prove nervous shock. ('Nervous shock' must consist of a recognisable medical condition with physical symptoms, not merely 'shock' as ordinary people would use the term, see **3.19**.)

Some examples

2.8 Various other cases have recognised tort liability for something akin to unlawful harassment or deliberate humiliation of P.

> *Thomas v National Union of Mineworkers (South Wales Area)* (1985) Thomas and others were bused into work in the course of a national strike and their travel to work was much inconvenienced by an

unlawful picket. Held: this was an actionable interference with their right to use the highway.

Khorasandjian v Bush (1993)   Bush 'stalked' Khorasandjian, by following her around, sending her unwanted messages and telephoning her and her relatives. Bush admitted he could be restrained from using violent threats and acts, but argued that he committed no tort by mere harassment. Held: harassment was a tort whether or not it involved violence or the threat of violence .

Bayliss and Barton v Home Office (1993)   On visiting a relative in prison, Bayliss and Barton were subjected to strip searches, to which they submitted. The searches were conducted in private rooms, but the doors had windows not entirely covered by curtains. Held: assuming that the searches were unlawful, the searchers were acting tortiously.

These cases seem to suggest that there may be a tort of subjecting P to humiliation or severe embarrassment. However, each of these authorities (and other similar ones) is rather weak. The facts of *Thomas* are very different from those of most likely harassment cases. *Bayliss* is the decision of a county court and thus of weak value as a precedent. *Khorasandjian* has been heavily criticised by the House of Lords in *Hunter v Canary Wharf Ltd* (1997) and is no longer justifiable on the reasoning given in the report (see **7.21**). However, in *Canary Wharf* Lord Hoffmann hinted ([1997] 2 All ER 452hj) that the result in *Khorasandjian* could be justified either under the new statutory tort of harassment (**2.10**) or under the doctrine in *Wilkinson v Downton* (**2.7**). It must therefore remain an open question whether there is a 'tort of harassment' as such.

Sexual harassment

2.9   It is sometimes argued that the law pays insufficient attention to issues of gender relations and is too ready to accept D's story that his harassment was (at worst) a joke and (at best) secretly welcomed by P, rather than P's story that it was unlawful aggression against her. However, there is a problem here, that the law of tort is usually an awkward method for controlling sexual harassment and is therefore little used for that purpose. In practice, issues of sexual harassment usually surface either as issues in employment law (with the employer being accused of exercising insufficient control over male employees who harass female employees) or, in extreme cases, in the criminal courts. Suing in tort is costly. This ensures that it is very much a weapon of last resort in the armoury of the victim of assault – even though it can occasionally be used with devastating effect.

Harassment: legislation

2.10 Under the Protection from Harassment Act 1997, a course of conduct amounting to deliberate or negligent harassment of P is forbidden (s 1). 'Harassment' is not defined, but includes alarming P or causing P distress, whether by speech or by other conduct (s 7(2) and (4)). The Act seems to require that any alleged harassment involve at least two distinct incidents (s 7(3)), though how this provision will be interpreted in practice is unclear. D has a defence if it can be shown that D's conduct was reasonable, or was designed to comply with some rule of law, or was for the prevention or detection of crime (s 1(3)). So harassment is now both a crime (under s 2) and a tort (under s 3). If P treats it as a tort, P may obtain an order restraining D from further harassment, as well as damages, which may include an element for 'any anxiety caused by the harassment' (s 3(2)). At the time of writing, the provisions on restraining orders are not fully in force; and the overall impact of the legislation has yet to emerge.

False imprisonment

Definition

2.11 D is liable for false imprisonment where D deprived P of the liberty to go where he or she wished. No special damage need be proved before P may recover damages for this tort, and in an appropriate case aggravated damages may be awarded (**10.16**).

Completeness of the restraint

2.12 The tort consists of depriving P of his or her liberty. It is not committed by mere obstruction of *one* route P could have followed, so long as others are reasonably open to P.

> *Bird v Jones* (1845) Part of a bridge was unlawfully fenced off, for watching a boat race. Bird climbed over the fence, following his normal

route, but was prevented from following the path he wished, being told to go back and cross outside the fence. Held: Bird had not been falsely imprisoned.

However, if there was a clear intention to restrain P, it seems to be irrelevant how D proposed to enforce this, or what would have been the likely outcome if P had resisted the restraint. If D says to P 'you are under arrest', it appears to be irrelevant whether D was in a position to restrain P. Conversely, if P is *in fact* under restraint, it appears to be irrelevant whether P knows this. So in *Murray v Ministry of Defence* (1988) the House of Lords would have been prepared to hold that false imprisonment is committed where soldiers would have refused to release P had she demanded it, whether or not she realised that this was the case. (On the facts, however, the restraint was held to have been authorised by statute.) Of course, whether P knows about the restraint will affect the degree of humiliation suffered, and consequently the level of damages P can expect if liability is established.

Entry subject to conditions

2.13 Some authorities suggest that if P enters D's premises, knowing that D intends to impose conditions, then P cannot later complain when D insists on compliance with the conditions, at least if the court considers the conditions to be reasonable ones.

> *Robinson v Balmain New Ferry Co Ltd* (1910) A ferry company ran ferries from its wharf across a river. It charged one penny to enter or to leave the wharf. Robinson paid one penny to enter the wharf and then changed his mind and tried to leave, but refused to pay another penny. Held: the ferry company did not commit false imprisonment by refusing to let him pass.

Up to a point this decision can be based on the defence of consent (11.2): P knew or ought to have known how D proposed to act and seems to have consented to the arrangement. But the decision has also been applied, more controversially, to cases where P certainly did not consent.

> *Herd v Weardale Steel, Coal and Coke Co Ltd* (1915) Herd, a coal miner, decided that conditions in the pit were unsafe and demanded

that he be allowed to return to the surface immediately. His employers refused, returning him only at the end of his shift. It would certainly have been possible to return him before. Held: Herd had not been falsely imprisoned down the pit.

Considerable stress was placed on the point that Herd was in breach of his employment contract. Today, the courts would be unlikely to hold that anyone had contracted out of their right to reasonably safe employment, even if it is lawfully possible to do so (on which see *Johnstone v Bloomsbury Health Authority* (1992)).

D's responsibility

2.14 Probably D can only be liable for *deliberately* imprisoning P. However, this is not beyond all doubt; when the question whether negligence was enough came up in *Weldon v Home Office*, Gibson LJ left it open ([1990] 3 WLR 465, 470). Where someone else, acting on D's instigation, unlawfully detains P, it is sometimes possible to make D liable, but D's responsibility for the actions of the imprisoner must be clear.

> *Davidson v Chief Constable of North Wales* (1994) Yates, a store detective, observed Davidson in a shop and formed the inaccurate impression that Davidson had stolen a tape cassette. She passed this information on to the local police, who arrested Davidson. Held: Yates was under no liability for false imprisonment, as she had merely passed on information to the police, rather than providing encouragement to them to commit unlawful acts.

The reasoning in *Davidson* seems unsatisfactory. Yates could surely guess what the police would do with her information. It was perfectly true that the police did not take orders from Yates, but it seems strange to deny that she encouraged them to make an arrest. The difficulty was that the police had a defence to any action (as they had acted on reasonable suspicion), whereas Yates, not being a police officer, would not have been able to take advantage of that defence, even if her belief had been reasonable. Can Davidson's arrest be 'lawful' when she sued the police, but 'unlawful' when she sued Yates? Sir Thomas Bingham MR thought it would be 'somewhat anomalous' if it were so ([1994] 2 All ER 601), yet this may be the result of the case.

Defences

2.15 General defences are dealt with below (11.1), but there are several defences peculiarly relevant to false imprisonment. Powers of arrest are governed by the Police and Criminal Evidence Act 1984: extensive powers are given to the police, including powers of search, and much more limited powers of 'citizens' arrest' to persons generally. Restraint in prison is authorised by Prison Act 1952, s 12 and the Prison Rules 1964. In the light of those rules, the House of Lords has ruled that there is no 'residual liberty' left to prisoners. Accordingly, no rights are infringed by keeping them in one part of the prison, rather than another where they would prefer to be (*R v Deputy Governor of Parkhurst Prison, ex p Hague* (1992)).

Invasion of privacy

No general tort

2.16 The orthodox view is that there is no tort of invasion of privacy at common law.

> *Kaye v Robertson* (1991) Kaye, a famous comedy actor, was in hospital after a road accident. A journalist and a photographer, acting on Robertson's instructions, entered the private ward where Kaye was. They interviewed Kaye (or so they later claimed), and took a number of photos before being evicted. Held: no tort had been committed against Kaye, nor could they be restrained from printing the photographs, so long as they made it clear that they were taken without Kaye's consent.

Bingham LJ commented that:

> If ever a person has a right to be let alone by strangers with no public interest to pursue, it must surely be when he lies in hospital recovering from brain surgery and in no more than partial command of his faculties. It is this invasion of his privacy which underlies the plaintiff's complaint. Yet it alone, however gross, does not entitle him to relief in English law ([1991] FSR 70).

Particular examples

2.17 Nonetheless, it has sometimes proved possible for P to use other torts or legal doctrines to remedy what amounts to an invasion of P's privacy.

- Where D publishes photographs of P or P's family, P may sometimes be able to assert breach of copyright (*Williams v Settle* (1960)).

- Surveillance of P or P's property may sometimes amount to trespass (**7.2**) or nuisance (**7.11**).

- P's privacy may sometimes be protected by the new statutory tort of harassment (**2.10**).

- Unwelcome phone calls may sometimes constitute public nuisance (*R v Johnson* (1996); **7.30**).

- The publication of private information may sometimes be restrained as being a breach of P's confidence (*Duchess of Argyll v Duke of Argyll* (1967)).

Reform? Waiting for developments

2.18 Whether the law should be reformed, by introducing a tort of invasion of privacy, is a matter of some debate. Considerable judicial distaste at intrusive press behaviour has become apparent, particularly in *Kaye v Robertson* and similar cases. It is clear that certain judges at least would welcome the creation of a tort of invasion of privacy, and might apply it with some enthusiasm.

There are no immediate plans for government legislation, but nonetheless change may be expected from two statutory sources. First, while the impact of the Protection from Harassment Act 1997 is as yet unclear (**2.10**), it is plainly capable of applying in some instances of invasion of privacy. Second, the planned introduction of enforceable human rights into domestic law is likely to impact on protection of privacy in some way, though precisely how remains to be seen. When the dust has settled, it may then be appropriate to ask whether there is a need for additional protection from invasions of privacy. It is certainly clear that the difficulties in defining any such protection would be considerable, as would also be the dangers of going too far in restraining press freedom.

Further Reading

Relevant sections of tort reference books may be supplemented with:

Conaghan 'Gendered harms and the law of tort: Remedying (Sexual) Harassment' (1996) 16 OJLS 407.

Trindade 'Intentional Torts: Some thoughts on assault and battery' (1982) 2 OJLS 211.

Allen 'Look who'stalking: Seeking a solution to the problem of stalking' (1996) 4 WJCLI (http://www.ncl.ac.uk/~nlawwww/1996/issue4/allen4.html).

Self-test questions

1. If P complains of invasion of his or her privacy, which torts, if any, are likely to be applicable (**2.17**)?

2. Why might P be interested in establishing that D was liable for assault, even if D is entirely without funds (**2.6**)?

3. What is the mental element of assault (**2.5**)?

4. Is it possible to falsely imprison P without P's being aware of it (**2.12**)?

5. What are the essential requirements of harassment under the Protection from Harassment Act 1997 (**2.10**)?

CHAPTER THREE

Negligent harm to the person: general considerations

SUMMARY
Redressing personal injury is the most important application of negligence law. This chapter describes the general rules on establishing duty and breach of duty. It then describes the system of recovery for injuries in negligence. It then covers certain special categories of plaintiff: those who suffer nervous shock, those complaining of negligence in relation to birth, and rescuers.

Introduction

Negligence: the scope of the following chapters

3.1   In chapter 1, the basic concepts of negligence law were reviewed: existence of duty, breach of duty, causation, defences. But some areas of the law are better worked-out than others. So it is necessary to discuss both general principles, and their application to particular areas. To put some flesh on the bones, we have to start distinguishing between different classes of case. This chapter and the following one deal with negligence as it relates to plaintiffs who have suffered personal injury. Property and economic losses are left to a later chapter (**5.1**), and damages and defences to still later ones (**10.1**, **11.1**).

This chapter deals with general principles of recovery for personal injury; the following chapter deals with the most common duty situations. The law is a lot clearer in some areas of this than others. Very roughly, the better-worked-out areas are so because most of the litigation occurs there. It is *because* there is so much litigation relating to road accidents that it is possible to be fairly precise about how the courts react to them

(**4.12**); similarly with claims by employees against their employers (**4.32**). The general principles of negligence, by contrast, are most useful when the court is in unfamiliar territory.

Duty

Foresight of the particular plaintiff

3.2   P can only sue for personal injury in negligence if P was a foreseeable victim of D's activities (**1.23**). In many situations, it is enough simply to ask whether D was careless: did D's behaviour create unreasonably large risks for others, or not? Yet while adequate for most purposes, the question is often insufficient. A more focused one must be asked: was it foreseeable that D's behaviour would injure P? By asking specifically whether D's behaviour threatened P in this way, we focus on the legal relation between those two people. This is sometimes more generous to P than simply asking whether D was 'careless', sometimes less generous.

> *Wright v Lodge* (1993)   Shepherd's car ground to a halt on a busy A-road, due to mechanical failure. Rather than push her car onto the hard shoulder, which she could easily have done with her passengers' help, she simply sat in it. Lodge, a lorry driver who was going much too fast for the foggy conditions, swerved to avoid Shepherd's car, skidded across the central reservation and collided with other cars, including Wright's. Held: Wright was not a foreseeable victim of Shepherd's misconduct.

The question is therefore whether D ought to have foreseen danger *to* P. So even though D's behaviour is plainly careless, and in fact causes P's injury, nonetheless a court may refuse to compensate P, on the ground that P was an unforeseeable plaintiff, so that D owed P no duty. But equally, focusing attention on the relation between P and D may allow P to recover even where people generally cannot.

> *Haley v London Electricity Board* (1965)   Manual workers excavating an electricity cable made a sizeable hole in the road, which they indicated to passers-by by leaving a long-handled hammer in front of it. Haley, who was blind, did not realise that there was a hole and walked into it. Held: even though the precautions taken were adequate

to warn sighted people of the danger, they were inadequate to protect Haley and others like him. Blind people were not so rare as to be unforeseeable.

So duty is owed to each possible plaintiff individually. This is none the less so because the court discusses P as part of a class or group of people. Of course, what it is reasonable to expect of D is limited by human capabilities. If no reasonable person would have thought of P or of P's special needs, then a court is unlikely to consider that a failure to consider P's position amounts to a breach of duty.

Adequacy of the 'foresight' criterion

3.3 The notion of 'reasonable foresight' has been much criticised, particularly on the ground that it is very loose, so loose that it enables the courts to do whatever they want with it. This is absolutely true. But it entirely misses the point. It is not a mechanical formula leading to definite results in each case. But it is a little hard to see how a liability as broad as negligence *could* be regulated by mechanical formulae. It is pointless to criticise the looseness of the criterion in the abstract; we must first see how the judges have *in fact* used the considerable discretion it gives them.

We have already seen a great deal of how the judges use their power to declare events to be 'foreseeable' or unforeseeable' (**1.23**), and it is clear that in personal injury matters at least they take a very broad view. It is always easy to be wise after the event and so to say that D 'should have foreseen' events which must have seemed very unlikely to someone thinking about matters before the event. This is quite different from the position as to pure economic loss, for example (**5.7**). So it is often said that the courts take an unrealistic view of what D can be expected to foresee before the event and are much too demanding in the level of care D is expected to give. But the law of negligence serves many purposes (**1.12**). It is not a case of the judges' being 'unrealistic', but of their making a particular value-judgement about the availability of liability. Of course the standard of care prescribed by the tort of negligence is far higher than anything most defendants are in fact likely to achieve, and indeed in some cases the law's prescribed level of care is actually *impossible* to achieve (**1.37**). It is not hard to see that a finding of 'negligence' is nonsense as a comment on what D 'should have done'. The challenge is to think of something that would be less ridiculous!

Omission

3.4   As already explained (**1.26**), it is a complete misconception to say that negligence law imposes no duty in respect of omissions. Once it is established that D owes P a duty, then the duty may be broken by omission as much as by action. Once we have concluded that manufacturers of ginger beer owe a duty not to include snails in their product, it hardly matters where snails get there by omission (the manufacturer fails to stop snails slithering in) or by action (the manufacturer carelessly inserts them into the bottle). Unreasonable omissions are as culpable as unreasonable actions, and just as likely to lead to legal action by the victim. However, there is a kernel of truth in the 'no liability for omissions' rule. If D's behaviour has in no way added to the dangers which P faces, then prima facie D is under no duty at all. If P argues that D is under a positive duty to save P from dangers created by others, then P must give a very specific reason for this. It is not enough that D could easily have helped P. If a duty is found, it will usually be because D had control over the source of danger to which P succumbed, or should have had control of it.

- Where D carelessly abandons his horse and it runs off, D owes a duty to those who make reasonable attempts to re-capture it (*Haynes v Harwood* (1935)).

- Where children at D's primary school escape and run across roads, causing P's lorry to swerve and crash, D owes a duty to P to prevent his injuries (*Carmarthenshire County Council v Lewis* (1955)).

- Where P seeks a divorce from her violent husband and D, her husband's solicitor, gives undertakings relating to her personal safety, breach of those undertakings may constitute actionable negligence (*Al-Kandari v JR Brown & Co* (1987)).

- Where D admit hooligans to their football matches and the hooligans throw pieces of concrete left around through the poor state of the premises, injured spectators may sue in negligence (*Cunningham v Reading Football Club* (1991)).

- Where D usually lock gates leading onto their railway line whenever there is a train coming, then their failure to do so on one occasion may constitute a breach of duty to P, who is misled into thinking it is safe (*Mercer v South Eastern & Chatham Railway Co's Managing Committee* (1922)).

- Where P is a mentally unstable prisoner lawfully in D's custody, D may owe P a duty to prevent him from injuring himself (*Kirkham v Chief Constable of the Greater Manchester Police* (1990)).

- Where P is a player at a rugby match and D a referee, D owes a duty to P to act carefully in relation to particularly dangerous situations, such as by taking reasonable precautions to avoid the collapsing of scrums (*Smoldon v Whitworth* (1996)).

In all of these cases, then, D was held liable for an omission, on the ground that D ought to have controlled some source of danger to P. However, the limits are quite unclear. Suppose a bus company carelessly leaves its bus in a public street, with the doors unlocked and the keys still in the ignition. If a joyrider seizes this opportunity and drives off, running over P, may P sue the bus company? The Court of Appeal initially thought that P could (*Hayman v London Transport Executive* (1982)), but has now reversed this (*Topp v London Country Bus (South West) Ltd* (1993)). Again, it is usually assumed that D will not be liable to rescue P from danger. In *The Ogopogo* (1970), the Canadian Supreme Court was prepared to hold that a duty arose. It held that the host of a boating expedition was under a duty to rescue guests who fell in the water – though on the facts it held that the host had done all that could reasonably have been expected of him, and so was not liable for the guests' death. It is quite unclear whether the English courts would follow this ruling.

Public policy

3.5 *Statutory authorities*   The courts are usually reluctant to impose liability on public authorities for misuse of statutory powers (**1.49**). The courts are reluctant to put broad duties on public authorities, or to allow particular individuals to skew broad questions of governmental policy round to the question whether they, personally, have done well out of them. The law is confused, however, and each regime of statutory powers and duties requires separate consideration.

X v Bedfordshire County Council (1995)   Children who suffered injury as a result of misconduct by their local authority in its role under the

Children Act 1989, sued the authority. Held: in the light of the elaborate range of remedies available under that Act, a tortious duty of care was incompatible with the remedies provided by Parliament.

M v Newham Borough Council (1995)   Children complained that their special educational needs had initially not been diagnosed by their local authority and that when ultimately diagnosed they had wrongly been told that their existing schools were adequate. They sued in negligence. Held: a duty of care by the authority was owed to the children.

Stovin v Wise (Norfolk County Council, third party) (1996)   Wise negligently drove out from a side-road onto the main road, causing injury to Stovin who was carefully driving down it. Wise sought to join the local transport authority as co-defendant, arguing that the poor road design had significantly contributed to the accident. Held: the highway authority did not owe a duty, or if it had, it had not broken it.

The police

3.6   One particular set of public authorities who are treated especially generously by the courts are the police authorities.

Hill v Chief Constable of West Yorkshire (1989)   A serial killer, the 'Yorkshire Ripper', murdered a number of women in the Wigan area before being apprehended by the police. The estate of his last victim sued the police authority, arguing that, with the exercise of reasonable care, he would have been caught earlier. Held: the police owed no legal duty to individual members of the public who might be affected by their failure to apprehend the killer.

Ancell v McDermott (1993)   Ancell was involved in a road accident caused by a leaking oil tank. The accident would have been avoided if certain police officers had acted more promptly in reporting the leak. Held: the duty of the police to road users did not extend to a tortious right of action by injured parties.

Various factors were suggested in these cases, as tending towards a finding that there was no enforceable duty. It was said that there was a risk of 'defensive policing', the police being more concerned with warding off legal action than with doing their proper duties. It was also said that there was no need for tort liability as a spur to make the police do their job, as they were already adequately motivated in that regard. Finally, it was suggested that the appropriate bodies to monitor police efficiency were the bodies appointed for that purpose, rather than the courts. None of this has convinced very many legal commentators, who cannot see why this is true of police authorities when it could equally be said of many other tort defendants. Are the police really so different from other major classes of defendants, such as employers (**4.32**)? If the police are different, this should be a matter of evidence, rather than of *ex cathedra* pronouncements from the bench. Does 'defensive policing' exist? Can the incentives on the police be improved? These are factual questions, not purely legal ones.

The overall climate of liability is chilly, then. Nonetheless, if a distinct and dangerous line of conduct by the police can be demonstrated, there may be liability.

> *Knightley v Johns* (1982)   A road crash occurred, blocking a road tunnel. However, traffic was still entering the tunnel, unaware of the crash. One officer, Johns, instructed his subordinate Knightley to ride his motorcycle against the flow of the traffic, to reach the head of the tunnel and close it. Held: Knightley could sue for his injuries which resulted from this very dangerous manoeuvre.

So it seems easier to establish liability in such a case, which involved an on-the-spot decision. This is not quite the 'policy'/'operational' distinction, however. *Knightley* was clearly operational, but arguably so was *Hill* (though views differ on this), and certainly *Ancell* was. As it is, the law is in a fluid state.

> *Swinney v Chief Constable of the Northumbria Police* (1996)   Swinney passed on to the police information about a man who had killed a police officer. Relevant documents were left in a police car, in an area notorious for theft. The documents were stolen and found their way into the hands of the killer, who terrorised Swinney and her husband. Could Swinney sue the police? The police tried to strike out Swinney's claim as showing no reasonable cause of action. Held: her case was arguable and should be allowed to proceed to trial.

Concurrent liability

3.7   Liability here may overlap with that in other areas of law. So, private medical patients whose doctors are guilty of extreme carelessness may sue in breach of contract or in negligence, entirely as they wish. Care is sometimes needed, however, in distinguishing a personal injury claim from a pure economic loss claim, where concurrence still needs careful consideration.

> *Van Oppen v Clerk to the Bedford Charity Trustees* (1990)   Van Oppen, a pupil at Bedford school, was injured in the course of a rugby game. No negligence in the running of the game was alleged on appeal, but Van Oppen claimed that the school should have insured its pupils against injury. Held: such a duty could only arise, if at all, under a contract with the school, not in tort.

Claims for purely economic losses, then, are treated with much less generosity than are claims for personal injury. The matter is dealt with in more detail in a later chapter, at **5.1**.

Breach of duty

Duty is owed to each individual plaintiff

3.8   While it is often enough simply to ask whether D was 'negligent' or 'careless', strictly speaking the question is whether D was negligent *in relation to a particular plaintiff* (**3.2**). It follows that each plaintiff's case is different, even where the same 'negligence' is in issue.

> *Paris v Stepney Borough Council* (1951)   A garage hand lost the sight of one eye when a metal chip flew off the axle he was hammering. His employer had not provided him with safety goggles. His other eye, as his employers knew, was not good. Held: his employers' knowledge that one eye was bad placed them under a higher duty than they owed to their other employees, and they were liable.

Again, in *Excelsior Wire Rope Co Ltd v Callan* (1930), children playing on D's machinery were injured when it was unexpectedly turned on. The risk of injury was in one sense the same to both adults and children; but the House of Lords held that the children's propensity to fool around near machinery meant that the duty owed to them was greater. Accordingly, the children recovered damages in circumstances where adults certainly would not.

This principle can work either for P or against P: the question is whether D broke the duty owed to P, and it is irrelevant whether the duty owed to others is higher, lower or merely different.

> *Bourhill v Young* (1943) Young drove his motorcycle recklessly, causing a collision from which he died. Bourhill, who was eight months pregnant, was some way away at the time of the accident, but saw the aftermath, including large quantities of blood. She suffered nervous shock and miscarried. Held: she was not a foreseeable victim of Young's negligence and so could not recover.

The standard of care: 'subjective' or 'objective'?

3.9 The standard of care is that of the reasonably experienced person in D's position (**1.37**). The duty is 'subjective' in the sense that it relates to the reasonable person *in D's position*. So if D has to make a decision on the spur of the moment, this will not be regarded as negligent merely because a reasonable person with more time to consider the matter would probably have done something different.

> *Watt v Hertfordshire County Council* (1954) A fire fighter was injured when a heavy jack loaded into the fire engine moved and fell on him. He sued the fire authority, arguing that a different engine, which was designed to transport the jack in safety, should have been used for this job. Held: the decision on which engine to use had not been unreasonable, in the light of the short time in which a decision had had to be made.

However, the duty is 'objective' in the sense that D's own character and dispositions are irrelevant. If reasonable people would regard D's conduct as rash and dangerous, it is no defence that D was a rash person and that, by his own lights, what he did was rather restrained. And *if D undertakes a job requiring professional skill, D will be judged by the standard of the reasonably competent professional*, whether or not D in fact has that level of skill. So each patient is entitled to expect professional competence from a surgeon, even if this is the surgeon's first ever operation. The courts are very reluctant to dilute this rule in major areas of liability: they even hold learner drivers to the standards of experienced professionals (**4.14**). However, in more marginal situations they are more generous, demanding only that D come up to the level of expertise that an impartial observer would have assumed that D had.

Wells v Cooper (1958)   Wells was injured when a door handle in Cooper's house came away from the door. Cooper had fitted it himself. Held: Cooper need not attain the standard of a reasonably competent carpenter doing the work for another, but only the standard of a reasonably competent DIY enthusiast, which he had.

Philips v William Whiteley Ltd (1938)   Philips arranged for her ears to be pierced by Whiteley's staff. The jeweller concerned sterilised his needle by putting it in a flame and in disinfectant, but did not take the precautions which a surgeon conducting a similar minor operation would have done. Held: Whiteley were not liable when Philip's ear become inflamed, as they had never claimed to reach the standard which a surgeon would have done.

Magnitude of risk vs cost of precaution

3.10   The most important factors in determining whether there has been a breach are those suggested by the 'Learned Hand formula' (**1.35**). P must establish that there is some precaution against harm which D should have taken, and which would have prevented the harm P suffered. In considering whether D should have taken any particular precaution, the court will weigh up the cost of doing this, and assess the degree of protection it would have given. This will be a function both of the risk of harm, and of the degree of harm if it eventuates: '... the law in all cases exacts a degree of care commensurate with the risk created' (*Read v J Lyons and Co Ltd* [1947] AC 156, 173, Lord Macmillan). Where it is clear that *no* precaution would have avoided the risk flowing from D's activities, which are therefore *intrinsically* dangerous, then the question is whether the reasonable person in D's position would have carried out the activity at all, bearing in mind the degree of danger to others. In other words, the question is the same, but the 'precaution' in issue is the complete abandonment of D's activity — and the cost to D of abandoning it is a factor against liability.

The system generally

[*Warning: The figures in this section are very rough. They are derived from a number of surveys which were a good deal more precise, but which often give conflicting accounts. A full discussion of which surveys are to be preferred would be a very substantial enterprise indeed!*]

Numbers of victims

3.11   It is difficult to give a precise picture of the pattern of accidents and of how the legal system deals with them. Patterns of reporting vary; there is no obvious, precise definition of 'serious' injury; different bodies collect statistics for different reasons, and with different definitions.

A very vague picture is as follows. The number of accidental injuries in Britain each year, serious enough to merit a few days off work, is in the millions, though not the tens of millions. Perhaps one-fifth are the result of industrial accidents and perhaps one-tenth are the result of road accidents; a very large proportion, perhaps one-quarter, occur in the home or in residential institutions. The bulk of the accidents are at the more trivial end of the scale, with the result that numbers of accidents drop sharply as we raise the severity of accident we are interested in. Only about 1%–2% of victims of accidents still suffer from the effects after six months. 'For every person who is off work for months, hundreds are off work for weeks; and for everyone off for weeks, scores are off for days' (P Cane, *Atiyah's Accidents Compensation and the Law*, 5th edn 1993, p 19). At the extreme end of seriousness, perhaps 14,000 people die in accidents each year: maybe one-third in road accidents, one-third at home or in residential establishments and one-tenth in industrial accidents. Slightly over 1,000 are either homicides or deaths caused by reckless driving.

At all levels of seriousness, injuries in accidents are far outnumbered by injuries due to disease. Perhaps 20 working days are lost through disease for every one through accident. Cigarette-smoking alone accounts for more than 100,000 deaths a year.

Willingness to sue

3.12   There are a number of reasons why injured people may not sue, if indeed they realise that they might be able to. There is a huge reluctance to sue family or friends; understandably so, though sometimes this may indicate lack of understanding of the workings of liability insurance. There are noticeable differences between different classes of claimants: men are more likely to sue than women; those of working age are more likely to sue than are children or the old; the poor are more likely to sue than the rich. Levels of claims also vary with the context of the injury. Road accident and work accident victims are relatively ready to consider legal action: one in three road accident victims and one in four work accident victims, go so far as to consult a solicitor. Others who are injured are much less likely to consider legal action. It is not entirely clear why this is, unless it is simply a self-perpetuating fashion: 'everyone knows' that you can't sue for accidents in the home, even though perhaps one-fifth of home accidents are the fault of someone other than the victim. No doubt, without social security benefits, sick pay and the NHS, minor injuries would do more harm to people's pockets, and so would be more likely to prompt litigation. Numbers of participants in legal actions can be greatly raised by publicity, as those promoting mass actions over specific incidents or products have found. A leading example is the Dalkon Shield action, which attracted an estimated 250,000 plaintiffs worldwide.

Numbers who sue and who receive compensation

3.13 Perhaps 200,000 people per year receive compensation for torts, which is in the order of 5% of all those injured. It is not always necessary to go to court to secure an award. Legal proceedings are started in perhaps less than one-third of those cases, and very few of those proceed to trial: perhaps 10% of cases where proceedings are started end up in a full trial. Of all plaintiffs who seriously pursue a claim, whether they start legal proceedings or not, about 90% secure some sort of settlement or award.

So, roughly 5% of all those injured receive tort damages, but the total amount paid out by defendants is about half the total social security injury benefits paid to *all* those injured! Thus we see a clear (and rather controversial) value judgement effected through our system: that those injured by someone's fault deserve to recover more than victims of misfortune alone. The vast bulk of successful claims are for relatively small amounts, in the hundreds and low thousands of pounds. However, there is a 'long tail' of massive claims for permanent disablement: the top 1% of tort claims account for about one-quarter of the total amounts awarded. Road accident and employment-related claims account for over 90% of the total.

Defendants

3.14 There is rarely any point in pursuing a claim in tort unless it is absolutely clear that the defendant can meet it if it is established.

Accordingly, the overwhelming bulk of tort claims are, as a matter of financial reality, against insurance liability firms. Nearly all of the others are against substantial companies, organs of government, or others with substantial wealth. Both employers and drivers are required by law to carry liability insurance, and an insurance industry body, the Motor Insurers' Bureau (MIB) acts as defendant in cases where the driver concerned was uninsured. Perhaps 90% of tort claims are covered by liability insurance, nearly all of the remainder being against firms wealthy enough to carry the financial risk themselves. Probably less than 1% of tort claims are against private individuals.

The reality of most tort litigation, therefore, is that it usually involves P's solicitor negotiating with a solicitor acting for an insurance company. This reality is not usually mirrored in tort textbooks. From the textbook point of view, tort often seems like an exercise in determining whether D was at fault, and who is to meet the claim is a mere peripheral detail. From an insurance perspective, D's fault has very little to do with it – indeed, D has very little to do with the claim, which is dealt with between P and D's insurer. What the court is really discussing is not 'the extent of D's liability' – D will not be paying a penny, whatever happens – but rather the extent of the insurance company's liability. Which perspective is the better one is a matter of opinion, but it is certainly true that the elaborate system of fault-finding that is modern tort law would not exist in its current form without the laws which require compulsory liability insurance.

Plaintiffs

3.15　Plaintiffs are typically less well-organised than defendants. Very possibly the plaintiff had no particular interest in legal matters before the accident, unlike most insurance companies. Until recently, it would have been fair comment that solicitors acting for plaintiffs would typically be less experienced than solicitors acting for defendants – though as a result of various pressures towards specialisation, this is less true today, if it is true at all. Financing an action is a hurdle many plaintiffs are unable to get over. Some plaintiffs negotiate with the insurance company directly, in some cases with success. There are also a number of 'claims assessors' who will act for a claimant, but as these assessors may have no formal legal qualification and therefore cannot lawfully start legal proceedings on their clients' behalf, their negotiating strength is limited. Some plaintiffs turn out already to have bought the right to legal services. It is comparatively rare to buy 'legal expenses insurance' for its own sake, but it often comes as part of wider insurance cover, or as part of a package of services offered by membership organisations, and especially by trade unions. Indeed, unions provide legal advice in a large proportion of work-related claims and a significant number of road accident claims, acting on behalf of their members. An uncomfortable illustration of this is in relation to the Hillsborough Stadium disaster, where claims were brought both by injured fans and by injured police officers. The Police Federation is a well-organised body, entirely familiar with the procedures for establishing legal rights on its members' behalf; whereas the fans are not normally organised for that sort of task at all. The greater success of actions by police plaintiffs is therefore no surprise.

These cases apart, either P must show that he or she is entitled to legal aid, or must pay the costs personally. Legal aid is means-tested and subject to strict limits. A significant number of plaintiffs, then, perhaps more than half, must pay for the services of a solicitor themselves. Most such work is done at an hourly charging rate for the solicitor's time. It has recently become possible for solicitors to charge on a 'conditional fee' basis, under which they charge nothing for their time unless they secure an award or a sum in settlement, in which case they charge rather more than their normal hourly rate. The scheme is still effectively experimental, and operates within financial limits, in that there is a maximum 'uplift' of 100% − in other words, the solicitor cannot charge a successful client more than double what they would have charged if working for their normal hourly rates. A plaintiff who sues but fails is liable for D's legal costs, whether P's own solicitor is working on a 'conditional fee' basis or not.

The settlement process

3.16 Personal injury claims typically take months or even years to resolve. A certain amount of delay is inevitable, unless (unusually) P's prognosis is clear from the outset. Delay may be increased by a wait for other legal processes to run their course, such as criminal proceedings arising out of the accident. Negotiations typically start with a standard letter from P's solicitor claiming damages, which receives a standard reply from D's solicitor denying liability and asking for details of the alleged negligence. Collection of evidence is often a slow and expensive process, and neither side will be willing to reveal the complete picture to the other even when they know it themselves; accordingly, there is usually a significant element of bluff and counter-bluff involved in the negotiations. As a rule, delay favours D rather than P, because P needs the money more than D needs to close the file. This is especially so where P's solicitor is charging P at an hourly rate. It seems that entirely hopeless claims are usually recognised as such at an early stage, which may explain why about 90% of cases actually proceeded with result in some sort of settlement. However, the costs involved even in a quick settlement are large. The total amounts received by successful claimants are only slightly more than the amounts paid to the firms representing them. If tort is contrasted with other mechanisms under which accident victims may receive cash payments, such as private insurance and social security, the relative inefficiency of tort is very apparent.

The future of the system

3.17 The increase in the number of legal claims generally has proved an increasing drain on the legal aid fund, and the response of government over the past decade has been to restrict access further and further. Whatever may be the future of the system generally, it appears that in its current form it cannot, for the foreseeable future, meet the legal needs of more than a small proportion of the population. Abolition of the current system of civil legal aid is under active consideration by the government. Various reforms for personal injury recovery have been mooted.

• Some commentators note the high success rate in personal injury claims and that settlement usually involves D paying for P's legal costs, which (if P is legally-aided) are then repaid to the legal aid fund. It is therefore suggested that with a slight increase in fees the system could be made self-financing. In other words, if successful plaintiffs paid slightly more back to the legal aid fund, this windfall to the fund would be enough to pay for the few claims which are unsuccessful. If the overall cost to the legal aid fund of personal injury cases is zero, then widening access should be a possibility. A variation of this scheme is the so-called 'contingency legal aid' fund, under which legally-aided clients would pay over the odds for their legal advice, but only if successful in their claim.

- Others suggest that the 'conditional fee' scheme should be expanded and developed, in the hope that more solicitors would be prepared to take on cases under it. If successful, this would make personal injury litigation a possibility for those who could never hope to qualify for legal aid.

Both schemes are open to objection. In particular, if either achieved its stated objective of making litigation affordable for larger numbers of people, then presumably the number of claims made would expand considerably, with unpredictable consequences. It remains to be seen how many firms of solicitors will be prepared to take on significant numbers of conditional fees cases, given the substantial financial risk they expose the solicitors to. Risk management of that type and severity will be new to many practices, and will require a cultural sea-change in the attitude of the legal professions.

In the following sections, I consider some special categories of personal injury plaintiffs.

Nervous shock

What is 'nervous shock'?

3.18 It is common to say of someone hurt in an accident that they were 'shocked' or 'in shock'. This is a vague usage, though the medical reality to which it points is definite enough. However, these cases do not pose particular problems for the personal injury lawyer: the 'shock' is compensatable as part of the action for the injury itself, probably as part of the claim for pain and suffering (**10.58**). Where personal injury lawyers talk of 'nervous shock', they have a different problem in mind. In some cases, P does not suffer any physical injury at all, but nonetheless emerges from the accident with psychiatric injuries of some gravity. Liability sometimes arises in this situation, but the law is not as generous to P as in cases of actual physical injury.

The need for a distinct psychiatric illness

3.19 P's case has to involve proof that P was mentally ill as a result of the shock, and it is axiomatic that pain, grief or distress are not enough in themselves to constitute 'nervous shock'. Currently, the lawyers' 'nervous shock' is roughly equivalent to the doctors' 'post-traumatic stress disorder' (PTSD), though any recognised psychiatric illness should usually be enough to establish action. The diagnosis of PTSD involves three major symptoms:

- persistent flashbacks or intrusive recollection of the traumatic incident, perhaps involving a re-experiencing of emotions felt at the time, or even a feeling that the trauma is recurring; and

- avoidance of people, places or activities which remind P of the traumatic events; and

- increased psychological arousal, manifested in sleep disorder, irritability, poor concentration or otherwise.

P's claim to suffer from PTSD is likely to be examined by the courts in considerable detail if it is disputed, and the law is no longer open to the criticism (if it ever was) that it allows a legal action to lie merely for grief or sadness. Two major problems persist.

First, there are many possibilities for fraud and for 'functional overlay' (roughly, unconscious exaggeration of symptoms). This is also true in other areas of personal injury law, but is particularly acute here. Sometimes P's illness can be shown to be a 'litigation neurosis' which will dissipate once the action is over. This is no bar to P's claim, though in those circumstances P's damages will certainly be reduced if any significant delay in the litigation can be laid at P's door.

Second, the courts, in their anxiety to avoid the charge that they are treating mere sorrow as if it were an illness, have drawn a sharp distinction between 'abnormal' mental diseases and 'normal' emotional reactions to distressing circumstances. But this distinction is in many contexts increasingly implausible. So the courts have refused the claim of a couple trapped in a hospital lift, on the ground that it was 'merely' claustrophobia complicated by anxiety connected to the heart condition from which one suffered (*Reilly v Merseyside Health Authority* (1994)). Yet the distress involved was as traumatic and as prolonged as many 'nervous shock' cases. And the Court of Appeal has recently been faced with the unedifying task of determining whether P's condition amounted to PTSD or 'merely' to a severe grief reaction at the drowning of his daughters

(*Vernon v Bosley* (1997)). The doctors are becoming less and less of a help in maintaining the distinction been 'normal' and 'abnormal' conditions. Perhaps the courts will soon be forced either to abandon the distinction, or to admit that it is legal and conventional, rather than rooted in medical reality.

Liability: basic principles

3.20 Until quite recently, the courts treated nervous shock as a distinct type of damage, quite distinct from other types of personal injury. Accordingly, it was said that 'the test of liability for shock is foreseeability of injury by shock' (*King v Phillips* [1953] I QB 429, 441, Denning LJ). However, the courts now recognise that this is unrealistic. The cases now distinguish between cases where D ought to have foreseen physical injury to P (where P is accordingly a 'primary victim') and cases where P can only say that D ought to have foreseen shock (where P is a 'secondary victim').

'Primary victims'

3.21 Where D's activities posed a foreseeable risk of physical injury to P, so that if P had been physically injured P could have maintained an action for those injuries, then P may sue for any proven psychiatric harm. In other words, if it was foreseeable that P would be injured, it is no defence that P's injury happens to take a psychiatric rather than a physical form.

> *Page v Smith* (1995)   Page and Smith collided in a car accident which was wholly Smith's fault. Page was physically unharmed, but subsequently suffered a recurrence of a pre-existing condition of myalgic encephalomyelitis (ME) as a result of the trauma of the incident. Held: Smith must take his victim as he found him and was accordingly liable for Page's condition.

It follows that where D's negligence creates a risk of physical injury to a group of people, then the main question for a plaintiff suffering nervous shock is whether he or she was within the 'zone of danger' which represented the limits of D's reasonable foresight. P can recover if within the zone, but otherwise not.

> *McFarlane v EE Caledonia Ltd* (1994)   Macfarlane witnessed the fire at the Piper Alpha oil rig, being about 100 metres away at the time.

He felt considerable anxiety for his own personal safety at the time, and later experienced psychiatric illness. Held: his fear for his own safety was unreasonable and his condition was not actionable.

However, while many cases are clearly one side of the line or the other, this doctrine still leaves a considerable grey area. Take the old case of *Bourhill v Young* (1943), where D's poor driving on his motorcycle led to an accident from which he died. P, who was eight months pregnant, was some way away at the time of the accident, but saw the rather gory aftermath. This had such an effect on her that she miscarried. The House of Lords in 1942 held that she was an unforeseeable plaintiff. Would the courts say the same today? It would have been very surprising if she had been physically hurt, but if she had been (say by a piece of debris from the collision, thrown on a freak trajectory) the courts would almost certainly have allowed her to recover. Does that put her within the 'zone of danger'? The courts have become much more generous towards 'nervous shock' claimants in the half-decade since *Bourhill*, but it is not entirely clear how far they are now prepared to go.

'Secondary victims'

3.22 *Introduction* Where P was not physically at risk from D's activities, but nonetheless suffers shock on witnessing them, then a duty may in principle be owed. But rather more is required than in cases of 'primary victims'. This usually involves two aspects:

- *A clear emotional connection between the traumatic event and the shock P suffers.* So witnessing injuries to a close relation is more likely to result in a successful claim than witnessing a stranger suffer.

- *Clear perception by P of the traumatic event.* Seeing your parents being crushed to death is more likely to lead to a successful claim than hearing via the radio that this has happened.

However, these are only factors in a larger question, and their relative importance differs from case to case. There is really only one question: ought D to have realised that a person of reasonable psychological firmness in P's position might suffer shock as a result of D's activities? Of course, people differ in their ability to withstand shock. Nonetheless, to ask whether P's firmness was 'reasonable' is rather odd. A plaintiff who is unusually susceptible to shock can certainly be regarded as *unlucky*, but it is a strong thing to regard P as *unreasonable*; what was P supposed to do about it? Are we simply asking whether P was average in this regard? Much is unclear here. However, one thing is clear: if the court considers that a reasonable person in P's position might have suffered shock, then it makes no difference that P's reaction is more than D might reasonably have expected. Once liability is established, defendants must take their victims as they find them.

Brice v Brown (1984)   Brice and her daughter were involved in a road accident which was wholly the fault of Brown. Brice already had a mild hysterical personality disorder. As a result of the injuries to herself and her daughter, Brice's psychological condition worsened considerably, involving her in bizarre and unsocial behaviour and a number of suicide attempts. Held: once liability for her nervous shock was established, damages were not to be reduced merely because P's behaviour was of an unforeseen type. It was enough that it was the direct effect of the psychiatric injury done to her.

3.23   *Close emotional link with traumatic event*   The archetypal 'secondary victim' is the plaintiff who sees a close relative suffer injury or death. The closer the emotional tie between P and the 'primary victim' of the accident, the more foreseeable is shock as a result.

Alcock v Chief Constable of the South Yorkshire Police (1991)   Ten plaintiffs alleging nervous shock arising out of the Hillsborough Stadium disaster sued the police authority in charge of the incident. Nine were relatives of primary victims, one the fiancée of a primary victim. None of the plaintiffs were spouses or parents of primary victims. Held: no duty was owed to any of the plaintiffs.

In *Alcock* the Lords seemed happy to endorse the result of the earlier case of *McLoughlin v O'Brian* (1982). There the Lords had granted a remedy to a woman who suffered nervous shock on the injury of her husband and three children. She had seen the news while in hospital, and later saw the injured bodies of those who had survived, still injured. However, *Alcock* is plainly a retreat from the position of Lord Scarman in *McLoughlin*, who was happy to declare that foresight should be the sole criterion, 'untrammelled by spatial, physical or temporal limits' ([1982] 2 All ER 311). It is clear that there is no fixed rule: the closeness of the relationship is only one factor, and the Lords in *Alcock* did not rule out the possibility of recovering for the effects of injury to a complete stranger, if it occurred in sufficiently disturbing circumstances. In some cases, such as brother and sister, the court is unlikely to be happy with a bare statement of the relationship, but will want some evidence of its closeness in fact.

There is obviously an element of arbitrariness in the test applied here, even if it is founded on straightforward, and apparently accurate, notions about when plaintiffs are likely to suffer shock. The Law Commission has mooted the idea of a fixed statutory list of relationships which are considered likely to give rise to shock. This would have the merit of clarity and is no more obviously arbitrary than current arrangements.

3.24 *Perception of the traumatic event*   P's chances of recovery improve with the clarity with which P was able to perceive the traumatic event. So shock occasioned by seeing a traumatic event at close hand may give rise to liability, even though hearing of the same incident by word of mouth may not. So in the *Alcock* case (**3.23**), it was made clear that plaintiffs who had seen the Hillsborough disaster on a TV screen, but not in person, could not possibly recover. However, it was also made clear that this was not a rule of law about TV transmission as such, but only because the images in the case had been censored. TV broadcasters are subject to a code which forbids (amongst other things) close-ups of people being crushed to death. Lord Ackner at least was clear that TV images might in appropriate cases give rise to claims in nervous shock, as where a balloon trip is filmed on live TV and a sudden catastrophe entails that parents watch their children plummeting to their death ([1991] 4 All ER 921).

This criterion of P's depth of perception is vague. It also reflects what is probably a psychological misconception. At least in the case of close relatives, it does not appear to be true that a better chance to view their injury results in an increased risk of shock. To be blunt about it, there is *no* pleasant or unstressful way to hear that your spouse or your child has been mangled to death. And it does not appear to be true that those who hear about it on the radio find the blow less severe than those who are on the scene to see it.

3.25 *Varieties of traumatic event*   Most cases of 'secondary victimhood' involve injuries to relatives, but there is no rule of law restricting liability to such cases. All that is required is that the event has such a direct and obvious effect on P that any reasonable person in D's position must have foreseen shock.

Attia v British Gas plc (1987) Due to the negligence of British Gas employees, a fire started in Attia's house. She arrived home to see it engulfed in flames. Held: her nervous shock was a foreseeable consequence of British Gas's negligence and she could recover damages accordingly.

In *A v Tameside and Glossop Health Authority* (1996), the defendant health authority discovered that one of their health workers was HIV positive. They decided to inform those he had treated of the (very slight) risk of infection, inviting them for tests. Some of the recipients of the letters sued for shock. In the event, the health authority admitted the existence of a duty, but successfully argued that they had acted reasonably in the circumstances. Obviously a court will be reluctant to find a breach of duty in that situation – What was the authority supposed to do? – but the existence of a duty is plain.

Reform

3.26 With every advance of medical knowledge in this area, the line between physical injury and 'nervous shock' has become harder to draw, as has the line between 'normal' and 'abnormal' reactions to disturbing circumstances. The drastic limitations on the forseeability of 'secondary' shock are not based on a realistic assessment of who is likely to suffer shock and who is not, but are the product of extreme judicial caution. Such caution is perhaps justified on questions where medical knowledge is far from complete, but are hard to justify in areas where it is more definite. Several legal commentators have urged that no firm line can be drawn between physical and mental trauma and that they should be dealt with by the same rules. However, even assuming that this is the right attitude to take (the matter is far from certain), it is another question whether the courts should say so all at once, or whether they are not doing plaintiffs a service by only slowly assimilating 'nervous shock' cases to liability generally. Can the court's current approach be regarded as a process of slow assimilation? If so, the pace is truly glacial. At the current rate of progress, we will be well into the twenty-first century before assimilation is complete.

Negligence and the foetus

Injuries suffered in the womb

3.27 *General*   Where, as result of D's activities, a developing foetus suffers an injury, can legal action be taken? Legal personality is not acquired until live birth; there is no such thing as an unborn plaintiff. In the early 1970s it was unclear whether or not a legal action vested in P on birth, in respect of matters occurring before it. Parliament therefore intervened to establish liability, by the Congenital Disabilities (Civil Liability) Act 1976, vesting a right of action in any child born alive for injuries suffered in the womb. It was later held that this was also the position at common law (*Burton v Islington Health Authority* (1992)), and accordingly a remedy is available whether D's negligence took place before or after the Act came into force.

The statutory right of action is derivative from the rights of the parents: D is liable for conduct which affected the ability of either parent to have a normal healthy child, or affected the mother during her pregnancy, and which resulted in disability to the child. The rule is, in effect, that if the parent could have sued had they suffered injury then the child can sue too. It is no defence that in the event the parent suffered no injury (s 1(3)). This derivative liability, in the Act as originally drafted, did not catch the case where D damaged gametes or eggs held in a laboratory and which were subsequently implanted and grew to form the child. This case is provided for expressly by Human Fertilisation and Embryology Act 1990, s 44, which introduces a new s 1A to the 1976 Act. An exception clause which would have barred action by the parent concerned also bars a claim by the child (s 1(6)). If the parent concerned was partly responsible for the damage, then the amount of the claim is reduced by whatever share the court thinks just and equitable (s 1(7)). No action lies if D's misconduct occurred before conception and at least one parent knew of the risk (s 1(4)).

3.28 *Claims against the parents*   It is clear from the Act that the father may be liable for injuries to the child. Where the father's breach of duty occurred before conception, the mother's awareness of the risk of disability is a defence (s 1(4)). The mother, by contrast, is liable in only one case: where, when she knew or ought to have known that she was pregnant, she drives a motor vehicle in a manner threatening the safety of the foetus. (In that situation she will have liability insurance and so will not pay the damages personally (**4.13**).) In this case, she owes a duty directly to the foetus, though it is actionable only in the event of a live birth (s 2).

'Wrongful life'

3.29 *Wrongful conception* Suppose that, but for D's negligence, the child would never have been conceived at all. The usual scenario is that D negligently performs a vasectomy or sterilisation operation. Action by the child in those circumstances seems unlikely to succeed, but actions by the parents are common. Initially there were doubts as to the propriety of this form of action, but it is now accepted, within limits.

> *Emeh v Kensington & Chelsea & Westminster Area Health Authority* (1985) In consequence of a negligent sterilisation by the health authority, Emeh had an unplanned daughter. Held: she was entitled to damages for *(i)* the pain, suffering and 'general wear and tear' involved in birth and parenthood, though with a deduction for the more positive aspects of the experience, and *(ii)* the financial cost of bringing up the unplanned child. Emeh's refusal to have an abortion was not considered a ground for reducing her damages.

Emeh was an example of a negligent failure to sterilise the mother. Action also lies for negligent failure of a vasectomy on the father and (presumably) for poor advice on how soon it is safe to have unprotected sex after a well-performed operation. In some cases, however, remoteness may be an issue.

> *Goodwill v British Pregnancy Advisory Service* (1996) MacKinlay underwent a vasectomy, and afterwards received advice from BPAS that it had been a success. Three years later he commenced a relationship with Goodwill. The couple assumed, on the strength of BPAS's advice, that no contraception was necessary. On becoming pregnant by MacKinlay, Goodwill sued BPAS in negligent misstatement. Held: there was no sufficient proximity between BPAS and Goodwill.

There has been some controversy over the nature of the action, in the context of limitation. If a woman is sterilised but then becomes pregnant, what injury has she suffered, and when did she suffer it? Is it *(i)* personal injury inasmuch as she is not sterile, or *(ii)* personal injury inasmuch as she is pregnant, or *(iii)* economic loss inasmuch as she has an unplanned child to look after? Controversially, the Court of Appeal has now selected option *(ii)* (*Walkin v South Manchester Health Authority* (1995)). It follows that the primary limitation period is three years, which runs from the time she first knew or ought to have known that she was pregnant and that there was a real possibility of suing the hospital over it (**11.36**).

3.30 *Deprivation of chance to abort* A rather different claim, more relevant where the foetus has severe abnormalities, is that while the foetus' disabilities are not D's fault, nonetheless if D had acted properly then the parents would have appreciated the position and arranged for an abortion. Such claims may in principle be brought by either the parents, or by the child, or by all three. Claims by parents have occasionally succeeded.

> *Thake v Maurice* (1984) On carrying out a vasectomy, Maurice negligently failed to warn Thake of the small risk of spontaneous natural reversal of the process. It was found that if Thake had been aware of this risk, he and his wife would have recognised her pregnancy earlier and would have been able to abort. Held: action lay in negligence.

However, while the principle of the case is still good, the courts are reluctant to find a breach of duty in this situation. In *Gold v Haringey Health Authority* (1987) a similar claim by a woman whose sterilisation reversed itself failed, because there was no unanimity amongst doctors that a warning was necessary in her case, and so it was impossible to prove breach of duty. And in *Rance v Mid-Downs Health Authority* (1991) further doubt was cast on this type of claim, the court suggesting that the mother might not be entitled to an abortion in those circumstances at all. Claims by the child have also received short shrift.

> *McKay v Essex Area Health Authority* (1982) McKay, who was pregnant, suspected that she had contracted rubella, but was wrongly assured by her health authority, after negligently conducted tests, that she had not. Her child was born with deformities. Held: neither mother nor child could sue the health authority.

Assuming that it is clear, as it was in *McKay*, both that the defendants were negligent and that the mother would have had an abortion had she known the truth, then the normal elements of a negligence claim are all present. Nonetheless, both claims were rejected in *McKay*, on the rather dubious ground that the loss in question is incapable of measurement. In other words, even though the law in other contexts accepts that it may sometimes be better to die than to live (eg *re J* (1991)), nonetheless some difficulty was felt in putting a price tag on this. Yet the law of tort seems capable of putting a value on life in other contexts (see **10.66**), and it is not clear why the task should be any more difficult here. So the reason given in the case is weak; which is not to deny that better reasons might be found.

It is not altogether clear whether a court today, convinced that *McKay* is wrong and wishing to depart from it, would be free to do so in the light of the terms of the 1976 Act. The Act purports to exclude the common law in the area to which it applies (s 4(5)), while itself only allowing a claim in respect of 'disabilities' 'which would not otherwise have been present' but for D's negligence. Will the courts be prepared to regard the fact that the child is alive at all as a 'disability' for which a remedy is available under the Act? This seems to strain the wording.

Rescuers

'Danger invites rescue'

3.31   Where D's negligence puts someone in danger, and P attempts a rescue, but is injured in the process, P may be able to sue D. If the creation of the danger was foreseeable, then equally it should be foreseeable that someone will try to save others from it.

The principle is obvious enough. But it reverses the value judgement normally made about people who deliberately go towards a source of danger. Normally, we would expect to say that it is not foreseeable that someone would deliberately increase the risks they were running; or that D cannot reasonably be expected to provide for such a person; or that P can be met by a defence, such as the *novus actus interveniens* principle (**10.41**), or the defences of contributory negligence (**11.17**) or consent (**11.2**). So if D is responsible for the occurrence of an accident, very probably D will also be responsible for the fate of those who rush in to alleviate the consequences, and will not be able to plead that these rescuers are the authors of their own misfortune.

Defendants who endanger themselves

3.32 Sometimes P sets out to rescue D, and then sues D for injuries received, on the ground that the entire incident was D's fault. While defendants cannot be said to owe duties to themselves, they may nonetheless be said to owe a duty to those who seek to rescue them.

> *Harrison v British Railways Board* (1981) Howard, a British rail employee, attempted to board a train just as it was leaving the station. Harrison, the guard, made an ineffective attempt to stop the train, then tried to pull Howard on board. They both fell off onto the track. Held: Harrison could sue Howard for his injuries, though with a 20% reduction for contributory negligence.

D endangers X, P rescues X, P sues D

3.33 A more common situation is where P is hurt attempting to rescue a third party, from a danger created by D. Generally speaking in this situation D has broken a duty to X, and what the courts are doing is effectively extending the benefit of that duty of care to P as well. If D is responsible for the injury to X, D is also responsible for P's response to it.

> *Baker v TE Hopkins & Son Ltd* (1959) Employees of Hopkins were overcome by noxious carbon monoxide fumes while at work, in circumstances which were held to be the result of negligence by Hopkins. Baker, a doctor, tried to rescue them, but was himself overcome by fumes, and died. Held: Baker's widow could sue Hopkins.

Very occasionally, the possibility of a rescue, or of its precise mode of execution, has been considered unforeseeable.

> *Crossley v Rawlinson* (1982) A lorry burst into flames due to the negligence of Rawlinson. Crossley rushed towards it with a fire extinguisher, but tripped over a concealed hole and injured himself. Held: this injury was an unforeseeable consequence of Rawlinson's conduct and there was no liability.

The decision is an unusual one, and is out of line with most authorities. If injury of some sort to P is foreseeable, generally speaking it is no

79

defence that P suffers a different sort of injury (**10.32**). It is to be expected that *Crossley* will not be followed.

Nervous shock

3.34 Suppose D creates a source of physical danger. P is well outside the 'danger zone' at the time, and so if P suffers nervous shock we would expect P only to recover damages if P satisfies the strict rules for 'secondary victims' (**3.22**). However, if P attempts a rescue of the primary victims and suffers shock, it seems that P is entitled to be regarded as a 'primary victim' as well. It is no defence that it was P's own act which brought P into the 'zone of danger'.

> *Chadwick v British Transport Commission* (1967)   Chadwick took part in the rescue operations following a rail crash near his home, where 90 people were killed and many more were trapped and injured. He subsequently suffered a recurrence of psychoneurotic symptoms from which he had suffered when younger, but which would not have been expected to recur under the ordinary stresses of life. Held: the BTC, who were responsible for the crash, were liable to Chadwick also.

The rule is well established, but it leaves difficult questions of who is a rescuer, and who is merely someone who arrives in the aftermath of the tragedy.

> *Frost v Chief Constable of the South Yorkshire Police* (1997)   A group of six police officers involved in the disaster at the Hillsborough football ground sued their Chief Constable for their nervous shock arising out of their work on that day. Held: recovery was merited by those who had attempted resuscitation at the ground, moved bodies there, and dealt with the crowd-control problems in the immediate aftermath of the disaster; also to those who had worked at the stadium later, moving bodies and attempting to revive bodies. But no recovery was allowed to one officer who had stripped and labelled bodies and dealt with distraught relatives.

> *Duncan v British Coal Corpn* (1997)   Duncan, a pit deputy rushed to help a colleague trapped in a conveyor machine. The incident occurred while he was 275 metres away. The victim was dead by the time

Duncan arrived, though this did not become apparent for a while. Held: Duncan was not a 'rescuer' and could only recover if he satisfied the tests for secondary victims.

Duty owed individually to the rescuer

3.35 In a sense, the duty just described is 'derivative', in the sense that P will usually prove that a duty was owed *to someone else* and that it was foreseeable that P would then help that someone. Usually this is an adequate description. However, it is not complete. Cases where P rescues the very person responsible for the danger (**3.32**) cannot be analysed this way: it is impossible to owe a duty to yourself. More generally, P is allowed to plead a duty arising on ordinary principles, and this may mean that P can recover *even though the endangered person cannot*.

> *Videan v British Transport Commission* (1963) Videan, a station-master, rushed onto the railway line in an attempt to save his two-year-old son who had wandered onto it. Both were crushed to death by a negligently driven motorised trolley. The son was an unforeseeable trespasser and so could not recover; it was argued that if the son was unforeseeable, then logically an attempt to rescue him was unforeseeable too. Held: the father was lawfully on the line and thus a foreseeable victim of bad driving. Accordingly, liability was established.

The law on trespassers has changed since the time of *Videan*: the fact that the son was a trespasser might not doom his claim today (**4.26**). But the main point is that the father could rely on his status as employee and lawful visitor on the premises of the main defendant. In that limited sense, the case was (as Pearson LJ said, [1963] 2 QB 682-683) not really a 'rescuer' case at all: the father could prove that a duty was owed to him and was broken, without adverting to the fact that he was engaged in a rescue. Similarly, in *Frost* (**3.34**), a majority of the judges hinted that the duty owed to the police at Hillsborough might be different from, and more extensive than, the duty owed to fans, as the Chief Constable was in the position of an employer to them. To judge from press comment, this is the most controversial aspect in all of the Hillsborough cases: to many minds, it seems strange that a duty is owed to 'professional' rescuers at all, let alone a higher one than to the people they are rescuing.

Further Reading

Relevant sections of tort reference books may be supplemented with:

Michael A Jones, 'Liability for Psychiatric Illness – More principle, less subtlety?' [1995] 4 Web JCLI (http://www.ncl.ac.uk/~nlawwww/articles4/jones4.html).

Harvey Teff, 'Liability for negligently inflicted nervous shock' (1983) 99 LQR 100.

Self-test questions

1.   Why do so few victims of personal injuries sue those who injured them (**3.12**)?

2.   Is it legally possible to sue for nervous shock consequential on what P has seen on a TV screen (**3.24**)?

3.   In the wake of the Hillsborough disaster, many plaintiffs sued for nervous shock. Why should you expect police plaintiffs to have a much better chance of recovery than spectator plaintiffs (**3.15**, **3.35**)?

4.   In what circumstances may P sue his or her mother for injuries inflicted while she was pregnant with P (**3.28**)?

5.   Give examples of defendants who have been held liable for inflicting harm on others by omissions rather than acts (**3.4**).

CHAPTER FOUR

Negligent harm to the person: special duties

SUMMARY
Litigation over personal injuries is much more common in some areas than others. The principles in the case law are correspondingly more detailed in some areas than others.

The areas considered in this chapter are:

- **Products liability**

- **Road accidents**

- **Occupiers' liability**

- **Employers' liability**

- **Medical care**

Between them, these heads account for nearly all personal injury litigation.

Introduction

4.1 This chapter considers a number of special cases of negligence liability. The basic principles have already been explained. The areas considered here include the major areas where litigation actually occurs. Nearly all of the cases considered here are concerned with personal injury, though they may sometimes involve property damage instead, or in addition. So a car accident typically includes both personal injury and property damage. While most of the chapter concerns negligence, there are various statutory liabilities which it is convenient to treat here, even though the liability is sometimes strict.

Products liability

Introduction

4.2   One of the most famous and influential cases in the whole of the law of tort, *Donoghue v Stevenson* (1932), was a products liability case. That case is the foundation of much of what is now understood about the law of negligence. Ironically, the context in which this leading case occurred was a highly atypical one. Defective products cases are only rarely brought before the courts: barely 1% of all injuries are caused by defective products, and perhaps only 5% of people so injured are successful in claiming any compensation. So despite the importance of *Donoghue* to the way lawyers approach the whole area of negligence liability, products liability cases are of relatively little importance when considering tort generally.

Now that we are well over half a century away from the seminal ruling in *Donoghue*, the legal system has outgrown it in a number of ways. We have already seen how it is misleading as a general indication of the scope of liability in negligence (**1.23**). In the area of products liability itself, the case has been superseded by new legislation, which provides for a broader liability for injuries caused by defective products, which in most situations removes the need for P to establish fault (**4.6**). Nonetheless, there are cases which the new legislation does not reach and so the discussion will start with the law of negligence, before moving on to the stricter duty which is in some cases prescribed by legislation.

Common law

4.3   *Who owes the duty?*   *Donoghue* itself involved the liability of the manufacturer of the defective product. But there is nothing in the reasoning to confine it to the manufacturer, and subsequent cases have allowed action against others with some influence on the state of the product when it ultimately reached the consumer. So those who assemble goods (*Howard v Furness Houlder Argentine Lines Ltd* (1936)) or repair them (*Haseldine v CA Daw and Son Ltd* (1941)) owe a similar duty to the ultimate consumer. Even those who merely distribute goods owe a duty to the consumer if in the circumstances they should have made a safety check — although of course the consumer's action will ultimately fail if the safety check would not have prevented P's injuries. There is no general duty on distributors to make a check, but the following special circumstances have been held to lead to a duty:

- where the goods came from another supplier with a dubious reputation (*Watson v Buckley, Osborne, Garrett & Co Ltd* (1940));

- where the manufacturer's instructions are that there should be a check (*Holmes v Ashford* (1950)).

It even seems that sellers of second-hand cars generally may be under a duty to make at least a superficial check by a competent mechanic on cars before they sell them (*Andrews v Hopkinson* (1957)).

4.4 *Content of the duty*   In *Donoghue*, great stress was placed on the facts that the product in question (a bottle of defective ginger beer) was sealed in D's factory. The point is that the bottle was opaque, and so there was no realistic prospect of intermediate examination before the product arrived in front of P. The point is a vital one, for the manufacturer will rarely have control over what is done to the product after it leaves their hands, and so can only be blamed for the most obviously foreseeable happenings thereafter. So if intermediate examination of the product seems probable, the manufacturer is not liable for any injuries which this examination would have prevented. Contrary to *dicta* in *Donoghue* itself, it is not enough that intermediate examination is merely *possible*, if it was most unlikely (*Griffiths v Arch Engineering (Newport) Co Ltd* (1968)). However, even when intervening conduct does not remove the duty, it may nonetheless make it harder for P to establish a claim.

> *Evans v Triplex Safety Glass Co Ltd* (1936)   The windscreen of a car shattered for no apparent reason, injuring the occupants of the car. They sued the manufacturer. Held: the claim failed. There were various opportunities for intermediate examination after it left the factory, and no evidence that the defect was caused by poor manufacture as distinct from poor fitting of the screen to the car.

Again, if the manufacturer issues a warning about the product's safety, which ought reasonably to have put the consumer on his guard, then there would be no liability for injuries which the reasonable plaintiff would then have avoided.

Hurley v Dyke (1979) Dyke sold a second-hand car to Hurley, the car being sold as seen and with all its faults. Hurley was then severely injured and rendered a paraplegic, after the car went out of control on the road. Held: the warning that the car came with all faults discharged the seller's duty, and subsequent injury to the buyer of the car did not give rise to an action in negligence.

Kubach v Hollands (1937) Chemicals used in a school laboratory exploded and injured Kubach, a 13-year old pupil. Held: as the manufacturer had warned retailers of the chemical that it should be tested before use, it was under no liability to Kubach in negligence.

Cases where liability will be found are likely to be ones where the consumer has used the product in a reasonable and foreseeable way, leading to personal injury.

Grant v Australian Knitting Mills Ltd (1936) Grant bought underwear in a shop, and soon afterwards began to suffer from skin irritation, which was caused by chemicals on the underwear left over from the manufacturing process. It was shown that there would have been no problem if Grant had washed the underwear once before wearing it. Held: as there was no warning when the product was sold that initial washing would be necessary, liability in negligence was found.

4.5 *What claims can be made* Any foreseeable victim of the defective product is within the scope of the duty, and may accordingly sue for personal injuries suffered. It is irrelevant whether that consumer bought the product in person, or was given it by a friend (*Donoghue v Stevenson* (1932)). Products such as cars obviously carry risks not only to their users, but also to others on the scene when they are used. So if P is injured in a car accident which can be traced to the poor state of another driver's car, P may be able to sue the repairer of that car (*Stennett v Hancock* (1939)).

Haseldine v CA Daw and Son Ltd (1941) Haseldine was injured when a lift in which he was riding fell. The defect in the lift was traced to poor repair work done the day before. Held: the repairers owed a duty to all who used the defective lift.

It appears that the manufacturer's duty may even extend for some time after the product leaves the factory, so that there is a duty at common law to recall unsafe products – even in respect of products which were reasonably believed safe at the time they were made.

> A manufacturer who realises that omitting to warn past customers about something which might result in injury to them must take reasonable steps to attempt to warn them, however lacking in negligence he may have been at the time the goods were sold (*E Hobbs (Farms) Ltd v The Baxenden Chemical Co Ltd* [1992] 1 Lloyd's Rep 54, 65, Michael Ogden QC).

So those who suffer personal injury are well protected. However, the claim does not usually extend to cover purely economic losses (**5.7**).

> *Muirhead v Industrial Tank Specialities Ltd* (1985)   Industrial Tanks supplied Muirhead with electrical pumps, which he used for a tank containing lobsters. The pumps supplied were however designed to run at the wrong voltage. They cut out and the lobsters died. Held: Muirhead could recover for loss of the lobsters (property damage) and loss of profit on them (economic loss consequential on property damage) but not for the cost of replacing the pumps (purely economic loss).

The line is sometimes hard to draw. In *M/S Aswan Engineering Establishment Co v Lupdine Ltd* (1987) buckets supplied for carrying waterproofing compound overseas melted when left on a quayside in Kuwait, spilling their contents. For various reasons, it was held that the buckets could not be considered defective. If they had been, could their owner have recovered for the lost compound? The issue did not directly arise; there are *dicta* both ways ([1987] 1 WLR 21, Lloyd LJ; 29, Nicholls LJ).

If P notices the defect in the product before it has the chance to do anyone any harm, P has no claim in tort. The loss suffered by that stage is purely economic (the product P owns is less valuable than it would have been had the manufacturer acted carefully). If P then proceeds to use the product anyway, any claim for later personal injury will be met by a defence of *novus actus interveniens* (**10.36**) or contributory negligence (**11.17**). If P has a remedy at all in that situation, it will be by a contractual claim against whoever sold P the goods.

Statute

4.6 *Introduction*   Attempts to harmonise the law of products liability across the European Communities led in 1985 to a Directive on defective products, requiring member states to enact a new regime of liability (Directive on Liability for Defective Products 1985, 85/374/EC). The Directive was made part of UK law by the Consumer Protection Act 1987.

The Act is rather more technical than the Directive, and rather restrictive in some of its provisions. Indeed, it has been suggested that the Act may put the UK in breach of its obligations under EU law, in not giving to consumers all the rights the Directive intended them to receive. To date, however, the European Court of Justice has accepted no such argument. It has ruled in particular that the UK government was entitled to introduce the 'development risk' defence protecting manufacturers who have complied with the best technical standards current at the time they made the product (4.11). The Consumer Protection Act 1987 can therefore taken as definitive for the present, although the Directive can certainly be used as a guide to the Act's interpretation (see s 1(1)). As will become apparent, the Act does not cover all possible cases and so the common law is not fully superseded in this area.

The main feature of the new regime is strict liability. The Mrs Donoghues of the new European age may sue the manufacturer without having to prove either the existence of a duty or negligent behaviour. However, this principle is hedged around with various qualifications and defences, and considered overall the new regime is not noticeably more generous than the old. In particular, the problems faced by P in proving that a product is 'defective' seem remarkably like the difficulties P would earlier have had in establishing that the manufacturer was negligent (4.10).

4.7 *What claims may be made* The new law is essentially concerned with consumer safety, and as such the main type of claim envisaged is a claim for personal injury. Claims for property damage are permitted within limits, but the limits are narrower than those of the common law, thus preserving a role for the law of negligence in this area. The limits are designed to exclude both trivial claims and claims for injury to business property, while preserving the right for consumers to complain about property damage. Claims for property damage are barred unless they exceed £275 (s 5(4)). Further, the property concerned must both be 'ordinarily intended for private use, occupation or consumption' and 'intended by the person suffering the loss or damage mainly for his own private use, occupation or consumption' (s 5(3)). Claims for damage to the product itself, or to articles supplied along with the product, or claims for purely economic loss, are not recoverable at all (s 5(1), (2)).

4.8 *Against whom may claims be made* The strict liability in the Act is aimed principally at the producer or manufacturer of the goods in question, rather than at intermediaries such as suppliers. However, there are often difficulties in establishing precisely who the producer is, or in taking legal action against them if they are not based within the European Union. Accordingly, the Act casts the net wider. In addition to the producer, the following are also liable for defects in the products:

- Anyone who holds themselves out as the producer (s 2(2)(b)). So if a supermarket sells 'own brand' goods, they are liable for defects, whether or not they produced the goods themselves.

- Anyone who imported the goods into the European Union (s 2(2)(c)). However, if the goods were merely imported from one EU country to another, only the manufacturer is liable, not the importer.

- Anyone who manufactured a defective component which was incorporated into the product; though the component manufacturer is responsible only for their own component, not the whole product into which it was incorporated (s 4(1)(f)).

A mere supplier of goods is not usually liable under the Act. However, suppliers are bound by the Act to keep records of the producers of goods they supply, and if they fail to hand over this information to the victim of a defective product when so requested, they are themselves liable as producer (s 2(3)).

4.9 *What is a 'product'* 'Product' is defined broadly as including all goods (s 1(2)). 'Goods' may include 'substances, growing crops and things comprised in land by virtue of being attached to it and any ship, aircraft or vehicle' (s 45(1)). It is not restricted to manufactured goods, but also includes goods produced by mining or quarrying (s 1(2)(b)). It also includes electricity (s 1(2)). Certain products are exempted from the scope of the Act:

- *Agricultural produce and game* are excluded except where they have been subjected to an 'industrial process' (s 2(4)). Moreover, the process must be responsible for 'essential characteristics' of the resulting product before liability will attach (s 1(2)(c)). There are difficult questions here. If the case involves tinned vegetables, is the fact that they are tinned an 'essential characteristic', or are they essentially agricultural products, and so outside the Act? Or are genetically modified tomatoes to be regarded as essentially agricultural or essentially the result of an industrial process?

- *Buildings* are 'goods' within the meaning of the Act, but nonetheless someone who does building work is only caught by the Act insofar as the work 'involves the provision of any goods to any person by means of their incorporation into the building' (s 46(3)). Cases where the supply involved 'the creation or disposal of an interest in ... land' are excluded (s 46(4)). The overall effect of these provisions is that consumers can complain that individual items incorporated into a building (such as doors or windows) are defective, but the Act cannot be used to complain that an entire building is a 'defective product'. In such a case P would have to invoke the law of contract, or possibly the Defective Premises Act 1972 (**5.39**).

- *Books* are undoubtedly 'products', and presumably *computer programs* are too, at least if they are supplied on physical media such as a floppy disk or CD. It is, however, not clear at all whether damage caused by either is recoverable under the Act. Is information a 'product'? The issue has yet to be decided.

4.10 *What is a 'defective' product?* A product is defective 'if the safety of the product is not such as persons generally are entitled to expect' (s 3(1)). Matters stated in the Act to be relevant include:

- The way the product has been marketed, including 'its get-up' (s 3(2)(a)).

- Any instructions or warnings supplied with the goods (s 3(2)(a)).

- '[W]hat might reasonably be expected to be done with or in relation to the product' (s 3(2)(b)).

This test is obviously a vague one. Presumably, though the Act does not say expressly, the cost of making the product safer is relevant.

Accordingly, there does not appear to be a huge difference between asking whether a product is defective under the Act, and asking whether the manufacturer was negligent at common law. Plainly the Act does not mean that products will be *absolutely* safe, but only that they are as safe as reasonable people would expect. The test is designed to do many things at once. In particular, it seeks to encourage manufacturers to make goods safer, and accordingly provides that subsequent improvements to safety should not lead to the inference that the product was formerly unsafe (s 3(2)).

4.11 *Defences* Various matters amount to defences. Some arise under the general law. If the matter is in dispute, it would be for P to prove a causal connection between the defect and the loss suffered (**10.21**). It is not clear whether remoteness is a defence under the Act. Contributory negligence by P may lead to a reduction in damages (**11.17**). It is no defence that others contributed to P's damage, though this might enable D to claim contribution from those others (**9.26**). In addition, there are various special defences mentioned specifically in the Act:

- that the defect was attributable to D's compliance with some requirement of the law (s 4(1)(a));

- that D never in fact 'supplied' the product at all (s 4(1)(b)), for example where it was stolen from D;

- that the supply was not in the course of a business, and was not done with a view to profit (s 4(1)(c));

- that the defect did not exist at the time of the supply (s 4(1)(d));

- that the defect was effectively undiscoverable by producers of the type of goods concerned given 'the state of scientific and technical knowledge at the relevant time' (the 'development risk' defence) (s 4(1)(e)).

It is the last defence that is the most controversial. It is effectively a plea of lack of negligence at the design stage, so that the much-vaunted 'strict' liability under the Act is strict only as regards production defects, not design defects. In cases of design defects, then, the only difference effected by the Act has been to put the burden of proof onto the producer of the dangerous goods rather than the injured consumer. Yet the main economic justification of the Act was to place both the costs and the benefits of technical innovation on the shoulders of the manufacturers, whereas the 'development risk' defence seems to leave them with the benefits while placing the risks on the consumers of their products.

Many commentators have suggested that the defence as enacted in the Act of 1987 is broader than that contained in the Directive it is meant to implement. The Act talks about the knowledge available to manufacturers, whereas the Directive talks rather of the state of scientific and technical knowledge generally. The European Court has however now rejected this argument, while emphasising that the UK courts will need to refer to the Directive in deciding precisely how the statute should be interpreted (*Case C-300/95 EC Commission v United Kingdom* (1997)).

Road accidents

Introduction

4.12 The roads are a major source of accidents. Indeed, they always were, even before the invention of the motor car. Under modern conditions they are all the more dangerous. And these accidents are very much the concern of tort law. Perhaps a quarter of a million people are injured on the roads each year, though most of these injuries are trivial. Perhaps one-quarter of all those injured in road traffic accident take legal action. Nearly all of those who start a claim obtain damages of some sort. This suggests that the law is in practice highly predictable, with lawyers on both sides being able to tell with high reliability which claims have some prospect of success, and which ones are bound to fail. Yet there is surprisingly little to say about road traffic cases that is not true of negligence claims generally. They are simply the application of general principles to this one special, if rather common, case. Reported cases concentrate on the novel and the marginal. In particular, the courts are very reluctant to lay down precise rules as to the standards applicable to drivers. Indeed, a judge who thinks that he or she has identified a hard rule is probably slipping to error.

Worsfold v Howe (1980) Howe was attempting to turn right out of a minor road onto a major road; a petrol tanker which had stopped just to his right obscured his view. Inching his car forward, Howe collided with Worsfold's motor cycle, which was passing the tanker at an excessive speed. The trial judge considered both parties equally at fault, but thought himself bound by a rule that all someone in Howe's position is bound to do is to inch forward with all due care. Held: no such rule was apparent in the authorities and so the judge should have found the parties equally liable.

It is significant that the Court of Appeal in the case was anxious not to re-try it. 'I am not saying for a moment that if I myself had been trying this case I should have apportioned the responsibility fifty-fifty, but it is not possible for this court to go into the question of apportionment or alter the judge's view about that' ([1980] 1 All ER 1033, Browne LJ). There is little to say about these cases in very general terms; everything turns on the precise facts and circumstances, which are not very reportable. So this very major class of negligence litigation in fact appears in the law reports much less often than its importance suggests it should.

Emphasis on compensation, not deterrence

4.13 Ever since the Road Traffic Act 1930, car drivers have been required to be insured against possible tort claims that might result from poor driving on their part. (The modern law is stated in the Road Traffic Act 1988, Part VI.) Compulsory insurance for the population generally is therefore achieved, not by first-party insurance (making pedestrians and drivers insure against possibility of injury to themselves), but by third-party insurance (making wrongdoers insure so that they can pay damages to their victims). When compared to other areas of tort, the function of tort as insurance system is very much to the fore. The courts are noticeably more generous to plaintiffs than they are in other areas, perhaps because they are far more concerned with P's need for compensation than with determining whether to punish D by imposing liability. As the claim will be met by D's insurers, an order to pay damages is not much of a punishment; and if D has behaved in a way meriting punishment, this can be done through the criminal law and need not concern tort lawyers. Nonetheless, if tort law here operates as a system of insurance alone, it is a very imperfect system. P's claim is still nominally based on D's fault, and so if P cannot prove fault in some shape or form P will receive no compensation. What of the plaintiff who cannot prove which driver inflicted the injuries, or where the driver at fault failed to purchase insurance? Before 1946, P would have been without a remedy, but now under the Motor Insurers' Bureau (MIB) scheme, P has a right to receive compensation from a fund established by the major insurance companies to cover this gap in insurance provision.

Application of negligence law

4.14 With the need to compensate P very much to the fore of their minds, and questions of whether D was morally to blame largely irrelevant, the courts apply ordinary negligence rules in a very generous spirit indeed. Many rulings are hard to make sense of as a moral judgement on D's behaviour; making this sort of judgement does not seem to be what the court is about.

> *Roberts v Ramsbottom* (1980)   Ramsbottom suffered a stroke while at the wheel of his car. Out of control, the car cashed into another, injuring Roberts and others. Held: from an objective standpoint Ramsbottom's behaviour amounted to negligence and accordingly he was liable for Roberts' injuries.

The court indicated that the case might have been different if Ramsbottom had become unconscious through his injuries. He would then have been in a state of 'automatism' and not responsible for his actions. But as he was in fact unable to control the car, it is not clear why it matters whether he was conscious or unconscious throughout.

> *Nettleship v Weston* (1971)   Nettleship, an experienced driver, was giving driving lessons to his friend Weston, a learner. On the third lesson, Weston failed to straighten out after turning left, mounted the curb and collided with a lamppost. Held: Nettleship could recover in negligence from Weston for his injuries, as she had failed to attain the standard to be expected of a reasonably experienced driver.

The latter result is all the more surprising, as learner drivers can hardly be accused of concealing their lack of skill; the function of 'L'-plates is precisely to warn other road users that they are not reasonably skilled drivers. Ironically, the law insists that they advertise to the world that they do not have ordinary driving skills, yet regards them as negligent if they do not display those skills anyway! However, despite the marked generosity of the courts to plaintiffs, the basic test is still whether negligence can be found. The courts have applied the negligence standard generously towards plaintiffs, but it is still the negligence standard, and P cannot recover unless D was in some sense at fault.

Liability of occupiers to those on their land

Introduction

4.15 The following sections deal with the liability of occupiers to those who suffer injury while on the land. The main focus is on personal injury, though many of the same principles apply to injury to property, as where a visitor tears her coat on a dangerously placed nail on D's premises.

Last century, the common law developed an elaborate scheme of different classes of entrants, the duty varying with each class. Modern cases and statutes have amalgamated several of these classes. The result is a simpler and rather more pro-plaintiff set of rules. It is still necessary, however, to distinguish between three classes of entrants:

* those to whom P has given permission to enter the land ('visitors');

* those who have a legal right to be on the land, regardless of P's permission; and

* those who entered with neither permission nor a legal right to enter ('trespassers').

Liability of occupiers to their visitors

The modern law

4.16 The law here was much simplified by the Occupiers' Liability Act 1957. This Act provides that the occupier of premises owes a 'common duty of care' to all visitors. This duty is stated in terms which are very similar to the common law negligence duty. The duty applies quite generally, in contrast to the earlier law, which distinguished different categories of visitors. The duty arises in tort even when there is a contract between D and P relating to P's admission to the premises. Indeed, it has been held (controversially) that the tortious duty in that situation is quite independent from any contractual duty of care (*Sole v WJ Hallt Ltd* (1973)). The pre-1957 law distinguished not only between different classes of visitors, but also between the 'occupancy duty' relating to the state of the premises and the 'activity duty' relating to what D did there. Most commentators now agree that all of this has been swept away, as indeed the wording of the Act suggests: the Act governs in its entirety.

'Premises'

4.17   The duty is imposed on the occupier of 'premises'. This word includes everything which is within the ordinary meaning of the expression, and more. It seems that any piece of real property is caught. The Act itself says that it applies to 'any fixed or moveable structure, including any vessel, vehicle or aircraft' (s 1(3)(a)); so the duty that car drivers owe to their passengers could technically be described as an occupier's duty. More generally, it seems to be a matter of degree what can be regarded as 'premises'. A tunnel-cutting machine has been so regarded (*Bunker v Charles Brand & Sons Ltd* (1969)); so has a ladder (*Wheeler v Copas* (1981)).

'Occupier'

4.18   The 'occupier' of premises is the person who has the legal right of control over it. This is logical enough: the Act imposes the duty on the person legally entitled to do something about the dangerous state of the premises or the activities carried on there.

> *Wheat v E Lacon & Co Ltd* (1966)   Lacon owned a pub, which it hired a manager to run. The premises included a private flat, which the manager was entitled to occupy and to use for paying guests. One such guest fell down an unlit defective staircase in the flat. Held: as Lacon had the legal right to control the flat, it was its occupier and so was liable in respect of the state of the premises.

The emphasis here is on the *legal right* of control, rather than actual control. Lacon was held responsible because it had retained the legal right to do repairs on the flat. It might have been different if it had leased the flat to the manager and entirely relinquished legal control over it. So it is perfectly possible for D to be held to be 'in control' of premises, on the ground that he ought to be in control, even though in fact no-one is in control.

> *Harris v Birkenhead Corpn* (1975)   As part of a slum-clearance scheme, Birkenhead Corporation served a notice on a house, requiring the tenant to vacate the property. The tenant did so; however, the corporation did not follow its usual policy of bricking up such premises. Harris, four and a half years old, entered the premises and fell out of a top-story window. Acting through her mother, she sued the tenant, the landlord and the corporation. Held: only the corporation was 'occupier' and therefore liable to Harris.

However, there is no rule that only one person may be occupier at any one time; indeed, a majority of the Lords in *Lacon* considered that the manager of the pub was also 'occupier' for the purposes of the Act. Where occupancy is shared in this way, the rule seems to be that each occupier is under a duty, though the duty is not necessarily the same: the greater the degree of *actual* control, the higher the duty (*AMF International Ltd v Magnet Bowling Ltd* (1968)). Or again, if there is a clear division of labour between occupiers as to responsibility for different aspects of the premises, the duty may be split in the same way.

> *Collier v Anglian Water Authority* (1983)   Collier was injured while walking along a seaside promenade, the injury being attributable to the state of repair of the promenade. The promenade was controlled jointly by the water authority, as it formed part of the area's sea defences, and the local authority, who swept up accumulated rubbish. Held: as Collier's injuries were attributable to the state of the promenade rather than to rubbish, it was the water authority which was liable and not the local authority.

'Visitors'

4.19 *Persons with express permission to enter*   The most obvious members of the class of 'visitors' are those who have been given express permission to come onto the land. It does not matter today whether this permission was granted as part of a contract with the occupier; the duty is the same (s 5(1)). Where the occupier places some limit on the permission, the entrant becomes a trespasser when the limit is exceeded. So permission to enter for a short time does not justify an indefinite stay. 'When you invite a person into your house to use the staircase, you do not invite him to slide down the banisters, you invite him to use the staircase in the ordinary way in which it is used' (*The Calgarth* [1927] P 93, 110, Scrutton LJ).

4.20 *Persons with implied permission to enter* Permission to enter the land need not be given in any particular form. So if it is clear that the occupier is extending permission to P to enter, P will be a visitor when he or she enters, whatever the occupier may or may not have said. In particular, it will usually be assumed that anyone who wishes to talk to the occupier has implied permission to come onto the land to call on him. If in fact certain types of enquiries are not welcome, the occupier must make this clear in advance (eg by posting a notice saying 'No canvassers').

Difficult questions can arise where the occupier knows that P has entered or plans to enter, but says nothing. Cases early in this century seem very willing to infer that permission has been given, even where the occupier had earlier made determined but futile attempts to keep people out (eg *Lowery v Walker* (1911)). The courts seemed particularly anxious to hold that children entering the land had implied permission, especially where there was some sort of 'allurement' there which children found particularly attractive (eg poisonous berries, *Glasgow Corpn v Taylor* (1922)). No doubt this attitude of the courts had much to do with the fact that *trespassers* could not sue the occupier no matter how shocking the latter's neglect of their safety. Now that trespassers have a right to sue, we can expect that the courts will not strain to find an implied permission where none is very obvious. Nonetheless, the courts still show some generosity here. So, for example, if D hands over the manage-ment of land to X, who then lets in P, it may be held that P has D's implied permission to be there − even if D made it clear to X that P was not to be let on (*Ferguson v Welsh* [1987] 3 All ER 777, 785, Lord Goff).

4.21 *Persons with a right to enter* What if P has a right to enter the land, but nonetheless does not have the occupier's permission? The Occupiers' Liability Act 1957 itself states that anyone who enters land under a right conferred by law is to be treated as a visitor (s 2(6)). So if D carelessly starts a fire on his land and P, a fire-fighter, is burned while putting it out, D is liable for P's injuries (*Ogwo v Taylor* (1987)). This is the general rule. But a few cases fall outside the scope of the Act. Users of rights of way across the land are not 'visitors', whether the right of way is private (*Holden v White* (1982)) or public (*Greenhalgh v British Railways Board* (1969)). And by s 1(4), the Act does not apply in favour of those who enter the land under an access agreement or by virtue of an order under the National Parks and Access to the Countryside Act 1949. The precise duty that is owed at common law under these circumstances is not entirely clear. What little case law there is suggests that the occupier of the land is bound to abstain from positive, dangerous acts but is not liable for failure to act. In other word, the occupier is liable for 'misfeasance' but not for 'nonfeasance'. So if P is injured on a public right of way going across D's land, P has no right to complain that D should have maintained the right of way (*McGeown v Northern Ireland Housing Executive* (1994)). In some of these cases, the duty is the same as that owed to trespassers (**4.26**); but the limits of this are unclear, and certainly those using the highway are not so protected (Occupiers' Liability Act 1984, s 1(7)).

The standard of care

4.22 *General*   The occupier of premises owes visitors the 'common duty of care' (Occupiers' Liability Act 1957, s 2(1)). This is a duty 'to take such care as in all the circumstances of the case is reasonable to see that the visitor will be reasonably safe in using the premises for the purposes for which he is invited or permitted by the occupier to be there' (s 2(2)). The burden of proof is on P to demonstrate that the duty has been broken. The test is the same as in negligence generally (**3.8**). Relevant factors include the size of the risk and the cost and practicability of taking precautions against it.

> *Simms v Leigh Rugby Football Club Ltd* (1969)   In the course of a rugby game, Simms was tackled, breaking his leg, allegedly after coming into contact with a concrete wall slightly over seven feet from the touchline. Held: even if he in fact hit the wall, this was such an unlikely event as to be unforeseeable by the occupier of the ground and so it was not liable to him.

This does not mean, however, that P must necessarily show precisely how the accident happened; it is enough that D was probably to blame.

> *Ward v Tesco Stores Ltd* (1976)   Ward was injured when she slipped on some yoghurt spilled on the floor of Tesco, where she was

shopping. Tesco gave evidence that the floor was generally brushed six times a day, and that staff were instructed to deal with spillages if they saw them. Held (by a majority) there was sufficient evidence of negligence, and in the absence of explanation Tesco would be held liable.

4.23 *Care expected from visitors* The occupier is bound to take due care for the visitor, but the visitor too is expected to exercise due care. Accordingly, in assessing the steps the owner is bound to take, the court will have regard to what the visitor should reasonably be expected to do for himself. So the content of the duty depends on 'the degree of care, and of want of care, which would ordinarily be looked for in such a visitor' (s 2(3)). This is a principle of general application. The Act mentions two special cases by way of example.

- *Children* The occupier 'must be prepared for children to be less careful than adults' (s 2(3)(a)). So the occupier must make allowances for behaviour which would be unreasonable in adults. In particular, D must make allowances for so-called 'allurements', which might attract children but not adults; poisonous berries are an obvious example (*Glasgow Corpn v Taylor* (1922)). Nonetheless, the courts are reluctant to put the onus for children's safety entirely onto the occupiers of land they happen to wander onto. 'It would not be socially desirable if parents were, as a matter of course, able to shift the burden of looking after their children from their own shoulders to those of persons who happen to have accessible bits of land' (*Phipps v Rochester Corpn* [1955] 1 QB 450, 472, Devlin J). Note, however, that in *Phipps* Devlin J nonetheless found liability, in a case where P fell into a trench on D's land. The existence of the trench would have been obvious to an adult, but Devlin J held that the occupier owed a duty to the 5-year old P to guard him against it.

- *Workers* Conversely, those who come on to the premises to do a job of some sort are expected to know the risks of their job, and how to minimise them. The occupier 'may expect that a person, in the exercise of his calling, will appreciate and guard against any special risks ordinarily incident to it, so far as the occupier leaves him free to do so' (s 2(3)(b)). So it has been held that a claim by chimney sweeps against a householder for dangers arising from fumes was not available (*Roles v Nathan* (1963)). Likewise, we would not expect electricians to have much success in suing for injuries caused by bare live wires. However, it is not a blanket defence to all risks which P ought to anticipate, if in fact there is little P can do about them. So where D carelessly start a fire on their premises and P is injured fighting the fire, D cannot defeat the claim merely by saying that the risk is inherent in the job of a fire-fighter (*Salmon v Seafarer Restaurants Ltd* (1983)).

4.24 *Liability for misconduct by others* The duty owed by the occupier to the visitor is non-delegable. That is to say, if no due care was in fact taken of P, it is no defence that D had done his best to make sure that care would be provided. Suppose that a court holds that P, who is 10, would only have been reasonably safe on D's land if D had provided some sort of supervision. If D did not in fact provide supervision, it is no defence that D had made reasonable efforts to hire a supervisor, or that the supervisor failed to turn up at work through no fault of D's. This matter is dealt with in greater detail below (**9.24**); it is important, because many occupiers are companies, which cannot 'personally' look after P's safety but must necessarily act through others. In addition, an occupier may be vicariously liable for misconduct by one of D's employees (**9.2**). What if the danger to P arose from misconduct of some independent contractor? In that situation, D is not directly liable for the contractor's misbehaviour; however, D cannot wash his hands of the matter simply by entrusting it to a contractor. D is expected to use all due care in selecting an appropriate contractor; D is also expected to make reasonable checks that the work has been done properly (s 2(4)(b)). Accordingly, if P is injured as a result of poor workmanship by an independent contractor, P may sometimes be able to sue the occupiers as well as the contractor, but only by showing that the occupiers are themselves at fault.

Warnings and exclusions

4.25 The basic principle is that if D gives P a warning of the danger, which gives P a fair chance to escape it, then D will not be liable. However, there are actually quite a number of different legal rules at work here, and it is important not to confuse them. Suppose D warns P of a danger, to which P subsequently succumbs. What defences will D raise?

- *Satisfaction of duty* D may argue that the only thing the reasonable occupier could be expected to do in that situation was to give a warning and so, having given that warning, D has done everything the duty requires (eg *Titchener v British Railways Board* (1983)). The Act itself makes it clear that this is a perfectly good argument, provided that the warning was 'in all the circumstances ... enough to enable the visitor to be reasonably safe' (s 2(4)(a)).

- *Consent*   D may argue that P agreed to run the risk (s 2(5)). Agreements of that sort usually have to be express, though in extreme cases P may be held to have agreed impliedly to run a risk which was very obvious (**11.6**).

- *Causation or remoteness*   D may argue that P's decision to ignore the risk was unforeseeable, or at least broke the chain of causation and relieved D of responsibility for the consequences which followed (**10.35**). This argument is unlikely to succeed unless P's conduct was irrational and reckless in the extreme.

Sayers v Harlow UDC (1958)   Sayers became trapped in a public lavatory because the lock was defective. After shouting for help for 10 or 15 minutes, she attempted to climb out and injured herself in the process. Held: the occupiers of the premises were liable for her injuries, though the damages would be reduced by 25% for contributory negligence. 'I do not think that the plaintiff should be adjudged in all the circumstances to have acted unreasonably or rashly or stupidly ... Indeed, she showed a very considerable measure of self-control' ([1958] 1 WLR 631-632, Morris LJ).

- *Contributory negligence*   D may argue that P is partly to blame for the accident, through the failure to heed the warning. The effect of this argument is only to reduce P's damages, not eliminate the claim entirely, and so does not take extraordinarily strong facts to back it up (**11.17**).

- *Exclusion of liability*   D may argue that a warning of danger constituted an exclusion of D's liability. The relevant principles are discussed below (**11.2**); where the premises are business premises, the argument is almost certain to fail.

The law is rather elaborate here, arguably too elaborate; it is trying to achieve a number of different objectives. The main point is perhaps that warnings can take many forms. At one extreme, D may warn P of the precise danger to which P ultimately fell victim; in a case like that, D will have a serious argument that the injuries are all P's own fault. At the other, D has simply posted a notice disclaiming all responsibility for the state of the premises. Notices of that sort, which are of no help at all in enabling P to avoid the danger, are generally ineffective today.

Liability of occupiers to trespassers

Introduction

4.26 Until recent years, the general position was that no duty was owed to trespassers, unless the occupier recklessly injured a trespasser they knew to be present (*Robert Addie and Sons (Collieries) Ltd v Dumbreck* (1929)). Some particularly deserving plaintiffs had a remedy found for them by devious means: so, for example, the courts were very willing to find that young children were not trespassers at all, even in cases where D had expressly prohibited their coming onto the land. The decisive break came in 1972, when the House of Lords held that there *was* a duty owed to trespassers. This was not the 'common duty of care' in the Occupiers' Liability Act 1957, but a 'duty of common humanity' which provided for a bare minimum of care (*British Railways Board v Herrington* (1972)). This duty was re-stated and extended in the Occupiers' Liability Act 1984, which is now the governing legislation. The duty is somewhat similar to the duty owed to visitors. Nonetheless, much less care is owed. Injuries caused to adult trespassers who well knew that they had no business to be on D's land are likely to receive little sympathy; though even there, liability may be found if the facts are strong enough. The duty does not extend to protect the trespasser's property (s 1(8)); so while an injured trespasser may possibly have an action against the occupier on the principles discussed in this section, there can be no action for the trespasser's ripped or damaged clothing.

Duty

4.27 Rather than the general duty owed to visitors under the Act of 1957, the duty under the Act of 1984 is more narrowly focused. The duty is owed to a particular trespasser only if three conditions are satisfied (s 1(3)):

(a) the occupier knows of the danger, or has reasonable grounds to know it exists;

(b) the occupier knows the trespasser is, or may in the future, come into the vicinity of the danger, or has reasonable grounds to know it;

(c) it is reasonable to expect the occupier to offer some protection to the trespasser against the risk.

The general lines of this are clear: the duty is a duty to act reasonably in the light of what the occupier knows. No doubt in time the bare bones of the statutes will be fleshed out by case law. One issue which will need to be resolved is the scope of (a): in particular, to what extent it imposes a duty on the occupier to check the premises for dangers. Or (to put it the other way around), to what extent does (a) allow the occupier to leave his own land well alone, at least if he has no lawful visitors? Proving that the occupier is, or should be, aware of trespassers (require-ment (b)) is usually difficult. The Court of Appeal has refused to assume that an occupier who took steps to keep out trespassers necessarily fell within requirement (b). Whether the requirement is satisfied 'had to be answered by looking at the actual state of affairs on the ground when the injury was met with' (White v St Albans City and District Council (1990), Neill LJ).

Standard of care

4.28   The duty owed to trespassers is specific to the danger: P will only have been able to establish a duty in respect of a particular danger (**4.27**). If P has done this, then the content of the duty is straightforward: it is 'to take such care as is reasonable in all the circumstances of the case to see that [the trespasser] does not suffer injury on the premises by reason of the danger concerned' (s 1(4)). This is obviously very similar to the duty owed to visitors. The real work of prescribing a different regime for trespassers, as distinct from visitors, is borne by s 1(3), the matter being ignored in s 1(4). Much that is stated in the 1957 Act is left unstated in the 1984 Act, though probably the courts will imply it anyway. In particular, presumably they will hold that the occupier 'must be prepared for children to be less careful than adults', just as under the 1957 Act (**4.23**). An important unanswered question is whether the occupier can plead lack of resources as an answer to P's claim. Before the Act, it was thought that lack of resources would be a defence (*British Railways Board v Herrington* [1972] AC 877, 899, Lord Reid). The matter is not addressed in the Act.

Warning and exclusions

4.29 Just as for the case of visitors, the law here is complex, though most of the complexities are the same as for the case of visitors (**4.25**). A warning alone may be sufficient to discharge D's duty of care, if that is all that a reasonable person in the occupier's position would do (s 1(5)). In appropriate cases, P's claim may be defeated by defences of consent (s 1(6)) (**11.2**) or contributory negligence (**11.17**), or by the doctrines of causation or remoteness (**10.35**). A difficult question is whether it is possible to apply the principles of exclusion (**11.13**), so that an occupier may avoid the duty entirely by posting a prominent notice denying the duty. The Act itself does not say either way. It would be very surprising if the duty could be excluded in this way, as by definition D has already made it clear that P should keep out. If posting a notice saying 'No Trespassers!' does not exclude the duty, why should a notice saying 'No Trespassers and No Writs either!'? Yet there are still cases where it is possible to exclude the duty owed to lawful visitors (**11.14**), so why not to trespassers as well? The neatest solution, from a logical point of view, would be that the duty to trespassers is not excludable, and applies *also* in favour of visitors against whom the normal duty is excluded – so the higher duty owed to visitors is sometimes excludable, the lower duty never. However, there is absolutely no warrant for this solution in the Acts themselves, and the matter remains shrouded in mystery.

Liability of non-occupiers to those on the land

General

4.30 Suppose P is injured while lawfully on land, and wishes to sue D, who was not the occupier. Most of the law applicable in that situation has already been described. So if P is injured by the activities of an independent contractor on the land, P's action against the contractor is the standard negligence action against those who engage in dangerous activities. Earlier in the century, judges were reluctant to allow action against builders and others whose carelessness had injured those other than the current occupier (eg *Bottomley v Bannister* (1932)), but any immunity they may have had is now abolished by statute. The careless builder is liable for negligence even if the premises have since changed hands (Defective Premises Act 1972, s 3(1)).

> *Rimmer v Liverpool City Council* (1984)   Shortly after moving into his new council flat, the tenant complained of a particularly dangerous panel of breakable glass, which he argued was a danger to his young son. He was told that it was a standard installation, and could not be changed. Nineteen months later, his son was injured by putting his hand through it. Held: the council was liable for negligence, in its capacity as designer and builder of the flats.

However, there is still a reluctance to allow action against builders for purely economic losses such as a failure to do adequate repairs; after the *Murphy* decision (**5.4**), action lies under statute, if at all.

Landlords

4.31   At common law, it was almost impossible to sue landlords in tort for injuries to those on the premises (eg *Cavalier v Pope* (1906)). Today, action can be maintained in two situations.

- *Landlord created the danger* (eg *Rimmer v Liverpool City Council*) (**4.30**).

- *Landlord under a duty to repair*   By statute, a landlord who is bound to repair owes a duty to all who might reasonably be expected to be affected by defects in the premises (Defective Premises Act 1972, s 4(1)). The duty applies in all cases where the landlord knew of the defect, or ought to have known of it (s 4(2)). Note that in the case of residential leases of less than seven years, there is a statutory obligation on the landlord to repair (Landlord and Tenant Act 1985, ss 11, 12; and see Housing Act 1988, s 16), and so the negligence duty applies. Even if the landlord is not bound to repair, nonetheless if the landlord has power to enter and repair, a duty of care is owed to everyone except the tenant (s 4(4)).

Employers' liability

Introduction

4.32 The liability of employers to their employees is ancient. But for most of its history, the potential of the law of negligence to protect employees from workplace accidents was held back by the existence of very broad defences. Since the 1940s, the defences have been considerably narrowed, and in some instances abolished. Liability insurance, already very common, was made compulsory by the Employers' Liability (Compulsory Insurance) Act 1969. Employers' liability is now one of the most important heads of negligence liability. The total number of work injuries in any one year is probably about 500,000. Perhaps 10% of those injured at work obtain tort-based compensation for it; the more serious the injury, the more likely is the victim to consider legal action. A Trades Union Congress study found that employers paid out £335m in damages to employees in the year 1993–94.

The privileged position of employees

4.33 The liability described in this section is in favour of employees only, not other grades of workers. (For the precise distinction between 'employees' and other workers, see **9.4**.) The protection afforded to other workers is distinctly less generous, though far from useless in all situations. Some, but by no means all, of the industrial safety legislation applies to other workers as well as to employees. The negligence duty discussed in this section does not apply, but in the case of an injury on work premises a similar duty will be owed under the law of occupiers' liability (**4.16**).

The duty generally

4.34 Each employee is entitled to expect from his employer that reasonable care will be taken to ensure his safety. The duty is imposed by the law of negligence and is not absolute; the general principles of negligence liability need to be borne in mind. It is usual today to consider the employer's duty under four heads: the duty to provide safe premises; the duty to provide safe plant, materials and equipment; the duty to provide competent staff; and the duty to institute safe work practices. These are, however, not distinct duties, but rather different aspects of the same duty. 'They lie within, and exemplify, the broader duty of taking reasonable care for the safety of his workmen which rests on every employer' (*Winter v Cardiff RDC* [1950] 1 All ER 819, 823, Lord MacDermott). Very often, what is in essence the same complaint can be raised under various different heads. So a complaint by P that she suffers from Repetitive Strain Injury (RSI) as a result of using machines in D's factory can be put in various ways. It may sometimes be put as a complaint that the equipment provided is not reasonably safe, but in other cases it may be better to plead it as a case about poor work practices, as where D did not provide proper breaks from using the machine, or proper medical care. There is only one duty, namely to take reasonable precautions to ensure P's safety. The duty is quite independent of statutory duties on the employer. If the employer is in breach of the common law duty, it is no answer that the employer has done everything that statute requires in the matter, even if the statute addresses the very danger to which P succumbed (*Bux v Slough Metals Ltd* (1973)).

The duty cannot be delegated

4.35 P is entitled only to a reasonably safe working environment, not an absolutely safe one. However, if the environment is not reasonably safe, it is no defence that this was the fault of someone other that P's employer. This is sometimes summed up by saying that the duty is non-delegable (**9.22**). So if P is injured by the acts of a fellow employee, it is usually possible to argue that the employer is liable directly, without having to argue that the employer is vicariously liable for the other employee's behaviour. The principle is most important in the case where the employer temporarily posts an employee to another firm. Assuming that the relationship of employer and employee continues, then so does the duty, even though the employer may have no control over the employee's work environment.

McDermid v Nash Dredging and Reclamation Co Ltd (1987)   McDermid was injured when the tug on which he was working as a deckhand started unexpectedly. He was pulled into the water, suffering a serious leg injury as a result. The accident was the fault of the tug's master, who was employed not by McDermid's employer but by the employer's parent company. Held: McDermid's employers were liable for his injury.

The result in *McDermid* is unsurprising. P and the man who injured him were part of the same small work team, and to refuse P a remedy merely because they have different employers sounds like a rather undeserving technicality, given that both firms were part of the same group. However, the reason given for imposing liability – that the employer's duty is not delegable – is plainly capable of applying in other cases, and it is not clear to what extent it will be applied. In the earlier case of *Davie v New Merton Board Mills Ltd* (1959), P was injured by defective equipment while at work; the equipment had been negligently made, but it was not reasonably possible for P's employer to spot the defect. On those facts, the House of Lords refused to find P's employers in breach of their obligations. This approach clearly conflicts with that taken in *McDermid*; it was not commented on by the Lords in *McDermid*, perhaps because this has been reversed on its facts by statute (**4.38**). It is an open question how far each approach will be taken. The signs are that the courts are very reluctant to find employers liable in a case where in reality they have no control at all over P's safety.

> *Square D Ltd v Cook* (1992) Square D employed Cook as a field service electronics engineer. He was sent out to Saudi Arabia to work on a client's computer control systems. In the course of his work, Cook injured himself through the poor state of the premises in which he was working. Held: his employers had no control over his conditions of work and were accordingly not liable. Farquharson LJ commented that 'the suggestion that the home-based employer has any responsibility for the daily events of a site in Saudi Arabia has an air of unreality'.

Safety in all respects?

4.36 Nearly all of the cases involve threats to employees' health through physical impact of some kind, as whether P accidentally comes into contact with dangerous machinery. In principle, however, any threat to P's physical health is within the law. Claims for illness caused by work conditions are perfectly standard, though they are usually hard to prove. Claims for nervous shock (**3.18**) may also be brought. In exceptional circumstances, it is even possible to sue for the consequences of extreme stress due to work conditions.

> *Walker v Northumberland County Council* (1995) Walker, a social services manager, suffered a nervous breakdown through overwork.

He returned to work after his employers gave him specific promises of extra assistance. The promises were broken, and six months after his return he suffered a second breakdown which permanently disabled him from working. Held: his employers were liable for the consequences of the second breakdown.

However, there is no claim for purely economic loss based on the employer-employee duty (*Reid v Rush & Tompkins Group* (1989)). Such a claim is only justified either on normal principles (**5.1**), or through the law of contract (eg *Scally v Southern Health and Social Services Board* (1991)).

The duty in detail

4.37 *Safe premises*   The place of work must be maintained in a reasonably safe condition. In many respects this aspect of the employers' duty is no different from that of an occupier to his or her visitors generally (**4.16**). But the fact that P is there to work is of course one factor in what it is reasonable to expect by way of provision for safety. Where there is a known source of danger, the employer is required to act reasonably in the face of it, and the court will pay attention to the practicality of the various options available.

Latimer v AEC Ltd (1953)   The floor of a factory became wet and slippery through flooding. The owner put down sawdust, but did not have enough to cover the entire floor. Latimer, an employee, slipped on a wet patch and injured himself. Held: the employer had done everything possible short of temporarily shutting the factory, which in the circumstances would have been an overreaction. Accordingly, Latimer could not sue for his injuries.

Very often, the nature of the job requires P to work in an inherently unsafe position. In cases of that sort, the duty is likely to require that the employer provide instruction and safety equipment. Where the danger is obvious and easy to avoid, it is possible that a court might be persuaded that any accident to P was P's own fault. But it would be unwise for an employer to rely on that.

General Cleaning Contractors Ltd v Christmas (1953)   Christmas, an experienced window-cleaner, was injured when the window he was cleaning suddenly and unexpectedly moved. He was not wearing a safety-harness, because there was nowhere to which it could be attached at that location. Various precautions his employers could have taken to prevent such an accident were suggested. Held: failure to attach to the building hooks for a safety harness was not a breach of duty. However, his employers were in breach for *(i)* failure to warn their employees to test windows before cleaning them and *(ii)* failure to provide wedges to keep windows still.

Recall that the duty in negligence is owed to each individual plaintiff (*Paris v Stepney Borough Council*) (**3.8**), and accordingly the duty to relatively inexperienced employees may be higher than that owed to the experienced.

4.38 *Safe plant, materials and equipment*   Reasonable steps must also be taken to ensure that plant, materials and equipment also are reasonably safe. The common law is here enhanced by the Employers' Liability (Defective Equipment) Act 1969, which provides (reversing *Davie v New Merton Board Mills Ltd* (1959)) that the employer is liable for equipment which is defective through the negligence of third parties. 'Equipment' is broadly defined in the Act as including 'any plant and machinery, vehicle, aircraft and clothing' (s 1(3)). The equipment must be 'provided by [the] employer for the purposes of the employer's business' (s 1(1)(a)). Case law has taken a broad view of the provision, making it clear that it covers not simply the tools P uses but also whatever P was working on.

> *Knowles v Liverpool City Council* (1994)   Knowles, a labourer involved in repairing pavements, was manhandling a flagstone into the shovel of a JCB mechanical digger. The flagstone broke, injuring Knowles. The cause was a negligent defect in the manufacturing process, which Knowles' employers could not reasonably have discovered beforehand. Held: the flagstone was 'defective equipment' and so his employers were liable for his injuries.

(Note also the possibility of an action against the manufacturers of the flagstone (**4.2**)).

It has also been held that a ship can be 'defective equipment' under the Act (*Coltman v Bibby Tankers Ltd* (1988)).

Difficult questions sometimes arise here where the equipment P uses cannot do the job, because P is using it for a job it was not designed to do. The court would have to ask whether the equipment was in any real sense 'defective', and if so whether that led to liability. The courts will not find liability if the main cause of the accident was P's own foolish selection of the wrong tool for the job (*Leach v British Oxygen Co Ltd* (1965)). An interesting, if not particularly realistic, hypothetical (suggested in Dias (ed), *Clerk and Lindsell on Torts*, 16th edn 1989), is as follows: suppose two employees on a factory floor quarrel. One attempts to hit the other with a hammer. He misses and the hammer hits the wall; because of a defect due to negligent manufacture, the hammer splinters, and the fragments injure a third employee. Can the injured employee sue the employers? On the literal wording of the 1969 Act, it appears that he can. Whether there is any escape from this rather surprising conclusion must be in the realms of speculation, but none is very obvious. (Of course, if the employers are liable they will be able to claim contribution from the hammer-throwing employee and possibly from the manufacturer of the hammer too.)

4.39 *Competent staff* Each employee is entitled to expect that reasonable care will have been taken in the selection and training of other employees. Where P is injured by the misbehaviour of a fellow employee, very often P may sue the employer on the basis of vicarious liability for the other employee's tort (**9.2**). But, where necessary, P can plead that poor selection or control of the other employee constituted a breach of duty, quite regardless of any vicarious liability.

> *Hudson v Ridge Manufacturing Co Ltd* (1957) Hudson was injured while fending off a mock attack by Chadwick, another employee. Chadwick's propensity for practical jokes was well known, but his employers had taken no steps to discipline him. Held: Hudson's employers were liable for his injuries.

However, isolated instances of misconduct by a particular employee will probably not be enough to lead to this result (*Smith v Crossley Bros Ltd* (1951)).

4.40 *Safe work practices* The final respect in which employers are bound to provide a reasonable level of safety is in the work practices they maintain. This is traditionally called the duty to maintain a 'safe system of work', although that phrase is also used to sum up the entire duty on the employer. The content of the duty varies considerably with the type of work. It will include a duty to issue standing orders in safety matters and to supervise employees to prevent dangerous situations from developing. There is no conclusive rule, but a number of considerations are relevant on a routine basis.

• Where there is an obvious risk to the safety of employees, much will turn on whether it is reasonable to leave avoidance of the risk to the employees themselves.

Nolan v Dental Manufacturing Co Ltd (1958) Nolan was sharpening a tool on a grinder. A splinter of metal flew out and entered his eye. Nolan's employer never issued goggles to workers in his position. Held: the employers should have issued goggles and enforced strict orders to wear them, and accordingly were in breach of duty.

(Compare *McWilliams v Sir William Arrol & Co Ltd* (1962), a case on similar facts which has often been criticised precisely because the House of Lords seemed to conclude too hastily that P would never have used the safety equipment provided, and so there was no causal connection between his employer's breach of duty and P's death (**10.25**). Right or wrong, the case is certainly unusually generous to employers.)

• 'Workmen are not in the position of employers. Their duties are not performed in the calm atmosphere of a board room with the advice of experts. They have to make their decisions on narrow window sills and other places of danger and in circumstances in which the dangers are obscured by repetition' (*General Cleaning Contractors Ltd v Christmas* [1953] AC 180, 190, Lord Oaksey).

• Standard practice in the industry concerned is a weighty, though not a conclusive, factor. If the danger to P could only be avoided by taking precautions which few or no employers actually do, then a court will hesitate long before deciding that this particular employer should have done it. Nonetheless, the courts are prepared to hold even well-established industry practices to be negligent if the facts justify this (*Brown v John Mills and Co (Llanidloes) Ltd* (1970)).

Newly-emerging dangers to employees

4.41 The employer's duty includes a duty to keep abreast of new developments and knowledge which may reveal new threats to their workers, or improved ways of combating old threats. Where a danger has only recently emerged, it may sometimes be necessary for a court to identify the precise point at which the reasonable employer ought to have realised the problem and done something about it. Prominent examples of this type of litigation in recent years have included repetitive strain injury (RSI) (eg *Pickford v Imperial Chemical Industries* (1996)), vibration white finger (VWF) (eg *Bowman v Harland and Wolff* (1992)) and the effects of noise on ship-building workers (*Thompson v Smiths Shiprepairers (North Shields) Ltd* (1984)):

> 'The employer is not liable for the consequences of [apparently inescapable] risks, although subsequent changes in social awareness, or improvements in knowledge and technology, may transfer the risk into the category of those against which the employer can and should take care. It is unnecessary, and perhaps impossible, to give a comprehensive formula for identifying the line between the acceptable and the unacceptable. Nonetheless, the line does exist ...' (*Thompson v Smiths Shiprepairers (North Shields) Ltd* [1984] 1 All ER 889, Mustill J).

The armed services

4.42 Until quite recently, a common law immunity barred action by active service personnel for injuries suffered. This immunity was however removed by the Crown Proceedings (Armed Forces) Act 1987. The quantity of litigation unleashed as a result has surprised many observers, and is certainly by any standard large. The 'Gulf War Syndrome' action alone has already resulted in the expenditure of millions of pounds in legal fees, and that is very far from a conclusion. This new head of liability has involved the courts being invited to apply concepts of employers' liability to rather non-standard situations.

Barrett v Ministry of Defence (1995) Barrett, a naval airman, drank heavily on the night he was celebrating his thirtieth birthday, while at a Royal Navy establishment in northern Norway. He choked to death on his own vomit. Held: no breach of duty by failure to control drinking at the base generally was established, but inadequate care had been taken of Barrett after he had become unconscious through drink.

Liability was established, but reduced by two-thirds for Barrett's own contributory negligence.

Mulcahy v Ministry of Defence (1996) While Mulcahy was engaged in cleaning a howitzer with a mop and bucket, the gun commander ordered it to be fired at Iraqi troops. Mulcahy suffered various injuries, including substantial damage to his hearing. Held: the duty of an employer to provide a safe system of work did not extend to cover soldiers in the course of hostilities.

This area of the law is very much in its infancy. It would of course be very strange if an army fighting a war were to be subject to the same duties as a peacetime employer. But equally it is not obvious that there should be no liability at all no matter how clear the evidence of guilt in the way P's injuries happened.

Defences

4.43 Defences to negligence actions generally are discussed below (11.1). In theory, an employer can plead either consent or contributory negligence wherever the worker knew of the risk concerned. In practice, successful pleas of consent are virtually unheard-of today (11.2), and while the 'contributory negligence' plea tries to strike a rough balance between D's lack of care and P's lack of care, the scales are heavily, and intentionally, weighted in P's favour (11.17).

Statutory duties

4.44 Alongside the general common law duty to take care is a wide array of statutory duties in relation to health and safety of employees. The principles under which these statutory duties can sometimes give rise to a civil right of action have been discussed above (1.42). The most important statutes for this purpose are the Factories Act 1961 and the Mines and Quarries Act 1954. There are also some very broad general duties in the Health and Safety at Work etc Act 1974, though breach of them does not give rise to civil liability (s 47(1)). However, breach of more specific regulations made under that Act gives rise to a civil action unless the regulations themselves provide otherwise (s 47(2)). The specific duties set out in the Acts and regulations vary considerably, some of them being framed in terms of negligence, others in absolute terms, and yet others in an intermediate style, such as by requiring an employer to achieve a certain result 'so far as is reasonably practicable'. The entire area is currently in transition, with the gradual implementation of the EC Framework Directive on Health and Safety (Directive 89/391), which should generally lead to a general code of rules applicable to all workplaces, as well as specific regulations on particular industries.

Medical care

Introduction

4.45   Actions for medical negligence form a substantial part of the overall total of tort claims. Perhaps £30m is paid out by the NHS every year as compensation, and legal and other related costs push the total bill much higher. Injuries induced by medical care are as old as medicine itself. Nonetheless, the current relatively high level of litigation has only been reached over the past half-century. At the start of the twentieth century, many factors inhibited litigation. Key factors were difficulty in finding funds to sue; also social deference to doctors, which made plaintiffs reluctant to sue and courts reluctant to find doctors liable. Courts were also unhappy at making large damages awards against charity hospitals, then very common institutions. The introduction of both civil legal aid and a National Health Service in the late 1940s transformed the area. And ironically, advances in medicine mean *more* dissatisfaction with medical care. Expectations are higher, and with better tests available it may be easier to demonstrate what has gone wrong and whose fault it is.

Hospitals and their staff accordingly protest that there has been a massive increase in their legal liabilities, which has nothing to do with any rise in injuries suffered. Lawyers retort that the low level of litigation in earlier years was not an indication that all was well in medical circles, but demonstrated rather the huge difficulties facing anyone who wished to sue. Meanwhile, medical negligence is probably the least efficiently run of all areas of negligence law. Barely 10% of plaintiffs who start proceedings obtain any kind of compensation, which suggests that their lawyers are remarkably bad at spotting which cases have a real chance of success and which do not.

Breach of duty

4.46 *The Bolam test* The level of duty owed by doctors, surgeons and other health professionals is in many respects unremarkable. Any health professional must act as the reasonable health professional would act in that situation. What is reasonable is judged by the standards current at the time, not later knowledge and understanding (*Roe v Minister of Health* (1954)). All of this is what one would expect from general principle (**3.8**). The level of duty has, however, a peculiarity, normally known as the *Bolam* test (after *Bolam v Friern Hospital Management Committee* (1957)). The test is not whether *all* health professionals would approve of what this particular health professional did. It is a defence if what they did was thought adequate by a significant number, *even if most competent professionals would disapprove*. Or as it was put in the *Bolam* case itself, a doctor

> … is not guilty of negligence if he has acted in accordance with a practice accepted as proper by a responsible body of medical men skilled in that particular art … Putting it the other way round, a man is not negligent if he is acting in accordance with such a practice, merely because there is a body of opinion which would take a contrary view ([1957] 1 WLR 587, McNair J).

Subsequent cases have not only endorsed this but have gone further, saying that it is not enough that some sort of error can be shown, if it is not of the requisite seriousness. A 'mere error of judgement' is not necessarily negligence, even if its consequences are gruesome (*Whitehouse v Jordan* (1981)). The level of duty owed is therefore in practice rather low by the standards of negligence law generally.

4.47 *Will the Bolam test survive?* Until recently, the courts stoutly resisted attempts to water down the *Bolam* test. The test was endorsed and extended in *Whitehouse v Jordan* (1981). The same thing happened in *Sidaway v Board of Governors of the Bethlem Royal Hospital* (1985), where P's argument that her rights as a patient included a right to be informed of the risks of treatment was defeated on proof that current medical practice was the contrary. There were some discordant notes in the case – a strong dissent ([1985] AC 876, Lord Scarman) and a recognition that steps would sometimes be 'so obviously necessary' that a court would require them no matter what clinical practice prevailed ([1985] AC 900, Lord Bridge). But overall the case was yet another endorsement of the *Bolam* approach.

Nonetheless, the principle is subject to obvious criticisms. The courts do not allow such a high degree of autonomy to other professions, and give no very clear reason why the medical professions should be special in this respect. By treating medical judgement as a black box which the courts will decline to open, they effectively allow doctors to continue to use outdated notions, so long as they can find others who have not updated their knowledge either. In recent years, the courts have shown increasing dissatisfaction with the *Bolam* test, though equally they are reluctant to set the law on a collision course with medical practice generally. In *Newell v Goldenberg* [1995] 6 Med LR 371, 374 Mantell J noted that 'the *Bolam* principle provides a defence for those who lag behind the times'. He refused to allow the doctor in the case to rely on the principle, the doctor having admitted that he followed an older practice not through intellectual adherence to it, but simply by accident. In *Bolitho v City and Hackney Health Authority* (1997), the House of Lords denied that professional opinion would always be conclusive:

> ... if, in a rare case, it can be demonstrated that the professional opinion is not capable of withstanding logical analysis, the judge is entitled to hold that the body of opinion is not reasonable or responsible ([1997] 4 All ER 779, Lord Browne-Wilkinson).

Important though this statement is, Lord Browne-Wilkinson stressed that it would only be rarely that a court would go so far as to override professional opinion in this way. Whether this new way of thinking will turn out to be significantly different from the old remains to be seen.

Alternatives

4.48 Dissatisfaction with the law on medical negligence is nearly universal. Much can be done to improve the working of the law, even on the assumption that the main principles are to remain as they are. In particular, there seems to be plenty of scope for encouraging more co-operative pre-trial procedures, the better to identify which cases have a real chance of success and which must ultimately fail. Whether the standard of care needs attention from reformers is not so obvious. Even if hospitals were made strictly liable, so that injured patients could recover merely by showing that the care they received caused their injuries, without proving fault, this would still be a complicated and expensive area for litigation. In practice, proof of causation in this area is far more time-consuming and wasteful of resources than proving fault.

There seems to be a high, though admittedly not universal, agreement that providing monetary compensation for plaintiffs is much lower down the scale of desirable objectives here than it is in other areas. There are certainly cases where P's desperate need after incompetent care is for money, as where D's lack of care severely damaged P's earning power, or created the need for long-term treatment, or both. But in most cases, money does not seem the right remedy. On D's side, the money must come out of their resources generally, and so ultimately from the same pot as that for money for the care of other patients. If P succeeds, this success is at the expense of other patients. And on P's side, all he is likely to get from a legal action is money; whereas what many plaintiffs say they want is rather an explanation of what happened. If plaintiffs in these cases often seem too eager for money, it should be remembered that nothing else is on offer. What direction reforms should take, therefore, depends on what we are trying to achieve. If the object is to provide compensation for injured patients, the system is a very bad one, for few patients receive compensation; but are we prepared to pay the bill for greater compensation? Alternatively, if the object of damages awards is to provide pressure towards greater safety, the criticism would be that it is a rather indirect way of doing that, and alternatives need to be considered. In particular, legislation has only recently permitted the disciplining of doctors for 'seriously deficient performance' (see Medical (Professional Performance) Act 1995, in force 1 July 1997). Perhaps experience of the operation of the new law will show whether this is a better route for the control of dangerous medical practices.

Further Reading

Relevant sections of tort reference books may be supplemented with:

Hoyte 'Unsound practice: The epidemiology of medical negligence' [1995] Med Law Rev 53.

Self-test questions

1. If the facts of *Donoghue v Stevenson* (1932) were to recur, what defences would potentially be open to Stevenson (**4.11**)?

2.   In what circumstances is an employer liable to the employee for the fault of others (**4.35**)?

3.   In what circumstances is a landlord liable for injuries to the tenant's guests (**4.31**)?

4.   Can the driver of a car be said to 'occupy' it for the purposes of the Occupiers' Liability Acts (**4.17**)?

5.   Why may an occupier's warning of danger be held to defeat an action by a visitor who falls a victim to that danger (**4.25**)?

CHAPTER FIVE

Negligence: property and economic losses

SUMMARY

A duty in negligence will usually exist where P can show:

- **that D injured P's property; or**

- **that there was a sufficiently close relationship ('special relationship') between P and D.**

Liability will not always be refused in cases falling outside those two categories, but the law is in an advanced state of confusion from which it currently shows no sign of recovering.

Introduction

The outward drift of the law

5.1 From *Donoghue v Stevenson* (1932) onwards, the tort of negligence has expanded greatly. However, that development has never been smooth. There have been many judicial disagreements over how, or whether, to expand it in particular areas, or indeed whether particular bold decisions of earlier years should not be reversed by later, more cautious judges. This is not a legal history text. Nonetheless, some understanding of the key decisions of the last few decades is necessary for understanding where the law has got to and how it might progress in the future.

5.2 *Spartan Steel and Alloys Ltd v Martin & Co (Contractors) Ltd (1973)* In this case, electrical contractors carelessly cut through a power cable, with the expensive consequence that P's foundry was deprived of power. P's molten metal cooled and solidified where it was. An expensive cleanup operation was necessary after power was restored. Profit was lost on these melts; and yet further profit was lost on melts which could have been performed but for the power cut. How much of this was recoverable in a legal action against the contractors? To award nothing, and therefore to put the whole cost of the accident onto P even though it was D's fault, seemed unpalatable. But equally it seemed excessive to put the entire cost on D, leaving D with a huge bill for a relatively small error. In the event, the Court of Appeal in effect imposed a compromise. The physical mess left by the accident was chargeable to D; and all economic costs which flowed directly from that physical situation could also be recovered. But purely economic losses – losses which neither consisted of property damage nor flowed directly from it – were held irrecoverable.

The arbitrariness of the line being drawn was obvious enough. The reasons given for the result hardly suggest a great degree of judicial unanimity. Lawton LJ relied heavily on the absence of precedent:

> Water conduits have been with us for centuries; gas mains for nearly a century and a half; electricity supply cables for about three-quarters of a century; but there is not a single case in the English law reports which is an authority for the proposition that mere financial loss resulting from negligent interruption of such services is recoverable. ([1973] QB 47)

Lord Denning MR preferred to stress policy considerations. He noted that the power might have been cut for many reasons and that there was a risk of a large number of relatively small claims. These claims, he thought, could better be met by letting the loss lie where it fell, rather than by concentrating it on a single individual, who might not be able to bear it ([1973] QB 37-39). Edmund Davies LJ dissented:

> ... if economic loss of itself confers a right of action this may spell disaster for the negligent party. But this may equally be the outcome where physical damage alone is suffered, or where physical damage leads directly to economic loss. ([1973] QB 40)

The distinction between physical damage and purely economic loss has a certain attraction on the facts of *Spartan Steel* itself. But it is another question whether it should have wider application. Nonetheless, the case played an important part in establishing the modern orthodoxy that *foreseeable injury to property is usually recoverable,* whereas foreseeable injury to purely economic interests is not. The first part of the proposition is as important as the second and is now very well established. The controversies in the following years have been over the second limb: when and how the courts will allow a remedy for purely economic losses.

5.3 *Hedley Byrne & Co v Heller & Partners Ltd (1964)*   If *Spartan Steel* is now the general rule, then the earlier decision of the House of Lords in *Hedley Byrne* can only represent a major exception to it. P had doubts about the creditworthiness of one of its clients and, through an intermediary, asked D for a credit reference. D responded that 'We believe that the company would not undertake any commitments they were unable to fulfil', though they added that 'Your figures are larger than we are accustomed to see'. They added that their reference was 'For your own private use and without responsibility on [our] part ...' P lost significant sums when its client went into liquidation, which it sought to recoup by action against D. The action failed, largely because of the way in which D had qualified their reference, but a majority of the House made it clear that negligent misstatements of this sort could give rise to liability in tort. D had only narrowly escaped liability. The Lords tried to meet the danger of an indeterminate liability to a wide class of potential plaintiffs by stress on the close association ('special relationship') which must have existed between D and P if action were to be possible.

There have been many later controversies over the limits of this liability. One open question, indeed, is whether the same result would today be reached on those facts, or whether it would be held that D had in fact assumed responsibility to P (**5.15**). But the basic principle has not been doubted, and is the starting point for modern discussions of the recovery of purely economic losses.

5.4 *Anns v Merton London Borough Council (1978)*   This case represented a serious, if slightly indirect, challenge to the line drawn in the *Spartan Steel* case. P bought a flat, but later realised that its foundations were utterly ruined: the builders had not dug deep enough for such soil and the local planning authority had not checked up on the builders. P sued both the builder and the planning authority, and succeeded. Lord Wilberforce, who delivered the leading judgment in the House of Lords, declared that P's loss was in fact physical rather than purely economic, but that it did not matter either way ([1978] AC 759). He proposed a two-stage test for duty, under which the main question was whether loss to P was a foreseeable consequence of D's action, but under which liability could then be limited if there was something in the situation to require it. Whether P's loss was physical or purely economic was not, for him, a matter of great importance.

Anns was initially followed with enthusiasm, notably in Junior Books Ltd v Vietchi Co Ltd (1983), which concerned the owner of premises suing sub-contractors for defective building work. Nonetheless, there was a strong dissent by Lord Brandon in that case, and later cases showed increasing dissatisfaction with it. These cases culminated in Murphy v Brentwood District Council (1990), when Anns was definitively overruled. The division between property damage and purely economic loss was re-asserted as fundamental. However careless the defendants, no duty was owed in relation to purely economic loss.

There is a certain irony in the reasoning in Murphy. The opinions place much stress on the need for certainty in the law – a strange point to emphasise when overruling a decision which had stood for 13 years. They also stress the desirability of the 'incrementalist' approach of building on past precedents – again not what we would expect when overruling one of the most significant holdings of recent years. The opinions also stressed the need for orderly development of the law and respect for what Parliament had laid down. Yet legislation had already been passed which plainly assumed that Anns was law (Latent Damage Act 1986), whereas the distinction between property damage and economic loss, right or wrong, is the courts' creation, not the legislature's! Whatever the Lords were paying respect to, it does not appear to be anything of Parliamentary origin.

5.5 *White v Jones (1995)*   Here, D acted as solicitors for P's father, and showed gross negligence by failing to carry out his instructions to draw up a will for him. The father died before the will was drawn up and P, who would have benefited from a legacy in it, sued D for negligence. The father's estate could not sue D, as it was no worse off than if D had acted carefully; but a majority of the House of Lords was prepared to compensate P. The case is notable for its close con-centration on D's legal situation, which is analysed in considerable detail. The major point of disagreement between the Lords was whether a duty to someone other than D's client was compatible with proper execution of the duty to the client, which all agreed was primary. Nonetheless, the case plainly indicates a willingness to extend liability to fresh situations, even where the loss is plainly economic rather than physical. This is none the less so because it was rapidly distinguished by the Court of Appeal, in a case where the deceased person's estate had an effective remedy against the solicitor for the negligence (*Carr-Glynn v Frearsons* (1997)).

The position today

5.6 These famous decisions form the backdrop to any discussion of the modern law and they establish many important points. Negligence liability for physical loss or damage will be easy to establish, and so will liability where P suffers loss after a defendant with whom P is in a 'special relationship' negligently misrepresents the truth. But how much wider can liability stretch? Would a court today refuse liability on the facts of *Hedley Byrne* (**5.15**)? Was it right for the Lords in *Murphy* to overrule *Anns*, or might not the 'two-stage' test of duty be superior to anything *Murphy* sought to replace it with (**5.34**)? And was *Junior Books* not perfectly right, on its facts if not in its reasoning (**5.4**)? These are all open questions under the current law, which is characterised by a high degree of doubt and uncertainty. In the sections which follow, I will review the more established areas of doctrine, before proceeding to the wilder regions at the edge of the modern law.

The distinction between property damage and pure economic loss

Definition and terminology

5.7 'Purely economic' losses are economic losses which cannot be described as physical damage to the person or to property. In other words, all economic losses are either personal injuries, or property damage, or *purely* economic losses. Economic loss which is consequential on physical damage is not caught by the restriction here described: so if P is injured in the leg and has to take a less well-paid job as a result, P need not fear that this loss of wages will be thought 'purely economic'. It results from a physical injury and the damages for the injury will include it (**10.59**).

Some confusion is caused by shorthand references to 'economic loss', meaning *pure* economic loss. This is obviously a confusing usage. If P's car, worth £1,000, is destroyed, then obviously P has suffered an economic loss. The car cost money to buy and will cost money to replace. But it is not a *purely* economic loss, but rather damage to P's property. (Indeed, most of the losses for which the law of tort allows compensation are economic, in this sense only.) The precise terminology is perhaps not important; what is important is to remember that the objection is not to losses which are economic, but to losses which do *not* constitute either personal injury or damage to property and are not losses consequential on such damage.

The restriction on recovery

5.8 At this stage, I will simply discuss whether particular situations are regarded as examples of purely economic losses, or whether they will be placed in another category. It would be quite wrong to suggest that, having classified a particular loss as purely economic, the court will *always* go on to deny liability. On the contrary, several judges have in particular contexts denied that it is of any significance at all whether the loss is purely economic. Whether liability will be allowed despite this is discussed below (**5.33**).

Contractual rights are not 'property'

5.9 The rule requires not merely damage to property, but that the property must have belonged to P at the time when it was damaged. It seems not to matter that the property was at P's risk, so that P must bear the loss if it is damaged, if P was not its owner.

> *Leigh & Sillavan Ltd v Aliakmon Shipping Co Ltd* (1986) Aliakmon Shipping injured a cargo of steel which they were carrying. The steel was at Leigh's risk, though ownership had not passed to them at the time of the damage. Held: Leigh's loss was a purely economic loss, and accordingly irrecoverable from Aliakmon.

This principle sometimes entails a minute analysis of the nature of P's interest in some property which has been damaged.

> *Candlewood Navigation Corporation Ltd v Mitsui OSK Lines Ltd* (1985) Mitsui owned a ship, which they chartered (by demise charter) to Matsuoka;

Matsuoka immediately chartered it back (by time charter) to Mitsui. The ship was then damaged through the negligence of Candlewood. Held: as a time charter, unlike a demise charter, did not give a property right to the charterer, Mitsui's claim was for a purely economic loss and therefore could not succeed.

These decisions show the rule against pure economic loss at its most technical and arbitrary. If in fact the cost of certain property damage is borne by P and the (technical) owner does not suffer any financial loss at all, then a refusal of compensation is impossible to defend on grounds over over-broad liability, and very hard to defend on any other grounds. Lord Goff, who in the Court of Appeal had argued for liability in the *Aliakmon* case (see [1985] 2 All ER 44) subsequently promoted legislation which has the practical effect of reversing it on its facts (see Carriage of Goods by Sea Act 1992).

Failure to provide proper services

5.10 It is at first sight strange that Anns and other plaintiffs, who find their houses crumbling about their ears, are refused a claim in tort because their loss is purely economic, rather than an injury to property. Indeed, some judges in earlier decades were prepared to regard this sort of loss as physical. The orthodox reasoning today is, however, that the loss is not physical, but rather a complaint of the lack of proper professional service by D. *Anns* would have been quite different if P had at one time owned good foundations, which D ruined. Rather, there never was a good set of foundations. Whether P's claim is good or not, it is not a claim for damage to property, for there never was a good piece of property which D injured. When D supplies a defective article which ends up with P, we must therefore ask whether D's negligence damaged P's property, or whether P is simply complaining of the low value of the article P now has.

Muirhead v Industrial Tank Specialities Ltd (1986) Muirhead bought pumps as part of his system for storing live lobsters in an aquarium, for later sale. The pumps failed and the lobsters died. Muirhead sued Industrial Tank, the manufacturers, who were found to have been negligent. Held: Muirhead could recover the value of the dead lobsters, but not the purely economic loss of having to repair or replace the defective pumps.

Possible exceptions

5.11 *'Complex structures'* If we consider Anns to own a single structure – a house with foundations – then clearly he suffered no property damage, for he never had a house with good foundations. If, however, we say he owned two things – bad foundations, with a perfectly good house sitting on top of them – then the case is altered, for while Anns cannot argue that his foundations were damaged, he can argue that the house was. Accordingly, by the mental device of separating the good from the bad, what was apparently a purely economic loss can be converted, at least in part, into property damage for which a claim can be made. This line of argument has received some support from the House of Lords (eg *D & F Estates Ltd v Church Comrs for England* (1988)). However, it obviously subverts the approach the Lords sought to establish in *Murphy*, where Lord Bridge disapproved it, at least insofar as it gave any support to *Anns* ([1990] 2 All ER 928). Yet he and his colleagues stopped short of condemning it outright, and its status today is somewhat obscure. Probably the idea will be of most value in cases where different parts of the structure were built by different firms.

5.12 *'Pre-emptive damages'* If P, the owner of defective premises, allows them to crumble, and rubble falls onto P's car, then certainly P has suffered physical damage. If the rubble falls on P personally, P has suffered personal injury, and so again may recover damages. It seems strange to hold that if P acts to obviate this threat of physical injury, this money is irrecoverable as being a purely economic loss. Accordingly, money spent in this pre-emptive way is treated by some judges as recoverable, as if it represented a physical loss. This was one strand of Lord Wilberforce's reasoning in *Anns*: Anns was paying to clear up a danger to his own and his family's health and safety (see *Anns* [1977] 2 All ER 492, 505). In *Murphy*, the Lords were obviously not anxious to lend any credence to *Anns*, and would not accept that P could recover if the danger were merely to P personally. Nonetheless, Lord Bridge at least seemed to accept that there might be something in the argument, in some circumstances at least:

> [I]f a building stands so close to the boundary of the building owner's land that after discovery of the dangerous defect it remains a potential source of injury to persons or property on neighbouring land or on the highway, the building owner ought, in principle, to be entitled to recover in tort from the negligent builder the cost of obviating the danger, whether

by repair or by demolition, so far as that cost is necessarily incurred in order to protect himself from potential liability to third parties ([1990] 2 All ER 926).

Conclusion

5.13 The line between property damage, on the one hand, and purely economic losses, on the other, is sometimes difficult to draw, and hard to justify once drawn. It is in some respects surprising that the more conservative judges have not allowed a looser definition of 'physical' damage, the better to reconcile the more radical judges to the continued existence of the distinction. As will be seen (**5.33**), it has proved impossible to hold the line.

'Special relationships' and negligent misstatement

Introduction

5.14 Where the relationship between P and D is such that P reasonably reposes a high degree of trust in D's advice, then bad advice to P resulting in loss may lead to an action in negligence against D. It seems to be irrelevant that the loss P suffers is usually purely economic. At this stage, the discussion will be confined to the case where D mis-advises P, rather than the case where P suffers because of bad advice D gave *to someone else* (that case will be considered below, **5.35**). It may also be assumed that the cases mentioned will concern purely economic loss, for while statements can certainly lead to physical damage, it does not appear that such cases are treated any differently from cases of physical damage caused by actions.

> *Clayton v Woodman & Sons (Builders) Ltd* (1962)   Clayton, a building worker, injured himself as a result of careless instructions from the architects of the building project. Held: the architects were liable for these injuries.

'Special relationship' or 'reasonable foresight'?

5.15 Even in the *Hedley Byrne* case itself, which first recognised this head of liability, there were considerable disagreements as to its nature, quite apart from disagreements about its limits.

- Lord Reid preferred to talk of a *special relationship* between P and D. The characteristics of this relationship are that P reasonably placed reliance on what D said, and D knew or ought to have known that that was so ([1964] AC 486).

- Lord Devlin said that the liability attached to relationships which were *equivalent to contract* ([1964] AC 529). It is unclear which relationships will be so regarded. It is obviously not enough to say that this means relationships which would be contracts but for the fact that they aren't. If Devlin meant relationships of close trust and confidence, then his *dictum* seems confused. Contracts are not necessarily relationships of trust and confidence – it may, indeed, be the parties' *lack* of mutual trust that led them to try to tie each other down by contract in the first place.

- Various *dicta* in the case tie the liability to an *assumption of liability*. D is liable not because the law seeks to impose a duty, but because D made it clear to P that D was *undertaking* a duty (eg Lord Reid [1964] AC 486). It is very unclear what this means, or how we are to recognise such an assumption when it is present. The 'assumption of responsibility' approach was rejected as not 'a helpful or realistic test in most cases' by Lord Griffiths in *Smith v Eric S Bush* [1990] 1 AC 831, 864.

- Lord Morris said that the true principle is simply *reasonable foresight* that P will rely on what D says ([1964] AC 503). Yet plainly liability is narrower than liability for negligent acts, which is also usually described in those terms. Yet again, we see that the range of foresight depends at least partly on policy considerations. Economic losses are treated as less foreseeable than personal injury.

It is impossible to reduce liability to a simple formula. The various theories mentioned are very little different in their practical effects. It is well to bear in mind that, quite apart from the general caution the courts exercise in relation to claims for purely economic losses, there are specific reasons for restricting liability in these cases. Words are easily passed on, and can have far greater consequences than individual acts. And while P presents the case as being that D did P harm, it would often be fairer to say that P did himself or herself harm by taking a bad decision (in which D's advice was merely one contributing factor), or that others harmed P (in a way which P might have been able to avoid if D had given better advice). If plaintiffs are to be treated as responsible for their own actions, the liability of defendants in negligent misstatement must be narrow.

The statement: addressed to whom?

5.16 In principle, the question should be whether *P* was entitled to rely on D's statement, and it is not obviously relevant whether anyone else can. In practice, the more generally D's statement is broadcast, the less likely is the court to hold that there is a 'special relationship' between D and any one person who heard it and relied on it. Sometimes this can be justified on the grounds that a statement addressed to many people will obviously not be tailored to their individual needs. In most cases it would be more realistic to say that the courts are scared of imposing too broad a liability. But there is no ban on liability merely because P is not the person at whom the statement is primarily aimed.

> *Smith v Eric E Bush* (1990)   Smith sought a loan on mortgage, to enable her to buy a house. Bush surveyed the house on behalf of the mortgage company, failing to notice fundamental structural defects. As Bush must have known was likely, Smith gained access to the survey and relied on it instead of having one of her own. Held: Smith's reliance was reasonable and Bush was liable to her.

However, it is important not to lose sight of D's position. The surveyor was paid to produce a report for the mortgage company, on whether it was good security for the amount they sought to lend. If that task had been done reasonably well, Smith would have had no valid complaint that she had been poorly advised on how comfortable or otherwise desirable the house was likely to be for her as purchaser.

Widely disseminated statements

5.17 Only rarely will information released to the public generally successfully be made the subject of an action in negligence. However, where D has compiled a semi-official and apparently authoritative report on some matter, it may be reasonable for P to rely on it. In those circumstances, the courts in recent years have tended to ask themselves whether P is the sort of person the report was prepared for.

Caparo Industries plc v Dickman (1990)   Caparo mounted a takeover of a firm, Fidelity, in which they already held shares. In their financial calculations, Caparo relied on Fidelity's statutory accounts as giving an accurate picture. On discovering that the accounts were in fact highly inaccurate, they sued Touche Ross, the firm's auditors, who had certified the accounts as being a true and fair view of Fidelity's position. Held: statutory accounts were produced to enable existing shareholders to safeguard their position, not to facilitate take-overs, and accordingly Caparo had no claim.

Mariola Marine Corpn v Lloyd's Register of Shipping (1990)   Mariola purchased *The Morning Watch*, a motor yacht, relying in part on its having received a glowing report from Lloyds' Register. The yacht turned out to be seriously corroded. Held: the purpose of Lloyds' surveys was to protect life and property when vessels were at sea, rather than to protect the economic interest of purchasers.

The principle is not an obvious one. If P's use of the circulated report is foreseeable, why should it matter that the original purpose of preparing such reports was different? Yet, even taking the principle of those decisions as a given, nonetheless its application to their facts is disputable. In particular, the view of statutory accounts taken in *Caparo* has been described by one commentator as 'an artificial interpretation which takes no account of commercial reality', especially since audited accounts are one of the few reliable ways by which outsiders may determine how well the company is being run (Percival 'After *Caparo* – Liability in business transactions revisited' (1991) 54 MLR 739, 742). The case was subsequently distinguished on very similar facts by the Court of Appeal.

Morgan Crucible Co plc v Hill Samuel & Co Ltd (1991)   Morgan Crucible made a take-over bid for FCE, an electronics firm. The directors and auditors of FCE released a 'defence document' advising rejection of the bid, and including various account information about FCE. Morgan Crucible increased its bid and completed the takeover. It later sued the directors and auditors, having discovered the account information to be inaccurate. Held: the case was distinguishable from *Caparo* and so need not be struck out.

The case suggests a rather different criterion, for which there is also support in the opinions in *Caparo:* that D will only be liable in a case where D has actual knowledge of P's plans.

Is a statement necessary at all?

5.18 If a sufficiently strong 'special relationship' is demonstrated, it might be thought that D could break the duty this relationship produces as much by silence as by bad advice. Liability for a failure to speak in pre-contractual negotiations was refused in *Banque Keyser Ullman (UK) Insurance Co Ltd v Skandia* (1990). This was, however, on the ground that it would unsettle what had long been understood to be the law on silence in negotiations; the case is no authority against liability for silence in other contexts. However, it has been said that there will only be liability if D has a duty to speak (eg Lord Scarman, *Tai Hing Cotton Mill Ltd v Liu Chong Hing Bank Ltd* [1986] AC 80, 110). It is entirely unclear when such a duty will arise, and despite occasional *dicta* in favour of such liability, there appears to be no clear example of it in this jurisdiction.

The special relationship

5.19 *The nature of the relationship* It is difficult to generalise on the nature of the relationship necessary to give rise to liability. The extent to which P relies, the reasonableness of so relying, and D's actual or reasonably-attainable knowledge of this are all relevant factors. But there is no simple formula to apply. Two sample cases where P relied on D, who was a solicitor acting for someone else, may be contrasted.

> *Gran Gelato Ltd v Richcliff (Group) Ltd* (1992) Gran Gelato took a sub-lease of premises, its landlord's solicitor having carelessly assured it that its head lease was good for ten years. After five years, the head lease was unexpectedly but lawfully terminated by the freehold owner. Held: Gran Gelato had no action against its landlord's solicitors.

> *Edwards v Lee* (1991) Lee, a solicitor, gave Edwards a reference for Hawkes, his client, on the strength of which Edwards allowed Hawkes to take away a Mercedes car on credit. Hawkes subsequently absconded; as Lee knew, he was on bail pending trial for criminal dishonesty. Held: even though legal professional privilege would not have permitted Lee to mention the charges against Hawkes, nonetheless the reference was misleading and Edwards could recover damages. They would however be reduced by 50% for contributory negligence.

In *Gran Gelato*, Nicholls V-C made much of the point that the client, rather than the solicitor, was the obvious person to sue. The same of course is equally true of *Edwards*, though possibly the case is different in that Edwards had asked for the reference precisely because the client's reliability was doubtful.

5.20 *Merely social relationships* If the relationship between P and D is purely social, then it is usually unreasonable to place much reliance on anything D may say, and accordingly no duty is owed. There will not be many cases where P can place much weight on what D may have told P off-the-cuff at a party. But there is no firm rule, except that P cannot sue unless P's reliance was, in all the circumstances, reasonable.

> *Chaudhry v Prabhakar* (1988) Chaudhry, who had just passed her driving test and knew little about cars, sought the advice of Prabhakar, a close friend with some knowledge of cars. Prabhakar subsequently recommended a particular Volkswagon Golf, making a number of careless statements about it. The Golf turned out to be unroadworthy and worthless. Held: a duty was owed to Chaudhry and was broken.

The case has been doubted, not least because counsel for Prabhakar appears to have conceded that at least some sort of duty was owed to Chaudhry. It remains the case that strong facts must be shown before any such plaintiff is likely to succeed.

5.21 *Potentially contractual relationships* For some years after *Hedley Byrne* it was generally thought that parties negotiating for the formation of a contract could not be in a 'special relationship'. It was thought that someone who shows enough self-reliance to negotiate terms with D is plainly *not* relying on D very much, if at all. There was also at that time a general wariness at letting tort seep into contractual contexts. However, this attitude oversimplified a number of issues and it was eventually established that one negotiating party can owe a duty to another.

> *Esso Petroleum v Mardon* (1976) Mardon sought the advice of an expert of Esso as to the likely sales at a particular filling station, of which Mardon was considering purchasing the franchise. On the strength of the expert's over-optimistic and careless prediction,

Mardon took the franchise and subsequently made large losses. Held: Esso owed a duty to Mardon, which had been broken by its expert's poor advice.

It has even been held that D might be in breach of duty for failing to advise P to enter into a contract with D!

Crossan v Ward Bracewell (1986)   Crossan consulted a solicitor for advice whether he should pursue a claim arising out of a road accident. After hearing the financial implications, Crossan decided that he could not afford to pursue the claim. The solicitor had, however, carelessly failed to appreciate that Crossan would have been entitled to have his legal expenses met from insurance. Held: the solicitor was liable to an action in negligence.

Relationships which later become contractual

5.22 It is no longer the law that the existence of contractual duties automatically excludes liability in tort in the context of the same relationship. So, for example, while it was held in *Groom v Crocker* (1939) that the duty owed by solicitors to their clients is contractual only, in *Midland Bank Trust Co Ltd v Hett, Stubbs & Kemp* (1979) this approach was repudiated. So there is no longer a general rule excluding tort liability. Nonetheless, in economic loss cases generally, and especially cases connected with construction work, the courts are acutely conscious that parties may have intended that their written contracts should be the definitive statement of their obligations. Accordingly, they may refuse to add others via the law of tort (**5.46**); and this may prevent P recovering damages.

Pacific Associates Inc v Baxter (1989)   Pacific Associates undertook dredging work in Dubai. Their employer hired a consultant engineer to supervise the work. Finding the work unexpectedly difficult, Pacific sought to sue the engineer for providing them with misleading geological data. There was no contract between Pacific and the engineer. Held: no duty was owed in tort either.

It was relevant that D had disclaimed all liability for this sort of loss under his contract with his employer (see [1989] 2 All ER 179), but very probably the case would have gone the same way in any event.

135

5.23 *Statutory remedy* Where D's poor advice results in P's forming a contract with D, there is a statutory remedy under the Misrepresentation Act 1967, s 2(1). If this remedy applies, P is almost certain to use it in preference to the remedy under *Hedley Byrne*. Under the statute, there is no need to establish a duty; lack of care is for D to disprove, rather than for P to prove; and damages are assessed on a more generous basis, as if the claim were one for deceit (see **6.2**; *Royscott Trust Ltd v Rogerson* (1991)).

Exclusion of liability

5.24 In the *Hedley Byrne* case itself, the claim failed because D had made it clear that it accepted no liability for its statement. However, in modern conditions, and especially given that not all judges accept that P's claim is based on an 'assumption of responsibility' by D (see **5.37**), this is no longer a very obvious conclusion. If D knows that P will rely on the information and that it is reasonable to do so (perhaps D is P's best or only source of information), can D escape all liability merely by stating that the information is given without responsibility? This is not obvious even so far as the common law is concerned. Moreover, legislation now forbids the exclusion of 'business liability' for negligence, except where the exclusion is a reasonable one (Unfair Contract Terms Act 1977, ss 1, 2 and 13). The precise effect of this is unclear, however. If D makes it clear that the advice is made without responsibility, is D excluding a duty, contrary to the Unfair Contract Terms Act 1977, or does the notice preclude P from establishing reasonable reliance, so that there is nothing to exclude? In *Smith v Eric E Bush* (**5.16**), the House of Lords preferred the first interpretation. Lord Griffiths mentioned various factors which needed consideration on whether the clause was un-reasonable within the meaning of the Act ([1990] 1 AC 858-859).

- 'Were the parties of equal bargaining power?'

- '[W]ould it have been reasonably practicable to obtain the advice from an alternative source taking into account considerations of costs and time?'

- 'How difficult is the task being undertaken for which liability is being excluded?'

- 'What are the practical consequences of the decision on the question of reasonableness? This must involve the sums of money potentially at stake and the ability of the parties to bear the loss involved, which, in its turn, raises the question of insurance.'

On the basis of these factors, he held unreasonableness established. Smith was in no position to object to the clause (first factor); she was relatively impecunious (second factor); this work was straightforward (third factor); and while insurance would undoubtedly raise costs somewhat, it should not be by much (fourth factor). (The generosity of the Lords here is an odd contrast to the restrictive attitude in cases like *Caparo* (**5.17**). Possibly the reasoning is that corporate raiders are less in need of protection than first-time house buyers.) *Bush* was not a case where the warning was very prominent. Conceivably D's claim that the duty was excluded might get a better hearing if D made it very obvious that no liability was accepted.

Must D be a professional?

5.25 A few years after the *Hedley Byrne* decision, the Privy Council ruled that P could not rely on any 'special relationship' unless D was some sort of professional person, exercising the relevant special professional skills (*Mutual Life and Citizens' Assurance Co v Evatt* (1971)). Accordingly, it refused to find liability when a life assurance company gave unsound advice to P about the financial standing of an associated company, as D's business was life assurance, not financial advice. However, there were powerfully-argued dissents in the case, and the majority's approach has been rejected in England. If D has special knowledge or expertise on which P relies, it does not matter whether D's career consists of utilising that knowledge or expertise (eg *Esso Petroleum Co Ltd v Mardon* (1976)).

Reliance in fact, and causation

5.26 Having established a duty and breach of that duty, P must also demonstrate a loss flowing from P's reliance on D's poor advice. This will be particularly difficult in a case where P takes an independent decision in reliance on a range of information, of which D's input is an important but not all-embracing part. The courts have occasionally reduced P's damages for contributory negligence (eg *Edwards v Lee* (1991), (**5.19**)), which seems to imply that it is not a complete answer to P's claim that P acted unreasonably in following the advice.

The cutting edge of liability

Introduction: continuity and change

5.27 Despite the confusion, there is a fair degree of certainty about the law of negligence. In many common situations, the existence and the limits of the duty are established with reasonable clarity. It is always true that the higher courts can overrule earlier cases, but for those cases which are not going to end up in the higher courts (the overwhelming majority) this possibility can be neglected. The best guide to what the courts will do in the future is to ask what they have done in the past. Moreover, the degree of confusion that remains is partly illusory: it indicates not an insoluble problem, but only that the higher courts prefer to delegate detailed application of their rules to lower courts. So while there is no denying that portions of the law are in a state of hideous confusion, it is important not to get it out of proportion.

Your examiners will not expect you to solve problems which have baffled judges and academics alike, and which have regularly led to furious dissension and argument. However, it is not unreasonable to expect you to be familiar with the leading cases, to be able to expound the major schools of thought and to venture a reasoned view of which you think preferable.

Philosophies of legal development

5.28 One major reason for dissension in the higher courts is differences of view over when, and by what methods, it is open to the courts to develop the law. To parody the opposing views (though not really by much), some judges are unimaginative book-worms, who stick closely to the text of past precedents and react with indignation at the idea that the courts might do something for which there was no precedent. Others, we might say, have forgotten that the courts are distinct from the Law Commission and draw no very obvious distinction between expounding the law and making it afresh. Throughout this area there is conflict between those judges who wish to develop the law in a relatively 'incrementalist' way and those who are bolder. Both types appeal to Parliament. The more timid judges insist that development of tort is a matter for the legislature not the courts, perhaps arguing that legislation can implement detailed restrictions and qualifications on liability which the common law cannot (eg *D & F Estates Ltd v Church Comrs for England* [1989] 1 AC 177, 210, Lord Bridge). The braver ones regard Parliament as a long-stop if the courts' attempts to develop the law go awry, and even threaten to introduce new legislation themselves if they cannot persuade their colleagues to develop the law through the courts (eg *White v Jones* [1995] 2 AC 207, 265, Lord Goff). Short of clear evidence that Parliament has already considered the possibility of negligence liability and rejected it as unsuitable, arguments of this sort cannot conclude the matter either way.

Few fundamental points are established

5.29   The disagreements in this area are not confined to the interpretation of agreed principles, but extend to fundamental disputes over what the relevant principles are. For example, some judges are happy to assert that there is a principle against the recovery of pure economic loss, whereas other judges deny that the distinction is of any importance at all. There is also little unanimity on the *function* of tort law in this area. For judges who stick closely to the precedents, this is perhaps not much of a problem: no policy not already endorsed in earlier cases need be adverted to. For judges who take a broader view of their responsibilities, however, there is a real problem and no agreed solution.

The leading cases are not final

5.30   The higher courts are frequently asked to pronounce on topical issues in this area, yet their rulings seem to have little finality about them. Indeed, many of the live issues are precisely over whether particular decisions should be overruled. At the time of writing, it is highly debatable (for example) whether *Murphy* was rightly decided, whether it was right to overrule *Anns* and whether the much-criticised *Junior Books* might not have been right for the wrong reasons. And while no-one supposes that the existence of dissenting judgments in itself calls decisions into question, nonetheless many of them are well worth reading. For example, Lord Mustill's dissent in *White v Jones* seems likely to be highly influential. As he noted, many disagreements in cases of this sort derive from a failure to agree on the justice of the claim itself. Assumptions on questions of that sort, he noted, 'dominate the landscape within which the whole inquiry takes place' ([1995] 2 AC 277).

The fear of indeterminate liability

5.31 *Too many cases for the courts to handle?* Many judges are concerned about over-extension of liability: that 'the floodgates of litigation' will be opened, with dire consequences for all. The argument is invoked rather too often to be convincing in all cases. Most professions are ready with arguments why the sky would fall if they were held responsible in damages for all of the consequences of their actions. If the argument is to be taken seriously, and sometimes it is so taken, then various different types of cases need to be distinguished.

First, the argument might be an appeal to the consequences *for the legal system* if liability is permitted. The court system would be deluged by claims, clogging up the arteries of justice and ultimately stopping the heart of our system of justice.

This argument can be overstated, and frequently has been. It is only rarely that the courts deal with any one case which in itself would have any significant impact on the total number of cases brought in any one year. No doubt it is true that the gradual broadening of the tort of negligence in this century is a factor in the gradual increase in the numbers of claims. But a problem as large as that requires a solution of more general import. Arguments that allowing a particular claim will lead to an unacceptable number of further claims are rarely supported by evidence of any sort, and are often merely a protest at a claim which is novel. In terms of number of claims, cases of purely economic loss are very much a sideshow to the main business of tort law: personal injury claims arising out of motor collisions and work-place accidents.

5.32 *Too heavy a liability on D?* A second, and quite different, argument is that it would be undesirable to make D liable for the large sums which would be assessed *against him or her* if liability were allowed: the classic case here being the *Spartan Steel* case. Here, the *number* of cases is not the point; rather, the argument is that the *total liability* on D will be more than D can pay, or more than D fairly should. The argument is often unattractive morally, as it suggests that the more harm D does, the less likely is D to held liable. However, it should not be forgotten that D's degree of fault is usually ignored in assessing damages – if D is found negligent, even in some relatively trivial respect, then D is liable for the whole of the loss caused, be it large or small. Arguably, to deny the relevance of degrees of fault is unfair and so it is not too surprising if, having thrown this principle out of the front door, some judges try to sneak it in through the back.

A related argument is that of the availability of insurance. Many judges would feel uncomfortable in holding D liable in circumstances where liability insurance was unavailable, or very costly. Courts have, however, not always found it easy to discover whether insurance is available; and of course the court's decision to impose liability will influence the availability of insurance, being one more circumstance to which insurers must adapt. Nonetheless, the availability of insurance is certainly a factor. It seems that the decision in the *Murphy* case was influenced by the fact that P was insured and D was not ([1991] 1 AC 458, Lord Keith). If the *real* plaintiff is an insurance company which has already been paid to bear the risk in question, and the *real* defendants are the local community charge payers, it is not too surprising if the courts seem sympathetic to the defendants.

Organising concepts

Introduction

5.33   No one set of concepts provides a magic key to this area. Certain ideas are, however, encountered again and again by those who study this area. Some of them concentrate on the relationship itself, asking whether there is *proximity* between P and D, or whether the relationship is a *special* one entailing a high degree of care. Others look at the matter from P's side, asking whether P has *reasonably relied* on the assumption that D will behave in a careful way. Or again, looking at it from D's side, some ask whether D has *voluntarily assumed responsibility* for safeguarding P's interests. Sometimes these concepts are used together, in various combinations; sometimes they are used alone. Each concept has its judicial supporters and detractors. Perhaps the truth is that each of them makes sense in some areas but not others.

'Proximity'

5.34   It is on any view relevant how close a connection there was between D's behaviour and P's financial or business well-being. It is also often the most obvious ground for liability, in cases where P's contact with D has been minimal.

Ministry of Housing and Local Government v Sharp (1970) Would-be purchasers of land applied to the local land charges registry to see whether any interests were registered against it. Due to the carelessness of a registry clerk, they were not told of the Ministry's planning charge, with the result that the Ministry lost the benefit of this charge. Held: the local registry was liable to the Ministry for this error.

Yet 'proximity' has been over-used. In the *Junior Books* case (**5.4**), a majority of the House of Lords was mightily impressed by the close degree of proximity between P and D. P knew D well and had indeed specifically instructed the head contractor to employ D as sub-contractor. The link between them was 'almost as close a commercial relationship ... as it is possible to envisage short of privity of contract' ([1983] 1 AC 542, Lord Roskill). Yet while this feature of the case was real enough, it is by no means apparent why it should make any real difference, or why P's case for compensation was any stronger than that of *any* owner of premises who hires a contractor whom P knows will himself hire sub-contractors. A high degree of proximity is necessary but not sufficient, and merely proving an exceptional degree of proximity cannot get around the need for additional factors. Equally, in *Ross v Caunters* (1980), where a solicitor misadvised his client with the effect that a legacy to P failed, Megarry V-C made the high degree of proximity between solicitor and legatee the main point in establishing liability. A subsequent House of Lords found this reasoning hopelessly unenlightened and preferred to ignore Megarry's judgment. 'It is better to start again' (*White v Jones* [1995] 2 AC 283, Lord Mustill).

'Special relationship'

5.35 The typical *Hedley Byrne* case is two-handed: D gives poor advice to P, who acts on it and suffers injury. Sometimes the advice follows a rather tortuous route on its way from D to P (eg **5.17**), but nonetheless the basic situation is still a two-handed one. The tort has occasionally been used in three-handed situations: D gives poor advice to X, who acts on it in some way which injures P. The analogy between the two situations is however somewhat imprecise. Some judges reject it altogether: in *White v Jones*, Lord Mustill reasoned that *Hedley Byrne* required some sort of reciprocity or mutuality between P and D, and thus considered it quite different from a three-party situation ([1990] 2

AC 287). The point of the analogy is unclear as well: is the 'special relationship' between P and D? Or is the relationship between D and X regarded as 'special' inasmuch as it has the capacity to harm others? The phrase 'special relationship' perhaps trips too easily off the judicial tongue. No doubt every relationship is special in some respect. It is very hard to understand the repeated suggestion that *Junior Books* may really be explained as a 'special relationship' case (eg *Murphy v Brentwood District Council* [1991] I AC at 466, Lord Keith). The relationship there was indeed close and special, but it is quite unclear why that should lead to the imposition of liability.

'Reliance'

5.36 Again, the idea of 'reliance' makes a certain amount of sense in the two-handed *Hedley Byrne* situation: P relies on D's poor advice and thereby suffers harm. It also makes a certain amount of sense in cases where D is doing work which is meant to benefit P, and for which P ultimately pays. Yet on that basis it is unclear why liability is sometimes established (eg *Henderson v Merrett Syndicates*(1995)) yet sometimes refused (eg *Leigh & Sillavan Ltd v Aliakmon Shipping Co Ltd* (1986)). It makes less sense in other cases, including some where liability has been established. For example, in what sense does a would-be legatee 'rely' on the testator's solicitor, given that the legatee has no legal right to check up on how the work has gone, and had no legal rights if the testator has a change of heart (*White v Jones*)? It is true that *after* the decision in *White v Jones* legatees are legally entitled to rely on the testator's solicitor, but to use that argument as a reason for establishing liability in the first place seems to be arguing in a circle.

'Voluntary assumption of responsibility'

5.37 This has proved to be one of the more fertile ideas in this area, but perhaps this is perhaps because of its inherent vagueness. Nearly all tort liability is 'voluntarily assumed', in the sense that D did not *have* to engage in the conduct of which P is now complaining. Nobody *forced* Stevenson to manufacture and market ginger beer (*Donoghue v Stevenson* (1932)). But equally, that observation is not enough in itself to justify a finding of liability, and presumably something more is meant by the phrase, though it is not always clear what. This explanation is at its strongest where D undertakes some professional task, in the knowledge that it is

P who is really paying for it (albeit indirectly), and P who will suffer if it is done poorly.

> *Henderson v Merrett Syndicates* (1995)   Henderson, as a 'name' at Lloyd's, entrusted considerable assets to his underwriting agent, who in turn entrusted them to Merrett for investment. Held: Merrett had undertaken responsibility to Henderson and the absence of a contract between Henderson and Merrett was no bar to action in negligence for mismanaging Henderson's assets.

It has also been suggested that this is the true explanation of the *Junior Books* case: D's communications with P arguably added up to an undertaking that the work would be done with reasonable care. Nonetheless, the notion plainly cannot explain all cases – where, for example, was the 'assumption of responsibility' in cases like *Smith v Eric S Bush* (**5.16**)? – and there are also recurrent problems with this notion.

- *Precisely what responsibility is assumed?*   The test of 'assumption of responsibility' is vague in its details. For example, are employers under a duty to their employees if they send them on foreign assignments, yet neither insure them against personal injury nor advise their employees to insure themselves? There might be arguments both ways, but it seems inadequate simply to say that this duty was not within the scope of the duty assumed by the employer (*Reid v Rush & Tompkins Group plc* [1989] 3 All ER 228, 239, Ralph Gibson LJ). (Similarly *Van Oppen v Clerk to the Bedford Charity Trustees* (1989), where the court denied that schools must insure their students against injuries in games. In both cases the court gave other reasons as well.)

- *To whom is responsibility assumed?*   D might admit that responsibility for a particular task was assumed, but deny that it was assumed *to P*. Sometimes this argument has been accepted, as where P asks X to sell his car and X delegates the task to D; if D loses the money, P cannot sue D, because D owed a duty to X only (*Balsamo v Medici* (1984)). Yet why, precisely, was this argument rejected in *White v Jones*, where equally the defendant solicitor could say that the duty he assumed was not a duty to the testator's daughters, but to the testator himself? Lord Mustill, dissenting, took precisely this point: the duty 'is between himself and his client' ([1995] 2 AC 281). Lord Nolan observed the solicitor had talked to the daughters and said that it would be 'astonishing' if the family solicitor owed a duty only to the head of the family and not to all members of it ([1995] 2 AC 295). Lord Goff side-stepped the issue, admitting that it was hard to see how there could be any assumption of responsibility here; but '[e]ven so it seems to me that it is open to your Lordships' House .. to fashion a remedy to fill a lacuna in the law and so prevent the injustice which would otherwise occur on the facts of cases such as the present' ([1995] 2 AC 268).

> To explain why none of these notions can be the complete explanation of the law of pure economic loss is rather easy. What is less easy to get over is how these concepts are actually used in judicial reasoning and how they are combined with one another to justify concrete results. There is no substitute for a close reading of the leading cases.

The influence of surrounding areas of law

The expanding tort of negligence

5.38   The tort of negligence has expanded. Aa a result it has repeatedly encountered questions of liability which are dealt with by other torts or other heads of the law. Negligence has raced ahead while other areas have stayed still. Whether negligence should be allowed into these other areas is not an easy question. Opposition is not necessarily based on blind conservatism. The intrusion of negligence law should be seen not necessarily as an opportunity for conflict, but rather an opportunity for reflecting what negligence law is for and what it can add. It is of course equally true that a willingness to let in negligence principles may well be a covert admission that the existing rules in an area are inadequate, or at least would benefit from being supplemented through negligence.

A thorough survey of all the areas on which negligence might have some influence would be beyond the scope of this book. I will review those areas where the possibility for conflict with other areas has been most obvious. I have dealt above with the general question of tort and the liability of statutory authorities (**1.49**).

The Defective Premises Act 1972

5.39 This Act gives a remedy to any person acquiring an interest in a 'dwelling' who then finds that D undertook building work on it but did not do it 'in a workmanlike or, as the case may be, professional manner, with proper materials and so that as regards that work the dwelling will be fit for habitation when completed' (s 1(1)). The duty is similar to a duty in negligence, but there are various limits on liability. It only applies to 'dwellings', not premises generally. The limitation period runs from the date of the defective work, not its discovery, and accordingly will often be unrealistically short.

The operation of the Act is wholly excluded if the house is subject to an approved National House Building Council scheme (s 2); compensation is then under the scheme, rather than under the Act. In the early years of the Act, most houses were so covered, making the remedy virtually useless. However, while a revised NHBC scheme remains on the books (approved by SI 1979/381), it appears that in the late 1980s the builders privately decided that they would no longer follow the terms of the scheme. So the official approval effectively became a dead letter (see Duncan Wallace (1991) 107 LQR 228, 243). It appears that the builders do not intend to seek official approval of their current scheme or subsequent modifications to it, and accordingly the Act applies in full force. It makes an occasional appearance in the law reports (eg *Andrews v Schooling* (1991)).

Was the 1972 Act a factor in the development of the case law? In *Anns*, neither counsel nor judges referred to the Act at all. In *Murphy, Anns* was criticised on that ground, the Lords arguing that it was not for the courts to rush in where Parliament had feared to tread. There was, however, no very full discussion of whether Parliament had intended to exclude a common law remedy, or whether Parliament's intervention in relation to domestic housing should be thought to exclude a remedy in relation to all building work. The Lords also seemed unaware of the builders' decision to dispense with official approval for their schemes.

The Hague Rules 1924

5.40 The terms of certain international trade transactions are standardised by treaty. One such treaty embodies the Hague Rules, regulating liability between ship-owners and cargo-owners. A broad view has been taken of the policy of this treaty.

Marc Rich & Co AG v Bishop Rock Marine Co Ltd (1995)   Cargo was lost on the sinking of the bulk carrier *The Nicholas H*, when its hull cracked. Possible cracking had been suspected, but the ship-owner's classification society had surveyed the vessel and agreed it could sail. The cargo-owners claimed from the ship-owners the maximum damages permitted under the Hague Rules and sued the classification society for the balance. Held: to allow such a claim would subvert the Hague Rules.

The law of negligence is accordingly excluded from the area, because the principles of liability are already settled and it would be undesirable for negligence law to unsettle them again.

The administration of justice

5.41   It would have startling consequences if individuals engaged in the justice system could sue one another for paying insufficient attention to one another's interests. The courts have usually refused to find any such liability. So the Crown Prosecution Service does not owe a duty to those it prosecutes (*Elguzouli-Daf v Metropolitan Police Comr* (1995)); nor does a police authority owe a duty to officers it investigates for alleged misconduct (*Calveley v Chief Constable of the Merseyside Police* (1989)).

Lawyers are certainly liable in general for bad advice to their clients, but whether they are entitled to any immunity on this public policy ground is a much-disputed question. Before the *Hedley Byrne* decision, it was assumed that the absence of a contract between barristers and their clients prevented action for shoddy work. Plainly that explanation would not do after *Hedley Byrne*, but the House of Lords accepted in *Rondel v Worsley* (1969) that most such actions would simply be attempts to re-litigate issues which should be regarded as settled, and accordingly denied liability. However, it followed that the true distinction was not between work done by barristers and work done by solicitors, but between court work and other work. It is not a barristers' immunity but an advocates' immunity.

Saif Ali v Sydney Mitchell & Co (1980)   On being asked to advise on the legal consequences of a road accident, a barrister advised suing the husband of one of the drivers, but no-one else. It was subsequently alleged that this advice was bad, though this was not discovered until it was too late to add either of the two drivers as defendants to the

147

action. Held: the advocates' immunity covered arguments in court and preliminary work which amounts to decisions on how to proceed in court, but did not cover other legal advice such as that given in the present action.

The climate of liability has changed a good deal since that time. It is now possible for judges to make *wasted costs orders*, under which costs attributable to the incompetence of a particular advocate must be paid by that advocate personally. It is an open question whether the advocates' immunity would withstand a modern challenge in the House of Lords, or in Parliament. Nonetheless, there are obvious difficulties involved in any claim which can only succeed if it is shown that *another* court reached a wrong decision. The Court of Appeal has recently re-affirmed that the advocates' immunity prevents action in negligence, where P's case depends on showing that his earlier conviction was wrong (*Smith v Linskills* (1996)) or that a settlement approved by a civil court was wrongly assented to (*Kelley v Corston* (1997)). However, Chadwick J has allowed a claim where P has already succeeded in having his conviction set aside by the Criminal Division of the Court of Appeal (*Acton v Graham Pearce & Co* (1997)).

Defamation

5.42 The harm that D might do to P by sending out an inaccurate job reference is obvious enough. Nonetheless, it is not an obvious subject for a remedy in negligence, as it seems classic defamation territory. Nonetheless, the House of Lords has been prepared to hold that action lies in negligence (*Spring v Guardian Assurance plc* (1994)). The decision would be very hard to understand if defamation were an area of law held in high regard by lawyers generally. But in fact the law of defamation is notoriously unsatisfactory (**8.43**), and this may well have been a factor in the Lords' decision. Nonetheless, the decision is a little startling. If P had sued in defamation, he would almost certainly have been met by a defence of qualified privilege, which would have defeated the action (**8.35**). An action for negligence is very different from an action in defamation, in many respects. It is much cheaper to mount; damages will only be for proved financial loss, with no sum for injury to feelings; and the main issue is likely to be whether D was careless, which in an action for defamation is not usually relevant.

Equity and property law

5.43   The divisions between legal subjects are often hard to justify except as the product of a long and complicated history. The notion that there is a very close relationship between D and P, and that it is accordingly reasonable to hold D to be under a duty to look to P's interests, appears under various guises. It appears in tort as the '*special relationship*'; it also appears as the idea of a *fiduciary relationship* between them, entailing a *fiduciary duty* to take due care. Indeed, it seems unlikely that the common law would have waited for so long to recognise a tort of negligent misstatement, had not this gap in the law been partly filled by the fiduciary duty (as recognised in cases such as *Nocton v Lord Ashburton* (1914)). The tort of negligence has been expanding at the same time as the fiduciary duty has been going through a (noticeable but more modest) period of expansion. In both *White v Jones* and *Henderson v Merrett Syndicates* either development could be used to justify liability. Which the individual Law Lords chose reflected their different legal specialisms (compare, in both cases, the opinions of the common lawyer Lord Goff with the equity specialist Lord Browne-Wilkinson). There seems in general to be little scope for conflict between the two different areas of the law, and they can exist side by side, or indeed overlap, with no problems.

One interesting puzzle is why no conflict between different areas of law was perceived in *White v Jones*, where P's complaint was that her father's legacy would not reach her as he intended. Yet *why* was the legacy not payable? It is because the doctrines of property law stopped it. The law of tort and the law of property approach the case with quite different presuppositions: the tort lawyers were happy to rely on whatever the evidence discloses, whereas the property lawyers will only act on a testator's supposed intention if it is embodied in a will. In other words, the court deciding the tort claim was assuming that the property lawyers would get the testator's intention wrong! This is a curious state of affairs indeed, and some have suggested that the defendant solicitors should have remedy against those who actually received the settlor's money, on the ground that they were unjustly enriched. It is, however, hard to see how this claim can lie under the law as it now stands. Moreover, while the result is strange, it is by no means indefensible.

Contract

5.44 *Introduction* Whether tort and contract are distinct subjects, and if so, how important the distinction is, are questions which different generations of lawyers have answered in very different ways. At the present day, there would be few who would deny that tort and contract are distinct, but the distinction is accorded less weight than it has been at any point in the last two centuries. Traditionally, it has been thought that unrestricted extension of tort liability undermines fundamental doctrines such as consideration and privity. But most lawyers today would answer that those doctrines are themselves distinctly unsatisfactory and that the tort of negligence very often is the simplest vehicle for avoiding their least satisfactory aspects. Accordingly, the old objections to 'concurrent liability' – that is, liability in contract and tort at the same time – have largely fallen away, as has the idea that there might be an 'exclusive contractual zone' where liability must be based on contract if there is to be liability at all.

5.45 *How might negligence interfere with contract?* The existence of a possible remedy in contract is still relevant in determining liability in negligence. There seem to be four ways in which the law of contract can still restrict the availability of a remedy in negligence and the following paragraphs set them out in more detail. First, if there is reason to suppose that any contract between P and D was meant to be a definitive statement of their entitlements as against each other, then the courts will not undermine this by granting additional rights under the tort of negligence. Second, and analogously, if there is no contract between P and D, and there is reason to believe that this is because they did not mean to have mutual rights, then again the courts will not impose them despite this. Third, where the task which D is expected to perform is one D contracted to do, then the courts will look to the contract to define the nature and detail of the task. Fourth, where D only agreed to do the task subject to conditions limiting D's liability, those limitations will probably apply to restrict any tort liability as well.

There are common themes running through all of these cases. The most obvious is that P will not be allowed to go against rules which are agreed, or at least generally accepted, in that particular area of work. Another theme, rather more muted but nonetheless an influence, is that negligence is a relative newcomer to many areas of law and should only be allowed in where this would improve the law's panoply of remedies.

5.46   *Contract intended to be definitive*   Where there is a contract between P and D, which was meant to be a complete statement of the parties' entitlements against each other, then the courts will respect that bargain. The courts will assume that no rights were meant to be available beyond those in contract, and accordingly they will not impose additional rights and obligations through the tort of negligence. Contract lawyers have in the past been too ready to assume that the contract was meant to be definitive. This approach seems most likely to succeed today in areas where the case law is of long standing and already denies tortious liability.

> *Tai Hing Cotton Mill Ltd v Liu Chong Hing Bank Ltd* (1986)   An employee of Tai Hing forged cheques on the company's accounts with its bank. The bank paid on the cheques, and on discovering the truth sued Tai Hing to recover the money. Held: it was settled law that in general banks were responsible for paying out on forged cheques (subject to exceptions irrelevant here) and there was no general duty of care on its clients to prevent this.

The result may be right, though some of the reasoning of the Privy Council in that case is unacceptably broad. If, for example, it is true that '[t]heir Lordships do not think that there is anything to the advantage of the law's development in searching for a liability in tort where the parties are in a contractual relationship' ([1986] AC 107, Lord Scarman), then they are at odds with a very large number of their colleagues (see for example **5.5**, **5.21**). The truth is that it is often very difficult indeed to determine whether or not the parties meant their contract to be the definitive statement of their rights.

5.47   *Absence of contract as definitive*   It may be that the *absence* of a contract between P and D was also meant to be definitive: in other words, they entered into no contract because they did not wish to have any mutual rights and obligations, and it would therefore be wrong for the courts to imply any. Again, the argument is sometimes plausible, but has been overused. If it deserves to be taken seriously, this will presumably be in a case where it would have been relatively easy for P and D to contact one another and negotiate terms (the case involving low transaction costs).

The argument has been used the most in cases concerning the construction industry, where there is typically a strong chain of command

– each contracting party knows to whom they are responsible – and so the absence of a contract between any two parties is probably not an accident. This argument was deployed again and again in the cases which came after *Anns* and eventually led to its overthrow: notably *Simaan General Contracting Co v Pilkington Glass (No 2)* (1988) (main contractor vs. supplier of glass to a sub-contractor). The logic of such cases is not compelling. It is one thing to point out that there is a precise chain of command, quite another to deny liability to someone who cannot give orders to D, no matter how obvious it was that they will suffer from D's carelessness. The absence of a contract between D and P *may* be because they intended no mutual obligations, but that should not be an obvious inference without more to support it.

5.48 *Contract defining D's task*   Where the principal reason for supposing that D has undertaken a particular task is that D has entered into a contract to do it, then it will be important to see precisely what that task is. D cannot fairly be blamed for failing to perform a different task from the one D was actually engaged on. Thus in *White v Jones*, it was emphasised that all P was demanding was that D do the job for which he had been paid. It would have been quite different if the argument had been that D should respect P's interests where they diverged from his client's.

> *Clarke v Bruce Lance & Co* (1988)   Clarke was the beneficiary under a will, under which he was to receive an interest in a petrol service station. The testator later instructed his solicitors to alter his will, to give a third party an option to purchase the service station. After the testator's death, Clarke argued that the solicitors had advised the testator poorly over the change to the will. Held: the solicitors owed Clarke no duty in the matter.

5.49 *Contract limiting D's liability*   Finally, where D undertook a duty by contracting to do it, then any limitation on liability in the contract will probably be held to limit the duty in tort as well. The argument was accepted by the House of Lords in *Junior Books Ltd v Veitchi Co* (1983), and even (controversially) in *Norwich City Council v Harvey* (1989), a case of property damage. It is not entirely clear how this doctrine is affected by modern legislation limiting the effect of exemption clauses (eg Unfair Contract Terms Act 1977, **11.4**). However, *Smith v Eric S Bush* suggests that exempting conditions which would be struck down in a contract action will also be ignored in tort (**5.24**).

Further Reading

Relevant sections of tort reference books may be supplemented with:

Steele, 'Scepticism and the Law of Negligence' [1993] CLJ 437.

Markesinis and Deakin, 'The random element of their Lordships' infallible judgment: An economic and comparative analysis of the tort of negligence from *Anns* to *Murphy*' (1992) 55 MLR 619.

Stapleton, 'Duty of care: peripheral parties and alternative opportunities for deterrence' (1995) 111 LQR 301.

Self-test questions

1. It seems strange that a house-owner with cracked foundations is not thought of as someone who has suffered property damage, but rather as someone who has suffered a purely economic loss. Why is this (**5.10**)?

2. The 'floodgates argument' is really several different arguments run together. Summarise the main strands of these arguments (**5.31–5.32**).

3. How satisfactory is 'voluntary assumption of liability' as a touchstone for liability in negligence (**5.37**)?

4. How was the result in the *Hedley Byrne* case justified by the judges who decided it (**5.15**)?

5. Is it true that liability for negligent misstatement cannot occur in the context of a purely social relationship between P and D (**5.20**)?

CHAPTER SIX

Deliberate infliction of economic loss

SUMMARY
Various torts protect P's economic interests against deliberate harm. Some are best defined as particular types of forbidden conduct: such as deceit, intimidation and conspiracy. Others are best defined as protecting particular economic interests, particularly P's interest in the performance of contracts to which P is party. It is an open question whether all these various instances of liability could or should be fused into a single 'genus' tort of unlawful interference with P's legitimate interests.

Introduction

6.1 Tort can be looked at from two quite different points of view. From D's point of view, it can be seen as marking out certain types of *conduct*, forbidden on pain of being held liable to P for the consequences (1.3). From P's point of view, tort can be seen as protecting certain *interests* from infringement (1.4). The choice between the two perspectives is often arbitrary and more a matter of educational technique than legal principle. For the torts in this chapter, I have chosen a mixture of techniques. First, some of them are best summarised as defining particular prohibited practices: notably the telling of lies, though also the formation of conspiracies and the practice of intimidation. (Very often these practices constitute crimes as well, though that is not particularly relevant here.) Second, some are best seen as defining particular interests: principally in the due performance of P's contracts. Finally, I consider the 'genus' tort of unlawfully inflicting harm to P's legitimate interest: an attempt to fuse the two perspectives.

155

Deceit

Basic definition and terminology

6.2 Where D dishonestly misinforms P and P suffers loss through relying on this misinformation, then P may sue D for the loss suffered. D is said to have committed the tort of 'deceit'. D's conduct is also sometimes labelled 'fraud', but 'fraud' has several possible meanings in legal contexts, of which this is only one. ('Fraud' may also refer to crimes, such as the offence of obtaining property by deception contrary to Theft Act 1968, s 15; further, it may refer to equitable wrongs such as undue influence or breach of fiduciary duty. The treatment here is limited to civil law, not criminal law; and to 'common law fraud', not 'equitable fraud'.) Deceit is a serious matter, requiring clear proof: indeed, arguably the law is too strict, as proof is required from P at every turn, even where it is already clear that D is an out-and-out fraudster. Jury trial is still sometimes available for this tort.

Fraud and other torts involving misrepresentation

6.3 The distinguishing features of the tort of deceit are that *(i)* D has misled P and *(ii)* D's behaviour is dishonest. Where P suffers loss because D has misled others, P may have a remedy in defamation (**8.1**) or malicious falsehood (**8.42**), but not in deceit. Where D's conduct was not dishonest, P's remedy, if any, will be in negligence. (In relation to contracts, there is an exception: careless statements which result in a contract may sometimes be treated *as if* fraudulent, by virtue of Misrepresentation Act 1967, s 2(1). For a full treatment, see your contract text.)

A misrepresentation of fact or law

6.4 *The basic requirement* This basic requirement is easy to state, and in many cases easy to apply as well. D is liable for misleading P, but *not* for failing to correct P's misconceptions – even if D knows of them and could easily have set P straight. It seems to make no difference whether D misinforms P as to facts or as to law (*De Tchihatchef v Salerni Coupling* (1932)). A misrepresentation can be made implicitly, or even by conduct. In one famous old (criminal) case, D orders goods at P's shop dressed in a student cap and gown; as he knows, P is prepared to give credit to students, but not to others. This was a fraud whether or not D *said* he was a student (*R v Barnard* (1837)). In general, it makes no difference what form the misrepresentation takes. However, by statute a misrepresentation as to the financial standing of a third party is actionable only if in writing and signed (Statute of Frauds Amendment Act 1828, s 6; oddly, this provision does not bar action in negligence: *WB Anderson and Sons v Rhodes (Liverpool)* (1967)).

6.5 *Problem cases* The basic rule is that misrepresentation is actionable, but silence is not. The borderline between the two is vague, however, and many issues are matters of degree. A good rule of thumb is that D is likely to be held liable if D has exploited P's ignorance – but not if D knows no more than P about the matter in question. Certainly if D set out to mislead P and was successful, it will rarely be a defence that what D said was *literally* true.

- *Where D takes active steps to mislead P*, a court is likely to find a misrepresentation. This is so whether D does so by making true but misleading statements, or by actively concealing inconvenient facts (as in *Gordon v Selico Co* (1984), where Selico deliberately hid patches of dry rot in a house to induce Gordon to take a tenancy there).

- *Where D makes ambiguous statements*, then D is liable only if D *meant* to mislead P and P was *in fact* misled (*Smith v Chadwick* (1884)).

- *Where D makes a statement to P and only later discovers that it is false*, D is treated as having made a false representation to P *at the time when D could have corrected P's mistake* (*Briess v Woolley* (1954)). Conversely, if D makes a statement fraudulently, but by the time P acts on it circumstances have changed and it is the truth, no fraud is committed (*Ship v Crosskill* (1870)).

- *Where D makes a false statement of intention*, this is deceit: 'the state of a man's mind is as much a fact as the state of his digestion' (*Edgington v Fitzmaurice* (1885) 29 ChD 459, 483, Bowen LJ). But if D has merely changed his mind at a later point, this is not deceit, however awkward it is for P, or however weak D's excuse for failing to mention it.

- *Where D makes a promise to P and then breaks it*, generally speaking this is not deceit (though it may be breach of contract). Deceit will only be established where D can be shown to have misrepresented some fact. This would occur if, for example, P could show that D never intended to keep the promise (eg *Re Eastgate* (1905)).

- *Where D expresses an opinion*, this will not be deceit merely because the opinion is wrong. It will be deceit if D did not in fact hold the opinion expressed. It will also be deceit if D deliberately implies something D knows to be untrue, such as that he has solid grounds for what he says (*Brown v Raphael* (1958)).

'Dishonesty'

6.6 *Knowledge of falsity* The requirement that D make the misrepresentation 'dishonestly' involves proof either *(i)* that D knew the representation was false or *(ii)* that D made the statement without belief in its truth. This last case includes the case where D doesn't know, and doesn't care, whether it was true or not. (This is often styled 'recklessness', but that word has too many meanings in law to promote clarity here.) Negligence, even gross negligence, is not enough for liability (*Derry v Peek* (1889)), except where statute makes it so (Misrepresentation Act 1967, s 2(1)).

6.7 *Inducing reliance* The requirement that D make the misrepresentation 'dishonestly' also involves proof that D meant P to act on the statement. This is usually clear, though it is less so where the statement is communicated to P indirectly.

> *Peek v Gurney* (1873) Gurney and others issued a company prospectus containing false statements. Held: those who subscribed to shares on the strength of the prospectus could sue for loss suffered, but Peek and others who had bought shares later had no claim, as the prospectus was not intended to affect market dealings.

Plainly, this rule can involve wafer-fine distinctions over what D intends. While the rule in *Peek v Gurney* is undoubtedly still law, it seems open to argument on its facts. There is no additional requirement of intent to *harm* P, or of 'malice', however defined (*Brown Jenkinson & Co v Percy Dalton (London)* (1957)).

Assessment of P's loss

6.8 P is entitled to recover the amount by which P would have been better off had D not engaged in fraud. P may recover for any form of quantifiable loss caused by fraud, including personal injury, but in practice the loss is almost invariably purely economic. In principle, calculation is straightforward. Difficulties arise in cases where D has fraudulently induced P to invest in a particular business, at least if it is not clear what P would have done with his or her money but for D's inducement.

East v Maurer (1991) Maurer induced East to buy one of his hair styling salons, falsely representing that he meant soon to discontinue working at the other. He did not, and East's business suffered as a result. Held: but for the misrepresentation East would probably have bought another salon elsewhere. The appropriate figure for damages was the amount the transaction had cost East *plus* the estimated profit she would have made had she bought another, similar salon elsewhere.

Smith New Court Securities v Scrimgeour Vickers (Asset Management) (1996) Scrimgeour fraudulently induced Smith to buy a large block of shares at 82p per share. The shares were then trading at 78p on the stock market. Soon afterwards, another fraud (not related to Scrimgeour's) was revealed, which took the trading price of the shares down to 44p. Held: Smith could recover for the entire drop in value from 82p to 44p, even though as a general rule it would fall on Smith as owners of the shares.

Downs v Chappell (1996) Downs bought a bookshop from Chappell for £120,000, after fraudulent representations as to its turnover. On discovering the truth, Downs tried to sell the business, but refused two offers of £76,000, eventually being forced to accept an offer of £60,000. Robert Owen QC found that Downs would probably have bought the business anyway had he known the business's true value, and accordingly gave no damages. Held: on appeal, the truth was that the value was unknown at the time Downs bought, so this was not the right approach. Damages were assessed at £44,000 (ie £120,000 less £76,000).

Other torts of making false statements

6.9 Where P suffers loss because D has made false statements to others, various torts are potentially relevant, none of which will be treated in detail here. Where D does injury to P's reputation, then the torts of *defamation* (**8.1**) and *malicious falsehood* (**8.42**) may be relevant. If D casts aspersions against P's business or against goods P sells, this will not usually be defamation. It may, however, be malicious falsehood; and there is a distinct but related tort of *slander of title*, which consists of creating doubts whether P has the legal right to sell his goods. Another highly specific tort is *passing off*, where D sets out to confuse his or her own products with P's in the eyes of the public. (See for example *Taittinger v Allbev* (1994), where Allbev described its carbonated drink as 'Elderflower Champagne', thus risking confusion with real champagne made by Taittinger and others.)

Intimidation

Definition

6.10 Where D makes an unlawful threat which induces someone else to harm P, D has committed the tort of intimidation. Usually D makes the threat to some third party, who then harms P ('three-party intimidation'); occasionally the threat is addressed to P personally, who feels compelled to act contrary to his or her own interests ('two-party intimidation'). It is sometimes said that the action induced by the threat must itself be lawful; but this simply seems to reflect the obvious point that if it is not, P will have a simple and obvious remedy for it without resorting to this rather arcane tort.

The 'unlawfulness' of the threat

6.11 D's threat is not actionable unless it was to do something contrary to law. However, it need not be something in itself actionable by P (and it will rarely be necessary to invoke this tort if it is). It seems that crimes and torts are for this purpose 'unlawful'. A threat to break a contract made with the party threatened will also be sufficient, even though P would have had no legal ground of complaint if the parties to the contract had voluntarily agreed to terminate it.

> *Rookes v Barnard* (1964) Rookes' employer sacked him, to avert a threat of strike action by Barnard and others, officials of a union seeking to impose a closed shop on the firm. Held: the threat of a strike, being a threat to breach an employment contract, was

sufficiently unlawful to found an action by Rookes, even though the sacking was itself perfectly lawful.

So the definition of 'unlawfulness' is broad, and while the authorities are unclear, there does not seem any reason in principle why it cannot cover breach of any duty under common law, equity or statute. But the matter is not so simple. Often it is legitimate to ask, How does it happen that D's threat is 'unlawful' and yet P has no remedy unless it is for 'intimidation'?

• In the *Rookes v Barnard* type of case, the reason why P has to resort to 'intimidation' is because the doctrine of 'privity of contract' prevents P complaining more directly that D has threatened to break his contract. There is considerable academic debate on the merits of the 'privity' doctrine and whether it should also prevent action in intimidation.

• Where the 'unlawfulness' consists of breach of a duty imposed by statute, the courts often ask whether Parliament also intended to create a private right of action (eg *Lonrho v Shell Petroleum Co (No 2)* (1982)). Simply because Parliament intended a duty, even a duty backed up with criminal sanctions, by no means necessarily implies that a private right to sue was meant as well. But it cannot be pretended that it will always be clear precisely what Parliament intended. This issue has already been discussed above, in connection with the tort of breach of statutory duty (**1.43**).

Intent to injure P

6.12 Action lies only if D intended to injure P. Difficult questions arise where it is clear that D deliberately set out to injure P, but was not motivated by personal spite, but rather by some economic objective. Do we regard the deliberate infliction of *economic* harm as 'intentional injury'? In what little case law there is, it seems to be assumed that pursuit of one's own economic interests is no defence. So in *Rookes v Barnard* (**6.11**) it was assumed that Barnard and his colleagues meant to injure Rookes, even though it appears that their sole motive was to dispose of an individual inconvenient for their scheme for a closed shop. Dicta in *Rookes* and elsewhere suggest that there may sometimes be a defence of justification, excusing quite deliberate harm, perhaps as a response to provocative behaviour by P (compare **6.26**).

The effectiveness of the threat

6.13   It is clear that D's threat must place considerable pressure on the person to whom it is addressed, if it is to be the foundation of an action in intimidation. Mere idle abuse, however humiliating, will not do, unless it is clearly meant to push the victim in the direction of certain conduct. There is no clear test in the authorities, however. Some judges distinguish between a 'threat' and a mere 'warning'. But while the manner in which D expresses himself or herself is a relevant circumstance in assessing D's behaviour, this is hard to apply as a test. A polite threat is still a threat; nor is it any the less so for being accompanied with a statement that D is highly reluctant so to act and would far prefer that the threat were unnecessary. No doubt a genuine willingness to explore alternatives other than submission to the threat or its execution goes a long way towards minimising its coercive character.

Is two-party intimidation different?

6.14   Intimidation is usually a three-party affair: D threatens X, inducing X to harm P. But it is clearly stated in *Rookes v Barnard* and other authorities that an action lies equally in the case where D unlawfully threatens P directly. This is odd, however, because we would naturally expect an unlawful threat against P directly to be actionable in itself, without the need for a distinct tort of 'intimidation'. So if for example D threatens some tort against P, we would expect P to be able to claim a *quia timet* injunction against D to prevent the threat becoming an actuality (**10.3**). And where D threatens P with breach of a contract between them, a remedy for 'intimidation' might be thought undesirable. Any such remedy undermines the more sensitive and complex enquiries usually thought necessary today where one party to a contract demands its renegotiation (for example under the doctrine of 'economic duress', on which see any contract textbook). The 'two-party' version of the tort is hardly ever invoked, and remains highly controversial.

Conspiracy

Introduction

6.15   Where two or more people agree to act in a way which they know will injure P, then in certain circumstances P may sue any or all of them for the loss caused by this 'conspiracy'. It may fairly be asked why conspiracy should be any concern of the law. If the loss would not have been actionable in itself, why should it matter that there was a 'conspiracy' to do it? There is no very obvious answer to this point. It is sometimes said that two or more people may do more harm than one, and so represent a special danger, to which the law must give particular heed. But this is absurd. If two market stall-holders attempt to drive a third out of business, this may be an actionable conspiracy; if a single chain store attempts to do the same, it is not. Yet which situation represents the more serious abuse of economic power?

Agreement

6.16   Whether there was in fact an agreement is usually a purely factual question. It was at one time thought that an agreement between a wife and her husband could not constitute a conspiracy, because of the ancient maxim that husband and wife are one person. But this contention has now been rejected: 'The gravity of the injury sustained does not vary according to whether those who inflict it are casual acquaintances or are indissolubly conjoined in wedded bliss' (*Midland Bank Trust Co v Green (No 3)* [1979] 2 All ER 193, 219, Oliver J).

Can a business be regarded as a conspiracy between the various people who constitute it? Cases on businesses are confused. It is said that the employees of a firm cannot be treated as conspirators in the execution of a business plan (eg *Crofter Hand Woven Harris Tweed Co v Veitch* [1942] AC 435, 468, Lord Wright). However, a plan hatched by the directors may constitute a conspiracy between themselves and the company too (*Belmont Finance Corpn v Williams Furniture (No 2)* (1980)); though it was also said in that case that the company would *not* be regarded as a conspirator if it was *itself* the intended victim of the conspiracy. It has been held (in a criminal case) that a one-person company cannot be treated as conspiring with the person who controls it, on the ground that it has no independent mind (*R v McDonnell* (1966)). But this reasoning is unsatisfactory, as contract lawyers have no difficulty with the idea that a one-person company can contract with the person concerned. Cases of this sort emphasise the oddity of the requirement adopted. Why should liability for particular harm vary depending on whether the person inflicting it acted alone?

Two types of liability for conspiracy

6.17 There is a division in the law, depending on whether the means adopted by the conspirators were in some sense unlawful.

'Conspiracy to injure'

6.18 Where the predominant purpose of the conspiracy was to injure P, then the conspiracy is actionable *whether or not* unlawful means were employed. The difficult question has always been over the necessary intent. A narrow view was taken in a famous case last century.

> *Mogul SS Co v McGregor, Gow & Co* (1892)   One shipping company, Mogul, was driven out of business by the concerted action of others, including McGregor Gow. It used a variety of tactics, including the offering of special rebates to customers not to deal with Mogul, and arranging services and prices in such a way as to deprive Mogul of custom rather than to run at a profit. Held: as no illegal means had been employed, no action lay.

Obviously we cannot explain this result by saying that the conspirators meant their victim no harm (plainly they did) or even that they bore no personal ill-will (they may well have done). Rather, it is a defence that they were motivated by self-interest rather than spite, *even though Mogul's ruin was a necessary part of their self-interested plan*. This has obviously gone beyond a proposition about the meaning of 'intent'. What would we make of an argument that a mugger does not 'intend' to harm his victims if he does not hate them personally, and does not care *how* he obtains their money? His indifference to his victim's fate is precisely what makes him dangerous. Yet in the case of purely economic harm, a different attitude is taken. Public policy towards competition has changed somewhat since 1892, and we would today expect McGregor, Gow and their co-conspirators to receive some attention from the Monopolies and Mergers Commission. But *Mogul* still represents the common law.

'Intent to injure'

6.19 The narrow rule on 'intent' stated in the previous paragraph has had its ups and downs in this century, but represents the current law. *Allen v Flood* (1898) was taken to establish that conduct by trade unions that stayed within the law would not be tortious merely on the ground that it was clearly meant to harm P. However, some outrageous bench-packing by the Conservative Lord Chancellor Lord Halsbury secured a contrary result in *Quinn v Leathem* (1901), where conduct designed to coerce P into accepting a closed shop was held to be an actionable conspiracy. (See Stevens, *Law and Politics* (1979) pp 93-94.) Only by slow stages (culminating in *Crofter Hand Woven Harris Tweed Co v Veitch* (1942)) were the courts prepared to apply the same rule to trade unions as to others, namely that pursuit of their own economic interests protected them from a charge of 'intent to injure'. But the 'pursuit of economic self-interest' defence does not protect those whose behaviour has no rational economic basis.

> *Gulf Oil (GB) Ltd v Page* (1987)   Page was involved in a commercial dispute with Gulf, in a case where Gulf was found by a court to be in breach of contract. Page and others hired a light aircraft to tow a banner saying 'GULF EXPOSED IN FUNDAMENTAL BREACH' over a race meeting where Gulf was entertaining clients. Held: even though the banner told the truth, nonetheless there was an actionable conspiracy to injure.

However, since that case it has been stressed that action lies only where loss is proved, and so a mere general allegation of 'injury to reputation' will not do (*Lonrho v Fayed (No 5)* (1993)). This is one more *ad hoc* limit on the tort, which is now in practice very hard to establish. Views differ considerably on whether this tort is a useful legal institution unreasonably hedged about with technicalities, or whether it is fundamentally anomalous and is rightly kept within narrow bounds.

'Unlawful means'

6.20   Liability is easier to establish where the means employed by the conspirators are themselves unlawful. However, the leading case puts strict limits on liability under this variety of the tort.

> *Lonrho v Shell Petroleum (No 2)* (1982)   Lonrho constructed an oil pipeline running from Rhodesia to Mozambique. However, this pipeline stood idle for many years, as a consequence of international sanctions applied to Rhodesia after its declaration of independence (UDI). Lonrho alleged that Shell had illegally supplied oil to Rhodesia, thus prolonging the life of the regime and incidentally lengthening the

time for which Lonrho's pipeline lay idle. Held: no action lay, first, because Shell had no intention to harm Lonrho, and second, because breach of the sanctions legislation did not count as 'unlawful means' for this purpose.

On the 'intent' point, this comes close to smuggling the defence of economic self-interest into this variety of the tort too. It is not clear that the Lords were applying the full rigours of the *Mogul* test, but the fact of the matter is that Shell were not treated as intending the harm to Lonrho, even though they appreciated very well the harmful effect of their actions. The Lords have since that time slightly backed away from that conclusion. They have now said that 'when conspirators intentionally injure the plaintiff and use unlawful means to do so, it is no defence for them to show that their primary purpose was to further or protect their own interests' (*Lonrho v Fayed* [1992] I AC 448, 465-466, Lord Bridge). But the Lords did not criticise *Lonrho v Shell*, and plainly a strict line is still being taken.

As to 'unlawful means', it seems that not only should D's conduct be in some sense illegal, but also it should be actionable in a civil court. So conspiracy to commit torts will usually be actionable, but conspiracy to commit crimes will not be, unless they are torts as well. In *Lonrho v Shell* it was said that statutory crimes only constitute 'unlawful means' for this purpose if, on its true construction, the statutory provision affords an action for its breach. (On the action for breach of statutory duty see above, **1.42**.) Certainly the current position is confused, and confusing.

Interference with contractual rights

Introduction

6.21   This tort is defined as protecting a specific interest – namely, P's interest in the performance of any contract to which P is a party. Where D intentionally interferes with performance, P may have an action for the loss which results. This tort has its origins in the mediaeval law of enticing away P's servant or a member of P's family. In principle, today it applies to any type of contract, though the cases are still heavily concentrated in the employment field.

Need D induce a breach of contract?

6.22 This tort is sometimes called 'inducing breach of contract', but this suggests too narrow an ambit for the tort, which today may also protect P against interferences falling short of breach.

> *Torquay Hotel Co v Cousins* (1969)   Cousins and other members of the same union disrupted oil supplies to the Torquay Hotel, by persuading lorry drivers not to carry it. There was a *force majeure* clause in the oil supply contract, so the supplier was not in breach for failing to deliver. Held: the hotel could nonetheless recover damages for the interference with the performance of the contract.

So it appears that interference with one party's performance of a contract is actionable, even if that party would themselves have a defence. But some care is needed. For example, it has been said that persuading a contractor to use an option as to performance of the contract might give rise to an action by the other party (*Torquay Hotel* case [1969] 2 Ch 147, Winn LJ). But this surely cannot be right. If D tempts away P's employee by the offer of higher wages, and the employee was entitled to terminate the employment with P, surely it cannot be the law that P may sue D for the loss of the employee. There is no action merely because D has made P's contractual right less valuable (*Rickless v United Artists Corpn* (1988)), or has helped to evade the consequences of a breach which took place some time ago (*Law Debenture Trust Corpn v Ural Caspian Oil Corpn* (1995)).

The mental element

6.23 It is sometimes said that the interference must be intentional, though if so 'intent' is being used in a very broad sense. If D knows of the contract, and that his or her conduct is certain to interfere with it, that is quite enough. There is no additional requirement that D's conduct be 'aimed at' P. It does not matter whether D knows the precise details of the contract concerned (*JT Stratford & Son v Lindley* (1965)). Where D must have known that there was a strong possibility of interference, intent may be inferred merely from indifference to this possibility, or from a deliberate failure to enquire further (*Emerald Construction Co v Lothian* (1966)).

Direct persuasion inducing breach

6.24 One variety of the tort is where D convinces a contracting party to breach it, or at least not to go through with it. It is then irrelevant whether D used unlawful means or not, or whether D's behaviour would more accurately be styled as 'coercion' or 'persuasion'. It is sometimes said that mere advice will not do: 'To induce a breach of contract means to create a reason for breaking it; to advise a breach of contract is to point out the reasons which already exist' (Heuston and Buckley, *Salmond and Heuston on the Law of Tort* (20th edn, 1992) p 363). This appears to be the law, though it is a difficult distinction to apply.

Inducement by unlawful act

6.25 If there is no persuasion, P may sue D only if the means D employed were 'unlawful'. It was at one time common to distinguish between 'direct inducement', where D gets at the other party to the contract, and 'indirect procurement', where D induces others to thwart the contractual performance. It is sometimes said that the courts will require a higher degree of knowledge in the second class of the case than in the first. There seems little point in such a distinction today, except by way of emphasising the range of different situations to which the tort is relevant. In any event, it is most unclear what is meant by 'unlawful' here, though it appears that most torts will do (eg trespass to goods, *GWK v Dunlop Rubber Co* (1926)). It would be surprising if breach of a penal statute which did not itself give rise to civil liability would be sufficient; but in the current state of the authorities it is hard to be very definite on the matter.

A defence of justification

6.26 In certain circumstances, D may be able to argue that the interference was justified. The defence relies on a thorough examination of the precise facts of each case. Numerous attempts by trade unions to argue that individual actions are justified have failed. The one exception was a case where counsel scared the court with the suggestion that the union's members would be forced into prostitution if they could not induce their employers to raise their wages (*Brimelow v Casson* (1924)). More successful are defendants who have argued that they were merely seeking to vindicate a legal entitlement of their own.

Edwin Hill and Partners v First National Finance Corpn (1989)   First National lent money to Leakcliff, a developer, secured by a charge on the land Leakcliff intended to develop. Later, under a debt re-structuring plan, it was agreed that First National would themselves develop the land. One condition of the plan was that the architect, Edwin Hill, would be replaced. This constituted a breach of the contract between Leakcliff and Edwin Hill. Held: Edwin Hill's action against First National for inducing breach of their contract with Leakcliff could be met by a plea of justification.

This variety of the defence is said to lie where D's right is an 'equal or superior' entitlement to that of P. The range of different circumstances in which the defence might be invoked means that this is a rather opaque phrase. It seems doubtful whether even a *very* superior entitlement could justify the use of unlawful means.

The 'genus' tort

Introduction

6.27   We have now looked at a number of torts which start from particular types of misconduct by D ('intimidation', 'conspiracy', etc), and at one which starts from the infringement of P's legitimate interests ('interference with contractual performance'). There is potential for considerable overlap between these torts. It has been suggested that each of these individual torts is merely a 'species of [a] wider genus of tort', that wider genus being interference with P's trade interest by unlawful means (*Merkur Island Shipping Corpn v Laughton* [1983] 2 AC 570, 609-610, Lord Diplock). In time, the 'genus' may come to be stated in sufficiently precise terms for it to swallow up the individual species. For the present, however, it has to be treated as a distinct category.

Definition

6.28   D commits this 'genus' tort by deliberate interference with P's trade or business interests by unlawful means. D's conduct must actually be unlawful, not merely antisocial: 'There is no tort of unfair trading' (*Associated Newspapers v Insert Media* [1990] 1 WLR 900, 909, Mummery

J). Despite its uncertainty, the 'genus' tort plainly has the ability to reach facts that other torts cannot reach.

> *Lonrho v Fayed* (1992)   Lonrho was in competition with the Fayed brothers to take over House of Fraser. Lonrho's bid was delayed by being referred to the Monopolies and Mergers Commission; the Fayeds avoided this, allegedly as the result of fraudulent misrepresentations, and were therefore able to make a successful bid. On these assumed facts, the Fayeds were liable for unlawful interference with Lonrho's business.

It appears that most torts (such as fraud in *Lonrho v Fayed*) and (probably) breach of contract, will constitute 'unlawful means'. There is little to suggest that breach of a statutory duty will do, unless actionable as such. The required degree of intent to harm P is unclear, though manifestly there is no *Mogul*-type defence of pursuit of economic self-interest.

The interest protected

6.29   In many cases, there is no doubt that D's conduct was 'unlawful' under some specific head of the law (such as a definite statutory provision), or that the harm it caused P was deliberate. There are, however, two obstacles to P's case, one being that it is unclear whether there is the right sort of 'unlawfulness', the other being lack of clarity whether P's legitimate interests have been infringed. In that situation, P must make the specific legal duty do double duty: not only as showing that D has acted unlawfully, but also that P's right has been infringed. This is difficult to do, unless there is something in the way the provision is formulated to suggest that it was meant to confer a right on P. Cases of equitable wrongs such as breach of confidence and breach of fiduciary duty fit neatly into this approach. In cases of that sort, it is easy to see both that the breach is a wrong and that it can be said to damage the rights of specific people (*Boulting v Association of Cinematograph, Television and Allied Technicians* [1963] 2 QB 606, 636, Upjohn LJ). But misbehaviour in the course of a court case, while obviously wrong, might be seen as harming the public interest rather than the rights of any one individual. So it has been held that there is no liability where D punishes P for giving evidence in a legal action, even though this is a contempt of court (*Chapman v Honig* (1963)). But exceptionally, misconduct in litigation may be held to infringe individual rights.

Acrow (Automation) v Rex Chainbelt (1971)   Acrow obtained an injunction against SI Handling Systems, to force it to honour a licence agreement it had entered into with Acrow. Rex, a company associated with SI, attempted to subvert the injunction by refusing to supply Acrow with essential equipment. Held: Acrow could sue Rex for deliberate interference with its business.

Statutory interests

6.30   Difficult problems arise where P relies on the same statutory provision both to establish the 'unlawfulness' *and* the legitimacy of the interest interfered with. The cases where this is easiest to do is where the statute was meant to grant P an interest in property, or something analogous. So in *Ex p Island Records* (1978) it was held that breach of the Dramatic and Musical Performers' Protection Act 1958 gave an action to the performers and record companies affected. But Shaw LJ dissented in that case, arguing that the statute could not be read as conferring a right to sue for breach of its provisions. The Lords have since confirmed that Shaw LJ's is the right approach (*Lonrho v Shell Petroleum Co (No 2)* [1982] AC 173, 187, Lord Diplock).

It remains controversial whether P has to show that the statute was one on which a civil action lies, or whether it is sufficient that the statute confers a right on P with which D has interfered. A good example of the sort of statute that will do is provided by *Associated British Ports v Transport and General Workers' Union* (1989, CA; reversed HL on grounds irrelevant here). The statute in the case established a dock labour scheme. Interference with this scheme was held capable of giving rights to the employers affected, *even though* there was no action for breach of statutory duty available. More controversially, it has been held that the making of an agreement which is 'unlawful', in the sense of contravening legislation on anti-competitive practices, is sufficient to give a competitor a right of action (*Daily Mirror Newspapers v Gardner* (1968)).

'Eurotorts'

6.31   Breach of EU law, a specialised form of breach of statutory duty, can give rise to an action, so long as the *Lonrho v Shell* test, that the duty was meant to give rise to rights, is satisfied (*Garden Cottage Foods v Milk Marketing Board* (1984)). But this is a highly complex area, which is still developing; and consideration must be given to the range of remedies available for breach. So in one context at least the Court of Appeal has ruled that action for damages is not available against the government, the alternative remedy of judicial review being adequate to achieve justice (*Bourgoin SA v Ministry of Agriculture, Fisheries and Food* (1986)).

Assessment

'The economic torts are in a mess'

6.32 The confusion of the economic torts is manifest. The confusion is partly linguistic, partly over how creative we want our judges to be, and partly over the merits of various proposed patterns of liability. Nor is it obvious that squeezing all the economic torts into a single 'genus' tort of unlawful interference with trade or business will improve matters. What is 'unlawful'? Why 'trade or business' and why not other losses? How does 'interference with trade' differ from mere competition? 'The economic torts are in a mess. The acceptance, without definition, of the genus tort ... only adds to that mess. Definition of this tort is vital' (Carty 'Intentional violation of economic interests: The limits of common law liability' (1988) 104 LQR 250, 278).

Liability for lawful behaviour

6.33 *Should it exist at all?* Cases where D neither commits nor induces any unlawful act at all, and yet is still held liable for an economic tort, are rare. Many consider them anomalous. In these cases – 'conspiracy to injure' (**6.18**) and cases of interference with contract without inducing a breach (**6.22**) – there is a strong case for there being no liability at all. Certainly Harman J was of the opinion (which he confessed he had learned from his nanny) that the answer to complaints of mere unfairness was 'The world is a very unfair place and the sooner you get to know it the better' (*Swedac v Magnet & Southerns* [1989] FSR 243, 249, Harman J). Yet to others it seems a pity not to have the option of finding liability for conduct which was intended to cause harm and which serves no conceivable beneficial purpose.

6.34 *Can we trust the judges?* An entirely different kind of objection to this type of liability is that, while it might often be a useful addition to the law, its development should be left to Parliament and not to the judges. The development of this head of the law over the past century is no glowing advertisement for the merits of the common law system. The issues it raises are broad and complex. So while it seems worrying that the common law gives no remedy in the *Mogul* type of case (**6.18**), it would be even more worrying if the courts attempted to fashion a remedy without due regard to the many policy issues involved. To act as if regulation of anti-competitive practices were unknown to the law would in truth be to re-invent the wheel. Many consider that the judiciary is not capable of doing this properly, at least without the aid of a statutory framework of ideas. So while the ability of a busy legislature to keep every part of the common law under its eye must be doubted, nonetheless there is a strong case for the judges leaving well alone.

Liability for unlawful behaviour

6.35 It seems less problematical to impose liability where D's conduct was in some sense unlawful, and judicial creativity here is correspondingly less worrying. Again, however, the over-enthusiasm and lack of rigour displayed in the deployment of the economic torts against trades unions throughout this century have not enhanced the judiciary's reputation in this area. The adoption of the 'genus' approach is welcome, but only against the background of highly, almost whimsically, specific torts it aims to swallow up. What can it matter whether D's conduct is rightly described as 'intimidation' or not? Why should it matter whether D had help or acted alone? If the 'genus' approach is right, then perhaps we can abandon the other, more specific torts entirely – and good riddance.

Yet what job should the 'genus' tort be doing? Time and again, we find the 'unlawfulness' issue turning on matters which should surely be resolved under another head of the law. Few think it enough that D was engaged in activity which was undoubtedly illegal. The question is not merely whether D's behaviour is illegal, but also whether P is entitled to complain of it. It is not enough that D has done wrong, if P has suffered no infringement of rights. This leads many to suspect that the emphasis is entirely wrong, and that the 'genus' tort is a mistake. If the question is whether D's procurement of a breach of contract should enable P to sue, then we should look for the answer to that question in the policies and purposes of contract law, not tort. If D has infringed a statute, then the matter should turn on whether the statute is one breach of which gives a right to sue, or whether the imposition of liability can be said to further the policy of the statute (**1.43**). On this view, the establishment of the 'genus' tort would be an intellectual error of the highest order: an attempt to generalise about the effects of 'unlawfulness', when what we should be doing is to enquire into the origins and rationale of the type of 'unlawfulness' we have on the facts.

Further Reading

Relevant sections of tort reference books may be supplemented with:

Carty 'Intentional violation of economic interests: the limits of common law liability' (1988) 104 LQR 250.

Craig 'Once more unto the breach: The Community, the State and damages liability' (1997) 113 LQR 67.

Self-test questions

1. Why is it misleading to talk of a tort of 'inducing breach of contract' (**6.22**)?

2. Is it possible to sue D in deceit when all D has done is express an opinion (**6.5**)?

3. Can the tort of conspiracy be used to protect P's reputation (**6.19**)?

4. How much does D need to know about a contract before he or she can be said to 'intentionally interfere' with it (**6.23**)?

5. Why is action over 'two-party intimidation' rare (**6.14**)?

CHAPTER SEVEN

Land use and the environment

SUMMARY

Various torts provide a patchwork of protection in respect of land use:

- **Trespass to land**

- **Private nuisance**

- **Public nuisance**

- **Strict liabilities for dangerous activities**

The torts here have only a small part to play in the law's protection of the environment, and have little overall coherence in themselves. Arguably, however, they remain a useful supplement to the law's general provision in this area.

Introduction

7.1 The law of tort has some impact on the protection of the environment. However, the law is complex and uncertain, even by the charitable standards which must be applied to tort law; and the rules have traditionally been seen in a quite different light, protecting the rights of individual landowners rather than 'the environment' as such. The result is that several quite distinct torts, each of considerable age, provide a crazy quilt of protection for land use and environmental interests. No-one would argue that these miscellaneous torts make any overall sense as a response to the problems of protecting the environment; but it is another question whether they form a valuable, if small, part of the law's overall response to the problem. This matter is taken up when the individual torts have been considered (**7.51**).

Trespass to land

Intrusion

7.2 D commits trespass by any unjustified intrusion onto P's land. P need not prove loss or damage, and the intrusion may be trivial – though P may also use the tort to remedy damage deliberately done by D while trespassing. The tort catches not only intrusion by D in person, but also intrusions for which D is responsible. So D may commit trespass if D's animals stray onto P's land; and if D leaves property on P's land, there is a continuing trespass, with a fresh cause of action every day, until it is removed.

Below and above

7.3 In principle, P may sue for an intrusion at any height or depth above or below the land; but some qualifications must be made. Different strata or levels may have different owners, and so might need to be treated as separate territories: for example, different floors of the same building may be in different ownership, and each owner can complain only of trespass to their own area. Cases of split levels aside, intrusion below the surface of P's land is actionable unless permitted by statute; though who is entitled to any minerals may be a complicated question. Intrusion above the surface is actionable as well, at least in the case where the intruder is still attached to the ground. So where a crane used for building on D's land swings its jib over P's land, this is usually trespass: *Woollerton & Wilson v Richard Costain* (1970). But where the intruder is not attached to the ground, this is not always the case.

> *Bernstein of Leigh v Skyviews and General* (1978)   Skyviews took aerial photographs of Bernstein's mansion, with a view to selling them to him. Instead, Bernstein sued in trespass. Griffiths J held that the action failed because *(i)* there was no evidence that the aircraft was ever directly above Bernstein's land, *(ii)* if it was, Bernstein had no reasonable use for the air space at that height and so no right to complain of a trespass, and *(iii)* Skyviews were protected by statute.

This statutory provision (now embodied in Civil Aviation Act 1982, s 76) gives a complete defence to trespass for an aircraft flying at a height which is reasonable in all the circumstances, though there is strict liability for any actual physical damage caused.

Whose land?

7.4 P is entitled to complain of intrusions onto any land of which P is in possession – that is, land over which P has physical control. Where P is not now in possession, but has a legal right to go into possession, then if P does so the possession is, by legal fiction, backdated to the time when P's right arose, and so P acquires a right to sue those who trespassed since that time. (This is called 'trespass by relation'.) There is no defence that P ought never to have been in possession of the land (no defence of '*jus tertii*'), unless D personally has a better right to possession. If land is subject to a lease, it is the tenant, not the landlord, who is legally in possession and can sue for intrusions. Those with lesser rights, such as lodgers, do not displace the owner's possession and have no remedy in trespass for intrusions – though conceivably the owner's failure to expel the intruders might be a breach of contract with the lodger.

7.5 *Need D be at fault?* Deliberate conduct by D which is *in fact* an intrusion is actionable. It is no defence that D did not appreciate that it was an intrusion, or realise that it was unlawful. It is no defence, therefore, that D had lost his or her way, even after taking the greatest of care not to do so. However, D has a defence if the intrusion was an involuntary act, as where D is pulled onto P's land despite protests and struggles. Where the intrusion is by D's property (usually D's animals), the courts ask whether the intrusion was the product of intention or carelessness on D's part, or whether D was blameless.

> *League Against Cruel Sports v Scott* (1986)   In the course of hunting, Scott's staghounds ran onto the League's deer sanctuary. Park J held that Scott would be liable if he meant the hounds to trespass or had been negligent in failing to prevent trespass. Persistent hunting in circumstances where trespass was impossible to prevent was evidence of intention to trespass. £180 damages and an injunction were awarded.

Defences

7.6 *General* The main defences open to D are: (i) exercise of D's own property rights, such as a private right of way, (ii) putting right some wrong which is P's responsibility, such as by 'abatement of nuisance' **(7.29)**, (iii) statutory authority to enter P's land, such as under the Police and Criminal Evidence Act 1984, (iv) public right, such as the right to walk the highway, *(v)* permission (**7.7**), and *(vi)* necessity (**7.8**). These rights to enter land are very specific and D must stay within their limits. Simply because D has the right to walk the highway going over P's land does not entail a right to spy on P – even if D is careful to keep walking as he spies (*Hickman v Maisey* (1900)). If D's intrusion is initially justifiable but then D does some positive and unlawful act, then D is treated by fiction of law as having been a trespasser all along. (This is called 'trespass *ab initio*', 'trespass from the very beginning'.)

7.7 *Permission*   P cannot sue D in trespass if D had P's permission ('licence') to be on the land. Permission can be implied from circumstances: this is why D does not usually commit trespass by walking onto P's land and knocking on the front door, unless P has already made it clear that D is unwelcome. D will become a trespasser if D acts in a manner not permitted by the terms of the licence. If P revokes the licence, then D becomes a trespasser if still present after a reasonable time for leaving has expired. However, P may surrender this right by contract.

> *Hurst v Picture Theatres* (1915)   During a cinema show, Hurst, sitting in the audience, was suddenly and unjustifiably told by one of the staff to leave. When Hurst refused, he was forcibly ejected. Held: Hurst could sue in assault.

7.8 *Necessity*   Necessity is usually said to be a defence to an action in trespass, but the courts are not always very consistent in their treatment of the defence. So it has been held that a need for shelter, however desperate, cannot justify D's trespass, because to hold otherwise would be open to abuse (*Southwark London Borough Council v Williams* (1971)). Yet it has also been held that the defence is available to a police force using inflammable CS gas against a psychopath on P's property, even though their use of it was held negligent (*Rigby v Chief Constable for Northamptonshire* (1985)). It is safe to say that extreme circumstances are needed before D will have a defence of necessity (**11.42**). There is no general right at common law for D to enter P's premises to effect repairs to D's own property, though by statute (Access to Neighbouring Land Act 1992) a court may grant D access for this purpose.

7.9 *Damages*   P may claim damages from D for any trespass. P may recover any financial loss proved to flow from the trespass, or (if none) a nominal sum. If D took over property which had some value in the rental market, P may also recover a reasonable rental for the period of D's occupation (this remedy is called 'mesne profits'). Some cases apply this principle also where D wrongly acted as if D had a right of way, allowing P to charge the market value of such a right ('wayleave'). There will not usually, however, be any question of an award of exemplary damages (**10.10**).

7.10 *Other remedies* In appropriate cases, P may seek a court order evicting D from the land. Self-help to achieve the same result is tightly controlled by Criminal Law Act 1977, s 6: it is an offence to use or threaten force to enter premises occupied by another, subject to a rather limited defence for displaced residential occupiers. In any event, P must use no more force than the circumstances reasonably justify. Where P never ceased to occupy, an injunction may sometimes be necessary to curb D's trespassory activities (**10.2**), or again P might use self-help, provided again that P uses the minimum force reasonably necessary for the purpose. Where D's property is trespassing on P's land, P has the right to impound it and retain it until paid compensation (the remedy is called 'distress *damage feasant*'), though P has to keep good care of it in the meantime.

Private nuisance

Definition

7.11 A private nuisance consists of an unjustified interference by D in P's enjoyment of land. The remedy usually consists of an award of damages or an injunction to force D to rectify the situation. The tort is 'private' in the sense that it is a right of one private individual (P) against another (D); a nuisance which affects a significant section of the public is 'public' and so may involve criminal proceedings against D as well (**7.30**). It is not always clear where nuisance (= interference) ends and trespass (= intrusion) begins. One old case holds that if D lets a pile of rubbish fall onto P's wall, this is trespass (*Gregory v Piper* (1829)), but the modern position is unclear. The test is usually said to be that of directness. So if D deliberately throws a cricket ball into P's garden, this is trespass; but if D organises a cricket match and balls are hit over the boundary, this is nuisance, if anything (*Miller v Jackson* (1977)).

Varieties of nuisance

7.12 Nuisance may take many forms. Perhaps P's land has been physically damaged, say by the emission of poisonous fumes from D's factory; or perhaps noise and smell from D's farm has ruined P's enjoyment without any discernible physical damage. Nuisance tends to involve continuing sources of annoyance, but one-off events may constitute nuisances if sufficiently severe. The older cases sharply distinguish between actual property damage, on the one hand, and mere aesthetic offences, on the other. Modern cases place less emphasis on this distinction, which is in any event hard to apply in many cases.

Balancing the rights of the parties: relevant factors

7.13 It is impossible to give a definitive account of which activities constitute nuisances, beyond saying that D's behaviour must be unreasonable in view of the damage it does to P's interests. In each case, the court balances D's right to act against P's right not to be injured, and decides whether D has overstepped the line which the court (retroactively) draws. The court usually asks the general question whether D acted 'reasonably' in view of the harm to P. However, there is some constancy in the factors the courts regard as relevant to this balancing process, and in that limited sense it is possible to generalise about the way the courts resolve disputes of this kind.

7.14 *How severely did D hurt P?* The seriousness of the injury – both its extent and its duration – is a major factor in the balance. If D temporarily delays in removing piles of manure, rendering nearby conditions very unpleasant, this may not be a nuisance, even though there would undoubtedly be a nuisance if D left them there permanently (*Swaine v Great Northern Rly* (1864)). Some judges have insisted that there must be a 'continuing state of affairs' before action will lie in nuisance. Yet it is hard to see why this should be necessary, particularly as a 'state of affairs' can be discovered in retrospect. So in *Spicer v Smee* (1946), where fire in D's house spread to P's and damaged it, the defective state of D's electrical wiring, which caused the fire, was found to constitute the 'continuing state of affairs' for this purpose. In practice, despite occasional dicta to the contrary, there seems to be no difficulty in suing for one-off incidents, provided they are sufficiently severe. It is also sometimes said that private nuisance requires material damage to P's property; but anything serious enough to constitute a nuisance is likely to have an effect on the value of the property, and that seems to be enough.

7.15 *What was the type of injury?* Different types of injury are treated in different ways, partly because of current judgments as to which injuries are serious, and partly as a reflection of the judgments of previous generations of judges. It is no longer realistic (if indeed it ever was) to draw a very sharp line between physical injury to property and merely aesthetic offences. However, the Law Lord who drew that distinction was undoubtedly right that P will have an easier time of it in private nuisance if physical damage can be proved (Lord Westbury LC in *St Helens Smelting Co v Tipping* (1865)). Property rights are much better protected than the right to leisure activities.

> *Hunter v Canary Wharf Ltd* (1997) Several hundred plaintiffs complained that the Canary Wharf building development had created clouds of dust which deposited itself on their property, and that Canary Wharf Tower, the centrepiece of the development, interfered with their TV reception. Held: the dust was actionable if it could be shown to have damaged plaintiffs' property (by impairing the utility or value of whatever it was deposited on), but the interference with TV reception was not actionable.

But even on those facts, the distinction between cases involving damage to property and other cases is no magic talisman. The House of Lords ruled against the TV claim principally because it seemed analogous to a claim that D's building has ruined P's view, which the courts have always rejected. It might be different, hinted Lord Hoffmann, if D had interfered with P's TV reception through electrical machinery.

7.16 *How valuable is D's activity?* D has a better chance of winning the case if D's activity has some obvious and significant utility to the public. However, it must not be forgotten that P, too, is part of the public; D cannot usually cast a significant loss on P by a simple plea of 'public interest'. Moreover, there is often scope for disagreement about what constitutes a valuable activity.

> *Miller v Jackson* (1977) The Millers complained that cricket balls from matches organised by Jackson often landed in their garden, and that a few had done damage to their house. Held (by Geoffrey Lane LJ):

an actionable nuisance had been committed and the Millers were entitled to damages and an injunction to prevent repetition; (by Cumming-Bruce LJ) that damages could be awarded for the nuisance, but it would be against the public interest for an injunction to issue; (by Lord Denning MR) that the social utility of cricket outweighed the inconvenience to the Millers, who accordingly had no remedy.

7.17 *What sort of locality did the events happen in?* The less pleasant the area in which the alleged nuisance occurred, the worse must be D's behaviour if it is to be held a nuisance. Accordingly, what is permissible behaviour in one place might be a nuisance in another.

> *Laws v Florinplace* (1981)   Laws complained of the opening of a sex shop and cinema club by Florinplace, in premises close to his home; he relied particularly on the adverse effect on property values and the attraction of undesirables to the previously placid residential area. Vinelott J held that it was arguable that a nuisance had been committed, and restrained Florinplace from continuing its activities pending full trial.

Several old cases suggest that the character of the locality is irrelevant if P is complaining of actual physical damage, rather than less tangible matters. Views differ on whether this is still the law, if indeed the distinction can sensibly be drawn at all. The general character of the area will, of course, be under the oversight of the local planning authority. It is not strictly relevant in nuisance whether D had planning permission. Nonetheless, a grant of permission *which was intended to change the character of the neighbourhood* may form an important part of a case that the neighbourhood's character has in fact changed – with the result that what would earlier have been a nuisance is not now a nuisance (*Wheeler v Saunders* (1995)).

7.18 *How sensitive is P?* A claim in nuisance may be rejected on the ground that P's unusual sensitivity to D's activity gives no right of action. This may sound at first like an obvious deduction from the first factor (**7.14**) – that P cannot complain of trivial inconveniences – but it is in fact a quite different idea. Unusually sensitive plaintiffs are not protected *even if the effect of D's activities is catastrophic.*

> *Robinson v Kilvert* (1889)   Kilvert heated his premises to assist him in his trade of making paper boxes. Robinson, who occupied the floor

above, complained that the heat affected the brown paper he ware-housed there, drying it and considerably reducing its value. Held: activities which would not injure any but the most sensitive of trades were not actionable as nuisances.

It is quite different if P successfully establishes nuisance, but D then pleads that the extent of the injury was much greater than would have been suffered by most plaintiffs. D's plea is then one of remoteness of loss, and will fail unless P's loss is of a *different type* from that which was foreseeable; it is irrelevant whether D could have foreseen the extent (**7.23**, **10.32**).

7.19 *Did D set out to hurt P?* Conduct which might be unexceptionable in normal circumstances might be a nuisance if intentionally used to provoke, annoy or harm P: see *Christie v Davey* (1893) (loud domestic noises) and *Hollywood Silver Fox Farm v Emmett* (1936) (shooting rabbits near P's farm and disturbing his stock). An apparent exception is provided by one old case (*Bradford Corpn v Pickles* (1895)), where D del-iberately diverted water running under his land away from P's reservoir, in revenge for P's refusal to pay D for it. The House of Lords held that no action lay. The exception is only apparent, however. If in principle P and D both have a right to do what they have been doing, the presence of malice is helpful in striking a balance between them. But, as the Lords pointed out in *Pickles*, P had no legal right to the water at all – and so there was nothing to balance.

Who can sue?

7.20 *The traditional view* It is usually considered that P can only complain of a private nuisance if P has either possession of the land or a property right in it. The typical plaintiff will therefore be the freehold owner of the property, but those with subsidiary property rights can also sue if their interest is affected: for example a tenant, or the holder of a private right of way. A landlord can sue for injury to the residual rights not leased (the landlord's 'reversion'). But others with no property right may not, on the traditional view, sue, however good their right to be on the premises: the tenant's spouse, for example (*Malone v Laskey* (1907)). This traditional view has now been re-affirmed by the House of Lords in *Hunter v Canary Wharf* (1997).

7.21 *A controversial case* P complains that D has threatened her with violence, followed her about, and persistently harassed her in person and over the phone. She seeks an injunction to prevent a repetition. D admits that an injunction is available to prevent violence or threats of violence (**2.3**), but denies that it is available against non-violent harassment. This cannot be nuisance, he says, because P did not own the property at which she was harassed: she lived at home with her parents. Controversially, and by a majority, the Court of Appeal held that P may sue despite this objection (*Khorasandjian v Bush* (1993)). The Lords in *Hunter v Canary Wharf* (1997) have now said that this is wrong. D would today almost certainly be caught by the new law on harassment (**2.10**), but as to the tort of nuisance D's argument was perfectly correct.

Must P prove that D was negligent?

7.22 *Clarifying the issue* It is sometimes said that liability in private nuisance is 'strict' and is therefore quite different from negligence liability, which requires proof of fault. However, two careful qualifications must be made, before we can see what the true issue is.

- First, it is absolutely true that D may blunder into liability for private nuisance through ignorance of law, or through practical inability to meet the law's standard of fault. If D lights a bonfire which is a nuisance to P's neighbouring land, it is irrelevant whether D knew enough law to appreciate the possibility of liability. So certainly nuisance is in that sense 'strict', but so too is negligence. For example, the learner driver is liable for not attaining the law's standard of the reasonably experienced and careful driver, whether or not the driver appreciates that, or is practically able to attain that standard (**4.14**).

- Second, where P is claiming an injunction to prevent or suppress a nuisance from D's land, it is irrelevant whether the nuisance is D's fault. The injunction looks forward to demand that D ameliorate the situation, not backward to whose fault it was (**10.2**).

A quite distinct question, however, is whether if P sues for the loss caused by D's nuisance, D may plead *lack of fault* as a defence.

7.23 *A narrower question* P complains of a nuisance from D's land and sues for the loss caused. D admits that the situation amounts to a nuisance, but denies fault in the way in which it came about. Must the court investigate D's plea, or can P retort that liability is 'strict'? This is a controversial question; all that can be said with certainty is that when the courts have been asked this question in recent years, they have tended to treat the liability as a negligence liability:

> *Leakey v National Trust* (1980) A mound of earth on the National Trust's land collapsed onto Leakey's land. Held: the Trust had anticipated the danger and, as they had unreasonably done nothing about it, they were liable.

This assimilation of private nuisance with negligence has been adopted in several leading cases, including *Bolton v Stone* (1951) (**1.36**) and *Cambridge Water Co v Eastern Counties Leather* (1994) (**7.36**). Of course, to say that the liability is 'negligence-based' rather than 'strict' is only the beginning of the enquiry. Negligence law is hardly static or settled, and many of the unanswered questions it poses resonate in nuisance cases – particularly the question of when D may plead that removing the risk to P would have been too expensive. Nonetheless, it seems likely that future issues will be fought about in that framework and not on the assumption of 'strict' liability. In particular, it is settled that, just as in negligence, D has a defence that the type of loss caused was unforeseeable and hence too remote (*The Wagon Mound (No 2)* (1967)) (**10.30**). (For the contrary view, that liability in nuisance is still strict, see eg Cross, 'Does only the careless polluter pay? A fresh examination of the nature of private nuisance' (1995) 111 LQR 445.)

Defence: D not in control at all

7.24 *Generally* It follows that it will be a defence to an action in private nuisance that D had not, and could not reasonably have had, control over the land from which the nuisance arose. So P will have to prove either intention or lack of care on D's part. D may be liable if D directly created the nuisance, whether from D's own land or elsewhere (*Hubbard v Pitt* (1975)). If a nuisance occurs on land which D occupies, D may be liable if D knew or ought reasonably to have known of it in time to do something about it, but not otherwise (*Sedleigh-Denfield v O'Callaghan* (1940)). If D instructs others to do building work, D will be liable if the work would have resulted in a nuisance however it was done. And some authorities say that if the project obviously risks creating a nuisance, D will be liable for any negligence on the part of those doing the work, *whether or not* D can be said to be vicariously liable for the workers' actions (*Matania v National Provincial Bank* (1936); for vicarious liability see **9.2**).

7.25 *Landlord and tenant* Where D1 leases land to D2, and a nuisance then emanates from that land, liability in nuisance follows the legal right of control. D1 (landlord) is responsible if:

- D1 knew or ought reasonably to have known about the nuisance at the time of letting (*Brew Bros v Snax (Ross)* (1970)); or

- D1 retains a right to repair, and the nuisance arises from failure to repair (Defective Premises Act 1972, s 4); or

- the nuisance arises directly from D2's activities, of which D1 knew before the letting (*Tetley v Chitty* (1986)).

D2 (tenant) is responsible if:

- the nuisance is the result of D2's own activities; or

- the nuisance results from the state of any part of the premises which D2 knows about or could reasonably be expected to know about. There are *dicta* (in *St Anne's Well Brewery Co v Roberts* (1928) that D2 may be liable even where D1 has a duty to repair, though D2 can then sue D1 to pass the loss on).

7.26 *Prescription* D has a defence if D has carried on the nuisance now complained for at least twenty years (Prescription Act 1832, s 2). However, it is not enough that D has been carrying on the same activity for twenty years if it is only more recently that it became a nuisance; time runs only from the point at which P was first unlawfully affected, not from when D began the activity.

7.27 *Statutory authority* Whether a statute relating to D's activities provides a defence in nuisance depends on its construction. As a rule, P may not sue for a nuisance if D's activities were authorised by statute, either expressly or by necessary implication. So statutory authorisation to build an oil refinery bars action both for building and for ordinary operation of the refinery (*Allen v Gulf Oil Refining* (1981)). P's claim will therefore fail if the nuisance is an inevitable consequence of the type of activities the statute authorises. However, authority to carry on a certain type of activity is not to be equated with authority to carry it on carelessly. More generally, if D had appreciable freedom of action under the statute, P may demand that D use it with due regard to P's interests, and sue if D's activities are unreasonable in relation to P's interests (*Metropolitan Asylum District Managers v Hill* (1881)).

7.28 *Consent* P's consent to D's activities is a defence, and consent need only be tacit. Two major qualifications must be made, however. First, consent to D's activity being carried on at all is not the same as consent to D's running it carelessly. If D was in fact careless, and the loss would probably not have occurred if D had acted carefully, D will have to prove consent *to carelessness*; which may be difficult. Second, it is traditionally said that consent cannot be inferred merely from the fact that P has 'come to the nuisance' by acquiring property near it, even with full knowledge of D's activities. If D then has a defence at all, it is by reference to the 'character of the neighbourhood' (**7.17**). This is controversial. In *Miller v Jackson* (1977), where P bought a new house just next to a cricket ground where cricket had been played for over sixty years, Lord Denning MR held that there was consent. Geoffrey Lane and Cumming-Bruce LLJ, by contrast, held the defence inapplicable – though Cumming-Bruce sided with Denning in holding that the case was not appropriate for an injunction.

Remedies: Damages, injunction, self-help

7.29 Once nuisance is established, P may recover any proven financial loss, subject to a defence of remoteness (**7.23**). It will often be desirable to forestall a nuisance, or obtain an order to make D stop it: an injunction to that effect is very often available (**10.2**). Traditionally it was also said that P had the right, after giving D notice, to 'abate' the nuisance, that is, to enter D's land and use the minimum force reasonably necessary to stop it, or to curb its effects. However, a recent case suggests that this self-help remedy is rather narrow.

Burton v Winters (1993)   The Winters' garage, built by the people from whom they had bought the land, protruded some $4^1/_2$" onto Burton's land; Burton applied for, but was refused, an injunction to have it knocked down. Could Burton knock it down herself? Held: she could not.

The court seemed to think that the right to abate was available only in two cases: where the case was a simple one where legal proceedings would have been inappropriate, or where urgent action was plainly necessary. Where a legal action not only could have been, but actually was, brought before a court, there was no longer a right to private self-help.

Public nuisance

What is a 'public nuisance'?

7.30   Where a nuisance affects a substantial number of people, it is said to be a 'public' nuisance. The nuisance need not interfere with the use of land as such, but may interfere with any aspect of the public's rights, and may accordingly take many forms. Cases include obstructing the highway (*Chaplin v Westminster Corpn* (1901)), making obscene telephone calls (*R v Norbury* (1978)), and organising raves (*R v Shorrock* (1994)). The uncertain and broad ambit of the tort allows the judges to spring occasional surprises. So for example in *Thomas v National Union of Mineworkers* (1985) Scott J ruled that picketing might amount to a public nuisance. This was on the ground that it was an unreasonable harassment of those at whom it was directed – even though it did not constitute an assault on them and had no prospect of preventing them from going where they wished. In each case the court must if necessary go through the same process of balancing D's rights against those of others as in private nuisance cases. To many minds this notion allows too much scope for judicial creativity, and it is only the rarity with which it is invoked that saves it from being a serious infringement of civil liberties.

A crime, and sometimes a tort

7.31   If D is responsible for the public nuisance, D is liable to be prosecuted criminally. An injunction to prevent or curb a public nuisance can only be sought by the Attorney General or by local authorities (under Local

Government Act 1972, s 222), though a private individual may proceed with the Attorney General's permission (this is called a 'relator action'). Individual, civil right of action is more limited. First, the fact a nuisance may be public does not prevent P from arguing that it infringes P's private rights, protected by the tort of private nuisance. Second, if P has suffered some particular injury, in some way going beyond the loss inflicted on all affected by the nuisance, there is a right of action for public nuisance.

Who can sue?

7.32 If P is contemplating a civil action for public nuisance, P must show some loss resulting from the nuisance which goes beyond the loss suffered by all affected. However, it seems that the *type* of loss is irrelevant, and may include a purely economic loss. Liability relating to the highway illustrates the need to give separate consideration to public and private aspects of nuisance here. If D blocks P's access to the highway, this is an infringement of P's private rights, and P may sue in private nuisance; but if D blocks the highway just outside P's land, this is at most public nuisance, and P will have to prove particular damage.

> *Tate & Lyle Industries v Greater London Council* (1983)   The GLC were responsible for the construction of ferry terminals on the Thames, causing silting. Tate & Lyle paid large sums to dredge the Thames, without which the silt would have prevented large vessels from reaching their jetty. Held: there was no private nuisance, as there was no injury to Tate & Lyle's jetty. However, as there was a hindrance to navigation generally there was a public nuisance, from which Tate & Lyle had suffered an unusual degree of damage. Accordingly, they had a right of action.

Who is liable?

7.33 The test for liability is whether D had control over the nuisance. The question whether liability in private nuisance is 'strict' was discussed above (**7.22–7.23**), and much of that discussion applies also to public nuisance. Ignorance of law is no defence. But if D argues that D had no control over the events leading to the nuisance or could not reasonably have prevented it, the questions are, whether D could reasonably have been expected to foresee the nuisance; and, if so, whether D could reasonably have been expected to prevent it. However, there may be an exception where D erects an artificial projection overhanging the highway: D is sometimes said to be strictly liable for loss caused by these projections (per Lush and Quain JJ in *Tarry v Ashton* (1876); Blackburn J to the contrary). If there is such a special rule, it does not apply to natural objects such as trees, where D has a defence if all reasonable care was taken (*Wringe v Cohen* (1940)).

Strict liabilities relating to land

Introduction: scope of this section

7.34 We have already seen that liability for nuisance has often been thought of as 'strict', though today it is increasingly being assimilated to negligence (**7.22–7.23**). At common law, there were two cases where liability was on any definition strict: liability for damage caused by animals, and liability for fire. In the famous case of *Rylands v Fletcher* (1868), the House of Lords generalised from these instances to create a general principle of liability for the escape of dangerous things from D's land, a principle which was meant also to include the escape of dangerous products of new technologies. Since that case, however, the courts have tended to stress negligence rather than strict liabilities. Liability for animals is now statutory (**7.44**); whether liability for fire still has an independent existence is considered below (**7.42**). Various other special cases are dealt with by statute (**7.43**).

The principle in Rylands v Fletcher: escape of dangerous things

7.35 If D accumulates some dangerous thing, as part of some non-natural use of land, then D is strictly liable to P if the thing escapes and does damage to P. This rule was laid down in *Rylands v Fletcher* (1868), where D constructed a dam on his land to provide water for his mill. As a result of negligence by D's contractors (though not by D himself), the water burst through into P's mines and flooded them. The liability is strict, in the sense that P need not prove negligence, but there are extensive defences, which are considered below (**7.40–7.41**).

How 'dangerous'?

7.36 It is usually said that a thing is 'dangerous' for this purpose if it is likely to cause damage if it escapes, and there seems no advantage in expanding this definition further. The following have, at one time or another, been held to be 'dangerous': gas (*Batcheller v Tunbridge Wells Gas Co* (1901)), a poisonous yew tree (*Ponting v Noakes* (1894)), fumes from creosote (*West v Bristol Tramways* (1908)), and a fun-fair 'chair-o-plane' ride (*Hale v Jennings Bros* (1938)). However, the House of Lords now appears to have held that a thing cannot be 'dangerous' if its escape was not foreseeable at all.

> *Cambridge Water Co v Eastern Counties Leather* (1994)   Eastern Counties Leather used a powerful toxic solvent in their tanning process, much of which was spilled on the factory floor. Over several years of use, a large quantity of this solvent seeped under their property, several thousand metres along an aquifer, and into Cambridge Water's bore-hole. New EU regulations on water quality meant that the solvent rendered the water legally undrinkable. Held: no action lay, as the pollution was unforeseeable.

And in *Crown River Cruises v Kimbolton Fireworks* (1996), where D's fireworks display caused a fire on P's river vessel, Potter J was reluctant to base liability on *Rylands v Fletcher* principles. '[I]n the light of the current judicial and academic reserve which appears detectable towards extension of the principle' ([1996] 2 Ll 547), he based liability on nuisance instead.

Is there a requirement of 'non-natural use'?

7.37 It is not clear what, if anything, the requirement of 'non-natural use' adds to the requirement of dangerousness. Not all of the classic formulations of the rule mention it. It may have been meant only to imply that D must deliberately accumulate something, rather than fail to remove a pre-existing ('natural') accumulation. Most modern cases assume, however, that the test is one of how ordinary D's activity is and (possibly) of how justifiable. So activities such as erecting or demolishing buildings (*Thomas and Evans v Mid-Rhondda Co-operative Society* (1941)) or mining in an ordinary way (*Rouse v Gravelworks* (1940)) are not 'unnatural'. Indeed, it was even suggested that the manufacture and storage of high explosives might be 'natural', at least in war-time (*Read v J Lyons* (1947)). Yet in the *Cambridge Water* case it was said that the storage of chemicals was 'an almost classic case of non-natural use' ([1994] 1 All ER 79, Lord Goff). On this view, D would escape liability merely because it was common in that industry, or because it provided employment, or was otherwise to be encouraged. This all suggests that the true test is now dangerousness, though the Lords did not say so expressly. This area of the law is badly in need of clarification.

'Escape'

7.38 P cannot complain of events if their effects were felt only on D's land, or which affected P while on D's land: such as an explosion in D's factory where P is an employee (*Read v J Lyons* (1947)). The requirement is often confusingly stated to require an 'escape' of *the thing accumulated*, but that is not strictly accurate. An accumulation of explosives, which detonate causing damage to neighbouring land-owners, is actionable (*Miles v Forest Rock Granite Co* (1918)), even though it is at best a rather confusing metaphor to describe this as an 'escape' of the explosives. *Something* must escape as a result of the accumulation, but it need not be the accumulation itself.

Who may sue?

7.39 The usual plaintiff in these cases is a landowner (including anyone with an interest in the land) who has suffered property damage. Some authorities say there are no other possible plaintiffs (eg *Weller & Co v Foot and Mouth Disease Research Institute* (1966)). However, other cases hold that P may sue for damage to personal property, whether or not it was on P's land when damaged (eg *Halsey v Esso Petroleum Co* (1961)). Some cases also hold that P may sue for personal injury (eg *Hale v Jennings Bros* (1938)), though other authorities doubt it, suggesting that the tort concerns only the rights of property owners (*Read v J Lyons* (1947)).

Who is liable, and how strict is the liability?

7.40 The liability arises whenever D has control over land where there is a dangerous accumulation. The liability is usually described as strict. However, various defences together drag the tort in the direction of liability for fault.

- If the immediate cause of the incident was the act of a trespasser, there is no liability unless D ought reasonably to have foreseen and prevented the trespasser's action (*Perry v Kendricks Transport* (1956)).

- If the immediate cause of the incident was some unforeseeable natural cause ('Act of God'), such as unforeseeably heavy rainfall, D is not liable (*Nichols v Marsland* (1876)). The result, though not the principle, of *Nichols* has been questioned in later cases, which point out that the possibility of heavy rain should surely have occurred to reasonable people considering the matter.

- P cannot complain of an escape which was P's own fault. On the question whether P can complain of a loss which would not have happened but for P's abnormal sensitivity, the authorities conflict.

- If damage of the type P suffers was not foreseeable at all, P cannot claim (*Cambridge Water* case, **7.36**).

These rules do not *quite* add up to a general defence of due care by D, but their joint effect is somewhat similar in many cases. However, D remains liable if the risk to P was plain but D decided (reasonably or not) that the cost of defending P against the risk was more than D was prepared to pay; arguably that would be the case if the facts of the *Cambridge Water* case recurred today.

Other defences

7.41 D also has a defence on proof of any of the following:

- That P *consented* to the dangerous accumulation. Consent may often be inferred from knowledge of the accumulation. However, if P knows of the accumulation, but not that D has acted negligently, then D remains liable for negligence, to which P has not consented (*Peters v Prince of Wales Theatre* (1943)).

- If the accumulation was carried on for the *common benefit* of P and D, it can usually be taken that P has consented to it (*Prosser & Son v Levy* (1955)).

- That D had a *statutory duty or authority* to make the accumulation, despite the danger. But the case law is confused, and each statute must be interpreted on its own merits. It appears that if the statute places D under a *duty* to act (as where a water company is placed under an obligation to maintain pressure in its pipes), D will probably not be liable for the unavoidable risk of escape unless negligence is proved (*Dunne v North Western Gas Board* (1964)). But if the statute merely *authorises* D to act, then the authorities conflict on whether D is liable in the absence of negligence, though they are unlikely so to hold if the risk was obviously incidental to activities of the sort D was engaged in.

Special case: fire

7.42 Strict liability for fire pre-dates *Rylands v Fletcher*, and only fits rather awkwardly within it. Nonetheless it is customary today to discuss it as an example of *Rylands* liability, which exists alongside negligence liability for fire. So where the carburettor of D's car caught fire in D's garage and the fire spread to P's premises, the court applied *Rylands*. The court did not seem unduly bothered by questions of what precisely was the 'accumulation', whether cars are 'natural', or whether what escaped was the same thing as what was accumulated (*Musgrove v Pandelis* (1919)).

By ancient statute (Fires Prevention (Metropolis) Act 1774, s 86), there is no liability for fires which start 'accidentally'. But the courts have construed this narrowly, holding that no fire is 'accidental' if it starts or is made worse by D's negligence (*Goldman v Hargrave* (1967)), or falls within the *Rylands v Fletcher* principle (*Mason v Levy Auto Parts of England* (1967)). D is also liable for the negligence of all lawful visitors on the land. Who is a lawful visitor is sometimes a difficult question.

H & N Emmanuel v Greater London Council (1971) The GLC hired contractors to remove two prefabricated bungalows, prohibiting them from burning any rubbish involved. The workers nonetheless did so, and the fire spread to Emmanuel's property. Held: as the GLC had done nothing to guard against the obvious risk that the workers would disobey their instructions, they could not plead that the workers were trespassers when they burned the rubbish, and the GLC were liable for their actions.

Other special cases

7.43 Strict liability is imposed for particular hazards by statute: notably for underground storage of gas (Gas Act 1965, s 14), discharge of oil from ships (Merchant Shipping (Oil Pollution) Act 1971, s 1, amended by Merchant Shipping Act 1988, s 34 and Sch 4), illegal disposal of waste (Environmental Protection Act 1990, s 73(6)), and incidents involving radioactive matter (Nuclear Installations Act 1965, s 12). In each case there are certain defences and so the liability is not strictly 'strict'.

Liability for animals

Strict liability of the 'keeper' of animals

7.44 By the Animals Act 1971, the 'keeper' of animals is under a strict liability for damage caused by those animals, in two situations described in the following paragraphs. 'Keeper' is defined in s 6(3), and the definition is broad. D is 'keeper' of an animal if D owns it, or possesses it (except where D has temporarily taken possession of the animal to stop it from doing damage, or to return to its owner). If D is head of a household, D is 'keeper' of all animals kept by members of the household who are under 16. Once D is 'keeper' of a particular animal, D remains its 'keeper' for the purposes of the Act until the animal has a new 'keeper'.

7.45 *Animals of a dangerous species* If the animal of which D is the keeper is a member of a 'dangerous species', then D is strictly liable for any harm it does. A species is 'dangerous' if:

- it is not commonly domesticated in the British Isles; and

- fully-grown members of the species either are likely to do severe damage unless restrained, or are such that any damage they do is likely to be severe (s 6(2)).

'Species' is defined as including subspecies and varieties (s 11); so (for example) each different breed of dog is a different 'species' to a lawyer, even though a zoologist would have a different view.

7.46 *Individually dangerous animals* D is also strictly liable as keeper of an animal from a non-dangerous species, if three specific matters are proved by P:

- the damage the animal caused was of the sort it was likely to cause unless restrained, or which was likely to be severe if that animal did it; and

195

- the animal's dangerous characteristics are not usually found in animals of that species, or are usually found only in particular circumstances; and

- D knew of the danger, or (if the animal has been left in someone else's charge) the person in charge knew of the danger. If D is keeper because he or she is head of household and the junior keeper is under 16, it is enough that the junior keeper knew of the danger.

7.47 *Defences* The liability of the keeper under the Animals Act 1971 is strict, and it is quite irrelevant whether the harm done by the animal has anything to do with its dangerous characteristics. So if D's tiger escapes and ruins P's paintings by leaving paw-prints on them, D is strictly liable. Nonetheless, the Act recognises certain defences:

- *P's own fault* Damage which is wholly P's fault attracts no liability at all (s 5); damage which is partly P's fault may lead to a reduction in damages (ss 10 and 11; **11.17**).

- *P's consent* As with most torts, P cannot sue where P earlier agreed to run the risk of harm (**11.2**). Note that consent may very often be inferred where P runs a risk which is very obvious (**11.6**).

- *P is a trespasser* P cannot recover for an injury caused by D's animal if D shows that it occurred when P was trespassing on D's land. There is an exception if D kept the animal deliberately to guard the land: in that case, D has a defence only if D also shows that it was reasonable to use the animal in that way (s 5(3)). Note that the Guard Dogs Act 1975 strictly regulates the use of guard dogs. Breach of that Act's provisions does not in itself entail civil liability, but will almost certainly stop D from arguing that the use of the dog was reasonable – and so it indirectly gives an injured trespasser a right to sue under the Animals Act 1971.

Application of other torts

7.48 The Animals Act 1971 abolished the special common law rules on liability for animals. So we need no longer concern ourselves with the old rules, or their concern with distinguishing animals *ferae naturae* (= of a wild nature) from those *mansuetae naturae* (= of a peaceable nature). Nonetheless, the general law of tort still applies and so D's misbehaving animals may involve D in liability in a number of situations.

- If it was foreseeable that D's animals might become dangerous, D may be liable in negligence (eg *Draper v Hodder* (1972), the facts of which arose before the Animals Act 1971 was in force). In particular, D may be liable in negligence for leaving animals where they might stray onto the highway (s 8(1)), though there is a statutory exception where D lawfully left animals on common land, or on a town or village green, or in an area where fencing is not customary (s 8(2)).

- D's animals may involve D in liability for nuisance, as by creating noise, smells, obstruction, or other disturbances (**7.11**).

- Trespass to land (**7.2**) or trespass to the person (**2.1**) may be committed through an animal, as where D deliberately sets his dog on P.

For that matter, if D trains a mynah bird to repeat words which ridicule P, this might involve D in liability for defamation; though it might be a difficult question whether D is liable in slander or in libel (see **8.20**). Potentially, then, D's animals may make D liable for just about any tort, though some are a great deal more likely than others.

Special cases

7.49 *Dogs harming livestock* Where D is keeper of a dog which harms P's livestock, D is strictly liable to P (s 3). 'Livestock' is precisely defined in the Act, as meaning 'cattle, horses, asses, mules, hinnies, sheep, pigs, goats and poultry, and also deer not in the wild state and, while in captivity, pheasants, partridges and grouse' (s 11). This special rule is somewhat anomalous, for it means that property is better protected than the person. If D's dog bites P1's thigh and P2's turkey, P2 may sue without more but P1 will have to show that some part of the Animals Act 1971 applies.

7.50 *Straying livestock* Where D's livestock strays onto another's land, there is strict liability for property damage done as a result (s 4). There is also a statutory right to detain the offending animals, to charge for their care while so detained, and ultimately to sell them if not reclaimed (s 7).

Evaluation

Current trends in the law

7.51 The torts under consideration in this chapter develop slowly, receiving relatively little attention either from the legislature or from litigants. Various key points stand out. The torts are very diverse: they cover a wide range of situations, and because they must therefore be based on very broad principles, they are unpredictable. The torts by-and-large protect individual rights, not the public interest (**7.20**, **7.31**). It is true that the courts pay some attention to the public interest (**7.16**), but the courts seek no evidence on this from anyone but the parties. The question before the court is essentially whether one private individual has infringed the rights of another, rather than what the public interest in the environment requires. P is allowed only to protect P's own interests and is not a representative of all who might have some objection to D's activities. It is increasingly clear that the courts see the answer to such problems in the application of negligence principles, rather than in ideas of strict liability (**7.22–7.23**):

> ... I incline to the opinion that, as a general rule, it is more appropriate for strict liability in respect of operations of high risk to be imposed by Parliament, than by the courts. If such liability is imposed by statute, the relevant activities can be identified, and those concerned can know where they stand. Furthermore, statute can where appropriate lay down precise criteria establishing the incidence and scope of such liability ... [G]iven that so much well-informed and carefully structured legislation is now being put in place for [dealing with environmental pollution], there is less need for the courts to develop a common law principle to achieve the same end, and indeed it may well be undesirable that they should do so (*Cambridge Water Co v Eastern Counties Leather* [1994] 1 All ER 76, Lord Goff).

Part of a wider system

7.52 This narrow incidence of the law of tort would be impossible to defend if it were all the law had to say on the protection of land use and the environment; but it is not. The common law runs alongside an extensive system of 'statutory nuisances' for which local authorities may take proceedings; further powers are vested in the Pollution Inspectorate and the Environment Agency. There is also the all-pervasive system of planning controls, which pre-empt many issues of land use before they get the chance to raise issues of nuisance (**7.17**). Parliament has not neglected questions of civil liability either: one reason why catastrophes such as tanker disasters tend not to give rise to litigation is that Parliament has already settled the ground rules of civil liability, without the need for the courts to do so. When we consider, therefore, what the proper scope of common law liability should be, we are asking what should be done in the marginal or unexpected cases which have not *already* been provided for by legislation. What, in the light of that, should be done?

Distinguish more between remedies?

7.53 For some, the law on nuisance is unnecessarily complicated because the courts tend to pose the blanket question 'whether there was a nuisance', when they should ask simply whether P should have the remedy claimed. The question whether P can close D's factory down is quite different from whether P is entitled to loss caused by its operations. Yet as these both depend on whether these operations constitute a nuisance, arguably the courts are unfair to plaintiffs, as they hesitate to grant damages because that could open the way to a claim to an injunction.

Strict liability or negligence liability?

7.54 Others suggest that it is too ungenerous to plaintiffs to insist on proof of fault. The argument, which is at its strongest where D's activities carry obvious dangers to others, may be put morally or economically: that justice, or economic efficiency, or both, require that D must carry the costs as well as the benefits to be made from the dangerous activity. (How strongly the economist would put the argument would depend on several factors; if it is relatively easy for D to bargain with plaintiffs or potential plaintiffs, the 'Coase theorem' suggests that bargains made by the parties will settle the matter regardless of the law's allocation of risk. The law's main role, on this view, is to facilitate bargains between the parties.)

More public, less public?

7.55 Finally, it is often suggested the current law is defective for placing too much emphasis on individual rights, with the result that the public interest is neglected. There might be many reasons an injured party might not sue. If one injured party does sue, there is no enquiry into the loss D has caused generally – indeed, the court would not normally hear from other injured parties at all. Damages are awarded strictly for P's own loss, and there is no question of punitive damages, or the award of a 'global' sum to compensate all those injured by the activities complained of. Moreover, many interests, and in particular individuals' interests in their own health and safety, are barely recognised at all by the tort of nuisance. The same is true of interests such as good air quality: the air does not belong to anyone, and so has no-one to guard its interests unless a particular plaintiff can establish and quantify a loss to him personally. Many argue, therefore, that the current structure of liability almost invariably underestimates the harm done by environmentally dangerous activities.

Further Reading

Relevant sections of tort reference books may be supplemented with:

Gearty 'The place of private nuisance in a modern law of torts' [1989] CLJ 214.

Steele 'Private law and the environment: nuisance in context' (1995) 15 LS 236.

Self-test questions

1. Angie's factory, which has been operating for 30 years, last year added a new unit. The machinery makes a loud humming noise. As a result Bernard, who last month bought a house nearby, cannot get to sleep at night. Assuming that there is a nuisance, does Angie have a defence (a) of prescription (7.26); (b) of consent (7.28); or (c) that she obtained planning permission before adding the new unit (7.17)?

2. Is it a defence to an action in nuisance that D's conduct was, on the whole, for the public benefit (7.16)?

3. May the same conduct by D amount to both a public nuisance and a private nuisance (7.31)?

4. In what sense or senses is the liability for the tort in *Rylands v Fletcher* 'strict' (**7.40–7.41**)?

5. Charles, while exploring tunnels under his land, discovers a large and impressive cave, which he regularly visits on later occasions. It turns out that the cave is in fact directly under Donna's land. Has Charles committed trespass (**7.3**)? Does it matter whether Charles reasonably thought it was under his own land (**7.5**)? What damages, if any, may Donna recover (**7.9**)?

CHAPTER EIGHT

Protection of reputation

SUMMARY
A statement which lowers P's reputation may constitute defamation. Key points are:

- **Was D responsible for the statement?**

- **Did the statement lower P's reputation?**

- **What defences are available?**

- **What is the appropriate remedy?**

Other torts may occasionally be used to protect reputation. Reform of the law is highly controversial, particularly in relation to the size of awards and the legal costs involved.

Introduction

8.1 Reputation is protected principally by the tort of defamation, though a few other torts are relevant (**8.42**). Defamation is the most antique part of tort law you are ever likely to meet. The law is byzantine, the procedure archaic, and the remedies Draconian. Reforms have smoothed away the rougher edges of the law, but the result keeps few happy. The expense of the remedy pushes all but the very rich away. Legal aid has never been available, the framers of the scheme never believing the law was in a fit state to justify it.

Defamation is sometimes divided into slander (roughly, spoken defamation) and libel (roughly, written or broadcast defamation). But the law is very similar for both and it will only be necessary to distinguish the two when we consider damages (**8.20**).

Procedures

8.2 Defamation is almost unique among the torts: it is very often heard before a judge and jury, rather than a judge alone. The role of the jury is to determine matters of fact and to determine the level of damages. The role of the judge is to decide issues of law and procedure, including (if necessary) the decision to withdraw from the jury any questions to which there can only be one reasonable answer. This division of responsibility is a major factor in the complexity of defamation proceedings. Yet it also means that at least some of the major decisions are in the hands of a body representative of the public.

Liability

The meaning of statements

8.3 Much of the law of defamation assumes that we can give a definite meaning to what D said or wrote. The meaning will often be clear: D might say outright that P is a thief. But defamation may take any form, if a derogatory impression is given.

> *Monson v Tussauds* (1894) Monson was tried for murder by shooting; the (Scots) criminal court returned a verdict of 'Not Proven'. Tussauds exhibited a waxwork of Monson, with a gun, near the entrance of its Chamber of Horrors. This was held, for defamation purposes, to amount to a statement that Monson was a murderer.

Where the meaning of D's statement is disputed, it is P's job to specify what the meaning is, and the jury's to say whether P is correct. The judge may refuse to put the question to the jury if the suggested meaning is an unreasonable one. The form of the statement does not matter. The test is: *What meaning would reasonable people give to the statement?*

> *English and Scottish Co-operative Society v Odhams Press* (1940) A newspaper story about incorrect tax returns was headlined 'False Profit Return Charge Against Society'. The Society said that this amounted to an accusation that it had *deliberately* made false returns. Held: the headline could reasonably be read in that way, and the jury was entitled, having regard to the whole story, to treat it as an accusation of fraud.

204

The process of spelling out the supposed meaning often results in something barely recognisable to its original author. In *Cornwell v Myskow* (1987), the passage P complained of read as follows:

'WALLY OF THE WEEK

ACTRESS Charlotte Cornwell made a proper pratt of herself in Central's crude new catastrophe, No Excuses. And then she foolishly prattled about it pompously in public. This repellent rubbish about a clapped-out old rock singer is without doubt the worst I have ever clapped eyes on. It bears no relation to rock and roll today – all concerned must have been living down a sewer for the last decade – or indeed to human beings. As a middle-aged star, all Miss Cornwell has going for her is her age. She can't sing, her bum is too big and she has the sort of stage presence that jams lavatories. Worst, she belongs to that arrogant and self-deluded school of acting which believes that if you leave off your make-up (how brave, how real) and SHOUT A LOT it's great acting. It's ART. For a start, dear, you look just as ugly *with* make-up, so forget that. And as for ART? In the short sharp words of the series, there is just one reply. It rhymes.'

This contains a number of distinct assertions about P. Here is P's version of its meaning. Do you agree that it is the true meaning?

'(*i*) that the Plaintiff has taken part in a production so repellently filthy that she and the others taking part in it might have been living down a sewer, (*ii*) that the Plaintiff was a middle-aged failure as an actress and singer, with a stage presence that drove the audience to the lavatories, (*iii*) that the Plaintiff was a foolish, ugly woman whose pretensions at acting in an artistic manner were utterly bogus and unjustified, (*iv*) that the Plaintiff lacked any ability whatsoever as an actress and was guilty of arrogant self-delusion in presenting herself as an actress to the public.'

[At trial, the jury accepted P's version, awarding her £10,000. The Court of Appeal overturned this and ordered a re-trial, which collapsed after P made an inappropriate remark on the second day. At a second re-trial P again succeeded, winning £11,500, though her total legal costs were greatly in excess of this.]

Slang

8.4 P may rely on slang meanings, but must explain them to the court.

Allsop v Church of England Newspaper (1972) A newspaper published a hostile review of Allsop's performance on television ('We need religious television we can understand'), and complained of a 'pre-occupation with the bent'. Held: while this phrase was plainly derogatory, it was ambiguous. Allsop was ordered to spell out in more detail what he took it to mean, if his libel action was to continue.

Inferences

8.5 Perhaps D's statement does not appear defamatory in isolation, but reasonable listeners would nonetheless infer something against P. D is responsible not only for the statement, but also for reasonable inferences from it.

Tolley v JS Fry and Sons (1931) Tolley, a famous amateur golfer, was depicted in an advertisement for Fry's chocolate, with a limerick praising both Tolley and the chocolate. Held: reasonable readers might infer that Tolley had received money for allowing his name to appear in this way, and accordingly might believe that he had compromised his amateur status.

Gillick v British Broadcasting Corpn (1995) A participant in a live TV programme commented that 'there were at least two reported cases of suicide by girls who were pregnant'. Gillick, a prominent campaigner against contraceptive advice for young girls, claimed that these words accused her of being morally responsible for those deaths. Held: the words were capable of bearing that meaning.

But this is potentially a highly oppressive rule and the courts have refused to apply it to its fullest extent.

Lewis v Daily Telegraph (1964) The *Daily Telegraph* reported, accurately, that the Fraud Squad of the City of London Police were investigating a particular firm. Lewis, its managing director, sued, arguing that readers might believe that 'there was no smoke without fire', and therefore would infer that he must be guilty of something. Held: many people might draw that inference, but nonetheless it was not a reasonable inference. Lewis would not be allowed to treat the story as an allegation of fraud against him.

Inferences based on special facts

8.6 Sometimes the inference on which P relies could only have been drawn by someone with special knowledge, the statement appearing quite innocuous to someone without this knowledge. P must carefully plead this special meaning (known as an 'innuendo'), as well as the special knowledge on which it relies. Further, even if P succeeds in this argument, P has only been defamed in the eyes of those with this special knowledge – a point which may reduce the damages payable. However, there is no rule that D must have known of the special facts, and accordingly the principle may have unexpected results from D's point of view.

Cassidy v Daily Mirror Newspapers (1929)   The *Daily Mirror* published a photograph of Mr Cassidy with a woman, implying that they were engaged. Mrs Cassidy sued, saying that this gave her acquaintances the impression that she was not married to Mr Cassidy and so it amounted to a charge that she was 'living in sin' with him. The *Mirror* argued that, as they had not mentioned Mrs Cassidy, they could not be said to have defamed her. Held: to those who knew Mrs Cassidy, the photograph would have conveyed the meaning she argued for, and so she was defamed in the eyes of those people.

E Hulton & Co v Jones (1910)   The *Sunday Chronicle* published an account of a motor show in Dieppe, suggesting that one Artemus Jones, a married clergyman, was seen behaving immorally. A barrister called Artemus Jones sued, producing friends who swore they thought the story referred to him. The *Chronicle* pleaded that the account was light-hearted, and 'Artemus Jones' manifestly an invention. Held: the test was whether reasonable people would infer that P was meant; in view of the unusual name, the jury was entitled to infer that P had been defamed.

This rule is potentially a very harsh one. If either case were to recur, D might plead the statutory defence of Unintentional Defamation (**8.25**); though on the facts of the *Jones* case itself this would be unlikely to succeed, as Jones had worked for the *Chronicle*, which would therefore have difficulty arguing that they did not know of anyone of that name.

(The term 'innuendo' is sometimes also used to refer to slang, topical references or other meanings which might need to be explained to the judge, but which are nonetheless the ordinary meanings of the words used. These are technically known as 'false innuendoes', as distinct from 'true innuendoes' which rely on proof of extrinsic facts.)

Is D responsible for publishing the statement?

8.7 Distinguish carefully between the person with whom the statement originates (the 'primary publisher') and those who repeat it ('secondary publishers').

Primary publishers are strictly liable

8.8 Good motive is no defence, nor is a reasonable belief that the statement is true. Communication to a single person other than P is enough. If P shows that D put the statement into general circulation, it is for D to prove that no-one read it or understood it. Indeed, some old cases say that if D sends P an insulting postcard, defamation is established, unless D can prove that it was not read by postal workers *en route*, or that the insults would not have been understood by those readers. D is not necessarily safe even in the case of a sealed envelope.

> *Theaker v Richardson* (1962) Richardson sent an abusive letter to Theaker, correctly addressed. Her husband opened it. Held: Richardson was liable for the publication to Theaker's husband. While refusing to lay down a presumption that husbands read their wives' letters, the Court of Appeal did not fault the jury's verdict that this was a natural and probable consequence of Richardson's behaviour.

The primary publisher may sometime also be held liable for the greater harm done when the statement is repeated. Traditionally this is said to be so in three cases: *(i)* where D requests or authorises the repetition; *(ii)* where D means it to be repeated; and *(iii)* where the repeaters do so because they feel morally bound to do it. But in practice D seems to be held liable whenever repetition is a natural consequence of D's behaviour, and some authorities say that this is indeed the law. (Both views are expressed in *Speight v Gosnay* (1891).)

Secondary publishers are liable for negligence

8.9 At common law, those who merely repeat defamatory statements may have a defence if they neither knew nor could reasonably have known that they were repeating defamatory matter; but they are otherwise liable (*Goldsmith v Sperrings* (1977)). The common law rule on the matter has now been replaced by statute (Defamation Act 1996, s 1); the new rule is somewhat more precise, but to the same general effect. 'Authors', 'editors' and 'publishers' of statements are strictly liable; others have a defence if they can show they took all reasonable care in relation to the statement, and did not know, and had no reason to believe, that they were contributing to the publication of a defamatory statement. The definitions used in the section are complex; how the courts will react to them can only be a matter for speculation at this early stage.

The liability of secondary publishers is one of the heavily criticised aspects of the modern law of defamation. It is not practical for printers and distributors to read everything they publish, let alone to check whether individual statements are true. The standard of care required from them has never been spelled out with any precision. Threats of action against distributors may be enough to suppress the offending publication entirely; yet the courts refuse 'prior restraint' when asked for it directly (**8.23**), and so should not allow it in through the back door. In fact, legal action is only rarely taken against distributors, but the threat is always there, and it is a potent one. (The issue is particularly topical in relation to the Internet: the author of a defamatory posting may be half a world away from P, who may therefore choose to sue the local internet service provider.)

The law's neat distinction between 'primary' and 'secondary' publishers sits rather uncomfortably with modern publishing practice. If a newspaper story criticises P, is there a 'publication' when the journalist types a first draft, another if a colleague sees it, another when seen by a sub-editor, another when seen by the libel reader? Technically speaking there is a fresh 'publication' each time the statement comes to someone's attention. However, most of the internal workings of the newspaper are covered by qualified privilege (**8.35**), and in practice P usually treats the printing of the newspaper as the 'primary publication'.

Does the statement defame P?

Introduction

8.10 It is not sufficient that the statement annoys or embarrasses P. The statement must lower P's reputation. In the traditional formula, it must stir up 'hatred, ridicule or contempt' against P. Yet this formula is misleading, for P is not bound to produce witnesses who say they are now inclined to loath, mock, or despise P. On the contrary, P often produces witnesses who say they never for a moment believed what D said. It is not any particular, real person who must feel these emotions of hatred, ridicule and contempt. Rather, the test is whether D's statement arouses them in the breast of The Reasonable Person.

The Reasonable Person

8.11 The courts have often acknowledged that The Reasonable Person differs somewhat from the citizenry at large. The Reasonable Person represents what people *should* be, in the court's eyes, even if they *are* rather different. If D accuses P of a particularly ingenious fraud, this defames P, because The Reasonable Person hates and despises those who commit fraud. It is irrelevant that many people might feel awe at the skill supposedly displayed (*Tournier v National Provincial Bank* [1924] 1 KB 461, 487, Atkin LJ).

To satisfy the 'hatred, ridicule or contempt' formula when P's property is disparaged, we must ask whether the state of affairs described reflects on P personally. So it is not necessarily defamatory to say of a shopkeeper that some of the goods he sells are defective, but it probably would be defamatory to say that they *all* were.

Beyond 'hatred, ridicule or contempt'

8.12 The traditional formula is at best a loose indication. It is impossible to be precise here, for a number of reasons. First, changing values mean that older cases are not a reliable guide. Second, whether a particular statement is defamatory is ultimately a jury question, and juries cannot give their reasons; the cases tell us only which cases are so clear that the judge can *withdraw* them from the jury. Third, the cases are often inconsistent. For example, some cases say that it is not defamatory to call P a bankrupt, because this could be for many reasons, not all of which reflect on P's character; whereas others say that this allegation obviously damages P's reputation, especially if P is involved in professional or commercial work.

As another example, is it defamatory to say that P is a homosexual? This is clearly stated in the older cases to be defamatory. Yet with modern changes in values, it is hard to imagine a court relying on them: '[t]here is no common view that sexual conduct of any kind between consenting adults is grossly immoral' (*Stephens v Avery* [1988] 2 All ER 477, 480, Browne-Wilkinson V-C). It does not follow, however, that D may allege homosexuality with impunity.

Donovan v 'The Face' (1992) A magazine, *The Face*, purported to 'out' the actor Jason Donovan. Donovan sued, saying that he had been accused, not merely of being homosexual, but also of concealing his supposed sexuality to preserve his stage image as a heterosexual. A jury found the statement defamatory, awarding £200,000.

Again, it has traditionally been assumed that it is defamatory to say that P suffers from a serious disease. There is no sign of a retreat from this position merely because hatred, ridicule and contempt are not today seen as appropriate responses to disease. And for a sufficiently shocking allegation, some judges will abandon the traditional formula entirely.

Youssoupoff v Metro-Goldwyn-Meyer Pictures (1934) MGM produced a film which, while it used fictitious names, nonetheless plainly portrayed the plaintiff, and suggested that she had been raped by Rasputin the Mad Monk. Held: this was a defamatory allegation because (per Scrutton LJ) the story was plainly to her discredit, or (per Atkin LJ) the law of defamation also protects plaintiffs from statements which would cause others to shun or avoid them.

Neither reason seems satisfactory. Scrutton's approach, which assumes that P herself was at fault, is strange. Atkin's formulation is more satisfactory, and also explains why it is defamatory to say that P has a serious communicable disease; but how was his criterion satisfied on the facts? This re-formulation seems to broaden the scope of liability very wide indeed, to include plaintiffs much less deserving than Princess Youssoupoff.

Berkoff v Burchill (1996) Burchill's review of a horror film *The Creature* compared the eponymous creature to the actor Steven Berkoff, though noting that the creature itself was 'marginally better looking'. Berkoff sued in libel. Held: on the assumption that the review meant that Berkoff was hideously ugly, it was capable of being defamatory.

There is much force in the dissenting judgment of Millett LJ, who concluded 'Miss Burchill made a cheap joke at Mr Berkoff's expense; she may thereby have demeaned herself, but I do not believe that she defamed Mr Berkoff. If I have appeared to treat Mr Berkoff's claim with unjudicial levity it is because I find it impossible to take it seriously' ([1996] 4 All ER 1020).

'Vulgar abuse'

8.13 Despite the traditional reference to 'ridicule', there is no liability for mere insults which no reasonable person would treat as factual allegations. It is sometimes said that there is no liability for 'vulgar abuse'. But that is misleading. Rather, the rule is that ridicule is not actionable if, rationally considered, it suggests nothing to P's discredit.

> *Blennerhasset v Novelty Sales Services* (1933)   Novelty Sales Services promoted their new toy, the yo-yo, with a poster depicting a fictitious Mr Blennerhassett, who was humorously suggested to have been driven insane by his devotion to the toy. A real Mr Blennerhassett, who in several respects resembled his fictional counterpart, sued, and could demonstrate that he had been subjected to considerable ridicule and humiliation as a result of D's poster. Held: there was no case to go to the jury.

> *Charleston v News Group Newspapers* (1995)   The *News of the World* portrayed the plaintiffs, who played a married couple in the soap opera *Neighbours*, apparently committing an indecent act. The headline was 'Strewth! What's Harold up to with our Madge?' The text made it clear that the plaintiffs' faces had been superimposed on pictures of pornographic actors. Held: the article must be read as a whole, and when so read was not defamatory.

'It is rumoured ...'

8.14 To repeat the defamatory utterances of others is usually regarded as attracting liability for defamation in itself. To preface a defamatory remark with the tag 'There is no truth in the vile rumour that ..' is likely to be regarded as a ploy, and no better than simple repetition without comment. A more tricky case was as follows. Rumours circulate in journalistic circles that the Prime Minister is having an affair. *New Statesman and Society* magazine suspects that these rumours have been manufactured to discredit the Prime Minister, and publishes a leading article saying so, necessarily repeating the rumours as it does so. Is this defamatory? The matter is unclear. The *Statesman* had a strong case, though they had certainly not done themselves a favour by their front-page reference to 'MAJOR'S "MISTRESS"'. The settlement gave Major only £1,001, though costs and compensation to their distributors drove the *Statesman's* total bill up to around £250,000.

Meanwhile, the courts have been sending out mixed messages as to whether someone who repeats a rumour may defend themselves on the ground that there was in fact such a rumour.

> *Aspro Travel Ltd v Owners Abroad Group plc* (1995) OAG, a package holiday business, approached various hoteliers and travel agents, suggesting that their rival Aspro might soon go bankrupt, and offering to take over Aspro's bookings. Aspro sued. OAG's pleadings argued that they had only spoken the truth, as there were in fact such rumours. Held: this defence could not be struck out as wrong in principle.

> *Stern v Piper* (1996) A columnist in the *Mail on Sunday* quoted allegations made against Stern, made in the pleadings of a legal action against Stern. Stern sued the newspaper. Held: the newspaper could not establish a defence of truth merely by proving that the allegations had in fact been made in judicial proceedings.

Values of particular class

8.15 P may argue that while D's statement does not defame P in the eyes of the general public, it nonetheless does so in the eyes of some smaller class. Stated baldly, this argument must be rejected. P must appeal to the values of the whole community – even if P and D both belong to some narrower grouping. Yet as we have seen (**8.6**), P is perfectly entitled to rely on matters of *fact* known only to a narrow class, and the line is often hard to draw.

> *Byrne v Deane* (1937) A private club had been running an illegal gaming machine, which the police confiscated. A satirical poem was

then prominently posted at the club, suggesting that Byrne had tipped the police off ('But he who gave the game away / May he byrnn in hell and rue the day'). Byrne sued the Deans, who ran the club. Held (by a majority): no reasonable person would regard it as wrong to inform the police of illegal conduct, and so the poem was not defamatory.

Yet Greer LJ was able, on those facts, to find liability. Byrne had in effect been accused of disloyalty to other members of the club, which is a sin in the eyes of the whole community. 'Whether that was justified or not is quite another matter' ([1937] 1 KB 830). Some care is needed, therefore, in applying this rule.

Akram v Shah (1981)   Akram published a pamphlet attacking Shah's standing as a Muslim, saying that he had insulted Islam. Both were devout Muslims. Held: a reasonable person, of any religion or none, would think poorly of someone who insulted the faith of others. Accordingly, Akram's statement was defamatory by the standards of the community in general.

Group defamation

8.16   There is no rule that P must be mentioned by name. The same statement may defame tens or even hundreds of people, if reasonable hearers would take it to reflect on each one of them. Yet the courts are reluctant to treat insults against a class as defaming each member of it. If D broadcasts racial abuse against black people, P may not sue merely because he or she is black. But the same remarks might be defamatory if, in context, they single P out in some way.

Defaming corporate bodies

8.17   A statement that a corporate body is poorly or dishonestly run may reflect on its officers and be actionable by them.

Orme v Associated Newspapers Group (1981)   A newspaper alleged misconduct against the Unification Church (the Moonies). Orme, the Church's leader in England, was not mentioned in the piece, but said that it could be taken to mean that he knew about, and condoned, the conduct complained of. Held: the statement was capable of being read that way by reasonable readers.

Can the corporation itself sue? A corporation is a person in law (unlike unincorporated bodies such as trade unions), and it does not require excessive mental gymnastics to think of a corporation having a reputation of its own. So companies may sue in defamation. But it has been recently held that local authorities cannot, whatever the injury to their 'governing reputation', as this would have a chilling effect on political debate (*Derbyshire County Council v Times Newspapers* (1993)). For the same reason, a political party cannot sue in defamation either (*Goldsmith v Bhoyrul* (1997)). After the hugely unsatisfactory 'McLibel' case (*McDonald's Corpn v Steel and Morris* (1997)), there is certainly a school of thought that business corporations do not need the right to sue in defamation at all, and that this right is too much open to abuse.

Remedies

Financial loss: 'special damages'

8.18   A successful plaintiff in defamation is entitled to all financial loss that can be shown to flow from D's statement ('special damages'), subject to defences of remoteness (**10.28**) and mitigation (**10.36**).

Injury to feelings and other unquantifiable losses: 'general damages'

8.19   Defamation is sometimes 'actionable *per se*' – that is, actionable in itself, without proof of special damage. P is then entitled to a sum for injured feelings, lost dignity, and unprovable but likely financial loss ('general damages'). It is important for this purpose to distinguish between libel, which is always actionable *per se*, and slander, which is only actionable *per se* in certain situations.

Libel or slander?

8.20   Defamation by word-of-mouth is slander; written defamation is libel. The test is sometimes said to be that slander is temporary, libel permanent; but this is misleading. Defamatory newspaper stories are libel, even if every reader throws the newspaper away immediately on finishing it; speech is slander, even if it is remembered for many years after.

The following have been settled by case law to be libel, not slander: pictures, sculptures, films (with or without sound track), and reading out defamatory letters. Statute establishes that stage plays, TV and radio broadcasts for general reception are libel (Theatres Act 1968, s 4; Defamation Act 1952, ss 1, 16(3)). The status of e-mail is unclear, but it too is probably libel; several cases involving e-mail have already been decided, but seemingly without broaching the libel/slander issue. Sound recordings (records, tapes, CDs) are of uncertain status, as are radio broadcasts intended to be private.

When is slander actionable per se?

8.21 The following slanders are actionable *per se*: *(i)* that P committed an offence punishable with imprisonment; *(ii)* that P has a serious communicable disease; *(iii)* that P, being female, is guilty of 'unchastity or adultery' (Slander of Women Act 1891); *(iv)* that P does his or her job, or the duties of some official post, ineptly or dishonestly. As to the last exception, if D's statement plainly reflects on P's work, it does not matter whether D mentioned the job or post; so a charge of dishonesty is almost bound to fall within it. There is some dispute over the types of post covered by the exception; it seems that if the post is a purely honorary one, then a charge of dishonesty is actionable *per se*, but a charge of ineptitude is not.

General damages: relevant factors

8.22 Where general damages are available, the following are relevant: the number and identity of those who heard the statement; the reactions of particular hearers; evidence relevant to financial loss, such as a falling-off of custom after the statement; and whether, when and how D offered an apology. Where D's statement plainly contributed to a knock against P's reputation, it is irrelevant that others besides D made the statement, unless P obtains compensation from them as well; though it is open to D to join those others as co-defendants (**9.26**).

Large awards by juries have given rise to criticism. By statute, the Court of Appeal may reduce excessive awards (Courts and Legal Services Act 1990, s 8). The court has made it clear that this supervision will be strict, both as to compensatory damages and exemplary damages (*Rantzen v Mirror Group Newspapers* (1993); *John v MGN Ltd* (1996)). The largest award ever in a defamation case, £1.5m, was challenged before the European Court of Human Rights, which ruled that the jury's award

216

violated D's right to free expression under Article 10 of the Human Rights Convention (*Tolstoy Miloslavsky v United Kingdom* (1995)). However, while the issue was not before the court, there are hints in its judgment that the control of juries outlined in the *Rantzen* case ensures that the modern law is not subject to the same criticism.

Evidence as to P's *general reputation* at the time the statement was made is highly relevant, and may be introduced by D or P. There are three qualifications to this:

- The evidence must have some connection with the subject matter of the statement; evidence that P is reputed to be stingy is irrelevant if the charge was dishonesty.

- The question is as to P's *reputation*, and so evidence as to P's actual (but hitherto secret) conduct, or as to P's real character, is out of order. Specific instances of good or bad behaviour by P are admissible only as evidence of reputation.

- D will not be allowed to confuse the question of reputation with the separate question of whether the statement was true. So rumours and suspicions that P did indeed do what D said are only admissible, if at all, as part of a case that the statement was true.

The circumstances leading up to the statement are relevant, and D may produce evidence of provocation by P. D's behaviour and motivation are also relevant. In this respect defamation differs for other torts: if I smash your stereo, I pay the same amount whether I did it deliberately or merely clumsily. In defamation, compensation is for injured feelings, and so a defendant who is openly hostile inflicts a greater injury than a defendant who plainly made a slip of the tongue (**10.16**). D's manner, and any additional insults thrown in, may inflate the damages. Nonetheless, the goal is to *compensate* P, D's hostility is said to 'aggravate' the defamation, but the object of these 'aggravated damages' is still to compensate.

Occasionally, P can go beyond compensation and demand a sum explicitly meant to punish D. The rules governing these 'exemplary' or 'punitive' damages, which apply to all torts, are described below (**10.10**).

217

Q. Are awards in defamation truly compensatory, or truly punitive?

A. The line is always blurred – ordering D to compensate P necessarily deters others who might end up in D's position. In practice there are usually elements of both.

Injunctions

8.23 It is sometimes possible for P to obtain an injunction (a court order backed up with the threat of imprisonment) against repetition of the defamation (**10.2**). Pre-trial injunctions ('interlocutory injunctions') are very rare indeed, and are never granted where D intends to prove the statement true, unless this is clearly a hopeless endeavour (**10.4**). Post-trial injunctions ('final injunctions') are less tightly restricted in theory, but are nonetheless uncommon.

Absolute defences

Introduction

8.24 Some defences to an action for defamation are 'absolute', that is, they may be asserted whatever D's state of mind. Others are only 'qualified', that is, they are unavailable if D had an improper motive for making the statement. There are a number of specific defences, though they are rather narrow.

Unintentional defamation: offer of amends

8.25 The Defamation Act 1996, ss 2-4, introduce what amounts to a defence that D did not mean to defame P. D can, however, only take advantage of this defence if D is prepared to apologise and to offer a sum in compensation. (These new provisions replace the much more limited defence of 'unintentional defamation' under Defamation Act 1952, s 4, which is now abolished.)

To invoke this defence, D must make an 'offer of amends' to P, which must include a reasonable offer to make a correction and apology, to publish it, and to pay compensation and P's legal expenses.

- If P accepts the offer of amends, P cannot sue in defamation, but the terms of the offer of amends are enforceable by legal process (s 2).

- If P is minded to accept an offer but does not think the terms offered by D are reasonable, s 3 establishes procedures for resolving this dispute.

- If P refuses the offer and sues, then P can only succeed by proving that D knew or had reason to know that the statement referred to P, *and* that it was false, *and* that it defamed P. However, if D relies on the offer of amends as a defence, D cannot also rely on other defences, such as that the statement was true or privileged (s 4).

There is also provision for 'qualified offers', where D's offer of amends relates only to certain specified possible meanings of the defamatory utterance, but not others.

Consent

8.26 If P assented to the publication, no action lies. So if D privately insults P and P challenges D to repeat this before witnesses, no action lies if D does so. A borderline case is where the only person who saw the defamatory publication was acting on P's instructions to seek it out, for the very purpose of commencing a libel action. One old case holds that there is no defence of consent (*Duke of Brunswick v Harmer* (1849)); it is an open question whether this is correct today.

Truth ('justification')

8.27 As a rule, D has a complete defence on proving that the statement was true. The jargon is that D 'justifies' the statement, and this defence is often referred to as 'justification'. The onus of proof is on D, who must carefully set out what it is intended to prove. What D must justify is not the literal statement, but the defamatory allegation, which (as we have seen, **8.3**), may be very different. This has counter-intuitive results, illustrating the startling effects of the rule that D is judged as reasonable listeners understand the statement, and not as D reasonably meant it. If D says (correctly) that P was sacked for dishonesty, reasonable hearers might perhaps take this as meaning that P actually *was* dishonest – and if they would, D must prove *actual* dishonesty. (The same logic applies if D reports that P has been convicted of a criminal offence, though by Civil Evidence Act 1968, s 13, the conviction is conclusive evidence for this purpose that P is indeed guilty.)

Where D's statement was very specific, the court is concerned not so much with its literal truth as with the accuracy of its 'sting' – the reason why it is defamatory. So if D says that P raped a specified woman on a particular occasion, D may justify by proving that P raped *another* woman on that occasion, or possibly even on another occasion, so long as the court thinks that the 'sting' amounts to the same thing.

Alexander v North Eastern Rly Co (1865)   D said that P had been convicted of a criminal offence and had served three weeks in prison in consequence. In fact, P had served two weeks. Held: the jury was entitled to regard the statement as justified, if it thought this appropriate.

At common law, if D made several specific charges, each one has to be justified if the defence is to succeed. But by Defamation Act 1952, s 5, D may prove some only, and then invite the court to say that the 'sting' of the statement was true. So if D accuses P of five distinct thefts and then proves three, D may argue that P's reputation has not been unfairly or materially damaged by the other two charges, even if they are completely untrue. That case aside, however, a partial justification is no defence, though the evidence to support it may sometimes reduce the damages.

Where the allegation is vaguer, such as that P is generally dishonest, the range of admissible evidence is wider. Accordingly, in a case where D alleges a specific act of misconduct, but can only prove another and different type of misconduct, P will usually try to treat the issue as narrowly as possible, and D will seek to broaden it.

Bookbinder v Tebbit (1989)   Tebbit accused a local council of spending £50,000 on over-stamping its notepaper with 'Support Nuclear Free Zones', which he considered a 'damn fool idea'. Bookbinder, leader of the council, sued over that single allegation, even though this was only one of several charges on the same theme. Could Tebbit justify by proving that the council had wasted money in *other* ways, or did he have to prove over-stamping? Held: Tebbit could not broaden the issue, but had to justify what he actually said.

These cases are difficult, however, and a number of factors are relevant; for example, in *Bookbinder* Ralph Gibson LJ suggested the result would have been different if instances of actual dishonesty had been alleged.

220

When is truth not a defence?

8.28 In a sense, truth is fundamental: if true statements damage P's reputation, then it was plainly an inflated one, which the law should not protect. Nonetheless, two qualifications must be made, where the law pursues different policies from those usually at work in defamation cases.

First, criminal convictions committed very far in the past may become 'spent' under the Rehabilitation of Offenders Act 1974. This has a number of consequences, designed to discourage subsequent revelation of the offence. One consequence is that if D's statement reminds others of P's conviction, and P sues in defamation, D's plea of justification will be defeated if P proves that D was motivated by spite or other improper considerations (s 8). How quickly convictions become 'spent' depends on a variety of factors; no offence can ever become 'spent' if the penalty was prison for two and a half years or more.

Second, revelation of the truth very often allows P to sue in breach of confidence. Indeed, it is possible to combine this action with action for defamation. Lurid re-tellings of the life of pop stars have led to writs alleging breach of confidence insofar as the stories are true and defamation insofar as they are false (eg *Woodward v Hutchins* (1977)). For plaintiffs who wish no further intrusion into their private lives, however, the law's solution here may be worse than the problem they hoped to solve by invoking it.

Absolute privilege

8.29 Certain governmental duties attract absolute immunity from suit for participants. This privilege applies even if malice is proved. The potential for abuse is obvious; the traditional view, which is not without its critics, is that absolute freedom from suit is a necessary shield for those involved.

First, *proceedings in Parliament* are privileged (Bill of Rights 1688, article 9), as are the reports of the various Parliamentary Commissioners (Ombudsmen) (eg Parliamentary Commissioner Act 1967, s 10(5)). MPs accused of accepting bribes in return for asking parliamentary questions recently found that they could not sue their accusers, as the courts could not investigate the charges without infringing this privilege. They persuaded their colleagues to enact Defamation Act 1996, s 13, which enables individual MPs to waive the privilege insofar as it concerns them. The 'sudden and humiliating' collapse of the resulting libel action may possibly discourage other MPs from invoking the section in future (see Williams '"Only Flattery is safe": Political speech and the Defamation Act 1996' (1997) 60 MLR 388).

Second, *courts* attract immunity for those involved in their activities. Statements in court are privileged, as are statements at any stage of the legal process, and even conversations between solicitor and client when the client seeks advice. There is no clear definition of a 'court' for this purpose, and the same body may be a court or not, depending on the activity it is engaged in. Magistrates' courts are (for this purpose) courts when trying a criminal charge, but not when deciding whether to renew a liquor licence; the European Commission is not usually a 'court', but may be sufficiently like one when engaged in enforcing competition law (*Hasselblad (GB) v Orbinson* (1985)). The privilege does not apply to an outburst which is irrelevant to the court's proceedings — even an outburst by the judge.

Third, communications between *high-ranking officials* are privileged: it seems that a defamatory statement by a Secretary of State to a Parliamentary Under-Secretary is not actionable (*Chatterton v Secretary of State for India* (1895)). It is unclear whether or when, if at all, this principle protects officers at lower grades.

Qualified defences

'Malice'

8.30 Rather more extensive defences are available if P cannot establish 'malice'. The precise meaning of 'malice' in this context is much disputed. The core idea is that D's statement was motivated by improper considerations – usually, but not necessarily, hatred of P. Strictly speaking, the definition of 'malice' varies with each defence to which it is relevant: each privilege is granted for a particular reason of public policy, and 'malice' means attempting to use the defence for some other reason. But little clarity would be achieved by separating the defences in this way.

The burden of proof as to malice is usually on P, and it is heavy. Evidence to establish malice may include: lack of candour or reasonableness; violent or exaggerated language; previous or subsequent words or behaviour showing hostility against P; or lack of reasonable grounds for believing the statement. None of these is conclusive. P only establishes malice if it is more likely than not that D had an improper motive.

Fair comment

8.31 *Introduction* D has a defence if the defamatory remark was *(i)* a comment on facts, *(ii)* within the bounds of fairness, and *(iii)* on a matter of public interest. P may defeat this plea by showing malice, which usually means showing either that D did not believe the statement, or was hopelessly and unreasonably prejudiced against P. A purely factual statement is not comment; it is either true or false.

8.32 *'Comment' must be comment on facts* D must explain to the court the facts on which the comment was based, and (if they are disputed) prove them. For example, if D says that P is cruel to his children, this cannot be fair comment if P has no children, no matter what other evidence of cruelty D can produce. D is often driven to the so-called 'rolled-up plea', that insofar as the statement was factual it was true, and insofar as it was comment it was fair. It is sufficient if the 'sting' of the facts is true – details may be wrong, so long as the substance is accurate (Defamation Act 1952, s 6). It seems that D may comment on statements protected by privilege; so D may comment on a report published by Parliament without proving that what it says is true – so long as D does not personally assert that it is true.

Given this requirement of a factual basis, it follows that D cannot comment on P generally under the guise of commenting on more limited issues. For example, D cannot use a review of P's book to comment on P's sexual habits, unless they are relevant to the book; and the reviewer must distinguish carefully between saying that a *book* is absurd or immoral and saying that *its author* is absurd or immoral. It is often a very difficult question whether (say) the reviewer of a play, who says that one of the participants is a bad actress, is making a comment on the performance or a factual statement about the actress; see eg *Cornwell v Myskow* (1987) **(8.3)**.

It does not matter whether the relevant facts are common knowledge or not, so long as D can prove them at trial. D need not have set out in the statement the facts on which the comment was based, if they would have been clear to those who read it.

Kemsley v Foot (1952)   Foot wrote a newspaper article violently critical of another newspaper, heading it 'Lower than Kemsley'. He did not otherwise mention the Kemsley Press, or the newspapers it controlled. Lord Kemsley sued. Foot argued that the headline was fair comment on Kemsley's management of his newspapers. Held: Foot was entitled to put this defence to a jury. The headline sufficiently indicated the facts on which the comment was based.

Surprisingly, in a later case the House of Lords ruled that, where the statement was a comment on an earlier statement, the court had to determine whether the statement was fact or comment *without* looking at the earlier statement (*Telnikoff v Matusevitch* (1991)). The reason given was that not everyone who read the statement would have read the earlier statement too. But this seems to demand a great deal from critics; as Lord Ackner, dissenting, put it, it should be enough for D 'to have identified the publication on which he is commenting, without having [to] set out such extracts therefrom as would enable his readers to judge for themselves ...' ([1991] 4 All ER 830).

8.33 *Comment must be fair*   This is simply one aspect of absence of malice: comment is indefensible when it goes beyond the limits of fairness, even if D personally believes it fair. Nonetheless, these limits are broad, and even sustained ridicule or prejudiced, obstinate and eccentric remarks may be 'fair' for this purpose.

8.34 *Comment must be on a matter of public interest*   The defence of fair comment only applies to matters of public interest or importance. Any aspect of national or local government, or of the legal system, satisfies this requirement. Whether the running of a private concern is 'of public interest' depends largely on its size and significance.

South Hetton Coal Co v North-Eastern News Association (1894)   A newspaper criticised the sanitary conditions of cottages rented by a colliery, which was landlord to most of the village's 2,000 inhabitants, as well as the major local employer. Held: the conduct of such a firm could be a matter of public interest.

A plaintiff who has deliberately attracted the public's attention is a fit subject for public comment. So any published work, any newspaper article, any literary or artistic performance open to the public, and any advertisement is open to public criticism – as indeed is the criticism itself.

Qualified privilege at common law

8.35 *Introduction*   There is a defence if D was under a duty to make the statement, or had a legitimate interest in so doing, *and* the person to whom he made it had a duty to listen, or a legitimate interest in so doing. For example, if D honestly reports to the police that her property has been stolen and that she thinks P is responsible, the privilege is made out: D has a legitimate interest in reporting the theft of her goods, and the police have a duty to listen. D therefore has a defence, even if P is not the thief. However, D must confine herself to her legitimate interest, and must not be motivated by malice. So she has no defence if she did not believe P to be the thief, or she lied in any respect, or had some improper motive; and the privilege does not protect her in relation to irrelevant remarks, such as that P is a pervert.

8.36 *Duty or interest*   Duty and interest are matters for the court. They must rise in fact: a mistaken belief by D, however reasonable, that there is a duty will not do. However, the duty or interest need not be a legal one. Relatives may be candid with each other about matters affecting one another's welfare, such as whether P is a suitable husband for one of them; and employer and employee may be candid with one another when doing their jobs.

> *Bryanston Finance v de Vries* (1975)   Defamatory letters were dictated, typed up and sent. When was the tort committed? Held: each communication to a distinct individual amounted to a publication, but all the work before the letters were sent was covered by qualified privilege.

Defence of assets or reputation against P's attacks is a good ground of privilege, though criteria of appropriateness and relevance must be borne in mind. So if P attacks D's character and D tries to rebut the charges, this may attract privilege; D may even call P a liar, provided P's veracity is relevant. But the privilege cannot excuse a general attack on P's character; it is no defence to slander that it avenges earlier slander. One old case (*Coward v Wellington* (1836)) holds that if A makes an accusation against D and D retorts by (wrongly) blaming P instead, this is privileged; but it is doubtful whether the law extends so far today.

It is often legitimate to invoke the help of others in pursuing one's legitimate interests, even if this inevitably leads to the spread of defamatory material.

> *Beach v Freeson* (1972)   Freeson, an MP, wrote letters to the Law Society and the Lord Chancellor, repeating defamatory complaints made by a constituent. Held: Freeson had acted properly and was protected by qualified privilege.

8.37   *Connection between duty and interest*   It is not enough that D has a legitimate interest in the subject matter of the statement, if the communication does not serve it.

> *Watt v Longsdon* (1930)   A company director received a letter accusing the managing director of alcoholism, dishonesty and adultery. He passed on copies to the chairman and to the managing director's wife. Held: the communication to the chairman was privileged, but the communication to the wife was not; she had a legitimate interest in receiving the letter, but the director had none in sending it.

8.38   *Duty or interest in listening*   D must take care not to broadcast the statement too broadly; the recipients must each have a duty or a legitimate interest in the communication.

> *Chapman v Lord Ellesmere* (1932)   The Jockey Club 'warned off' Chapman from Kempton Park racecourse, in such a way as to suggest he was responsible for the doping of a racehorse. Held: publishing this by notices in the *Racing Calendar* was legitimate, as the racing public had an interest in the matter; but the general public had none, and so the publication in *The Times*, and to news agencies, was not privileged.

Where there is an official channel for complaints of the type D is making against P, use of that channel is usually privileged, and broader communication is usually not. It appears that the preparation of a petition to Parliament attracts a qualified privilege, if indeed it is not within the absolute parliamentary privilege. But the courts have, to date, set their face against any general defence of 'fair information on a matter of public interest'. The public is not regarded, for this purpose, as having a right to know.

> *Blackshaw v Lord* (1984) A newspaper named the plaintiff, a civil servant, as responsible for the loss of massive amounts of public money. Held: the public had no legitimate interest in hearing this accusation.

It might be different, the court added, if the case was one involving immediate public danger, such as cases of suspected terrorism, or contaminated food. A similarly narrow line has been take by statute: reversing earlier case law, Defamation Act 1952, s 10 disallows the defence of privilege in election campaigns where it relies purely on the voters' right to know about issues relevant to the election.

Privilege by statute

8.39 *Court reporting* Reports of legal proceedings attract privilege, which is now stated in the Defamation Act 1996, s 14. The privilege is stated to be 'absolute', though it applies only if the report is 'fair and accurate', and contemporaneous with the proceedings themselves. It is unclear how far a reporter can go with a fragmentary report, but plainly the privilege is lost if the reporter repeats allegations made against P but fails to mention evidence or argument on the other side. It is legitimate for a newspaper to report on a long case day by day, despite the inevitably partial picture given; but an account given after the trial is over is not allowed this leeway. It is unclear whether a paper which relates allegations against P on day one of a trial loses privilege retroactively if it fails to publish P's rebuttal on a later day.

It is unclear to what extent foreign legal proceedings attract the same protection. Pearson J in *Webb v Times Publishing Co* (1960) held that they would do so if the matter was one in which the public had a legitimate interest, and the motive for the publication was to give the public information; but mere gossip would not be protected.

8.40 *Parliament* Qualified privilege applies to fair and accurate extracts and abstracts of papers published by Parliamentary authority

(Parliamentary Papers Act 1840, s 3). Unusually, it is for D to establish absence of malice, not the converse.

8.41 *Other official bodies* Defamation Act 1996, Schedule, Part I extends privilege to reports of public proceedings of foreign legislatures, international organisations and courts, as well as copies or extracts from official registers and notices published by courts. In cases covered by Part II, there is a right to publish fair and accurate reports, but it is lost if D, being the original publisher of the statement, refuses to publish a reasonable letter from P by way of explanation or contradiction of what D published. This protects the proceedings of associations to promote science, religion or learning; trade associations; associations to promote particular sports; public meetings on matters of public concern; general meetings of public companies; local authorities, magistrates and committees of persons holding enquiries authorised by statute.

Other torts protecting reputation

Miscellaneous

8.42 Various torts in addition to the tort of defamation may be used to protect P's reputation. No detailed treatment will be given here.

- The tort of *malicious falsehood* is largely aimed at protecting business interests and requires proof of express malice. However, there is no reason why it cannot be used to protect personal reputation, and legal aid can be granted for it, even where it is inevitable that any sum won by P will be clawed back to the Legal Aid Fund to meet the cost of the action (*Joyce v Sengupta* (1993)). It appears that P cannot succeed without proving financial loss of some kind (*Allason v Campbell* (1996)).

- The tort of *negligence* may be invoked, even when an action for defamation on the same facts would be barred by privilege (*Spring v Guardian Insurance* (1994) (**5.42**)).

- False accusations of crime leading to an attempt to prosecute P may be remedied through the tort of *malicious prosecution*. The tort has strict requirements; in particular, it must be shown that D had an improper motive, and the criminal proceedings must ultimately have ended in P's favour. It used to be thought that the tort could only be used where D was actually the prosecutor. It now appears that it can also be invoked against those who make false complaints with a view to instigating a prosecution, at least where 'in substance' they are themselves prosecutors (*Martin v Watson* (1995)).

Reform of the law

Reforms: small or large?

8.43   The present state of the law pleases no-one. But there is no agreement on whether the problems are relatively minor, or whether they go to the roots of the present system. As to minor reforms, several have recently been made, such as widening the defence of unintentional defamation (**8.25**), and narrowing the liability of secondary publishers (**8.9**). Other reforms, such as allowing the Court of Appeal to reduce excessive awards by juries, have been enacted in recent years (**8.22**). And the Court of Appeal in *Rantzen v Mirror Group Newspapers* (1993) and elsewhere has proclaimed that in doubtful cases the courts will lean in favour of freedom of speech. But is this fine-tuning sufficient? To clarify the issue, compare the tort of defamation with the other torts you have already learned about. What are the main differences? Several stand out:

*   large awards for injury to feelings;

*   juries;

*   a complex and bewildering mix of strict and fault liability;

*   high legal costs.

These are all bound together. Juries are thought necessary because of the highly subjective level of the damages. Complex rules are necessary to control juries. And the high costs of administering these rules is only sustainable because the possibility of massive damages prompts parties to pay their lawyers well; no-one would contemplate incurring a legal bill in five or six figures unless the sum at stake was large as well.

229

Compensation or deterrence?

8.44 Let me briefly play devil's advocate, to show what the present system is good at. Compare a typical personal injury action with a typical defamation action. The personal injury plaintiff will recover a sum largely designed to reflect actual financial loss, though of course it may include a sum for pain and suffering as well. The defamation plaintiff will typically have suffered no financial loss at all, yet will receive an award despite this – possibly quite a large one. Plainly, then, the principal object of defamation is not to give compensation, at least not in any ordinary sense. If the current law is justifiable, it can only be on the ground that it deters potential defamers.

Seen this way, many of the more common criticisms of the law miss the point. Relatively few defamation cases reach court; if the sole deterrent against defamation is to be the court's reaction in those cases, that reaction must be correspondingly gruesome. It is unsurprising that awards in defamation cases are so much more generous than awards in personal injury cases. There is a battery of legal regulation on health and safety, with the result that the law on personal injury *damages* need not deter, but may simply ask how much each injured plaintiff deserves to get. The higher levels of damages in defamation therefore reflect the law's very different purposes. From this point of view, the unpredictability of jury decisions is an advantage rather than a disadvantage: few cases result in a really huge award, and the deterrent effect would be entirely lost if potential defendants *knew in advance* which of them were running a serious risk.

Options for change

8.45 None of this is to support the current law, but only to focus the issue. In most defamation cases, there is no injury to compensate for other than an injury to feelings; this requires some legal response, but it does not have to take the form of a large money award, or indeed any money award at all. The main issue is therefore over deterrence and what form it should take. There appear to be three main possibilities: *(1)* no fundamental change; *(2)* a considerable reduction in awards for general damages; *(3)* complete abolition of general damages and introduction of other forms of deterrence.

230

8.46 *Option 1: No fundamental change* The case for no fundamental change is not completely unarguable. Many blemishes in the law have been removed, especially by giving the Court of Appeal the power to correct excessive jury awards. And it is unfair to judge the current system by what happens in individual cases alone; it is the deterrent effect that has most impact on people in general. Yet by placing all the weight on deterrence before the event, the current law sadly neglects the position of those who have been defamed despite it. None but the very rich can afford to sue. Effectively, the more powerful an individual is, the more congenial he finds the law of defamation, which is arguably the wrong way round for a democratic legal system to be.

8.47 *Option 2: Substantial reduction in general damages* A defendant who stands to lose a very large sum is slow to settle, and inclined to spend correspondingly large sums on a defence. A sharp reduction in the range of possible awards could be a major part of a package to speed up procedure, widen the range of those who can afford to sue, and encourage rapid settlement. A range of measures to implement this change would probably involve the following and more: abolition of juries; explicit limits on awards for non-pecuniary loss; encouragement of arbitration; and simplification of the law, such as on the test for a defamatory utterance. Modern controls on jury awards and the pro-cedural changes in the Defamation Act 1996, go a long way down this road, accelerating the procedure and providing avenues to terminate more cases before they reach full trial. The overall effect should be to speed up and cheapen litigation, and to shift more of the disputes from the full trial to the preliminary (interlocutory) stages.

Changes of this sort would amount to a re-orientation of defamation law towards a relatively poorer clientele. The emphasis on deterrence would remain the same, as would the mechanism of deterrence: namely the impact of damages awards on the editorial budget of potential defamers. The law would be more predictable, less exacting, but also broader in its grasp. If the reform were done well, it would widen access to potential plaintiffs considerably. Many who can now do no more than write impotent letters of protest to their defamers would be able to start county court proceedings. Newspapers would still have to employ libel readers, and many would have to take on litigation managers as well. No-one can predict whether the impact on editorial budgets will ultimately be greater or smaller; it will simply be different, a drip-drip-drip of relatively small claims, rather than occasional thunderbolts threatening D's very existence. Which is preferable?

8.48   *Option 3: Abolition of awards of general damages*   Other means of deterring defamation exist, and are arguably preferable to a money award. Common suggestions are a right of reply; a right to an apology in some cases; a specific criminal offence of 'character assassination'; or a statutory Press Council to implement any or all of these changes and to enforce journalistic standards generally. All of these would rely ultimately on the criminal law for their efficacy, though the reforms would have failed in their purpose if recourse to the criminal law became an everyday event. (There is already an offence of 'criminal libel', though it is rarely prosecuted for.) This would bring the element of deterrence out into the open, and precisely for that reason would attract a great deal of hostility. The civil liberties implications of an extension of the criminal law would need careful thought, though they might on balance be thought preferable to the threat of bankruptcy implicitly wielded by the current law.

Conclusion

8.49   Reform of the law of defamation is much discussed, but little ever comes out of the discussion; when it does, it is usually fairly timid. Public discussion of the issues is dominated by the press itself, which often seems reluctant to accept even that the grossest cases of defamation should attract any legal response, and which regards any suggestion that it should apologise for misstatements as a breach of its human rights. Only an unusually powerful and self-assured government could push through any reform unacceptable to a large part of the press. As a result, the law is labyrinthine in its complexity, entirely unaffordable to most potential plaintiffs, and thoroughly capricious in its treatment of those who can afford it.

Further Reading

Relevant sections of tort reference books may be supplemented with:

Raymond Snoddy, *The good, the bad and the totally unacceptable: The Hard News about the British Press* (Faber & Faber, 1993).

Self-test questions

1.   Arnold insults Bernard before a large audience, but speaking in Swahili. Does this defame Bernard (**8.6**)? If yes, what factors are relevant in assessing damages (**8.22**)?

2.   Connie writes an editorial in the *Tiddlywinks Times*, claiming that only those brought up in the UK are likely to show sufficient commitment when part of the national team. Dot, a member of the UK Tiddlywinks Team, who spent most of her early years abroad, sues in libel. Will she succeed (**8.5**)? Does it matter whether her recent performance has been good or bad (**8.32**)?

3.   Edna states publicly that Frank is a thief who has often stolen money from his mother. When Frank sues, Edna cannot prove theft from Frank's mother, but has evidence of theft from Frank's former girlfriend. Can Edna use this evidence to support a plea of justification (**8.27**)? If not, can Edna introduce it to reduce Frank's damages (**8.22**)?

4.   Gordon chairs an official enquiry into whether Harry, Imogen and Jeremy broke the law by authorising arms exports to warring states. In what circumstances will Gordon's report be privileged (**8.41**)?

CHAPTER NINE

Parties, and liability for others

SUMMARY

D may be liable for torts committed by others, in a number of situations. These situations include:

- **where D's employee commits a tort;**

- **where D was under a duty to prevent others committing torts; and**

- **where D's duty was non-delegable.**

Where a number of different people are responsible for the same damage, then as between themselves the law may make a rough apportionment of blame. But each one of them is liable to P for the whole of the loss. The principles in this chapter vastly expand the range of tort liability, by making many beyond the obvious perpetrator of the tort liable to compensate P.

Introduction

9.1   Tort texts are often written as if the person who must pay damages for a tort is the person primarily responsible for it. This is not usually so, however. Most tort liability in practice is liability for the actions of others. There are a number of legal doctrines under which the tort of D1 may render D2 liable to compensate the victim. The discussion here commences with the most frequently encountered one, the doctrine of *vicarious liability*.

While much of the detail here may seem obscure, it is nonetheless one of the most practically important chapters in the book. It explains how to connect a tort committed by D1 to other defendants, who may in an ordinary sense be blameless but on whom the law nonetheless fastens liability. Very often the main perpetrator of a tort is penniless or un-traceable: establishing liability in tort might seem academic. Nonetheless P may be able to obtain an effective remedy against a solvent defendant.

Vicarious liability

Definition

9.2 Where D1 is engaged in carrying out his or her obligations under a contract of employment, and while doing so commits a tort against P, then P may sue not only D1 but also D1's employer. It is irrelevant whether the employer was at fault. However, the doctrine applies only where D1 is *employed* by D2; the mere existence of a contract between D1 and D2 is not sufficient, if it is not a contract of employment. It is also not enough merely that D1 committed the tort in work time: it must be committed 'in the course of the employment', a more demanding requirement.

Who is an employee?

9.3 *Background* The law in this area has its origins well before this century. Employer and employee (or, more probably, 'master and servant') may well have lived in the same house, and the employer's right to give orders to employees was seen as somewhat analogous to a husband's right to give orders to his wife and to his children. In that context, the distinction between an employee and an 'independent contractor' was simple enough. The employee's time belonged to the employer, who could therefore give precise orders as to how it was to be used, whereas an independent contractor was hired to achieve particular results without detailed direction. Therefore, if there was some doubt whether a particular contractor was an employee or not, it was usually sufficient simply to ask whether he was subject to the 'control' of an employer, or whether he was an 'independent' contractor. Did the employer control how the work was done, or only what results were to be achieved?

Ideas of social deference and hierarchy have changed somewhat in the intervening period. Moreover, in all but the simplest jobs the scope for detailed control of employees is rather limited. In *Mersey Docks and Harbour Board v Coggins and Griffith (Liverpool) Ltd* (1947) a crane driver had been temporarily seconded by his employers to a firm of stevedores. The issue was whether the stevedores had become his employers. Attempting to apply the 'control' test, counsel asked him which firm's orders he accepted. He replied 'I take no orders from anybody' ([1947] AC 4). Many employees would, no doubt, give this answer today; and the very idea that skilled employees such as surgeons or airline pilots might need detailed control would be a deeply worrying one.

Technically there may still be a right of control, but this is theory, not fact. Who is an employee, and who an independent contractor, remains an important question today, for many reasons: different taxation, health and safety, and employment protection regimes apply, quite apart from the issue of vicarious liability with which this chapter is concerned. But 'control' cannot be the sole or main criterion today.

9.4 *The modern law*   The courts have many times had to consider who is an employee and who is not. This has not always been for the purposes of the law relating to vicarious liability. Employment status is relevant for a wide variety of purposes, and the orthodox view is that the question of status has a unique answer in each case. X cannot be an 'employee' for one purpose but an 'independent contractor' for others: either X is an employee or X is not. Relevant factors are said to be the following.

• *How have the parties themselves described the legal relationship between them?*   The way in which the parties have themselves described the relationship is obviously a factor. Some care is needed, however. The question is not which category the parties would like their relation-ship to fall into, but rather, which category best describes the rights and duties they have created. So if the relationship is clearly an employment relationship, the court will not be put off by the parties' own description of it as a 'labour-only sub-contract' (*Ferguson v John Dawson & Partners (Contractors) Ltd* (1976)). The courts are also aware of the risk that the parties may deliberately have misdescribed their relationship, to secure tax advantages to which they are not entitled.

• *Is the work done an integral part of the business, or incidental to it?*   This test was enunciated by Denning LJ in *Stevenson Jordan & Harrison v Macdonald & Evans* [1952] 1 TLR 101, 111. It is also called the 'organisation' test: is the worker employed as part of a wider organisation, or a self-employed independent contractor?

- *Who has the risk of loss and the chance of profit?* This is the 'entre-preneur' test: is the worker simply selling a set proportion of his time at a fixed rate, or can the worker be said to be in business on his own account? So an architect who retains control over his own number of hours is likely to be an independent contractor, even when other factors point to his being an employee (*WHPT Housing Association Ltd v Secretary of State for Social Services* (1981)). The test is sometimes called the 'economic reality' test, though this label begs rather a lot of questions. Moreover, the distinction can be a fine one.

Ready Mixed Concrete (South East) Ltd v Minister for Pensions and National Insurance (1968)   A driver was hired by a concrete company on terms that he would always have his lorry ready to carry concrete. He was obliged to maintain the vehicle at his own expense, to have it painted in the company's colours, and he had to wear the company's uniform. He was, however, permitted to hire a substitute driver. Held: the driver was not an employee.

- *Is it sensible to speak of 'control' and, if so, who has control?*   It has been clear since *Cassidy v Ministry of Health* (1951) that control is not conclusive: there can be employment relationships where the employee is so skilled that control is obviously impossible. Control was still emphasised as a factor as late as the decision in *Market Investigations Ltd v Minister for Social Security* (1969), though that is probably the last major case to give it a prominent role. Nonetheless it can still be a significant factor. When a part-time drama teacher claimed he was an employee of the school which hired him, the lack of control the school exercised was an important consideration. The school did not prescribe a syllabus, and left him free to teach as he wished. He was held to be an independent contractor (*Argent v Minster for Social Security* (1968)).

- *'Borrowed' employees*   Control may also be relevant where there is no doubt that the worker is an employee, but it is unclear *whose* employee (eg *Mersey Docks and Harbour Board v Coggins and Griffith (Liverpool) Ltd* (1947)). But it is only one factor. *Thompson v T Lohan (Plant Hire) Ltd* (1987) appears to hold that clauses transferring control from the main employer to a temporary 'borrower' may sometimes be invalid under Unfair Contract Terms Act 1977, s 2. (Probably, however, the point of the case was that the main employer retained control and so the clause was a sham.) There is a strong presumption that the 'lending' company is still the employer, though there are occasional examples of the presumption being rebutted (eg *Gibb v United Steel Companies Ltd* (1957)).

No one test is conclusive. On one side, there is the stereotypical employee, who sells a certain number of hours of time, in which the employee does precisely what he or she is told. On the other side, there is the stereotypical independent contractor, who performs a set task, by his own methods and using his own equipment. Which stereotype is closest to the actual facts is largely a matter of impression. Modern judges still make some use of the tests outlined above, but they emphasise their limitations, and that the role of a higher court is only to correct manifest errors of law, rather than to substitute its own verdict on such an open-ended enquiry (eg *Hall (Inspector of Taxes) v Lorimer* (1994)).

'The course of employment'

9.5 *Introduction* The employer is liable for the employee's tort only if the employee was genuinely trying to do the job at the time. Or, as it is usually put, the tort must be committed 'in the course of the employment'. There is therefore no vicarious liability if the tort occurred while the employee was (in the antique but well-established phrase) 'on a frolic of his own'. Of course, no employer would want the employees to act so badly as to land the employer in court as defendant in a tort action. Nonetheless, the courts insist that there is a difference between doing a job badly and ceasing to do it all, and that is the distinction they apply. The basic idea is clear enough, despite numerous borderline cases, which are probably impossible to reconcile with one another.

9.6 *Honest attempt to do the job* So long as the employee was trying to do the job at the time when he or she committed the tort, the courts are likely to hold that the employee was still 'in the course of the employment'. Occasionally, the employee's actions are so outrageously dangerous that the court rebels and holds that the employee was outside the course of the employment. But such cases are rare.

Bayley v Manchester Sheffield & Lincolnshire Rly Co (1873)   A railway porter pulled a passenger off the train he was on, in the mistaken belief that he was on the wrong one. Held: his employers were vicariously liable for battery.

Keppel Bus Co Ltd v Sa'ad bin Ahmad (1974)   A ticket collector on a bus attacked Ahmad, a passenger, smashing his glasses. The ticket collector was under the mistaken impression that this was necessary to prevent a fight breaking out on the bus. Held: the bus company was not vicariously liable.

Allen v London and South Western Rly Co (1870)   A railway booking clerk accidentally gave Allen a foreign coin in his change. An argument followed; Allen then tried to take a replacement from the till, whereupon the clerk had him arrested. Held: prosecuting defaulting customers was not the clerk's job, and therefore his employers were not vicariously liable for assault and false imprisonment.

9.7   *Incidental activity while doing the job*   In general, activities which the employee carries out while engaged in work are treated as part and parcel of the work itself. The courts do not usually have any truck with the idea that the employee might be working with the right hand but 'on a frolic of his own' with the left.

Century Insurance Co Ltd v Northern Ireland Road Transport Board (1942)   Davison, a petrol lorry driver, was engaged in pumping petrol from his lorry into the tank of a filling station, while smoking a cigarette. Held: his employers were vicariously liable for his causing the ensuing explosion.

Photo Production Ltd v Securicor Transport Ltd (1978)   Musgrave, a security guard, was patrolling premises late at night, guarding them against fire. It was bitterly cold and he lit himself a small fire to warm his hands. The fire unexpectedly grew and engulfed the entire premises. Held: the employers were vicariously liable for Musgrave's misconduct.

The last is a very strong case, for the guard's carelessness was sufficiently gross to sustain a prosecution against him for arson! Perhaps the case would have been different if he had been a *deliberate* arsonist, though the distinction is rather a fine one. There can certainly be cases where the employee's tortious activities can sensibly be separated from work activities being carried on at the same time. For example, there was no vicarious liability for an office cleaner who used her time in the office as an opportunity to make long-distance calls from the office phones (*Heasmans v Clarity Cleaning Co Ltd* (1987)). Nor was the Post Office liable for an employee who scrawled racial abuse on a letter bound for his neighbours (*Irving and Irving v Post Office* (1987)). While in general an employee who does the job slowly is still doing the job, nonetheless there are exceptions.

General Engineering Services Ltd v Kingston and S Andrew Corpn (1989)   Firemen were in dispute with their employers and operated a go-slow policy. When summoned to a fire, they took about 17 minutes to reach it, rather than the 3 minutes it would ordinarily have taken them. Held: their employers were not vicariously liable for the failure to put out the fire.

9.8   *Forbidden method of doing the job*   Employees do not step outside the scope of their employment merely because they employ methods which their employers have forbidden. Difficult questions of degree arise when employer and employee have different conceptions of what the job entails.

Limpus v London General Omnibus Co (1862)   Omnibus drivers were specifically forbidden to race one another, even with the object of beating a rival omnibus to a group of potential customers. Held: a driver who caused an accident while racing under such conditions was still in the course of his employment.

One special case is where an employed driver is forbidden to carry extra passengers, but nonetheless does so. If the driver later injures the forbidden passenger through negligence, is the employer vicariously liable? Plainly on any ordinary interpretation the driver will usually have been driving in the course of the employment (as would quickly be made plain if the driver injured some other road user), but the courts have tended to ask the slightly different question whether *the offer of a lift* was made in the course of the employment.

Twine v Bean's Express Ltd (1946)   A driver picked up a hitch-hiker, despite express instructions not to do so. The driver's poor driving

241

injured the hitch-hiker. Held: the hitch-hiker was a trespasser in the employer's vehicle and so could not sue the employer.

Rose v Plenty (1976) Contrary to his employer's orders, Plenty, a milk delivery driver paid Rose, a 13-year-old boy, to help him with his deliveries. Rose was injured by Plenty's poor driving. Held: the employers were vicariously liable, despite their direct orders.

It is sometimes suggested that the case would be different if the passenger *knew* of the prohibition, but this suggestion has yet to be confirmed in an actual decision.

9.9 *Honest attempt to do someone else's job* The employee is likely to be held to have stepped outside the course of the employment if he or she attempts to perform some task which is *someone else's* job. This is especially so if the task is one requiring special skills which the defaulting employee does not have. So the employer will not be liable where a bus conductor attempts to move a bus (*Iqbal v London Transport Executive* (1973)). But where the employee was hired to move obstacles in a warehouse, and so ought to have pushed a lorry out of the way, the employee remained in the course of the employment when he attempted to drive it out of the way instead (*Kay v ITW* (1968)). It would be hopeless to attempt to reconcile all of the many and varied cases on this issue, though it is safe to say that an honest attempt to serve the employer's interests is likely to attract vicarious liability.

Poland v John Parr and Sons (1927) An employee thought he saw a boy stealing sugar from his employer's cart; he attacked the boy, who fell and injured his leg. The employee was off-duty, and in any event was not employed to guard the sugar. Held: the employer was nonetheless vicariously liable for the employee's act.

9.10 *The driver who frolics* Where employed drivers, for their own private purposes, deviate from the route they ought to be following, it is a matter of degree whether they can be held to be 'on a frolic of their own'.

Harvey v RG O'Dell Ltd (1958) A builder took a five-mile detour to buy tools and to get lunch. Held: he was still in the course of his employment.

Hilton v Thomas Burton (Rhodes) Ltd (1961) A lorry driver who had had lunch took a detour to get tea. Held: he was no longer in the course of his employment.

After some initial controversy, it now seems to be settled that driving to or from work is not usually travel 'in the course of the employment', unless the terms of the employment make it so.

Smith v Stages (1989) Employees were sent out to do emergency work about 200 miles away from their usual place of work. They used their own cars and were paid for their time while driving. Held: they were still in the course of their employment while driving.

9.11 *The criminal employee* The basic position seems to be that crimes committed as part of a *bona fide* attempt to do the job, or otherwise to serve the employer's interests, are within the scope of the employment. Crimes committed for the employee's own personal benefit or amusement will not be. So deceit by an employee will be in the course of employment if intended to benefit the employers, even though the employers did not know about it and would have forbidden it had they known (*Barwick v English Joint Stock Bank* (1867)). There are a few cases which extend liability beyond this, but it will be argued below that these cases are better explained on other grounds (see **9.18**, **9.19**).

The employer's indemnity

9.12 The employer is liable to an action by the victim of the employee's tort. However, the employee is still liable for the tort; moreover, the employer can, in theory at least, recoup any money paid out to P from the employee personally.

Lister v Romford Ice & Cold Storage Co Ltd (1957) The Listers, father and son, were employees of Romford Ice. The son negligently injured his father, who sued Romford Ice. Romford Ice paid the father, then sought to recoup the damages from the son. Held: the son's negligence was a breach of his employment contract, for which his employer could recover damages.

This claim can only be made if the employers were themselves blameless, their liability being vicarious only. In practice, such a liability would be very heavy for the individual employee to bear. Most employers find that the financial benefits of trying to pass on such liabilities to the employees concerned are far outweighed by the price they would have to pay in poor industrial relations. Their liability insurers might not always take the same attitude, but after the *Lister* decision the major liability insurers entered into a 'gentlemens' agreement' not to take advantage of it. Poorly-unionised employees are not always in a position to resist such claims if made. It is currently a particular grievance of trainee and newly-qualified solicitors that their employers regularly invoke the *Lister* decision in cases where the employee's negligence is not covered by the Solicitors' Indemnity Fund.

Joint and several liability

Introduction

9.13 There is a variety of legal doctrines under which one person may be liable for the tort of another. The doctrine of vicarious liability is the most important, but others are encountered on a regular basis. It was at one time necessary to distinguish carefully between 'joint liability', where there is a single legal wrong for which both D1 and D2 are responsible (as where they jointly planned and executed some dangerous building operation which injures P) and 'several liability', where the wrongs were entirely independent but led to the same damage (as where D1 and D2 both drive negligently and injure P when they crash into one another). The distinction is very hard to apply in practice, and in modern conditions it can usually be forgotten. It may, however, occasionally be relevant on the finer points of law. For example, there appears to be a rule that if P releases a claim against one tortfeasor, this operates to release claims against other *joint* tortfeasors, but not *several* tortfeasors responsible for the same injury (*Jameson v Central Electricity Generating Board* (1997)).

Joint tortfeasors: vicarious liability

9.14 This is the most common form of joint liability: employer and employee are jointly liable for the same tort. By statute, in certain cases, there is a liability analogous to vicarious liability, even though there is no employment relationship:

- Trade unions are liable for the acts of their officials, unless they repudiate them under a specific statutory procedure (Employment Act 1990, s 6).

- Chief Police officers are liable for the actions of constables under their direction and control (Police Act 1964, s 48). The liability attaches to 'torts committed ... in the performance or purported performance of their functions in like manner as a master is liable in respect of torts committed by his servants in the course of their employment'. It is unclear whether this envisages a broader inter-pretation of a constable's 'course of employment' than is usual for other jobs, though in practice a wide definition is assumed.

Joint liability

9.15 *Joint enterprises* Where D1 and D2 together carry out some risky enterprise, it appears that they may both liable for torts committed by one of them.

> *Brooke v Bool* (1928) His tenant being away, the landlord looked round the rented premises to try to locate the source of a gas leak. His lodger, who had come to help, lit a match to help them see where they were going. Held: the landlord was jointly liable with the lodger for the resulting explosion.

The principle is clear enough, though its application to the facts of *Brooke* is not. The full facts were not entirely clear. Joint enterprise is mentioned as one ground of liability; but so is agency; also the point that the landlord had legal and factual control of the situation – though it was unclear whether he realised what the lodger was up to in time to forbid him to do it.

9.16 *Extra-hazardous acts* Where D1 carries out an especially dangerous task on D2's instructions, it appears that D2 may be liable for D1's negligence, even though D1 is an independent contractor rather than an employee.

> *Honeywill & Stein Ltd v Larkin Bros Ltd* (1934) Contractors, hired to install sound equipment in a theatre, themselves hired photographers to take pictures of their work. At that date, flash photography was a risky operation, generating momentary quantities of very intense heat.

245

The photographers negligently set fire to some curtains and there was extensive fire damage as a result. Held: the contractors were liable to the theatre-owners for the photographers' negligence.

The doctrine is rarely invoked, and it is not entirely clear which activities are sufficiently 'extra-hazardous' for this purpose. However, it has been held to apply where the owner of a house hired a contractor to re-roof it, resulting in penetration of damp in his neighbour's property (*Alcock v Wraith* (1991)); though the court in that case relied also on the notion of a 'non-delegable duty' (**9.22**).

9.17 *Delegated duties* Analogously with vicarious liability, where DI commits a tort in the course of carrying out a task delegated to DI by D2, then D2 may be liable for DI's tort. Nearly all of the modern cases involve DI's temporary use of D2's car. The rule is that if DI drives it negligently while doing a job for D2, then D2 will be liable.

> *Ormrod v Crosville Motor Services Ltd* (1953) Murphie lent his car to the Ormrods, so that they could visit friends in Normandy and then drive on to meet him in Monte Carlo, where they would have a holiday together. Held: Murphie was liable for the Ormrods' poor driving en route.

However, attempts to extend the doctrine further were prevented by the House of Lords in 1972.

> *Morgans v Launchbury* (1973) A husband borrowed his wife's car to go to work and then to go on to the pub. He had promised her that if unfit to drive, he would not attempt to do so, but would get a friend to drive for him. Held: the wife was not liable for the friend's poor driving.

In particular, the Lords refused to hold that the wife's desire for her husband's safe return made the friend's driving a task 'delegated' to him; nor would they give any legal status to the notion of a 'family car'. The line the Lords drew in *Morgans* has forced later courts to make some rather fine distinctions, such as deciding precisely when a wife who has gone shopping has done so as a 'delegated task' and when she has gone on her own account (*Norwood v Navan* (1981)). As Ormrod LJ commented in the case, it is absurd that liability might turn on whether the driver's shopping basket contained a preponderance of goods for herself or for her family, if indeed the distinction can sensibly be drawn at all ([1981] RTR 461). It is not clear that this doctrine serves any useful purpose at all, given the existence of the MIB scheme for the protection of those injured by uninsured drivers (**4.13**).

9.18 *Agency* The legal concept of agency is primarily relevant to contracts. If A authorises B to make particular contracts on A's behalf, then if B negotiates contracts as A's agent, the contracts which result will bind A. No doubt it is possible for A to authorise B to commit torts, and no doubt A is liable in that case also, but these cases seem to be rare. However, the concept of agency may sometimes extend to cover acts which were never authorised. So if A invests B with a general authority to make contracts, A may sometimes be liable even if B makes contracts which A would certainly never have permitted had A known the facts. It is in this connection that a confusion with tort is likely.

> *Lloyd v Grace, Smith & Co* (1912)   Lloyd entered the offices of Grace Smith, solicitors, to ask for investment advice on property she owned. Sandles, the managing clerk, advised her to sell, and she signed documents which she supposed were necessary to effect a sale. In fact, they were conveyances of the properties into Sandles' own name, and he quickly disappeared with the proceeds. Held: the solicitors were liable for Sandles' fraud.

The result makes sense in terms of agency. The solicitors had left Sandles in charge of the office, and Lloyd's assumption that he was an authorised member of the firm was not an unreasonable one. As a decision on vicarious liability, it seems a little odd, as Sandles was plainly acting for his own benefit, rather than 'in the course of his employment'. Moreover, if the liability is based on vicarious liability then presumably it would have been quite different if Sandles had been an independent contractor rather than an employee – a surprising result from Lloyd's point of view. Nonetheless, even though the opinions in the case squarely base the liability on agency, it is often said to be an example of vicarious liability. The orthodox view at present is that it can properly be regarded as an example of vicarious liability, but that in this particular context the test for the existence of liability is not 'the course of employment' test. Rather, the test is whether the fraud was within the scope of the agent's authorisation (*Armagas Ltd v Mundogas SA, The Ocean Frost* [1986] AC 717, 783, Lord Keith).

Several liability

9.19 *Bailment and custody of goods* Where one person agrees to look after goods for another, various obligations arise under the law of bailment. In particular, there may be a duty to guard the property against theft or damage by third parties. Accordingly, where D1 steals or damages P's goods which are bailed to D2, then D2 may be liable for the loss. Where D1 happens to be D2's employee, this looks rather like vicarious liability.

> *Morris v CW Martin & Son Ltd* (1966) Morris left a fur stole with Beder for cleaning. Beder sub-contracted the work, with Morris's consent, to Martin. The job was given to Morrissey, an employee of Martin; but Morrissey committed theft. Held: Martin was responsible for its employee's theft.

Whether this is regarded as a special rule relating to bailment, or as an example of vicarious liability, may be a mere matter of taste. However, there are certainly some situations in which it would matter, and there are various questions which need to be asked:

- *Was the thief in the course of his employment?* Even after making full allowance for the rule that an unauthorised mode of performing the employment contract may still be 'in the course of the employment' (**9.8**), it seems strange to regard stealing an article as merely an unauthorised mode of looking after it. Equally, where P's car has been left with a garage for repairs, the garage is liable to its owner when one of their employees drives it around for his own purposes (*Aitchison v Page Motors Ltd* (1935)). If this is vicarious liability, then, it is of a special type, subject to its own special rules.

- *Does the nature of the bailment matter?* If this is truly vicarious liability for the tort of the employee, it is hard to see how the nature of the bailment matters. However, *dicta* in *Morris* suggest that it does. In particular, where D2 is looking after goods gratuitously, there would be no liability for theft by D1 even if D1 is employed by D2 (see [1966] 1 QB 725, Lord Denning MR, 737, Diplock LJ; though compare *Port Swettenham Authority v TW WU & Co (M) Sdn Bhd* (1978)).

- *Does it matter whether the thief is an employee or not?* If the basis of the liability is vicarious liability, then obviously it is vital; if the liability

248

is in bailment, it is not obvious why it should. The point appears to be open.

So there appears to be a special rule that where P entrusts property to D2 under contract and D2 entrusts it to its employee D1, then D2 is liable to P for D1's misbehaviour with it. This appears to be so even on facts where D1 was obviously on a 'frolic of his own'. There are conflicting *dicta* on whether D2 would be liable if the thief was an employee, but *not* the particular employee to whom the goods had been entrusted.

9.20 *The economic torts*   Under the so-called 'economic' torts, P may sue D for loss deliberately inflicted on P by 'unlawful' means (**6.27**). The precise meaning of 'unlawful' varies from context to context. Where the means adopted are 'unlawful' in the sense that they constitute a tort for which P could have sued someone else, then in effect the 'economic torts' are a means for imposing several liability for the tort.

9.21 *D2 negligently allows D1 to commit a tort*   At various points, we have already encountered situations where D2 is liable to P for failing to prevent D1 injuring P (**1.27**). There are always arguments against holding one person responsible for what another person did; when D2 is held responsible, it is usually on the ground that D2 was personally responsible for the circumstances in which D1 acted. The fact that D1's behaviour is tortious is usually completely incidental in such cases, though of course the possibility of suing D1 as well or instead of D2 is likely to have been very important to P when considering legal strategy.

- D1 may be incapable of looking after himself or herself, and it is precisely for that reason that D2 owes a duty to others, perhaps because D1 is a child (eg *Carmarthenshire County Council v Lewis* (1955) (**1.26**).

- D2 may be under a particular duty to prevent D1 harming others. Perhaps D1 is a prisoner (eg *Home Office v Dorset Yacht Co Ltd* (1970) (**1.29**)), or an irresponsible employee of D2's (eg *Hudson v Ridge Manufacturing Co* (1957) – where D1's behaviour would almost certainly have been held to be outside the scope of his employment).

- It may be D2's fault that D1 is so dangerous in the first place. Perhaps D2 carelessly hired D1 and put him in a position of trust, when a little care would quickly have established that D1 was a professional burglar (*Nahhas v Pier House (Cheyne Walk) Management Ltd* (1984)).

- D2 has ordered D1 to carry out activities which would be dangerous however carefully they were done. Perhaps D2 hires D1 for building operations inherently likely to create a nuisance (*Matania v National Provincial Bank Ltd* (1936) (**7.24**).

Non-delegable duties

9.22 Sometimes D2 is held liable because, while D2 reasonably delegated a legal duty to D1, nonetheless D1 failed to perform it. The reason for this is sometimes said to be that certain duties are 'non-delegable'. But this way of putting it leads to confusion. *All* duties are non-delegable, at least in the sense that they must be performed, and if they have not, it is no answer to say that someone else was (ineffectively) asked to do so. The practical answer to any question of 'delegation' is usually to ask precisely what the duty on D2 is.

An example may help. Take the (fictitious) Nutrition of Children (Civil Liability) Act 1998, which provides that if any children have not had their tea by 5pm on a given day, their parents have committed a tort against them. Plainly, there is a sense in which this statute imposes a duty on parents. Is this duty 'delegable'? There are really two questions:

- If the parents arrange for a neighbour to provide tea on a particular day, and the neighbour does so, are the parents in breach? The answer is that they are not, unless there is something in the legislation to say that the parents must provide tea *in person*. So if the statute allows others to perform the duty on the parents' behalf, it is in one sense a 'delegable' duty.

- If the parents arrange for a neighbour to provide tea, but the neighbour *fails* to do so, what is the position? Almost certainly, the next question is whether the Act imposes an absolute duty to provide tea, or only provides that the parents must act reasonably. In the first case the parents will certainly be in breach, in the second they are only in breach if their attempt at delegation was unreasonable. Only if the parents satisfy their duty by doing their best is the duty 'delegable', in this sense.

In general, tort lawyers are more interested in results than in who achieves them. And so it is the later distinction that is usually most important. Where tort law imposes an absolute duty to produce a certain result, then D is in breach unless it is in fact achieved; 'delegation' only avoids liability if it was successful. Where the duty is only to act reasonably, then D may usually escape liability by showing that the task was delegated to someone else, so long as that delegation was reasonable. However, there is a limited class of exceptional cases, where even a reasonable delegation will be held not to be a satisfaction of D's duty.

9.23 *Absolute liabilities* Where D2 is under an absolute duty not to harm P in a particular way, then it is no defence that D2 took a (reasonable but ultimately misguided) decision to tell D1 to deal with the problem. This rule applies to the strict liability for breach of statutory duty and to the strict common law liabilities such as nuisance liability for activities adjacent to the highway, *Rylands v Fletcher* liability, interference with a private right of support (*Alcock v Wraith* (1991)), and liability for fire. In these cases, then, the duty is 'non-delegable'. Two very minor qualifications need to be made to this proposition:

• Where an employer is in breach of statutory duty and an employee is injured as a result, it appears to be a defence that the task of complying with the statute was reasonably delegated *to the very employee who was injured*. However, this defence will only be success-ful where the entire responsibility both for the breach and for the injuries themselves can be put on the employee's shoulders.

    Ross v Associated Portland Cement Manufacturers Ltd (1964) Ross was killed when he fell off a ladder while repairing wire netting in Associated's factory. His widow sued for breach of statutory duty, saying that Associated had failed to 'provide a safe means of access to the place of work'. Associated replied that the decision to work at the top of a ladder was Ross's own. Held: the work had been beyond Ross's experience, and so responsibility for the breach of statute could not be attributed to him alone, though his widow's damages should be reduced by one-third for contributory negligence.

- Where D2 has a strict common law duty to render a harmful situation safe and hires D1 to put it right, it appears that D2 will only be liable for a failure by D1 to do the task properly. D2 is not liable for 'collateral' acts by D1, not intimately connected with the removal of the danger. The reason seems to be that D2 is not vicariously liable for the acts of D1, but is responsible only for the source of danger. So D2 should not be held responsible for misbehaviour by D1 which is unrelated to the task. There is no particular logic to this – the point that the danger cannot be removed except by workers who may misbehave is surely part of the reason why it is dangerous – but the exception seems well established.

Padbury v Holliday & Greenwood Ltd (1912)   Contractors were hired to put metal window frames into a building. One worker left a tool on a window-sill, not in the ordinary course of doing the work. The wind blew the tool off and it hit P. Held: the tool had not been left as part of doing the work, and therefore the owner of the building was not responsible for the worker's collateral negligence.

9.24 *Negligence duties*   In general, where D's only obligation is to act reasonably, D may sometimes satisfy the duty simply by instructing someone else to deal with the problem. This will of course only be so if this was a reasonable thing to do and there is nothing else that the reasonable person would do in that situation. If D's decision to delegate is reasonable, then it cannot retrospectively become unreasonable simply because the delegate turns out to be incapable of handling the situation. So, for example, if it is reasonable for the occupier of premises to turn over some repair job to an independent contractor, the occupier need not do it personally. He or she need only act reasonably in selecting the contractor and in checking the work after it was done (Occupiers' Liability Act 1957, s 2(4)(b)) (**4.24**).

There are a limited number of exceptions to this basic rule. It has been held that if D advertises that he runs a fleet of mini-cabs, then he owes customers a non-delegable duty to ensure that the cabs he refers them to are reasonably safe. If customers are injured, he cannot plead (contrary to the impression he deliberately fostered) that the cab drivers are all independent contractors over whom he had no control (*Rogers v Night Riders* (1983)). A broader exception relates to employment. Employers owe their employees a duty to make their work environment reasonably safe (**4.32**). This duty has been held to be non-delegable, in the sense that the employees are entitled to this safe environment wherever they have been sent, even if it is to some site over which the employer has no control. So if an employer temporarily 'lends' an employee to another firm, then the employer remains liable for any deficiencies in the employee's work environment (*McDermid v Nash Dredging and Reclamation Co Ltd* (1987) (**4.35**)). Further, by statute, if an employee is injured by defective equipment, the employer is liable if the defect was due to negligence, whether the employer's or anyone else's (Employers' Liability (Defective Equipment) Act 1969) (**4.38**).

9.25 *Conclusion* It is important to remember that there is no magic in delegation. If the duty is simply that D order someone else to perform a certain task and D does so, then D has discharged the duty the law imposes. But that is because D has *performed* the duty, not because D has 'delegated' it to someone else. In other cases, the duty may demand more. So the duty a hospital owes its patients is not merely its vicarious liability for the sum total of the duties the members of its staff owe. There is in addition a primary duty to care for the patient (*Cassidy v Ministry of Health* [1951] 2 KB 343, 363, Denning LJ). Again, if harm comes to a child at school, the school is vicariously liable for any misbehaviour by the teachers and other staff, but it also owes a primary duty to care for the children. To show that there was no one teacher whose job it was to guard against the particular harm that befell P may make the school's legal position worse, as it could be precisely what P is complaining of (*Carmarthenshire County Council v Lewis* (1955)).

Contribution

Introduction

9.26 If D1 is liable to P in respect of a certain loss, P is entitled to sue D1 for the whole of it. It is no defence that others too are liable. Nor is this a ground for reducing damages. P need not justify the decision to sue D1 rather than anyone else. However, it is open to D1 to seek a 'contribution order' against any other person whom P could have sued in respect of the same damage. If D1 can show that D2 was also liable to P, the court will divide ('apportion') the liability between D1 and D2. It is vital to appreciate that contribution does not usually affect P's position: P may sue D1 or any possible defendant, and it is no concern of P's whether that defendant manages to recoup a share of the damages from someone else. Indeed, P may sue *more* than one defendant, though P will not be able to recover legal costs in the second or subsequent actions unless the court agrees it was reasonable to bring them (Civil Liability (Contribution) Act 1978, s 4). In any event, P cannot recover more than 100% of the loss suffered. It is sometimes suggested that D1 should be entitled to a defence of 'proportionate fault', reducing D1's liability on the ground that D1 was not the only one at fault – *even if* P has no prospect of recovering damages from anyone else. But this is not currently part of the law (11.25).

Liability

9.27 D1 has the right to claim compensation 'from any other person liable in respect of the same damage' (Civil Liability (Contribution) Act 1978, s 1(1)). It is irrelevant whether D2 was liable as joint tortfeasor, several tortfeasor, or indeed was liable for breach of contract or breach of trust. The main situation the Act envisages is where D1 and D2 could each be sued by P, but it also allows for other cases:

- D1 does not lose the right to seek contribution merely because D2 has settled with P (s 1(2)). Indeed, where D2 has settled with P, D1 is entitled to claim compensation without having to prove that P could have sued D2 – even if D2 never admitted liability to P (s 1(4)).

- If D2 was at one point liable to P, then D2 remains liable to contribute even if P can no longer sue D2 (s 1(3)). There is an exception to this in a very limited class of case – 'expiry of a period of limitation or prescription which extinguished the right on which the claim against' D2 'was based'. This applies, however, only to the tort of conversion, the usual effect of limitation being merely to bar the claim, not the right on which it was based.

However, if P has already sued D2 and failed on the merits of the claim, it appears that D1 cannot claim contribution (s 1(5)).

Apportionment

9.28 The court may make any apportionment of liability 'such as may be found by the court to be just and reasonable having regard to the extent of that person's responsibility for the damage in question' (s 2(1)). This may be a high as 100% or as low as 0% in appropriate cases (s 2(2)). However, the maximum the court may order D2 to pay is the amount which P could have recovered from D2, even if D1's own liability is greater (s 2(3)). Express agreement between D1 and D2 as to apportionment, whether before or after P's injury, in effect excludes the court's discretion (s 7(3)).

Relation to contributory negligence

9.29 What is the correct approach when P also bears some of the responsibility for the accident? In *Fitzgerald v Lane* (1988) P attempted to cross a pelican crossing without waiting for the lights to change in his favour. D1's car ran into him and he was thrown onto the other side of the road, where D2's car ran into him. The trial judge found that D1 and D2 had both been driving too fast; he considered that all three of the parties involved had acted equally badly. Accordingly, he argued that each should bear one-third of the loss. In the result, therefore, P could recover one-third of the loss from each of D1 and D2, bearing one-third himself.

The House of Lords held that this was the wrong approach, as it telescoped two quite different questions. The first question was as to the proper size of P's claim. If P sues either defendant, then a court should say that that P and D were equally to blame, and therefore P is entitled to recover 50% of the loss he suffered. The result is the same whichever defendant P sues, and in neither case is the existence of another possible defendant relevant. Second, how is this claim to be apportioned between defendants? Since they are equally to blame, each must pay half. Accordingly, P must bear 50% of the loss himself, and D1 and D2 must each pay 25%.

Assessment

Introduction

9.30 Much of the material in this chapter may have seemed rather esoteric, or antiquarian, or simply marginal. Yet it is one of the more important chapters in the book. For it is only through the principles outlined here, and through the mechanism of insurance, that most tort plaintiffs are able to link the liability to a financially substantial defendant, and hence actually recover damages. Indeed, the whole edifice of tort liability, with its strong emphasis on concepts of personal fault, rests on distinctly collectivist foundations. Defendants are able to meet these awards because policy decisions were taken to force liability on those with deep pockets, rather than the more 'obvious' defendants.

Why is employment special?

9.31 The doctrine of vicarious liability makes much turn on whether or not the person whose fault the accident was is an employee of the defendant. Why should this be? The old idea that employees are 'under the control' of the employer, whereas independent contractors are not, is long discredited; in any event there is no suggestion that the liability should be any less where the employer was not in a position to prevent the accident. It is often suggested today that, whatever may be the orthodoxy, the courts do in fact ask themselves *why* it is necessary to determine, in any one case, whether a particular worker is an 'employee' or not, and adapt their answer to the policies relevant to that issue. Whether someone is an 'employee' or not does in reality, and arguably should, depend on why the question is being asked. But this approach, while probably correct, points an even sharper finger at the lack of principled reasoning behind vicarious liability. It is all very well to say that we should hold workers to be 'employees' when the proper policy basis to vicarious liability points in that direction: but when is that, precisely?

Tort as a just response to wrongdoing?

9.32 If we regard tort as society's response to wrongdoing, as a system for the ascription of responsibility, then it emerges as a (crude but workable) answer to the problem of how we make business enterprises liable. It says, in effect, that business enterprises are guilty of wrongdoing where one of their employees, attempting to do his job, is guilty of wrongdoing. This is obviously not perfect, but it is not easy to improve on, either. How else can we hold companies responsible, given that a company has 'no body to be kicked, and no soul to be damned'?

Tort as a system of deterrence?

9.33 Alternatively, we might regard vicarious liability as part of a system for deterring companies from wrongful behaviour. The threat that companies will be held responsible for the torts of their employees is supposed to terrify them into controlling the employees. It is possible that it has this effect to some extent; but it has to be said that there is very little evidence for it. A firm worried by this prospect is likely to insure against it, and while it is possible for an insurer to know enough about its client's business to recommend appropriate improvements to procedures and safeguards and hence to stop the problem at source, this seems to be relatively rare.

Tort as loss-distribution?

9.34 If we regard tort as a mechanism for spreading losses across society, we would see vicarious liability as merely one step in the chain linking the unfortunate victims of accidents to those who bankroll them, namely the general public. If particular industries or professions cause great harm to the population, then their extensive legal liability will ultimately be reflected in the prices they charge. By their individual decisions whether to buy the goods or services in question or to spend their money elsewhere, the individuals who constitute the market effectively decide whether society can afford it. This is not an implausible way of describing the modern system; but it suggests that the law is not only unduly complicated but also unduly narrow. Why should it matter whether the harm is done by employees or not? And why should it matter whether the harm was done 'in the course of employment'? Surely it should be enough if the employee's access to work facilities made it easier for him or her to do damage?

Conclusion

9.35 The various legal institutions described in this chapter extend liability considerably. Yet their basis and justification is rather obscure. Simultaneously, they cast into doubt the justification for many other areas as well, for they provide the mechanisms whereby doctrines seemingly aimed at imposing personal responsibility in fact impose it on those who bear no responsibility at all for the events in question.

Further Reading

Relevant sections of tort reference books may be supplemented with:

Kidner 'Vicarious liability: for whom should the "employer" be liable?' (1995) 15 LS 47.

Self-test questions

1.   Can an employee acting directly contrary to the employer's orders still be 'in the course of the employment' (**9.8**)? What about an employee who is acting solely for his own benefit (**9.11**, **9.18**, **9.19**)?

2.   What is the modern relevance of the 'control' test for vicarious liability (**9.4**)?

3.   Given that police officers are not employees, how do you account for the vicarious liability of their chief officers (**9.14**)?

4.   When can D defeat P's claim by pointing out that others are more at fault than P (**9.26**)?

5.   If P, D1 and D2 are all equally at fault for the accident in which P was injured, how are damages apportioned between them (**9.29**)?

CHAPTER TEN

Remedies

SUMMARY
The main remedy available to P is damages. Generally speaking these damages are calculated so as to provide a quite precise assessment of P's loss. After dealing with general principles of assessment, the chapter goes on to consider in detail methods of calculation of personal injury damages.

Introduction

10.1 There could in principle be many responses from the law to a tort committed by D against P. In practice, by far the most common is an award of compensatory damages. We will come to this possibility last (**10.18**). In a few cases, P may be able to exercise self-help (see **7.29**). P may sometimes be able to claim an injunction forbidding D to continue with tortious behaviour (**10.2**). Alternatively, P may seek an award of money not calculated on compensatory principles (**10.8**).

Injunctions

Definition and terminology

10.2 An *injunction* is a court order instructing D to behave in a particular way. Disobedience is a contempt of the court which issued the injunction: it is a criminal offence, and can be punished by imprisonment or a fine. Most injunctions are *prohibitory* injunctions, telling D to abstain from doing something or other, though some injunctions are *mandatory* injunctions telling D positively to do something or other.

The injunction is a discretionary remedy, but the principles on which the courts will decide its availability in any one case are relatively settled.

The principles on which injunctions are granted vary considerably with the point in time at which P claims the injunction. If no tort has yet been committed, but P has good reason to believe that it will be, P may claim a *quia timet* injunction to nip the tort in the bud. Where a tort has already been committed, P may start an action for damages and seek an *interlocutory* injunction, before trial. Alternatively, P may wait until trial and seek a *final* injunction.

Quia timet injunctions

10.3   Where no tort has yet been committed, the courts are reluctant to act without clear evidence that a tort is likely. It is not entirely clear how imminent a tort must be. Evidence that D's tree roots are likely to grow so as to infringe P's rights within three years has been held insufficient to justify an immediate court order to cut them back (*Lemos v Kennedy Leigh Development Co Ltd* (1961)). It has been said that the only rule is that no court will issue an injunction 'prematurely' (*Hooper v Rogers* (1975)). Certainly the court will consider possible alternative remedies, such as making a declaration of P's rights with liberty to apply for an injunction if circumstances later warrant it.

Interlocutory injunctions

10.4   Particular problems arise when P alleges that a tort has already been committed and seeks an injunction before the trial of the main action. Basic issues in dispute may not yet have been resolved. If an injunction is issued, it may turn out that P in fact did not have the right claimed and that D was perfectly entitled to act in the way the court forbade. So P will certainly not be awarded an injunction without making an undertaking to compensate D, should P's claim turn out to be misconceived. Further, while P is no longer put to proof that there was a *prima facie* case against D, nonetheless P must show that there is 'a serious issue' to be dealt with at trial. In deciding whether to grant an interlocutory injunction, the courts take into account various factors:

- If P's claim is right, will damages be enough to compensate P?

- If P's case is wrong, will P's undertaking adequately compensate D?

- Is the preservation of the *status quo* is a worthwhile objective?

These criteria were laid down in *American Cyanamid Co v Ethicon Ltd* (1975) as being of general application. However, it is clear that different approaches will be required in different kinds of case. In defamation cases, considerations of freedom of speech predominate. If D intends to prove at trial that the statement was true or was fair comment, a court will almost never restrain D before he or she has had a chance to do that (*Bestobell Paints Ltd v Bigg* (1975)). In labour law cases, by contrast, almost certainly the dispute will have been resolved long before the matter comes to a trial, and what the court says at the interlocutory stage will effectively decide the matter. Accordingly, a court will be strongly influenced by which side's case on the ultimate issues looks stronger at that stage (*NWL Ltd v Woods* (1979)). More generally, it has recently been doubted whether it is really necessary to ignore the apparent merits of P's and D's cases at the interlocutory stage, in the way *American Cyanamid* seems to suggest (*Series 5 Software v Clarke* (1996), Laddie J).

Final injunctions

10.5   *The inadequacy of damages*   The ordinary remedy for a tort is damages. P cannot claim an injunction unless P can show that damages alone would not be an adequate remedy. Where D is plainly doing serious and continuing damage to D's property, it is almost axiomatic that an injunction to stop the damage is a superior remedy to damages, and so an injunction is readily available (eg *Pride of Derby and Derbyshire Angling Association Ltd v British Celanese Ltd* (1953)). Differing views are expressed in cases concerning relatively slight property damage, often in the course of the same judgment. On the one hand, if the damage is truly trivial, it would be wrong to allow the heavy machinery of an injunction to be invoked. On the other, there is unease that a deliberate taking of P's property can in effect be condoned by the legal system, merely because P's loss is small in monetary terms. So if D deliberately extends his house in such a way as to diminish P's light, and then dares P to take legal action over it, some may doubt 'whether it is complete justice to allow the big man, with his big building and his enhanced rateable value and his improvement of the neighbourhood, to have his way, and to solace the little man for his darkened and stuffy little house by giving him a cheque that he does not ask for' (*Leeds Industrial Co-operative Society Ltd v Slack* [1924] AC 851, 872, Lord Sumner). Much depends on whether the court truly regards the claim as trivial. The monetary value of the loss is only one factor, and the fact that only a small sum would be awarded in an action for damages might be precisely why the court decides that an injunction is the most appropriate remedy.

10.6 *The court's discretion* It is sometimes said that the courts will only grant final mandatory injunctions if certain strict conditions are satisfied: that there is a strong probability of future harm to P, that D has acted 'wantonly or unreasonably', and that it is possible to state precisely what D is being required to do (*Redland Bricks Ltd v Morris* (1970)). Other factors may be taken into account in deciding whether to grant an injunction, including some factors which would be irrelevant if the action were for damages:

- *The degree of difficulty to which the injunction would subject D.*

- *P's behaviour* Misconduct by P, such as by leading D on or misleading D, may lead to the refusal of an injunction.

- *Public interest?* Some cases assert that the public interest can be a factor in deciding whether to grant an injunction, particularly where the activity P seeks to restrain benefits many besides D (eg *Miller v Jackson* (1977) (**7.16**)). Other judges have criticised this, however, as giving insufficient weight to P's rights in the matter (eg *Kennaway v Thompson* (1981)).

Substitution of a damages award

10.7 The courts have power to substitute an award of damages for an injunction (Supreme Court Act 1981, s 50). This is a curious provision, the origins of which go back to the days before 1875, when injunctions and damages had to be claimed in different courts. Judges sometimes assume that it applies in any case where a court could in theory have granted an injunction, whether or not it would have been wise to do so (eg *Hooper v Rogers* [1975] Ch 43, 48, Russell LJ). In cases of deliberate invasion of property rights, the orthodox position seems to be that if P has established a right to an injunction, the court will not substitute an order under s 50 unless damages would adequately compensate P, and it would be oppressive to D to issue an injunction (*Shelfer v City of London Electric Lighting Co* (1895)).

Types of damages

Introduction

10.8 Damages are usually compensatory. That is, they represent the value of something to which P was entitled, and of which D deprived P. While an award of damages always punishes D at some level, however they may be calculated, nonetheless the point of asserting that damages are compensatory is that they are measured by what P has lost, rather than as a measure of how wicked D has been. Where P's rights have been violated, but the court is unable to award any sum as compensation, the court may give *nominal* damages (currently £10); and where P brought the action simply to establish that the right exists, this remedy may be quite adequate for P's purposes. In defamation cases, it is open to the court to award *contemptuous* damages of 1p, to indicate that P was indeed defamed but that P should nonetheless never have brought the action. In such a case, P will probably find that the court is reluctant to award any legal costs against D.

General damages and special damages

10.9 A contrast is often made between *general damages* and *special damages*. These expressions are used in various different senses, though the underlying contrast is always the same: 'special damages' represent specific items of which P can give details, whereas 'general damages' represent some loss for which P is entitled to compensation without giving details. So, for example, some torts are said to be actionable 'without proof of special damage': action lies in assault (**2.1**) or defamation (**8.1**) without establishing any damage as such. Negligence, by contrast, is not actionable even in theory unless loss to P is proved. However, when discussing damages in negligence, it is common to distinguish between 'special' damages that can be itemised before trial (eg clothing torn in the accident) and 'general' damages which cannot (eg future wages, or damages for P's pain and suffering). It is not necessary for P to prove 'special damage' in *this* sense as a pre-condition of bringing the action.

The different uses of the 'general'/'special' distinction are slightly baffling at first. The root meaning is always the same and the distinction is about the duties of the lawyers involved in fighting the case. 'Special' damage is damage which P's lawyer must itemise and prove, 'general' damage is damage which P's lawyer is entitled to assert without proving, or at least without proving it in detail. But the precise nuances vary with the context.

Exemplary damages

10.10 *Introduction* In a very limited number of cases, P is entitled to an award of damages which exceeds the sum necessary for compensation and which is explicitly meant to punish D for misbehaviour. Exemplary damages are highly controversial, many arguing that the law of tort should only concern compensation. Put like that, the argument is rather circular: it does not give any reason why exemplary damages should not be available, or suggest any limit that should be placed on them, but merely asserts that they should not be regarded as part of the law of tort. A more sophisticated argument is that punishment of wrongdoing is more appropriately carried out through the criminal law. This is for several reasons, notably that better procedural safeguards are open to defendants in the criminal law and that if a criminal court orders D to forfeit money, it will go to the state rather than to P. How strong this objection is must depend on the context.

Exemplary damages are only available in a limited class of cases.

- First, where D acted on behalf of an organ of government, and committed the tort in an arbitrary, unconstitutional or oppressive way.

- Second, where D committed the tort after calculating that the benefit D would gain from the tort exceeded any likely claim for damages in respect of it.

These narrow limits to the doctrine were established in *Rookes v Barnard* (1964). That decision was much criticised, but the Lords re-affirmed it in *Broome v Cassell & Co Ltd* (1972). There are a few statutes which seem to authorise the award of exemplary, or at least non-compensatory, damages: Reserve and Auxiliary Forces (Protection of Civil Interests) Act 1951, s 13(2); and Copyright, Designs and Patents Act 1988, s 97.

10.11 *Arbitrary, oppressive or unconstitutional conduct* This category is traditionally stated to apply to 'servants of government', but it appears to apply to all governmental activity, whether or not the individuals who do it are technically 'servants' (employees). It is not always clear who is 'governmental' and who is not. It has been held that a (privatised but heavily regulated) public utility is not 'governmental' for this purpose (*AB v South West Water Services Ltd* (1993)). It appears to be enough if the conduct complained of is unconstitutional *or* oppressive *or* arbitrary (*Holden v Chief Constable of Lancashire* (1986)). It may be asked why oppressive and arbitrary behaviour by government entitles P to more generous remedies, when equally unpleasant behaviour from private bodies would not. A possible answer is that it is often very difficult to use the criminal law against governmental bodies, and especially against the police, whose conduct is often impugned in these cases. The law of tort is here being used as a substitute for the criminal law, and accordingly takes on rather crime-like characteristics.

10.12 *D sets out to make a profit* This category has been broadly stated to apply 'whenever it is necessary to teach a wrongdoer that tort does not pay' (*Rookes v Barnard* [1964] AC 1129, 1227, Lord Devlin). Provided that the wrong was clearly deliberate, it usually seems to be enough to show that D's motive was straightforwardly economic. Typical cases are where a landlord seeks to evict a tenant so that he can redevelop the property (*Drane v Evangelou* (1978)), or where a publisher includes libels in a publication to increase its circulation (*McCarey v Associated Newspapers Ltd (No 2)* (1965)). 'What is necessary is that the tortious act must be done with guilty knowledge for the motive that the chances of economic advantage outweigh the chances of economic, or perhaps physical, penalty' (*Broome v Cassell & Co Ltd* [1972] AC 1027, 1079, Lord Hailsham LC).

10.13 *The law set in concrete?* There are many examples of exemplary damages in the law reports; but not all the torts are represented. The decision in *Rookes v Barnard* (1964) certainly discouraged any further expansion. It is sometimes suggested that the existing cases should be regarded as definitive, so that exemplary damages will not be awarded for any tort unless there is a pre-*Rookes* authority allowing it for the same tort. This is a proposition it is hard to justify from *Rookes* itself, and is inconsistent with a number of cases since *Rookes* (eg *Bradford City Metropolitan Council v Arora* (1991)). Nonetheless it appears to be the current view.

> *AB v South West Water Services Ltd* (1993)   Various plaintiffs were injured by contamination from their local water supply, and damages

were obtained from the supplier for public nuisance. It was argued that exemplary damages should be awarded for the supplier's high-handedness throughout the affair, particularly in issuing denials of the contamination before it had carried out any checks into it. Held: exemplary damages are not available in public nuisance.

(And see to the same effect *Deane v Ealing London Borough Council* (1993), which held that earlier cases allowing exemplary damages of the statutory tort of racial discrimination were wrong.)

10.14 *Relevant considerations*   Where exemplary damages are available, the courts have tended to emphasise the need for restraint, once the remedy has been cut loose from the notion of compensation. Various factors are mentioned as relevant:

- P's own position must be considered. So it is a factor tending to reduce exemplary damages that P provoked D's conduct (*Lane v Holloway* (1968)). Where there are a number of plaintiffs, the appropriate course is first to calculate how much D should fairly pay, and then determine how it should be shared between the various plaintiffs (*Riches v News Group Newspapers Ltd* (1985)).

- Obviously D's own behaviour is a vital consideration. It is also appropriate to consider D's means in determining how much would be an appropriate punishment. If there is more than one defendant, then the award of damages should be that which is appropriate for the *least* blameworthy of the defendants (*Broome v Cassell & Co* (1972)).

- The court should first calculate a compensatory award, and then consider whether D merits further punishment beyond that. There is, however, a conflict of authority over the relevance of other punishments to which D was subjected. One case holds that if D has been criminally punished for his behaviour, there is no scope for further punishment through an award of exemplary damages (*Archer v Brown* (1985)).

There is currently considerable controversy over the level of damages in these cases, especially in cases brought against the police, where cases are typically decided by juries. Should jury awards be under the same rigid control by the courts as are now applied in cases of defamation (see *John v MGN Ltd* (1996) (**8.22**))? The two classes of case are not entirely analogous; most of the police activity in issue is straightforwardly criminal and tort is being used to redress the deficiencies in the criminal justice system that fail to deal with them as such. It seems very strange to lump the treatment of serious crimes by police officers in with the frivolities of defamation cases. Nonetheless, the Court of Appeal has recently ruled that similarly tight controls are appropriate in these cases too. And so exemplary awards against the police of £50,000 and £200,000 respectively were reduced, the court ruling that £25,000 and £15,000 were the right figures (*Thompson v Metropolitan Police Comr* (1997)).

10.15 *Reform* The Law Commission has recently proposed that exemplary damages (or, as it prefers, 'punitive' damages) will be available more broadly, at least in cases where D has deliberately flouted P's rights (Report No 247 'Aggravated, Exemplary and Restitutionary Damages' December 1997).

Injury to feelings, and aggravated damages

10.16 In a limited number of cases, P is treated as having suffered an injury for which substantial compensation should be given, even though there is no quantifiable pecuniary loss in any ordinary sense. So victims of defamation (**8.1**), trespass to the person (**2.1**) and trespass to land (**7.2**) may be entitled to substantial sums even though their wallets are none the worse as a result of D's behaviour. In those circumstances, if D has infringed P's rights in a particularly nasty way, the compensation may be correspondingly larger than normal. The damages are said to be *aggravated*.

Jolliffe v Willmett & Co (1971) A private detective entered Jolliffe's house; in the ensuing struggle, the detective gave Jolliffe a glancing blow. Held: Jolliffe was entitled to £250 compensation for the 'insolent and high-handed' trespass, and £150 for assault.

As well as the torts already mentioned, it appears that aggravated damages are available in deceit (*Archer v Brown* (1985)). But an attempt to claim them in negligence for 'horrific' pain failed, the court considering that they would serve no purpose not already covered by an award for

267

pain and suffering (*Kralj v McGrath* (1986); on pain and suffering generally see **10.58**).

Aggravated damages are technically compensation for a wrong, not punishment. An argument for aggravated damages is thus quite distinct from an argument for exemplary damages. Indeed, P is free to argue in an appropriate case first, that the damages are aggravated and, second, that even when so enhanced they do not adequately punish D for the wrongdoing in the case. In practice, however, exemplary and aggravated damages are available in much the same sets of circumstances, and it is often hard to say which is the more appropriate label for a particular award; cases before *Rookes v Barnard* (1964) often did not distinguish the two at all. The Law Commission has recently proposed that statute should rigorously divide up the two, by stating that aggravated damages can only compensate for mental distress and cannot be used to punish D (Report No 247 'Aggravated, Exemplary and Restitutionary Damages' December 1997).

Restitutionary damages

10.17　Where D tortiously takes some valuable asset from P, then the court may sometimes award P the amount P might reasonably have charged D for the use of the asset.

> *Swordheath Properties Ltd v Tabet* (1979)　Tenants became trespassers, when they stayed on in leased premises after their leases expired. Held: the landlords could recover the reasonable market rental for the period of occupation, as damages for trespass.

Such an award might be justified as compensatory damages if it is shown that P would have made this profit but for P's tort. However, this doctrine is not confined to cases of that sort, and may be available even if it is clear that P could not have used the asset profitably elsewhere. There has been considerable academic controversy over whether these cases should be regarded as compensatory damages, or as illustrating a principle of 'unjust enrichment' (compare Sharpe and Waddams 'Damages for lost opportunity to bargain' (1982) 2 OJLS 290, and Birks 'An introduction to the law of restitution' 330). While the cases could be fitted into either mould, they fit neither very well. The Law Commission has recently proposed considerable extensions to the availability of restitutionary damages, though their proposals would leave a great deal of discretion to the courts as to both the availability and the method of calculation (Report No 247 'Aggravated, Exemplary and Restitutionary Damages' December 1997).

Compensatory damages: general principles

For what should P be compensated?

10.18 We turn now to strictly compensatory awards, which form the bulk of claims in tort. It is first necessary to establish what P will receive compensation *for*. The basic principle is that P is entitled to be compensated to the extent that D's tort made P worse off. In other words, the courts will compare P's position as it is and P's position as it would have been had D's tort not occurred, and will compensate P for the difference between the two states. So if D destroys P's property, in principle P is entitled to the value of that property; if P suffers personal injury, P is entitled to the amount by which this injury makes P worse off. Personal injury damages are treated in detail below (**10.51**).

Destruction of P's property

10.19 P is entitled to the value of property which is destroyed by D's tort. But how is that value to be ascertained? An obvious measure, if it can be applied, is the market cost of a replacement. Indeed, the courts have applied this measure even where P was in a position to manufacture a replacement at a cheaper cost (*SmithKline & French Laboratories Ltd v Long* (1989)). When P buys a superior replacement, the courts have occasionally awarded P the entire cost of so doing, where P had no sensible alternative (*Harbutt's 'Plasticine' Ltd v Wayne Tank & Pump Co* (1970)). Where there is an appreciable delay before replacement, which P cannot reasonably avoid, the damages may include a figure for loss caused by the delay (*Moore v DER Ltd* (1971)), or for the reasonable cost of hiring a temporary substitute (*Martindale v Duncan* (1973)). In principle, P is entitled to all financial costs occasioned by the destruction of the property.

> *Owners of Dredger 'Liesbosch' v Owners of Steamship 'Edison'* (1933)   The *Edison* negligently sank the *Liesbosch*, which was engaged in profitable

contract work. Held: the owners of the *Liesbosch* were entitled to the cost of a replacement dredger, plus the costs of adapting it and transporting it, and for losses under the contract caused by the delay.

Damage to P's property

10.20 Where D has merely damaged P's property, without destroying it outright, the court will usually have to chose between two measures: the diminution in value of the property and the cost of putting the damage right. The diminution-in-value measure is most obviously appropriate if P does not intend to do any repairs, or intends to sell the property before any repairs are done, though even there *dicta* occasionally favour the cost-of-repair measure (eg *The York* [1929] P 178, 184–185, Scrutton LJ). Where P in fact repairs, the cost of so doing is the obvious measure of damages, though it can be displaced if D convinces the court that the amount spent on repairs was unreasonable. P may also recover for other losses which result from any delay while repairs are taking place, such as the need to hire a replacement. Such claims occasionally fade into claims for restitutionary damages (**10.17**).

> *Owners of Steamship 'Mediana' v Owners, Master and Crew of Lightship 'Comet'* (1900)   D collided with P's light-ship, damaging it and putting it temporarily out of action. While it was being repaired, P used a substitute ship, which it kept available for precisely this sort of emergency. The substitute ship would, but for the emergency, not have been used for any purpose at all. Held: P's damages could include a sum for the use of the substitute light-ship.

Probably the result on the facts is justifiable on ordinary principles, as the sum was mostly for additional expenses which P would not have incurred had it not had to push the substitute vessel into service. Nonetheless, it appears that the House of Lords meant to go further: 'Supposing a person took away a chair out of my room and kept it for twelve months, could anybody say you had a right to diminish the damages by showing that I did not usually sit in that chair, or that there were plenty of other chairs in the room? The proposition so nakedly stated appears to me to be absurd …' ([1900] AC 117, Earl of Halsbury LC). The precise rationale is unclear. Perhaps this means merely that where D has effectively deprived P of the use of an asset for a certain period, the courts will be inclined to award the value of that asset for the relevant period. The alternative is to engage in refined calculations which may, in the end, do no better justice than simply awarding the rough figure. After all, no one contends that the assessment of damages is a very precise process, and the more refined the procedure, the more it costs the parties to apply.

Causation

10.21 *Introduction* If there is no causal connection between P's loss and D's conduct, then D is not responsible for P's loss.

> *Performance Cars Ltd v Abraham* (1962) D damaged P's car, necessitating a re-spray. However, the car already needed a re-spray because of earlier damage for which D was not responsible. Held: D was not responsible for P's loss.

Problems in relation to causation are particularly acute for torts which require proof of special damage – a list headed, in terms of practical importance, by the tort of negligence. An entirely different approach is taken for torts which do not. So, for example, it is taken for granted that a defamatory statement 'causes' injury to P's reputation (**8.19**). It is in effect possible to deny causation between P's utterance and D's poor reputation, but it must be done indirectly, such as by arguing that D had no reputation to lose (**8.22**), or that the statement was spread about by persons for whom P had no responsibility (**8.8**). These problems are pursued in the chapter on defamation itself, as they raise problems peculiar to that tort.

10.22 *The 'but for' test* The starting point in causation is usually assumed to be the 'but for' test: D is liable to P only if P would not have suffered the injury but for D's tort. Many cases can be resolved on this criterion. Certainly, if the criterion is satisfied, D is unlikely to be able to deny causation; and few plaintiffs who fail it can hope to establish liability.

> *Barnett v Chelsea and Kensington Hospital Management Committee* (1969) Barnett was admitted to hospital with stomach pains and vomiting. The duty officer negligently failed to diagnose his condition, telling him merely to consult his own GP if the symptoms persisted. Barnett soon died from acute arsenic poisoning. Held: as Barnett's

death would have been a certainty even if the hospital had accurately diagnosed his condition, the hospital was not liable for the death.

In cases of that sort, the argument is really that D's conduct, however reprehensible, really had nothing to do with P's injury. It is not so much a factual argument as a denial of responsibility. Accordingly, it may sometimes be convincingly employed even in cases where it is entirely unclear what would have happened had D acted properly.

> *The Empire Jamaica* (1957)   The owner of *The Empire Jamaica* was in breach of statutory duty in not obtaining a certificate of competence for the mate on his ship. However, the mate was in fact perfectly competent. When the mate was in charge of the ship, it was involved in a collision due to his negligence. Held: the owner's breach of statutory duty was not a cause of the collision.

10.23   *Cases where there is no duty*   Confusion enters in some cases where D fails to prevent P coming to some kind of harm. Sometimes the court denies causation, but seems really to mean that there is no duty. So in *East Suffolk Rivers Catchment Board v Kent* (1941), where P suffered a long period of flooding which D could easily have prevented, liability was refused. This was put both on the ground that D had no duty to prevent the flooding, *and* that D's behaviour was not the cause of the flooding. It seems preferable to describe such results in terms of duty. Certainly P's loss was caused by weather conditions, but it was also caused by D's failure to act with due care; whichever way the question is asked, we come sooner or later to the question whether D had a duty to act, and 'causation' seems a red herring.

10.24   *Cases of multiple tortfeasors*   Many commentators have pointed out that the 'but for' test breaks down where D1 and D2 both engage in dangerous behaviour and simultaneously injure P. Say both are reckless members of a hunting party, who carelessly discharge their firearms in P's direction at the same time. Can each of them say that his bullet did not cause P's death, because the other bullet would have killed P anyway? Common sense suggests that neither defendant should be allowed to escape on that ground. But such cases are rare. Simultaneity of that kind usually suggests that D1 and D2 are acting in concert, and if they are then they will both be liable as joint tortfeasors (**9.15**). Indeed, sometimes the courts seem prepared to stretch a point in P's favour even though D1 and D2 have not acted together.

Lambton v Mellish (1894)   Mellish and Cox were rival merry-go-round operators, each of whom played pipe organs. Lambton, who lived nearby, argued that, while neither organ was loud enough to constitute a nuisance in itself, nonetheless their joint sound constituted a nuisance. Held: as Mellish had been aware of Cox's music but had continued, he was liable in nuisance.

In cases where D1 and D2 both shoot P, in practice D1's bullet will not be precisely simultaneous with D2's. So it appears that the earlier defendant will be liable, the later fortuitously being able to plead that the damage was done before he acted (*Performance Cars v Abraham* (1962) (10.21) is of that type). A more credible hypothetical case, though it is hard to find a case where it has occurred, is where D1 negligently disables the brakes on D2's car, and then D2 collides with P after negligently failing to apply them at all. It would be strange if P's case against either defendant were to fail on causation grounds, even though both can say that the 'but for' test was not satisfied.

10.25 *Factual uncertainty*   A further difficulty with the 'but for' test is that it is often very unclear what would have happened if D had not committed the tort. The court knows what *did* happen, but what would have happened if D had behaved carefully is often a matter of speculation. Generally speaking, P has to prove his or her case on the balance of probabilities. P will therefore lose unless it is more likely than not that proper conduct by D would have avoided the injury P suffered.

Hotson v East Berkshire Area Health Authority (1987)   Hotson fell from a tree and entered hospital in such a poor way that he had only one chance in four of ever being able to walk again. However, the hospital entirely failed to treat him, and his chances of avoiding being a cripple reduced to zero. Held: Hotson would probably have ended up that way even if the hospital had acted with reasonable speed, and accordingly the hospital was not liable.

This principle has been applied many times. An obvious criticism is that it is unreasonably generous to D. Where D is guilty of serious wrongdoing, which deprived P of a significant chance of avoiding injury, it seems wrong to give D the benefit of doubts over what precisely would have happened. But this is often what the courts have done.

- In *McWilliams v Sir William Arrol & Co Ltd* (1962), Arrol failed to provide safety harnesses for its employee scaffolders, including McWilliams. McWilliams later fell to his death. The House of Lords held that Arrol was without responsibility for the death, relying on evidence that McWilliams would not have worn a harness had one been provided. The decision has been much criticised. It seems a classic case of both P and D being to blame, and it is hard to see how ruminations about 'causation' take it out of that category (**4.40**). It may be true that scaffolders in general very rarely wore harnesses, leading to an 'irresistible' inference that McWilliams would not have done ([1962] 1 WLR 300, Lord Kilmuir LC). But those very facts seem to point to significant and widespread neglect of employers' obligations.

- In *Bolitho v City & Hackney Health Authority* (1997) a registrar was summoned to Bolitho's hospital bedside to advise on his acute respiratory difficulties. She failed to attend; Bolitho died. The registrar's evidence was that her presence would not have helped: in the event, the only thing that might have made a difference would have been if she had intubated, but (fully in accord with medical practice) that is not what she would have done. The court held that there was no causation: if she had complied with her duty of care, Bolitho would still have died.

10.26 *Factual uncertainty and 'material contribution to risk'* There is one leading case which departs from the usual approach.

McGhee v National Coal Board (1972) McGhee worked in a brick kiln. He contracted dermatitis due to the high concentrations of brick dust. There was evidence that the risk of the workers' getting dermatitis would be significantly reduced if the employer had installed showers for them to use at the end of their shifts. It was, however, impossible to say that if the showers had been available, then McGhee would never have suffered dermatitis. Held: there was sufficient evidence that the employer's breach of duty had made a contribution to the dermatitis, and the employers were liable.

Plainly, these facts are very similar to those in *Hotson* (**10.25**), and if there is a real difference it is hard to see what it is. In both cases, D deprived P of a chance; yet in both, P would probably have suffered the same fate whatever D did. The reasoning is a little obscure: it was assumed to be enough that the employers had made a 'material contribution' to the risk of dermatitis, and how this was to be reconciled with the 'but for' criterion was not spelled out. The case is similar to, but goes further than, *Bonnington Castings Ltd v Wardlaw* (1956), where P was injured by the escape of silica dust from two of his employer's machines. Neither machine was well ventilated, but the employer was only in breach as to one of them, as there was no practical means for ventilating the other. There too, it was thought sufficient to establish causation that there had been a 'material contribution' to P's injury by the machine in breach.

The present status of *McGhee* and *Bonnington* is unclear. Some of the reasoning was criticised in *Wilsher v Essex Area Health Authority* (1988). There, five independent causes appear to have contributed to the risk of the damage which P suffered while in D's hospital, but the House of Lords refused to hold the hospital liable simply because one of those causes was the result of negligence. *McGhee* was described as 'robust and pragmatic' ([1988] AC 1090, Lord Bridge). But the Lords specifically disapproved Lord Wilberforce's suggestion that where D neglects a precaution and then the precise thing that precaution was aimed at happens, then the burden of proof on causation is reversed. However, they did not rule that *McGhee* was wrongly decided. Nor did they definitively state that P's case must fail on grounds of causation; rather, they remitted the case for re-trial. So *McGhee* still seems to be rightly decided and has occasionally been applied (*Page v Smith (No 2)* (1996)).

10.27 *Factual uncertainty and damages for a lost chance?* Another approach to factual uncertainties would be to award P damages for lost chance. So a court faced with the facts of *Hotson* might argue that P had been deprived of a 25% chance of recovery, and accordingly award 25% of the amount P claimed as representing the whole loss. (Note that while support for loss-of-chance damages is usually regarded as a pro-plaintiff position, nonetheless it might reduce damages in cases where P lost a chance of more than 50% but significantly less than 100%.) Damages for lost chances are well established in some areas of damages assessment (eg **10.59**), but the controversial question is whether they can be awarded in a case where P's claim will otherwise fail completely on the ground that P's whole claim fails the 'but for' test.

The *Hotson* case itself provides no support for damages for loss of chance, but neither does it rule them out. Such cases are well established in the law of contract. In tort, there are a few recent examples, in financial contexts, where it is stressed that the loss of the chance has to be proved on the balance of probabilities; but if it can be so proved, then it can be sued for.

> *Allied Maples Group Ltd v Simmons & Simmons* (1995) Allied Maples took over Kingsbury, the subsidiary of a rival group, with a view to selling off unwanted properties and keeping the rest. However, they found that Kingsbury had certain onerous legal liabilities of which they had been unaware. They sued Simmons & Simmons, who had been advising them on the take-over, arguing that if they had been warned of these liabilities, they might have been able to secure indemnities against them. Held: as there would have been a substantial chance that they would have been able to secure an indemnity, they were entitled to damages to reflect that chance.

Allied Maples was a tort case rather than a contract case, but nothing seems to turn on the point.

> *First Interstate Bank of California v Cohen Arnold & Co* (1995) First Interstate Bank became concerned about the financial stability of one of its clients, to whom it had lent some £5m. It consulted Cohen Arnold, who negligently assured it that there was nothing to worry about. Accordingly, the bank waited rather longer than it would otherwise have done before realising property it held as security for the loan. Held: there was a two-thirds chance that it would have received more money but for Arnold Cohen's poor advice, and accordingly it could recover two-thirds of the likely extra amount.

> *Acton v Graham Pearce & Co* (1997) Acton, a solicitor, was convicted of legal aid fraud. His solicitors negligently failed to order an inspection of certain key documents, which might have shown that the most damning evidence against him was in fact perjured. If his solicitors had done their work more carefully, there would have been a 50% chance that he would never have been convicted. Held: he could recover 50% of the loss caused by his conviction.

Remoteness

10.28 *Introduction* Where D's tort has caused loss to P, D may sometimes argue that the loss was too remote a consequence of D's conduct. Too many other causes may have intervened, or the injury may be very unexpected, or it may simply be out of all proportion to the fault D was guilty of. The argument is often confused and undeserving, and many commentators have cynically concluded that 'remoteness' arguments are simply a device for controlling claims which seem too large.

10.29 *To which torts is it a defence?* In general, torts involving deliberate wrongdoing by D do not allow remoteness as a defence. This applies to assault and battery, deceit, and the economic torts. It is therefore enough in these cases if P establishes a causal link between D's conduct and P's loss.

> *Doyle v Olby (Ironmongers) Ltd* (1969) Olby sold Doyle an ironmongery business, making various false statements about its accounts. Doyle put considerable money into the business, but ended up making a loss. Held: Doyle could recover all sums he had expended on the business.

It is less clear whether torts of strict liability are subject to a remoteness defence. The tort in *Rylands v Fletcher* certainly is, as is liability for fire. It is unclear whether liability for animals is. Probably the tort of breach of statutory duty is not: it is no defence that a breach of duty was unforeseeable or unpreventable, and so it would be surprising if the consequences of a breach could be avoided by a plea of remoteness. But there is no clear authority on the point. In practice, the rule that P's loss must be of the same type as that which the statute was intended to prevent (**1.45**) fulfils a similar function. Most of the case law on remoteness concerns the tort of negligence; it appears that nuisance applies similar rules (**7.23**).

10.30 *Competing approaches* The actual test for remoteness is a matter of some controversy. In a leading case earlier in the century, the courts tended to stress causation issues: so long as D had committed a breach of duty against P, D was liable for all direct physical consequences of P's behaviour.

Re Polemis and Furness, Withy and Co Ltd (1921)   Furness Withy's employees, in the course of unloading Polemis's ship, carelessly dropped a plank into the hold. This caused a spark, which lead to an explosion which seriously damaged the ship. Held: Furness Withy was responsible for the entire loss.

It was stressed in the case that this doctrine applied only where 'the damage is in fact directly traceable to the negligent act, and not due to the operation of independent causes having no connection with the negligent act' ([1921] 3 KB 577, Scrutton LJ). Yet the case was subsequently heavily criticised, by a court possibly under misconceptions as to the breadth of the decision, and a test based on foresight was substituted.

Overseas Tankship (UK) Ltd v Morts Dock and Engineering Co Ltd, The Wagon Mound (1961)   OT(UK)'s employee deliberately discharged furnace oil into Sydney Harbour. The oil spread over the harbour. MDE's employees, seeing the oil on the water, consulted their manager on whether it was safe to continue welding; he said that it was. Held: the fire which resulted was too remote for MDE to recover from OT(UK).

However, there is a certain amount of ambiguity in the application of this test. In subsequent litigation over the same incident, another plaintiff, whose ship was some way away from where the fire started, and so who was presumably less 'foreseeable' and more 'remote', nonetheless established to the court's satisfaction that the fire *was* foreseeable. The reasonable person in D's position would have realised that there was a (small but non-negligible) risk of fire (*Overseas Tankship (UK) v Miller SS Co Pty, The Wagon Mound (No 2)* (1967)). Plainly, then, there is a certain amount of flexibility in the test. What may have been going on is that the plaintiff in *The Wagon Mound* was not anxious to obtain a ruling that D should have foreseen the fire, as D would then have retorted that P should have foreseen it too. D would then have raised a defence of contributory negligence, whereas the plaintiff in the second action laboured under no such handicap. But whatever may be the explanation of the discrepancy between the cases, it is clear that *The Wagon Mound* is not such a terrifying decision for plaintiffs as it was at first thought to be. Certainly it does not mean that the *precise* facts which happened have to be foreseeable before the event.

Hughes v Lord Advocate (1963) Hughes, an eight-year-old boy, was playing in a temporary shelter left by council workers digging up the road. He accidentally knocked over a paraffin lamp, which fell down an open access hole: the paraffin effervesced and there was a fuel-air explosion which injured Hughes. Held: the harm to Hughes was of a foreseeable type, and it was unnecessary for the extent of a foreseeable type of harm to be foreseeable.

Accordingly, the modern rule is sometimes stated to be that while the *type* of loss must be foreseeable, its *extent* need not be, nor need the precise manner of its infliction.

10.31 *Different doctrinal labels* Very often, essentially the same argument about liability can be put in various different ways, using different terminology. Where D injures P in circumstances where it is pretty amazing that P was affected by D's activities, it is common to discuss the issue as being 'whether P was too remote a victim'. But equally the issue might be discussed under the rubric of whether D was in breach of duty to P at all. For example, the 'rescuer' cases have this ambiguous quality (**3.31**). It is usually completely unimportant which classification is adopted. This book treats denials that P was in any way a foreseeable victim of D's activities as a denial of duty, rather than an assertion of remoteness. But this is purely a point about the arrangement of the book: if they were treated as 'remoteness' cases, as they are by many writers, the result would not be that the law was stated differently, but merely that it was stated in a different order. Again, where D's argument is that the chain of events leading from D's conduct to P's loss is too long and convoluted, in many situations it makes little difference whether we say that P's loss is 'too remote' or whether we say it is 'not caused' by D's tort. In this treatment, 'remoteness' and 'causation' are initially treated as separate notions, but the major part of the text treats them together.

A common talking-point here is the famous New York case of *Palsgraf v Long Island Railroad Co* (1928), where guards employed by the defendant railroad were careless in helping a passenger on to a train, just as it was pulling out of the station. A package was dropped. Unfortunately it contained fireworks, and the resulting explosion injured P (who was some distance away) by knocking over a set of scales standing next to her. No doubt liability would be refused in England, just as it was refused by Cardozo J in the New York Court of Appeals; but on what ground? No duty? No breach of duty? Remoteness? Insufficient causation? Lack of 'proximity'? Each solution has its supporters.

10.32 *Direct physical consequences of D's conduct* As a generalisation, if D is in breach of duty to P, D is liable for direct consequences of D's behaviour, except where the type of loss which occurred was of an unforeseeable type.

> *Doughty v Turner Manufacturing Co Ltd* (1964) A foundry worker accidentally knocked the asbestos lid of a cauldron into the molten metal in the cauldron itself. After a few minutes, an unforeseeable and violent chemical reaction between the metal and the asbestos took place, showering Doughty, who was working underneath, with molten metal. Held: the foundry owners were not liable for this unforeseen event.

Nonetheless, a broad view is taken of the 'type' of loss and, if the type is the same, the extent does not matter.

> *Vacwell Engineering Co Ltd v BDH Chemicals Ltd* (1971) BDH delivered chemicals to Vacwell, without a warning that they would explode on contact with water. One of Vacwell's employees put them in a sink, and there was an explosion of immense proportions. Held: BDH was liable for the whole loss.

> *H Parsons (Livestock) Ltd v Uttley Ingham & Co Ltd* (1978) Through its breach of contract when supplying farm equipment, Uttley Ingham poisoned Parsons' pigs. It was foreseeable that the pigs would be ill as a result, but the death of most of the herd was unforeseeable. Held (on the assumption that remoteness rules were the same in contract and in tort): the entire loss was recoverable.

10.33 *Remoteness and mere matters of assessment* What is sometimes treated as a variant on the 'type and extent' rule, but is perhaps better treated as a distinct notion, is that matters of mere assessment are not subject to a remoteness test. So if D negligently smashes P's vase, D is liable to pay for a replacement, even if (unforeseeably) it turns out to be an exceptionally valuable antique. Or if D negligently runs over P, who looks like a tramp, P may recover for the consequences of the personal injury, without having to meet any argument that it was 'unforeseeable' that he was in fact remuneratively employed (*The Arpad* [1934] P 189, 202-203, Scrutton LJ). Most such cases can be explained by arguments about the 'range of foreseeable consequences' of D's action, or considerations of the type of injury D could reasonably foresee. But it seems that P can recover whether or not those arguments could be made.

10.34 *The 'thin skull' rule* Where D is responsible for the infliction of personal injury on P, and then because of some pre-existing condition the damage is more extensive than could have been foreseen, D is nonetheless liable for it all. D must 'take his victim as he finds him', and cannot protest that it was unreasonable for P to have such a thin skull or such a delicate constitution.

> *Bradford v Robinson Rentals Ltd* (1967) Robinson Rentals sent out Bradford, an employee, in freezing conditions, in a van without a heater. Bradford sustained severe frostbite. Held: Robinson Rentals was liable for the full extent of his injury.

> *Smith v Leech Brain & Co Ltd* (1962) Smith, a factory worker, was burnt on the lip by a piece of molten metal, in an accident for which his employer was responsible. It turned out that Smith had a pre-malignant condition, which the burn turned into a full-blown and fatal cancer. Held: Smith's widow could sue for her husband's death.

There is an obvious incompatibility between the 'thin skull' approach and the general approach in *The Wagon Mound* (1961), at least in cases where P's injuries were of a type which could not have been foreseen before the event. One case has held that where the approaches conflict, there can be no recovery.

> *Tremain v Pike* (1969) Rats infested Pike's farm. They bit Tremain, one of Pike's employees. He then contracted Weil's disease, a rare condition transmitted through rats' urine. Held: Pike was not liable for this unforeseeable harm.

However, that case was decided relatively soon after *The Wagon Mound* (1961) itself. Later decisions tend to fudge the issue, wavering between a 'thin skull' approach on the one hand, or liability for loss of a foreseeable 'type', broadly defined. Either approach is more generous to P than was the court in *Tremain*, and it is very hard to see how the case can be regarded as rightly decided.

What happens after the accident

Introduction

10.35 In many cases, the measure of P's loss is immediately obvious. If D destroys P's car, the obvious measure is the value of the car, and often it will not matter what happens later on – the damages will be the same. However, sometimes the court looks further, particularly where P says that further loss occurred at a later stage. Many concepts are used in this enquiry. We might ask whether any additional loss is 'too remote' or was 'unforeseeable', or question whether it was really caused by D. In the following paragraphs I follow a thematic approach, rather than trying to isolate particular legal doctrines.

It is sometimes said that the results in these cases owe relatively little to legal doctrine and rather a lot to policy choices by the judges. However, even if that is a meaningful distinction to make, it is misleading, not least because it ascribes to the judges rather more clarity of thought than really seems to be the case.

P's subsequent conduct

10.36 *General* D is liable for all foreseeable consequences of the tort. So D does not cease to be liable for the consequences of the tort merely because P has reacted in some way, even in a way which increases the loss suffered. However, D may disclaim liability where P 'breaks the chain of causation', or commits a *novus actus interveniens* (a 'new and intervening act'), or acts in a manner which is unreasonable.

It is sometimes said that P is under a *duty to mitigate the loss*, that is, a duty to take reasonable steps to reduce the loss, or at least prevent it from getting any larger. However, this is a very confusing way of putting it. P is not under a *duty* in any normal sense: P commits no legal wrong by being extravagant. However, P is not entitled to be extravagant *at D's expense*. D can therefore refuse to pay any expenses which P could readily have avoided.

10.37 *Reasonable response to the accident*   Where P's increased loss is the result of P's own decisions in the wake of the accident, D's liability for the increased loss turns on the reasonableness of P's behaviour. The need to contain the loss is one factor which ought reasonably to influence P. But it is not the only one. The courts will not allow D to be charged for items of expense which P incurred unreasonably. Equally they do not expect P to sacrifice *all* other considerations to the reduction of the bill which D must pay.

> *McKew v Holland & Hannen & Cubitts (Scotland) Ltd* (1969)   As a result of negligence for which Holland was responsible, McKew suffered an injury to his leg which occasionally made it give way. McKew suffered further injury when he collapsed while descending some stairs, which he had tried to do without assistance. Held: Holland was not responsible for the further injury.

> *Wieland v Cyril Lord Carpets Ltd* (1969)   As a result of negligence for which Cyril Lord was responsible, Weiland had to wear a surgical collar, which made it hard for her to move her head, and hence to see around her. Held: Cyril Lord was liable for her further injuries when she fell over obstacles she could not see.

In cases where P becomes pregnant after D's negligent failure to sterilise her, it is sometimes argued that any loss which P could have avoided by abortion is her own responsibility, and cannot be laid at D's door. However, the courts have rejected this view, reluctant to say that it can be unreasonable to refuse an abortion (eg *Emeh v Kensington & Chelsea & Westminster Area Health Authority* (1984) (**3.29**)). Again, the courts almost never hold that rescuers are responsible for the injuries they suffer while rescuing (**3.31**). Indeed, anyone placed by D's behaviour in a life-or-death situation where he must act quickly can plead that his behaviour was not, 'in the agony of the moment', unreasonable – no matter how foolish it can be made to appear in retrospect.

10.38 *Mental disorder*   Where D's tort interfered with P's mental stability or mental health, subsequent activity by P will not necessarily be judged by ordinary standards of reasonableness, but is judged by more generous standards of 'foreseeability'.

Pigney v Pointer's Transport Services Ltd (1957)   After a head injury for which Pointer's was liable, Pigney became a depressive, and ultimately committed suicide. Held: his widow could sue Pointer's in respect of his death.

Brice v Brown (1984)   Brice had a hysterical personality disorder, though it was fairly moderate and well controlled. After suffering nervous shock for which Brown was responsible, her condition worsened considerably, including various examples of bizarre be-haviour, a suicide attempt and three admissions to mental hospital. Held: everything that had happened was within the range of the foreseeable, and Brown was liable for her condition.

A controversial decision holds D liable even for the consequences of very serious criminality by P.

Meah v McCreamer (1985)   Meah suffered brain damage as a result of an accident resulting from McCreamer's drunken driving. This led to a personality disorder, and Meah ended up as a category 'A' prisoner for life following a succession of sexual assaults. Held: Meah's damages could include an element to compensate him for his imprisonment.

This is a highly controversial result. The verdict left Meah considerably richer than most convicted rapists. This prompted his victims to sue him for assault and they obtained damages (*W v Meah, D v Meah* (1986)). Meah then sued McCreamer again, claiming that these additional sums were also recoverable. However, Woolf J held them too remote (*Meah v McCreamer (No 2)* (1986)), a result which it is hard to reconcile with the first ruling. (The correctness of *Meah (No 1)* is now in doubt, though on grounds not relevant here: see **11.31**.) There is similar judicial ambivalence in cases where P divorces, and alleges that his divorce is traceable to personality changes he suffered as a result of D's negligence. In *Jones v Jones* (1985), this argument was accepted, but in *Pritchard v JH Cobden Ltd* (1988), *Jones* was overruled. There are serious conceptual difficulties in these cases, not least because of the conflict between tort's usual assumption that people are responsible for their own actions, and the very clear psychiatric evidence that these particular plaintiffs were not.

10.39   *Financial decisions*   P must act reasonably when taking decisions which affect the amount P will subsequently be claiming.

Darbishire v Warran (1963)   Warran damaged Darbishire's car, valued at £85. Darbishire had it repaired at a cost of £180; he thought it impossible to get a replacement for £85, though it seems that there would have been other similar vehicles available at that price. Held: he could recover no more than £85.

The limits of the ruling are unclear. It appears that P had simply not looked for a replacement at all, and accordingly the court was unimpressed with his argument that none was available. It also seems that the court was unsympathetic to any argument that he attached sentimental value to the particular vehicle; though the court suggested that it might be different if the vehicle in question were unique (as in *O'Grady v Westminster Scaffolding Ltd* (1962)). It is unclear when, if ever, P is reasonably allowed to be motivated by non-financial considerations.

Admiralty Comrs v SS Amerika (1917)   A submarine was sunk, with the loss of all crew, by the negligence of the *SS Amerika*. One item of loss claimed was the pensions paid by the Navy to the crew's widows. Held: these payments were voluntary payments, which could not be added to the damages.

10.40   *The impecunious plaintiff*   Perhaps P chooses a relatively expensive solution to the problem caused by D's negligence, because P cannot afford the costs associated with a cheaper solution. For example, if P is forced into borrowing large amounts of money in a hurry, the total amount P will ultimately have to pay is likely to be more than if P could have paid the immediate expenses out of P's own capital. The view has traditionally been taken that P cannot pass these higher expenses on to D.

Owners of Dredger Liesbosch v Owners of SS Edison (1933)   The *Edison* negligently sank the *Liesbosch*. The owners of the *Liesbosch* could not afford to replace it immediately. They hired another dredger to complete their current contracts and borrowed money, eventually buying the hired dredger. Held: their damages could not include any element for losses which were the result of their own financial position.

The decision is sometimes justified on grounds of 'lack of proximity', but this seems rather circular. The connection between D's actions and P's loss is fairly direct. If it is not 'legally proximate', this must be because of some special legal principle as to the proximity of losses caused by financial difficulties. The *Liesbosch* decision has not been accorded much weight in recent years.

> *Dodd Properties (Kent) v Canterbury City Council* (1980) Dodd's property was destroyed by negligence in the construction of a car park. However, Dodd did not rebuild immediately, as it had not the funds to do so. In the event, as the defendants stubbornly denied liability for close to ten years, the building was delayed for a similar period. Held: Dodd could recover the cost of rebuilding after liability had been established.

The lack of a clear principle in the *Liesbosch* case has made it relatively easy to distinguish. In *Mattocks v Mann* (1993), where P's claim after a road accident was somewhat increased by P's decision to delay repairs until D's insurers would meet the bill, Beldam LJ noted that the authority of the *Liesbosch* case was 'consistently being attenuated in more recent decisions'. He added that

> ... in ... 'the varied web of affairs' that follows a sequence of events after an accident of this kind, it is only in an exceptional case that it is possible or correct to isolate impecuniosity, as it is sometimes called, or the plaintiff's inability to pay for the cost of repairs from his own resources, as a separate cause, and as terminating the consequences of a defendant's wrong ([1993] RTR 19).

Nonetheless, the *Liesbosch* case has yet to be overruled, and the suggested replacement rule – whether the additional loss was foreseeable – is rather vacuous. In a negligence case, it seems unreal to suppose that D was or should have been speculating over how P would meet any liabilities D happened to create for P.

Subsequent conduct of third parties

10.41 *Introduction*   Where D causes injury to P and subsequent activity by others (not under D's control) makes matters worse, P may sometimes argue that D is nonetheless responsible for the whole. Perhaps it is only because of D's activity that the other parties had the chance to injure P's interests at all. As noted above, the courts are generally reluctant to find D liable for wrongdoing committed by others (eg 1.27). So it is not unusual for the courts to hold that the third-party intervention is a *novus actus interveniens*, or is for some other reason not something which D can held responsible for.

10.42 *Criminal acts* No formal line is drawn between lawful and unlawful third party conduct, but nonetheless the courts are highly likely to hold that third party criminality breaks the chain of causation.

> *Lamb v Camden London Borough Council* (1981) Negligence by the local council in re-laying a water main lead to subsidence in Lamb's house. Her tenants deserted it and squatters soon moved in. Held: the council was not liable for damage done by squatters.

Each of the judges in the case gave a different reason, and the case is a puzzling one, especially since it is hard to deny foreseeability. The court's reluctance to hold anyone liable for the uncontrolled acts of squatters was palpable. But such claims do not inevitably fail.

> *Ward v Cannock Chase District Council* (1985) The council allowed its property to fall into disrepair. It collapsed, damaging Ward's house, which had to be abandoned. The council accepted responsibility, but did not proceed with repairs at any great speed. Ward's house, left abandoned, was vandalised. Held: the council was liable.

Scott J distinguished *Lamb* on the ground that the vandalisation of P's property was 'virtually certain' unless the council acted with great speed ([1985] 3 All ER 553).

10.43 *Criminal acts as supervening cause?* A slightly unusual argument was deployed in *Baker v Willoughby* (1970). D injured P's leg by poor driving. P permanently lost about 30% of the use of the leg, and in normal circumstances would have been entitled to damages to reflect this loss for the rest of his life. However, three years after the accident, P was attacked by armed robbers, who further injured the leg, so that it had to be amputated. D admitted liability for restricted use of the leg for three years, but suggested that after that time there was no further liability. P no longer had a leg at all, and to award him money for having *restricted* use of the leg was to compensate him for a loss which he had not, in the event, suffered. In other words, the argument was that the criminal attack on P was a 'supervening' cause, of such proportions that it made the earlier history of injury by D merely past history.

The argument failed and P kept the damages for 30% loss of use for the duration of his life. In other words, P recovered damages for having restricted use of his leg, when in fact (through no fault of D's) he had no leg at all. The case is unusual, and the reasons for sympathy to P are obvious enough. Perhaps the simplest explanation of the case is that as P's misfortunes were entirely the result of two torts, all his loss should be recoverable from the tortfeasors together; yet the robbers could not be sued for the loss of a good leg, for they had only deprived P of a 70%-useful leg. (The question of the robbers' liability was not academic, since it could then have been recovered from the CICB: see **2.6**.) Nonetheless, the reasoning in the case is rather obscure, and the result has been criticised.

10.44 *Responses to the crisis precipitated by D* By contrast, where the third-party conduct was an attempt to deal with the problem caused by D's own negligence, the courts will not be quick to call it unreasonable or unforeseeable.

> *The Oropesa* (1943) Bad navigation by the master of the *Oropesa* caused it to collide with the *Manchester Regiment*. The master of the *Manchester Regiment*, which was badly damaged, set out in a lifeboat to talk to the master of the *Oropesa* about saving it. The lifeboat capsized, drowning the occupants; the widow of one of them sued the owners of the *Oropesa*. Held: the decision to set out in a lifeboat had been a reasonable response to the situation, and did not break the chain of causation.

The courts have been reluctant to hold D liable for the consequences of bad medical treatment in response to an injury caused by D, perhaps because it is always open to P to sue the doctor. Nonetheless, where it must have been obvious that P would need medical treatment as a result of D's tort, D may sometimes be held liable.

> *Robinson v Post Office* (1974) Robinson suffered a cut for which his employer was responsible. A doctor gave him an anti-tetanus injection, to which Robinson suffered a violent anti-allergic reaction. Held: Robinson's employers were liable for all injuries.

10.45 *Market movements* Where D gives P bad advice in a financial matter, yet much of P's loss is due to subsequent market movements, it appears that that element of P's loss will not be recoverable.

South Australia Asset Management Corpn v York Montague Ltd
(1996) SAAM lent considerable sums of money to borrowers
offering property as security. It would not have made the loans but
for the over-valuation of the property by York Montague. The lenders
defaulted on the loans, and SAAM could not recoup all its money
because of the inadequate value of the property. Its loss was further
compounded by a steep fall in the property market. Held: SAAM could
not recover from York Montague any element of loss fairly attributable
to the fall in the property market.

Clearly the additional loss in the case is the result of third-party activities
in the market place, as the Lords stressed. However, stated in those
terms, the decision is hard to understand, because those third party
decisions were hardly unforeseeable or unreasonable. Market prices can
go down as well as up, as is well known. Perhaps the case is really about
P's own responsibility to manage his own assets, of which he is not
divested by one bit of bad advice by D.

Benefits subsequently received by P

10.46 *Introduction* P suffers injury; one consequence of the injury is
that P receives money or other benefits as compensation. Should these
sums go to reduce D's liability to P? In principle, the answer is yes: D
need only compensate P for loss actually suffered. To the extent that
the loss has been put right by others it is no longer something for which
P deserves compensation from D. However, there are two exceptions,
both of uncertain extent.

10.47 *Insurance and analogous benefits* Where a benefit P receives is
an entitlement for which P previously paid, then the sum does not reduce
damages. So if P pays for private insurance against accidents, sums
received from the insurer do not reduce P's damages. This rule is clear
enough where P deliberately purchased and paid for the insurance, but
it is unclear how far outside that it stretches.

Parry v Cleaver (1970) Cleaver's bad driving injured Parry, a
policeman. This resulted in Parry's premature retirement from the
force. Cleaver suggested that Parry's damages should be reduced
to reflect the invalidity pension payable to Parry in respect of the
years before Parry would have retired in normal circumstances.
Held: this sum should not be taken into account to reduce damages.

The decision is a controversial one, reached only by a majority. In justifying the decision, the majority emphasised that the entitlement was closely analogous to private insurance. It was therefore unfair, it was said, to penalise P because merely P takes the insurance as part of his or her remuneration package, rather than taking a higher salary and paying for insurance out of that. However, this approach has not struck all the judges as realistic, especially if there is no reason to suppose that P had the option of taking the money in higher salary rather than insurance benefits. Certainly the courts will not allow P to invoke the rule in respect of sick pay (*Hussain v New Taplow Paper Mills Ltd* (1988)), and why that situation should be any different from *Parry* is not altogether clear.

Where P is insured against the very sort of loss which D causes, typically the insurers will seek to be *subrogated* to P's claim, that is, they will stand in P's shoes for legal purposes and claim the damages which P could have claimed. In cases of that sort, P has in fact been compensated, and the real quarrel is between P's insurer and D. Can D argue that in those circumstances P has in reality suffered no loss, and so there is no claim for the insurers to be subrogated to? Usually the answer will be No, but the real question is as to the purpose of the insurance.

> *Europe Mortgage Co v Halifax Estate Agencies* (1996) Europe Mortgage lent money on security, but subsequently claimed it would never have done so but for the negligent valuation of the security by Halifax. Halifax pointed out that Europe Mortgage had already been fully compensated for this under its mortgage indemnity guarantee insurance. Held: this insurance was taken for the plaintiff's benefit, not the defendant's, and should therefore be ignored.

10.48 *Friends and family* Where P receives money freely given by others after the accident, and which was meant to benefit P rather than to reduce D's liability, then it will usually be treated as having that effect. It will accordingly be ignored in calculating the damages D must pay. The doctrine is simple enough where P receives cash or other gifts from family or relatives; these sums are simply ignored in calculating P's damages. More complicated considerations enter when the gift consists of services.

> *Donnelly v Joyce* (1974) Donnelly, aged six, was injured by Joyce in such a way as to require regular re-bandaging of the wound. This was

done by Donnelly's mother, who gave up her nursing job in order to find time to do it. Held: her loss of wages was recoverable as an additional item of damages by Donnelly.

It is obvious that torts involving personal injury will have some impact on P's family as well as P personally. Nonetheless it is not usual to regard them as victims of the tort, in the eye of the law. However, the reasoning in *Donnelly* was considered too artificial in later cases. The loss had in reality been incurred by his mother and the law should recognise that: it should 'enable the voluntary carer to receive proper recompense for his or her services' (*Hunt v Severs* [1994] 2 All ER 385, 394, Lord Bridge). One consequence of this is that where such damages are awarded, they are held on trust for the carer, rather than belonging to P beneficially.

A controversial case is where D is a member of P's family and provides part of the care P needs after the accident. In *Hunt v Severs* (1994) P fell off D's motor cycle on which she had been riding pillion; D was held responsible for her injuries. P and D later lived together, and eventually married. D in fact provided much of the nursing care P needed. Should P be able to include an item for nursing care in her damages claim, or could D's insurers retort that P had in effect already received compensation for that through D's care for her? The House of Lords ultimately held that she had no claim. P could not force D (or in reality, D's insurer) to pay for nursing care which had in fact been provided by D in person.

Subsequent natural events

10.49 Where D has caused loss to P, the courts are in principle prepared to hold D responsible also for subsequent physical consequences. Nonetheless, there comes a point at which they decide that P's problem is no longer one for which D can fairly be asked to take responsibility. D's tort becomes a mere part of the history, not a ground for further liability. The argument is usually made in the form that later supervening events 'submerge' the loss originally caused by P, making it irrelevant to what follows.

Carslogie Steamship Co Ltd v Royal Norwegian Government (1952) The *Heimgar* was damaged when it collided with the *Carslogie*, in an accident which was the fault of the *Carslogie*. The *Heimgar* headed into port for repairs, but was further damaged in stormy weather, necessitating further repairs. The *Heimgar* would have taken ten days to repair, but because of the storm damage was unavailable for thirty days. The owners of the *Heimgar* claimed for loss of profit over ten days. Held: no damages for loss of profit were recoverable at all.

The Lords stressed that the storm had turned the ship from a seaworthy, albeit damaged, ship into a ship that would not be seaworthy until repairs were completed, and accordingly they regarded the storm as supervening earlier causes of loss. D's tort had become a mere part of the history, rather than a cause operating in the present. The same point has also come up in relation to personal injury.

Jobling v Associated Dairies Ltd (1982)   As a result of an injury for which his employers were responsible, Jobling suffered partial disablement, being fit only for sedentary work. Three years after his accident, he was struck down by a spinal condition that made him unfit for any work at all. Held: his employers were not responsible for his injuries after the date when the spinal condition supervened.

There is much insistence in the case that P is expected to bear the ups-and-downs of life without attempting to pass them on to others. The legal problem in the case is caused by the factual uncertainties involved. If it had been clear that the spinal condition pre-dated the original accident and was all along inevitable, the employer would certainly not have been liable (10.21). If, by contrast, it could have been shown that it was an indirect and unexpected consequence of the work injury, then the employer would probably have been liable under the 'thin skull' rule (10.34). As it was, it was very hard to know what was going on. The result is easier to understand if we say, as some of the Law Lords did, that the total disability was 'inevitable' regardless of the work accident. But it is hard to see how the evidence justified that.

Jobling is obviously similar to *Baker v Willoughby* (10.43) where, however the supervening cause was the activities of armed robbers who attacked P. *Baker* was criticised in *Jobling*, but most of the criticism seems to miss the mark. It is not true, for example, that *Baker* created a risk of double compensation if P had claimed against both sets of tortfeasors. The robbers did not deprive P of a healthy leg and would not have been made to pay damages as if they had. If the result of *Baker* is wrong, then P would fail to recover the total loss suffered by suing all the tortfeasors, even though the tortfeasors' activities were the sole cause of the loss. Are the two cases consistent? They appear both to be still law, with the (rather unsatisfactory) distinction between them being that in *Baker* the allegedly supervening cause was tortious, whereas in *Jobling* it was not.

Subsequent events: taxation

10.50   If P loses earnings as a result of the tort, almost certainly P is also relieved of a tax liability. In other words, if P loses £10,000 in earnings then P does not have to pay the tax on £10,000. And so, to give P £10,000 in damages may amount to over-compensation. The inevitability of taxation is proverbial, and so it would be surprising if the effect of the tax system on P's loss was regarded as unforeseeable. However, there are substantial practical difficulties in asking what P's tax liability would have been in hypothetical circumstances, or which part of P's existing bill is attributable to D's tort. The case law is accordingly somewhat confused. However, there is one clear and common case where the courts will act. When P is deprived of some gain on which P would certainly have been taxed, but the damages D pays will certainly not be taxed at all, then P's damages must be reduced to reflect this. So if P claims for lost earnings, then P will receive the amount P would have received *after* tax (*British Transport Commission v Gourley* (1956)).

Personal injury damages

Introduction

10.51   The assessment of personal injury damages might seem one of the most uncontroversial areas of the law of tort. Once liability for P's personal injuries has been established, all that is left is the mechanical collation of information on P's resulting disability and its consequences.

Yet the stated goal of providing full compensation for P is taken for granted, rather than rationally demonstrated. Why should D have to pay for all the consequences of the wrong? Much press criticism of tort is ultimately aimed at this feature of the law, reflecting a sentiment that damages should reflect other features, such as D's relative blame-worthiness. And when we compare tort with other methods for securing just compensation – insurance, social security – tort's goal of full compensation begins to stand out as rather unusual. Worse, the goal is impossible. The court cannot restore to P what P has lost, but only give money. Where what is lost is non-pecuniary – freedom from pain, enjoyment of life, freedom of movement – it is obvious that no one sum of money will ever be quite right. Even where the loss is pecuniary, there are numerous problems of assessment. Moreover, it is never possible to know quite what would have happened but for the tort, or indeed what has happened with it except by waiting for events. Yet the whole point of the award is lost if it cannot be made within a reasonable amount of time following the accident. Many guesses, some of them quite arbitrary, must be made in the course of estimating the likely consequences of an accident. As one Law Lord has commented:

> The award is final; it is not susceptible to review as the future unfolds, substituting fact for estimate. Knowledge of the future being denied to mankind, so much of the award as is to be attributed to future loss and suffering – in many cases the major part of the award – will almost surely be wrong. There is really only one certainty: the future will prove the award to be either too high or too low (*Lim Poh Choo v Camden and Islington Area Health Authority* [1980] AC 174, 183, Lord Scarman).

Indeed, this understates the difficulty, because while P will eventually know what the future holds, P may never know what it would have held but for the accident.

The process of assessment

10.52 Damages are today calculated by a judge sitting alone, applying relatively fixed principles, and subject to appeal. This is a recent state of affairs. Before the 1930s, it was still common for juries to set damages awards, and they were not practically excluded from such cases until the 1960s (*Ward v James* (1966)). It is still theoretically possible for a jury to be summoned in such cases, but it is almost unheard of (see *H v Ministry of Defence* (1991)). It was not until *Jefford v Gee* (1970) that judges were required to itemise the awards they made. It then became the orthodoxy that 'plaintiff and defendant alike are entitled to know what is the sum assessed for each relevant head of damage and thus to be able on appeal to challenge any error in the assessments' (*George v Pinnock* [1973] 1 WLR 118, 126, Sachs LJ).

Today, the principles on which judges should act are stated with a fair degree of precision, though a degree of elasticity is well recognised. The appeal courts are unwilling to alter awards on appeal simply because it is rather more or less than the members of the court would themselves have awarded. The court will not interfere unless the reaction on hearing the figure awarded below is 'Good gracious me – as high as that' (*McCarthy v Coldair Ltd* [1951] 2 TLR 1226, 1229, Denning LJ). Consistency in practice results from past cases, especially as collected in the sizeable reference work *Kemp and Kemp on Damages*. The Judicial Studies Board has attempted to increase consistency in the award of damages.

Consistency, of course, is not the same thing as justifiability. Not all commentators agree that the principles of damages 'have few parallels outside the world of witchcraft and sorcery' (Conaghan and Mansell *The Wrongs of Tort* (1993) 56), but it is fair to say that few are entirely happy with them either.

Assessment in practice

10.53 Very few cases come to court, and the tort system would be unworkable if they did. In practice, therefore, most awards are settlements reached between P's lawyer and D's legal department or insurers. Most of the claims are for a relatively small amount. An authoritative survey carried out 20 years ago found that nearly three-quarters of all claims settled for under £1,000, the average claim (for claims which achieved any settlement at all) being £1,135. Large claims, while not irrelevant to practice, do not constitute a very large proportion of it. There is considerable delay involved in the system. The survey found that the average settlement delay was 19 months. Unsurprisingly, therefore, the tort system cannot provide help at an early stage. For that, the injured have to rely on sick pay and the social security system. The superior bargaining strength of defendants puts them in a strong position vis-à-vis plaintiffs, and therefore in a position to drive damages levels down. This is not in itself a ground for criticising the system, as strong centralised defendants are in a better position to meet damages awards than would be a more disparate grouping. But it is a point to be borne in mind when individual judicial decisions are criticised as too generous to plaintiffs.

The lump sum

10.54 Damages are nearly always in the form of a lump sum, representing all of P's loss. This sum will be received some time after the injury itself, and may represent items of loss sustained before and after the award itself. Where the money is being received later than the injury for which it compensates, interest may be payable, though the rates are rather low:

- Provable ('special') pecuniary losses attract interest from the date of the injury, at half the special interest rate for money paid into court.

- Non-pecuniary losses attract 2% interest from the date the writ was served.

Where money is paid early, as is common for compensation for injuries with long-term consequences, the damages will be lower to reflect this, though the calculations are rather crude. Where loss is recurrent, such as a loss of wages over a long period, the courts calculate a sum representing losses for a typical year (the 'multiplicand') and then select an appropriate 'multiplier' for the number of years over which the injury is suffered. This multiplier will usually be much less than the number of years involved. P is expected to invest the money to secure a reasonable return over the future years, and the multiplier will also be reduced to reflect various contingencies.

Whether this rather crude technique is adequate is a matter of some debate. It has been suggested that the courts should fix the multiplier by reference to official statistics of mortality rather than guesswork, and this is beginning to happen (see *Wells v Wells* (1997) (**10.56**)). There was controversy in the 1970s over whether inflation should expressly be taken into account in the calculations. The courts ultimately ruled that it should not, on the argument that if P invests the damages wisely the effect of inflation should be offset (*Lim Poh Choo v Camden and Islington Area Health Authority* (1980)).

Avoiding the inconveniences of a lump sum

10.55 Various devices have been proposed for avoiding the disadvantages of a single lump sum. The Pearson Commission recommended in 1978 that the courts should be empowered to order periodical payments, adjustable in the light of changing circumstances. But this has never been acted on. Various palliatives are in place:

- The court may order a *split trial*, to determine whether D is liable, but then postponing any question of the amount of liability (RSC Ord 33, r 4). This is most obviously appropriate where P's prognosis is very unclear.

- The court may order an *interim payment* to P where liability has been established or the court thinks it likely that it will be, so long as D is an insurer, a public authority, or otherwise capable of making the payment (RSC Ord 29, r 11). The court may order payment of a 'reasonable percentage' of P's likely eventual claim.

- If both P and D consent, any award of damages can include an order for *periodical payments* (Damages Act 1996, s 2), though there is no provision for adjusting the amount in the light of later events.

- Where there is a chance that P's condition will deteriorate seriously in the future, P may claim *provisional damages*, assessed on the assumption that the chance will not materialise. P has liberty to apply to the court again if it does (Supreme Court Act 1981, s 32A, inserted by Administration of Justice Act 1982, s 6). However, the courts have ruled that this provision can only be used in the case of 'clear and severable' risks, rather than in the more normal case where P's existing condition seems likely to degenerate. So where P has arthritis caused by D's tort, the risk that P will eventually have to stop work entirely is a matter for ordinary techniques rather than provisional damages (*Willson v Ministry of Defence* (1991)). If P later dies, there may be a further claim (Damages Act 1996, s 3).

For various reasons, however, none of these powers are much used. The lump sum is the norm.

Investments and structured settlements

10.56 The courts usually presume that P will invest the lump sum received in investments which will bring a return of between 4% and 5% per annum. They are resistant to arguments that P might reasonably prefer investments which bring a lower return but are safer (eg *Wells v Wells* (1997)). The Lord Chancellor has recently been given a power to set general rules in this area (Damages Act 1996, s 1), but it is not yet clear how they will be used.

In general, tax is not payable on damages, or on sums received in settlement of personal injury claims. However, if P uses the award to purchase a regular income, P would usually expect to pay tax on that income. The tax liability can however often be avoided by a so-called 'structured settlement', under which D pays a lump sum to purchase an annuity on P's life, and passes on the periodic payments to P. This arrangement has advantages to both sides. P has a regular income without the administrative difficulties involved in buying an annuity personally, and the amounts received are not subject to tax as (by revenue concession) they are treated as payments of compensation. D has the advantage of being able to treat the case as closed, its obligation being only to pass on the annuity payments as received. However, the system is far from perfect. The administrative burden on D is still substantial. Moreover, it does not solve the problem of future uncertainties. It is possible to index-link annuities to avoid the risk of inflation, but it is not usually possible to buy annuities which vary with future contingencies such as the progress of P's disease or the extent of the nursing care P needs. Structured settlements have received a great deal of official encouragement, but the courts do not have any power to force structured settlements on parties who do not wish to agree to them.

Assessment: the live victim

Introduction

10.57 Personal injury damages are calculated under different heads, in a standard way. Special damages compensate for specific items of pre-trial loss. General damages are roughly divisible into sums for injury to P's feelings, sums for lost income, and future expenses. Certain benefits received or likely to be received in the future must be deducted from the total. In what follows, we will first assume that P is still alive, or at least *was* alive in the period under consideration; the effect of P's death is considered below (**10.66**).

Injury to feelings

10.58 This is commonly sub-divided yet further, though it would be wrong to suppose that the division is very rigid or very rigorously applied. Some commentators have fundamental difficulties with this head: it does not represent a loss of money, so how can money replace what is lost?

However, the court has nothing else to give but money, and as such does its inadequate best to translate P's injury into a precise sum.

- *'Pain and suffering'*   The pain P has suffered is likely to account for the major part of the sum awarded. It is assumed that plaintiffs who are unconscious are not in pain, and accordingly nothing is payable for any period of unconsciousness, however prolonged. The courts also generally refuse to give damages for pain and suffering to a plaintiff who died quickly, even in extreme pain (*Hicks v Chief Constable of the South Yorkshire Police* (1992)).

- *'Loss of the amenities of life'* or *'loss of faculty'*   This refers to loss of enjoyment of life, or of the possibility of enjoyment of life, as a result of the injury. Typically, awards emphasise deprivation of the chance to pursue a favourite hobby or pastime. Controversially, the courts have insisted that the compensation is for the loss of amenity, not for *knowledge* that the amenity has been lost. Accordingly even a plaintiff who has remained unconscious since the date of the accident can recover the full amount under this head (*H West & Son Ltd v Shephard* (1964)). There are arguments both ways over whether this should be so. It is hard to justify such damages if compensation is the sole aim. But if other goals are relevant, it might be argued that damages should not be reduced because D has suffered a *more* severe injury – and indeed that the sum is as much to comfort P's relatives as it is to comfort P.

- *'Loss of expectation of life'*   Formerly, this was compensatable as a distinct item. However, this head of damages has been abolished by statute, which directs that P's knowledge that his or her life has been cut short is to be counted as part of the pain and suffering arising from the injury (Administration of Justice Act 1982, s 1).

A single sum is usually awarded for all of these items, to reflect losses both pre- and post- trial. It will often not be necessary and, indeed, may be pointless, to insist on the precise sub-division of damages mentioned. So, for example, where P is given damages for reduced likelihood of marriage following the accident, it is unnecessary to consider whether this is technically 'pain and suffering' or 'loss of amenity' (*Hughes v McKeown* (1985)). It appears to be irrelevant whether the money could be used effectively to alleviate the pain. Here are some fairly typical examples:

- Female, aged 17 at date of accident and 20 at date of trial, suffered whiplash injury to her neck and a sprain to her lower spine, with no broken bones. She wore a cervical collar for one week. The pain increased, becoming severe after two months but then decreasing. Full recovery to the neck within 12 months and to the spine after 18 months. General damages £2,500 (*Cliffe v Williams* (1996)).

- Male, aged 20 at date of accident and 23 at trial, suffered severe bruising of the left calf, minor bruising to right shoulder, and shock. Placing any weight on left leg caused pain. He was effectively house-bound for one month; symptoms finally disappeared after ten months, before which time he had to avoid his usual pastime of football. General damages £1,500 (*Gorry v Southern* (1996)).

- Female, aged four at date of accident and six at date of trial, suffered carbon monoxide poisoning at home. She was unconscious when the ambulance arrived but soon recovered consciousness. The poison was completely gone from her system within 24 hours, and no long-term effects were envisaged. General damages £1,250 (*Stibbs v British Gas plc* (1996)).

- Male, aged 54 at date of accident and 58 at date of trial, injured in the lower back. This accelerated an osteoarthritic condition by ten years. Sitting or driving for long periods were painful. He had to give up competitive cycling, at which he had been very proficient, and had to curtail his golf and his gardening. His condition was expected to be permanent. General damages £8,500 (*Canning v Roberts* (1996)).

Studies in the mid-1970s found that overall awards for non-pecuniary items made up about half the total amount of damages awarded, though a higher proportion of the smaller awards. The sums are fairly arbitrary. They 'could be multiplied or divided by two overnight and they would be just as defensible or indefensible as they are today' (Cane, *Atiyah's Accidents Compensation and the Law* (5th edn, 1993), 139). Such evidence as there is (though it is not overwhelming) suggests that, left to his own devices, the average member of the public would be more generous than the courts are. However, different members of the public feel differently, and so bringing back juries is likely to re-introduce an unacceptable level of uncertainty. It might, however, be possible to settle new guidelines for damages after some form of public consultation.

Loss of earnings

10.59 *General* Wages lost before trial are special damages, which must be itemised and proved. Future loss of earning is usually calculated on a multiplier-multiplicand basis. The multiplicand is usually P's net annual loss: salary lost, less tax which P no longer has to pay and expenses P no longer has to incur. All lost income can in principle be take into account, including perks and benefits in kind; equally, any income P seems likely to secure in fact must be deducted. No allowance is made for likely general increases in earnings generally; and most factors affecting P's own pay are taken into account via the multiplier, not the multiplicand.

Selection of the multiplier is a complicated affair. The figure is meant to reflect the number of years over which P suffers the loss, but there is no simple relation between the number of years and the number selected as the multiplier. If a multiplier of 23 was selected and P was able to invest the money at 4.5% interest per annum (which is what we would normally assume in this area, see *Wells v Wells* (1997)), then P would receive as yearly income the sum represented by the multiplicand, in perpetuity. Accordingly, the multiplier will be less than that (the practical maximum is 18).

The multiplier may be increased to reflect P's lost prospects of promotion. It may be reduced to reflect the risk of injury other than by D, the possibility of redundancy, and other 'vicissitudes of life'. There is some confusion over whether women plaintiffs should have their multipliers reduced to allow for the possibility that they might have given up work to have children. Some judges have done so, though where appropriate they have also added a sum for diminution of marriage prospects (eg *Moriarty v McCarthy* (1978)). But others have simply assumed in a rough-and-ready way that these two alterations to the figures will cancel one another out, and so both may be ignored (*Hughes v McKeown* (1985)).

The courts have maintained that the multiplier will not, exceptional circumstances aside, be increased to take account of future inflation. This was partly on the (incontrovertible) ground that the court does not know what the future level will be, sometimes on the (debatable) ground that, properly invested, the real value of P's money should be unaffected, and sometimes on the (despairing) ground that P's fellow citizens have to put up with inflation and P deserves no special protection. It is also not permissible to increase the multiplier to offset the higher rate tax P will pay on investing the sum the court awards (*Hodgson v Trapp* (1988)).

There is provision in the Civil Evidence Act 1995, s 10, for the use of official government statistical tables ('Ogden tables') for the selection of the appropriate multiplier. At the time of writing this provision is not in force, though the courts in this area now regularly use Ogden tables.

10.60 *The 'lost years'* Where one effect of the injury is to reduce P's lifespan, so that P is expected to die before P would (but for the injury) have retired from work, there is a problem in assessing P's loss of earnings in the period where P would have been earning but cannot because P is dead. This problem of 'wages in heaven' is solved by calculating P's net income over the relevant period on normal principles, but including in the deductions from income a sum representing P's ordinary living expenses. Where P was part of a family this will involve calculating an appropriate proportion of the family bill for food, housing, heating and lighting (*Harris v Empress Motors Ltd* (1984); though this approach has now been doubted by the Court of Appeal in *Phipps v Brooks Dry Cleaning Services Ltd* (1996)). Whatever is left is recoverable as damages, including sums which would certainly have been spent on P's dependants had P lived (*Pickett v British Rail Engineering Ltd* (1980)). The rule is plainly intended to safeguard the position of P's dependants, though it applies even if P has none. Where P is very young, the courts are in principle prepared to entertain claims of this sort. But they are likely to award nothing under it if there is no good evidence of what P's earnings are likely to have been (*Connolly v Camden and Islington Area Health Authority* (1981)).

10.61 *'Loss of earning capacity'* In rare cases, the courts award damages for 'loss of earning capacity'. This is not distinct from lost earnings, but rather a different way of calculating it. If there were too many uncertainties to calculate a sensible multiplier or multiplicand, the court may nonetheless award a lump sum to reflect the diminution in P's work prospects. This is usually because the loss involved will be suffered, if at all, far into the future. Perhaps P is very young, or the effects of the injury rather speculative, or P's employer has kept P on at the old wage but P plausibly argues that his or her future prospects have nonetheless been damaged. It is often arbitrary which approach is adopted. In one case where a 21-month old plaintiff was injured (he was seven and a half by the time of the trial), a majority of the Court of Appeal assessed damages on the basis of a multiplicand representing the national average wage and a multiplier of five (*Croke v Wiseman* (1982)); but an award for loss of earning capacity on those facts would not have been surprising. Almost by definition, awards are exceedingly imprecise; the courts tend to err on the side of caution.

Expenses

10.62   As with earnings, so with expenses. Actual expenses before trial must be proved as special damage. Future recurrent expenses will probably be calculated on a multiplier-multiplicand basis, with the multiplier being chosen to reflect the number of years for which the expense will continue. On general principles, P can of course only recover for expenses *reasonably* incurred, but that can be extensive, including (for example) the conversion of P's house to take account of her injury (*Moriarty v McCarthy* [1978] 1 WLR 155, 163, O'Connor J). A decision to obtain medical help privately is not be to be treated as unreasonable merely because the same help was available under the National Health Service (Law Reform (Personal Injuries) Act 1948, s 2(4)). Sometimes there is a danger of overlap between P's claim for expenses and P's claim for lost earnings. If P is hospitalised for a lengthy period and stays in a private hospital, P will not be allowed to recover *both* the cost of the hospital care *and* the lost wages in full, for while staying in hospital P presumably avoids a significant part of his or her ordinary living expenses (*Lim Poh Choo v Camden and Islington Area Health Authority* (1980)).

Deduction of benefits

10.63   *General*   The general principle has been explained above (**10.46**). In general, benefits received by P as a result of the tort must be deducted, but there are two exceptions, one for benefits funded by P at some time in the past, the other for acts of generosity to P after the accident. The latter exception has caused a great deal of confusion down the years. In *Roach v Yates* (1938), where P's wife and sister-in-law gave up their jobs to nurse him, a sum was added to P's damages because 'he would naturally feel that he ought to compensate them for what they have lost' ([1938] 1 KB 263, Greer LJ). But this precedent was rather neglected in the following few decades. The practice grew up whereby relatives who intended to care for the victims of torts would often be advised to sign formal contracts to care for them for specific sums of money, which could then be added to P's claim. In *Donnelly v Joyce* (1974) it was held that such contracts were unnecessary: where D's tort had created P's need for care, P could recover the value of that care. The amount it had cost P's relatives to provide it, whether by wages foregone or otherwise, was admissible as evidence of the proper amount of P's claim. However, this approach remained unsatisfactory, not least because it perpetuated the fiction that the loss involved was really suffered by P, whereas the reality was that P's need for care had been catered for, but the court considered that the carer deserved to be able to claim. The reality of the matter was acknowledged first in *Housecroft v Burnett* (1986), and then by the House of Lords in *Hunt v Severs* (1994). There are numerous problems with this analysis, though the worst of them will only arise if P and P's carer subsequently fall out over the precise ownership of the money.

Social security benefits

10.64 *The old law* The Social Security Administration Act 1992, Part IV, embodied a particular philosophy in the area of social security benefits. Where P had received benefits from the state, P would be receiving double compensation if these benefits were not deducted from damages; equally, if D were able simply to deduct benefits paid, then the state would be paying for a liability which was admittedly D's. In principle, the solution would have been to insist that benefits to the victims of torts should be paid solely by tortfeasors. However, this is impracticable, because of the delays involved in awarding tort damages. The solution adopted was to insist that any tortfeasor settling a tort claim should account to the state for the amount of benefits received by the victim. No payment of compensation could be made until D receives a 'certificate of total benefits' from the appropriate governmental department; the definition covered nearly all social security benefits, from the date of the accident for five years or up to the date of the compensation payment, whichever is sooner. The full amount of the benefits received by P were deducted, even in a case where the amount P received was reduced for contributory negligence. Certain benefits were excluded from the scheme: most important for present purposes are payments under the criminal injuries compensation scheme (on which see **2.6**), cases falling under the Fatal Accidents Act 1976 (see **10.67**), and cases where the compensation did not exceed £2,500. For those smaller payments, the compensation recovery rules did not apply and another, still older set of rules on deductions was left in force.

10.65 *The new law* After criticism of the old law, the law was re-stated and amended in the Social Security (Recovery of Benefits) Act 1997. There is no major change in the philosophy of the legislation, but the old law was seen as unfair to plaintiffs in various respects. The class of social security benefits deducted was seen as too broad; the relevant benefits are now more precisely and more narrowly defined. Second, the approach of the law was too broad-brush: the amount of benefits received were simply deducted from P's damages, whether or not P's damages related to the same head of loss as the social security benefits. So under the old law a plaintiff who has received invalidity allowance might find that amount being deducted from his or her damages for pain and suffering. The link must now be more direct. So social security benefits meant to provide the cost of care can only be deducted from P's damages for cost of care; benefits meant to reflect loss of earnings may only be deducted from P's damages for lost earnings; and P's damages for pain and suffering are in effect ring-fenced, as there is no social security payment which corresponds to them. Finally, the new Act is more comprehensive, the special provisions applying to awards of £2,500 or less now being abolished.

Assessment: the dead victim

Survival of actions in tort

10.66 At common law, P's death brought the action to an end. However, this rule has been reversed by statute (Law Reform (Miscellaneous Provisions) Act 1934, s 1). However, a claim brought by P's estate after P's death cannot include any element for:

• exemplary damages (Law Reform (Miscellaneous Provisions) Act 1934, s 1(2)(a)); or

• loss of earnings in respect of the period after death (Administration of Justice Act 1982, s 4(2)).

In practice, therefore, any claim brought by P's estate after the death will be restricted to claims in respect of the period before P's death. As to the period after, P no longer experiences pain or suffering and is taken not to merit a claim for lost amenities; claims for lost earnings are

305

excluded by statute; and P no longer has any expenses. General damages are therefore zero. A claim for special damages may succeed.

The Act specifically provides that where P's death was the result of the tort, a sum is recoverable for funeral expenses. This forestalls any argument that this payment was a mere anticipation of an inevitable expense, as P would undoubtedly have died at some time or other, tort or no tort. That special case aside, any gain or loss to the estate consequential on the death itself is ignored.

The Fatal Accidents Act 1976

10.67 *Introduction* Where P's death is the result of D's tort, then in addition to any claim by P's estate, there is a statutory claim available to P's dependants. This reflects the degree of the 'dependency', that is, the benefits which they would have received from the deceased had he or she not died. The claim is quite distinct from the claim by the estate. It is a claim for pure economic loss consequential on the death of a provider. However, the claim lies only if a claim could have been brought in respect of the tort at the date of the death. So if the deceased person had already successfully sued D, no additional claim arises on death, and conversely any defences which D could have raised against a claim by the deceased can also be raised against the Fatal Accident Act claim.

10.68 *Who can claim?* The claim is only for the amount of the dependency, and accordingly can only be brought by someone who was in fact a dependant of the deceased. Further, the Act demands that claimants must come from specific categories of dependant. The claimant must, by s 1, be one or more of the following:

- husband or wife of the deceased at the date of death, or former husband or wife (including cases where the marriage was annulled or declared void);

- any person 'living with the deceased in the same household' and so living 'as their husband or wife' at the time of the death and for the preceding two years;

- any parent of the deceased, or anyone treated by the deceased as his or her parent;

- any child of the deceased, or anyone treated by the deceased as a child of the deceased's family in relation to any marriage to which the deceased was party;

- any other ascendant or descendent relative; or

- any brother, sister, uncle or aunt, or the issue of any such person.

The section also provides that relationships by marriage ('affinity') count the same as relationships by blood ('consanguinity'), and makes provision for cases of relationships by half-blood. It adds (confusingly, given the earlier references to marriage) that an illegitimate child is to be 'treated as the legitimate child of [the] mother and reputed father'. The list is long, confused and confusing. It has been added to down the years, now being considerably longer than when the claim was first introduced in 1846. The Law Commission has provisionally recommended that the statutory list of dependants be abolished, the test in future being simply whether there is a dependency in fact (Consultation Paper No 148, 'Claims for wrongful death', September 1997).

In principle, each dependant has a distinct claim, but the act insists that procedurally there must be a single claim (s 2), and it is usual for the court to assess a single figure for the dependency and then divide it between claimants. The court has complete discretion as to the division of any sum received between multiple claimants (s 3(2)).

10.69 *Calculation of the claim*   The claimant is entitled to a sum representing the value of benefits which he or she would have received from the deceased but for the death. Where (as is usually the case) the benefits were expected to be received over a period, the courts will usually employ a multiplier-multiplicand basis for the calculation. Where the deceased had not provided any benefits in the past but seemed likely to do so in the future, it is a purely evidential question whether the facts justify a claim.

Taff Vale Rly Co v Jenkins (1913)   A 16-year old girl, living with her parents, was about to finish her apprenticeship as a dressmaker at the time when she was killed. It was expected that her wages would have risen sharply after qualification. Held: as there was a reasonable possibility that she would have supported her parents, an award to reflect this dependency could be made.

In cases where the deceased was a bread-winner, in theory the claim is for the amount the deceased brought into the house, less expenses attributable to his or her *own* upkeep as opposed to the upkeep of others in the family. In practice, the courts recognise that the family's bills may not decline very much merely because one member is dead. It would be unrealistic to expect that if one member of a two-person household dies, then future bills for rent, food and heating will decline by 50%. The courts usually start from the assumption that where there is a single dependant, the dependency will be two-thirds of the amount of money the deceased brought in, and that if there are children as well it will be three-quarters. The figure will then be adjusted up or down in the light of the evidence (*Harris v Empress Motors* (1984)). In cases where the deceased provided home-making services, the courts sometimes say that the dependency is to be estimated by the cost of buying replacement services commercially (*Hay v Hughes* (1975)). But if the services are in fact provided after the death by a partner or by relatives, a more obvious measure is any wages lost by that relative (*Mehmet v Perry* (1977)).

Losses which result from the death are not always part of the dependency. In particular, when one member of a family works for another, being paid the going rate for the job, neither side 'benefits' from the arrangement, and its loss is to that extent not a ground for a claim under the Act.

> *Malyon v Plummer* (1964)   A wife regularly performed some rather nominal services for her husband's one-man company, for which the company paid her £600 per annum; it was found that her services were worth about £200 per annum. On her husband's death, this arrangement ceased. Held: she could recover only £400 per annum as dependency.

> *Burgess v Florence Nightingale Hospital for Gentlewomen* (1955)   Husband and wife worked as professional dancing partners; the wife died through a surgeon's negligence and her husband claimed under the Act. Held: nothing was recoverable as compensation for the interruption of their professional relationship.

The award may also include a sum to cover burial expenses actually incurred by the dependants (s 3(5)).

10.70 *Loss of chance* The claimant does not have to show that the dependency would certainly have existed but for the death, or even that this is more likely than not; but any chances involved are part of the calculus of benefits. So where a husband and wife were separated at the time of the husband's death, the Lords held that it was wrong to deny the widow any dependency claim merely because a reconciliation seemed less likely than not – though, not insignificantly, they refused an award on the facts, as being too speculative a possibility (*Davies v Taylor* (1974)). The Act specifically directs the court to take account (in the case of a claim by a cohabitant living with the deceased as husband or wife) of the lack of any enforceable claim to support during life (s 3(4)).

10.71 *Disregard of benefits* Benefits received by dependants as a result of the death are to be disregarded in calculating the dependency (s 4). The Act also provides that the possibility, or indeed actuality, of re-marriage by a widow of the deceased is to be disregarded in calculating her dependency (s 3(3)). However, the Act makes no mention of claims brought by any children of hers, and so the widow's re-marriage to a man who turns out to be a better provider than her first husband may reduce the children's claim substantially. As drafted, the sub-section does not cover re-marriage by widowers, but in fact the same result has been reached in their case by broad interpretation of s 4 (*Stanley v Saddique* (1992)). The precise ambit of s 4 is unclear, and not all the decisions in that area seem consistent. So where her husband's death meant that a claimant would not receive the benefit of her husband's retirement pension, but she received a similar result from a death-in-service pension, it was said that overall she had suffered no loss and so had no claim (*Auty v National Coal Board* (1985)). Yet when the widow of a retired man died and accordingly lost the benefit of his occupational pension, her damages were not reduced by her receipt of a widow's allowance under the same scheme (*Pidduck v Eastern Scottish Omnibuses Ltd* (1990)). Since the abolition of the 'wages in heaven' claim by the estate, there is no longer any provision for deduction of benefits received in consequence of a claim by the estate under the 1934 Act (**10.60, 10.66**).

10.72 *Damages for bereavement* In addition to the claim for a de-pendency, there is now a claim for the non-pecuniary loss, called 'damages for bereavement'. The claim is for a fixed amount, which is the same in each case and set by the Lord Chancellor. At the time of writing it is £7,500. The claim can only be made by a narrow class of relatives:

309

- Where the deceased never married and never reached 18, the claim may be made by his or her mother and (if the deceased was legitimate) father.

- Where the deceased married, the claim may be made by the spouse at the date of the death.

10.73 *Defences* Any defence which would have defeated a claim by the victim of the tort also operates to defeat a claim under the Fatal Accidents Act 1976. If a claim by the deceased would have been met by a plea of contributory negligence, leading to a reduction in the damages payable, then the claim under the Act will be similarly reduced (s 5). There are also additional defences that can be raised.

> *Burns v Edman* (1970) A widow claimed for loss of dependency when her husband was killed in a road accident. It appeared that most, if not all, of his past earnings had come from criminal activities and that there had been no prospect of his earning a living in any other way. Held: no claim was maintainable.

An unusual situation arose in *Dodds v Dodds* (1978), where a wife's bad driving led to her husband's death. In a claim brought by her husband's estate, it was suggested that negligence by one of the dependants would weaken the claim. However, the court held that the negligence of one dependant could not affect the claims of the others, and the children all recovered for their dependency without any reduction. In that case, the wife was solely responsible for the accident, and it was conceded that she had no claim herself; it seems that where a dependant is partly responsible for it, that dependency claim may be correspondingly reduced (*Mulholland v McCrea* (1961)).

Further Reading

Relevant sections of tort reference books may be supplemented with:

Reed 'Exemplary damages: A persuasive argument for their retention as a mechanism of retributive justice' (1996) 15 CJQ 130.

Reece, 'Losses of chances in the law' (1996) 59 MLR 188.

Stauch, 'Causation, Risk, and Loss of Chance in Medical Negligence' (1997) 17 OJLS 205.

Self-test questions

1.   It is much easier to obtain a final injunction against libel than an interlocutory injunction against it. Why is this (**10.4**)?

2.   Why might P prefer to be the beneficiary of a 'structured settlement' rather than any other sort of settlement (**10.56**)?

3.   Is remoteness a defence to a claim for *any* tort (**10.29**)?

4.   In what circumstances will benefits received by P in consequence of the tort be ignored in assessing damages against D (**10.46**)?

5.   Are 'aggravated damages' intended to compensate P or to punish D (**10.16**)?

CHAPTER ELEVEN

Defences and other factors limiting damages

SUMMARY

A number of defences call for special attention. They are:

- consent and exclusion of liability;

- contributory negligence;

- illegality;

- limitation; and

- necessity.

They provide a number of safety valves for courts concerned to limit the scope of liability.

Introduction

11.1 This chapter covers defences to tort actions. This is a diverse area. A list of everything that has ever been counted as defence to a tort action would be very long indeed. For that matter, there is little agreement on where rules relating to liability end and rules relating to defences begin. For example, it was at one time thought that there was a defence of 'inevitable accident' to actions in negligence, and some of the more traditional texts still refer to it. But the more modern tendency is to say that this is a denial of negligence ('the accident was inevitable') or a denial of causation ('it would have happened anyway'). Little turns in practice on which approach is adopted. Again, it is not entirely clear that all defences apply to all torts. This chapter will consider five defences of fairly general application: consent, contributory negligence, illegality, limitation and necessity.

Consent and exclusion of liability

Definition

11.2 It is a defence to an action in tort that P consented in advance to the behaviour of which P now complains. The Latin maxim is *volenti non fit injuria*: 'No injury is suffered by one who consents'. A related idea (though not all would concede that it is precisely the same idea) is that P cannot sue if P has entered into a contract to give up any right of action.

In essence the idea is very simple, but a number of factors make it very rash to generalise about the defence:

• While the doctrine of consent supplies the explanation when D erects a warning notice which is held to absolve D from liability, *notices are of different types, and accordingly have different effects in law.* At one extreme, there are notices which give P precise warning of the physical danger P is running, in such a way as to enable P to avoid it. At the other are legalistic notices informing P that D does not intend to assume any legal liability, but giving no clue as to the danger P might be running. If either type of notice has any effect, it will be on the ground that P 'consented' to the terms of the notice. But the questions to ask in each case are different, and for a number of reasons the first type of notice is viewed with a great deal more sympathy than the second.

• *The defence of consent raises different issues in different contexts.* For example, a plea of consent in relation to a surgical operation where P was given a false idea of the nature of the operation (as where the surgeon removed the wrong leg) is very different from a consent plea where P's complaint is that the surgeon did not warn P in advance of certain risks of the surgery. These differences are partly, but not wholly, explained by the point that in the first case P would be suing in battery and in the second in negligence. In what follows, I will be assuming that there is a common core of principle in the area, applying to most cases, but discuss elsewhere individual situations and individual torts which need consideration.

The burden of proof on matters of consent is on D (*Freeman v Home Office (No 2)* (1984)).

P's ability to consent

11.3 P can sometimes pre-empt any argument for consent by showing that at the time at which P supposedly consented, he or she did not possess an adequate level of understanding to give a valid consent. So children may often be held not to have consented in circumstances where adults certainly would be. The leading case is *Gillick v West Norfolk and Wisbech Area Health Authority* (1986), and the question whether P has adequate understanding for this purpose is often called the question of '*Gillick* competence'. It is a matter of whether P has 'sufficient understanding and intelligence' to comprehend what is being proposed and to decide whether to agree to it. On or after their 16th birthday, it is taken that children are so competent in the case of medical procedures (Family Law Reform Act 1969, s 8).

Reality of consent

11.4 *General* An apparent consent by P may not count as consent for legal purposes. In principle P will not be held to have consented if her 'consent' was obtained by threats or bullying, though the leading case on the matter does not give much encouragement.

> *Latter v Braddell* (1881) Employers accused their maidservant of being pregnant, insisted on a medical examination to confirm their suspicions, and threatened to sack her if she did not consent to it. She underwent examination, protesting but believing she was legally bound to, and was found not to be pregnant. They sacked her anyway. Held: her consent, though reluctant, was genuine and she could not sue in battery.

It is often said that P's consent will be vitiated if it was obtained by misleading P on some fundamental matter. But examples are hard to come by. If D obtains P's consent to a surgical operation by telling P that D intends to perform *some other* medical operation, then D has no defence to battery; but that is usually explained by saying that what D did was not what P consented to. It is not that P's consent was vitiated, but rather that what D did was not what P consented to. The judges have resisted any broader notion of 'informed consent': it is enough that P knows in general terms what D proposes to do (eg *Freeman v Home Office (No 2)* (1984)). Again, judges in an earlier century held that P's consent to sex was effective even though she would certainly have refused had she known that D suffered from a venereal disease (eg *Hegarty v Shine* (1878)). There are good reasons for not treating that case, and others like it, as conclusive authority. They are antique. In any event, most of the authorities are from the criminal law: criminal lawyers are asking about 'consent' for different reasons and with different policy objectives. A judge who was reluctant to label D a rapist might none-theless be willing to order D to pay compensation. Nonetheless, action by P in fraud or negligence probably has a better chance of success than action in battery.

11.5 *Medical cases* If a doctor misleads P about the treatment the doctor is about to administer to P, then the operation may amount to a battery, on the ground that what D does is not what P consented to. The requirement is that P understands 'the general nature' of what D is up to (*Chatterton v Gerson* (1981)). Consent is not vitiated simply because D is not as open as D could have been about the operation, or did not explain all the risks associated with it. This seems to be so even if P specifically asked to know the risks (*Sidaway v Board of Governors of the Bethlem Royal Hospital* (1985)). Strong opinions are held on both sides of the question whether patients' consent should be 'informed'. Not everyone would agree with the view of the Lords in *Sidaway*, that confidence between doctor and patient can only be upheld by permitting systematic concealment of the risks inherent in whatever course of action the doctor proposes. It is sometimes said that fraud vitiates consent, but it is not clear whether this applies to all frauds, or simply to fraud as to the type of operation. Other torts may possibly be invoked: a doctor who lies about what is planned may be liable for deceit (**6.2**); a doctor who does not reveal facts which a reasonable medical practitioner would have revealed may be liable for negligence (**5.14**). However, in both cases, P would not be able to recover damages unless it can be proved that he or she would not have agreed to the operation but for the doctor's misbehaviour.

Doctors who act in circumstances where P is unconscious, or for some other reason cannot be asked or give consent, are sometimes said to act on an 'implied consent'. But this legal fiction is misleading: cases of this sort are dealt with here under the heading of 'necessity' (**11.42**). There is some scope for 'implied consent' so long as it is genuine: P's consent need not take any particular form, and consent to an operation will include consent to all procedures necessarily incidental to it.

Consent inferred from the existence of an obvious danger

11.6 *Introduction* In the mid-Victorian period, when actions by employees against their employers were a not altogether welcome novelty, it was common for actions to be defeated on the ground of consent. The consent was often inferred from the mere fact that the employee knew of the risk. Perhaps as a reaction against this, later cases stressed that mere knowledge of a risk was quite different from agreement not to sue anyone who created it (eg *Smith v Charles Baker and Son* (1891)). However, this can at best be described as a half-truth. Some potential plaintiffs have better reasons than others for taking risks, and this seems to play a heavy part in the court's decision whether to infer consent from knowledge of the risk. So while knowledge of the risk seems to be a pre-requisite for a finding that P has agreed to run it, it is not always clear what else is necessary.

11.7 *Car cases* The courts are reluctant to infer consent to bad driving, even where P is very well aware of an increased risk of danger.

> *Dann v Hamilton* (1939) Dann accepted a lift from Hamilton, whom she knew to be drunk, though he appeared to be still capable of exercising care. 'Hamilton seems to have been somewhere in the limbo which divides complete sobriety from mild intoxication'. Held: she did not consent to the injuries she suffered from his bad driving.

> *Nettleship v Weston* (1971) Nettleship, a driving instructor, was injured by the driving of his pupil Weston on her third lesson, when she crashed into a lamppost. Held: he could sue her for his injuries.

No doubt the existence of compulsory liability insurance is a factor here. In *Nettleship*, there was evidence that P had checked in advance that D was covered by insurance; however, it does not appear that the court's decision would have been any different if he had not. In any event, it seems that consent may today be irrelevant in car cases (**11.15**).

11.8 *Sporting cases* The courts take it for granted that sports are risky and that P has no business complaining of injury unless it was of a quite different type from that which P could reasonably have expected to encounter.

317

Simms v Leigh Rugby Football Club Ltd (1969)   Simms played rugby at an 'away' game in a field, with a concrete wall seven feet three inches from the touchline. He sued the occupiers of the field in respect of injuries sustained through his head colliding with it. Held: by playing he consented to this risk.

White v Blackmore (1972)   White was catapulted into the air after an accident with safety ropes at a jalopy race. He had been standing the wrong side of the ropes, but he would have been caught in the same way if he had been standing on the right side. Held: this risk was so unusual that he could not be taken to have agreed to run it. (Note, however, that White lost the case on another point (11.13).)

P cannot sue when the sport in question was an obviously foolish enterprise in the first place.

Morris v Murray (1991)   After an afternoon's drinking, Morris and Murray set out on a trip in a light aircraft, in conditions of poor weather and visibility which had grounded other air traffic. Held: neither could sue the other for injuries sustained.

11.9   *Employment cases*   Risks which are inherent in the job P is employed to do will not come within the defence. P will probably know of the risks all too well, but in reality has no choice but to run them, and so cannot be said to consent to them. However, where the risk in question is not only obvious but is also easy to avoid, then the courts may be able to infer consent to run it.

Gledhill v Liverpool Abattoir Utility Co Ltd (1957)   Gledhill was employed as a pig-slaughterer. He was injured when a pig he had just killed fell on top of him, falling out of the slip-ring attached to its leg. The rings were well constructed and Gledhill knew of the risk. Held: Gledhill had impliedly agreed to run the risk and could not sue.

However, in most such cases, D's real argument will be that the risk is inherent in the job and so not really avoidable by anything D did. It is really a denial that the employer's duty has been broken, rather than a defence of consent as such. Where D is in a position to do something to lessen the risk, the courts will usually insist that it is done. Note also that the Lords have rejected the so-called 'fireman's rule', that workers in dangerous trades such as firefighting cannot sue those who made their services necessary. So if D negligently starts a fire and P is injured in putting it out, P can sue (*Ogwo v Taylor* (1987)) (**4.21**).

A special case is where P's action is based on breach of a statutory duty by P's employer. It would offend against the policy of the employment safety legislation to allow a defence of consent to run the risks of the job. Accordingly, the defence is not usually available. In extreme circumstances, however, where the breach of statutory duty was itself P's responsibility, the courts consider that it would be unjust not to allow it. But strict requirements must be observed. Suppose P's complaint is that he was injured through working on an unsafe roof without using a crawling board, contrary to statute, and D's answer is that P could easily have used a board if he had chosen to. This is generally a matter for the defence of contributory negligence, which may reduce P's damages somewhat (**11.17**). D may, however, be able to defeat P's claim *entirely*, so long as P's failure to use the boards is itself a breach of statutory duty *by P*, and D, while technically in breach of the law, was in no way at fault (*Ginty v Belmont Building Supplies Ltd* (1959)). The defence of consent is therefore available to D where P is 'the sole author of his own misfortune'. It will be defeated if at least part of the blame lies with D, as where D failed to supply necessary equipment or training, or gave orders which contributed to the accident (see *Boyle v Kodak Ltd* (1969); *Imperial Chemical Industries Ltd v Shatwell* (1965)).

11.10 *Rescuer cases* In this area as in others (**3.31**), the courts are reluctant to condemn the behaviour of rescuers and would-be rescuers. The fact that P proceeded despite the obvious dangers might, indeed, be grounds for the award of a medal. Generally speaking, then, a plea of consent will fail where P is attempting to save others from a peril of D's own making. A fairly typical case is *Haynes v Harwood* (1935). A rare case where such a plaintiff fails is *Cutler v United Dairies (London) Ltd* (1933). Here P was injured during his rather inept attempt to catch D's runaway horse. Possibly the decision is to be explained by the point that no one was in immediate danger from the animal.

11.11 *The mentally unbalanced plaintiff* In cases where P was mentally ill and D knew it, the courts have been prepared to make D liable for the consequences of P's own voluntary act (*Reeves v Metropolitan Police Comr* (1997)) – even where P had committed suicide (**1.28**). Obviously it would have been futile to rule in P's favour on liability if the court were then to apply the defence of consent, and so of course they have refused to do so. The doctrinal basis for this is unclear, although presumably it is along the lines that D, at least, cannot treat P as a voluntary agent, whether or not P would for other purposes be so treated.

11.12 A redundant principle? It is not obvious that a principle of 'consent' is necessary to explain these cases. P does not very obviously 'consent', in any normal sense, in any of them. Where the courts refuse liability, this is usually better explained by the suggestion that D did not break the duty, perhaps because all that the duty required was to warn P of the danger. This is particularly obvious in the case of occupiers' liability, where the question whether P was warned is clearly part of the duty the occupier owes (**4.25**), but is a point of general validity. Given the existence of a defence of contributory negligence, many have suggested that the ability to infer consent from the existence of danger is quite unnecessary.

Consent inferred from the posting of a legal notice

11.13 A rather different situation is where D posts a notice which warns P, in general terms, that D accepts no legal liability to P or to others in P's position. The notice may or may not give any indication of what sources of danger D might be concerned at. This problem is of most relevance to occupiers' liability. A typical notice would be positioned at the entrance to D's land and grant general permission for entry on conditions, one of which would be that the occupier would be under no liability. By contrast with the cases discussed above, the case law discloses relatively little sympathy to P. If D is entitled to keep others out of his or her land, it follows that D is entitled to let them in only subject to conditions, some of which may restrict P's rights to sue. But these cases are old, and a very different attitude is taken today, at least if D is a business or governmental body. This change of heart has been achieved through legislation, which is described below:

- The test is said to be whether D has done enough to warn people generally that no liability is accepted. It follows that there is usually no very careful examination of P's own situation, to determine whether in fact P saw the warning. It seems clear that P cannot escape the effect of the notice if the reasonable person in P's position would have read it (*Ashdown v Samuel Williams & Sons Ltd* (1957)). It is unclear to what extent P can plead factors such as illiteracy or lack of age which made it impossible to read. In *Geier v Kujawa, Weston and Warne Bros (Transport) Ltd* (1970) an 18-year old German woman who spoke little English was held able to escape the effect of an exempting notice, in circumstances where it bound people generally.

- As the notice is a legal instrument removing P's rights, it is read against the person relying on it ('*contra proferentem*'). It is read as narrowly as possible, any ambiguity being resolved in favour of P rather than D. Nonetheless, prominently displayed notices exempting D from liability for accidents 'howsoever caused' have been held to mean just that and to exclude all liability (eg *White v Blackmore* (1972)).

- It is open to P to argue that, while aware of the conditions D meant to impose, nonetheless P had no real choice but to enter, and accordingly cannot be said to have freely accepted the terms. So when P entered D's dock in the course of his job as a lighterman and was injured by a defective rope, D was held unable to rely on exempting conditions displayed at the entrance to the dock (*Burnett v British Waterways Board* (1973)).

It is not entirely clear on what basis the doctrine defeats P's rights, when it does. The cases usually suggest that it is a doctrine of 'conditional licence': P is only allowed onto the land on condition that no cause of action arises. If so, it would be distinct from the doctrine of consent generally. This point matters, for if the true basis is conditional licence it is hard to see how it can apply to trespassers, as they enter without a licence and in defiance of the need for one. But there is no very obvious reason why trespassers cannot be subject to the doctrine of consent. The point is open (**4.29**).

11.14 *Unfair Contract Terms Act 1977* A major limit is placed on the doctrine of consent by the Unfair Contract Terms Act 1977, s 2. This section absolutely bars exclusion or restriction of personal injury liability in negligence by 'any contract term or notice' (s 2(1)), and subjects liability in respect of property damage or pure economic loss to a test of reasonableness (s 2(2)). 'Notice' is defined as including 'an announcement, whether or not in writing, and any other communication or pretended communication' (s 14). This provision is aimed primarily at formal notices of the *Ashdown v Williams* type, but it may have broader effects:

- The Act applies only to 'business liability' (s 1(3)), though 'business' is defined to include 'a profession and the activities of any government department or local or public authority' (s 14). D's business liability comprises 'things done or to be done by a person in the course of a business (whether his own business or another's)' and occupiers' liability in respect of business premises. But liability to those admitted only for 'recreational or educational' purposes can be excluded, so long as the admission cannot be treated as part of the business purpose of the occupier (amendments to s 1(3) effected by the Occupiers' Liability Act 1984, s 2).

- Where the test of reasonableness applies, various factors are relevant. In *Smith v Eric S Bush* (1990), Lord Griffiths mentioned particularly whether P and D were of equal bargaining strength, whether it would have been practical for P go elsewhere, how difficult it was for D to take good care and do the act properly, and whether it was open to D to insure ([1990] 1 AC 858-859) (**5.24**).

- It is not entirely clear where the Act leaves liability generally. The Act was meant to safeguard P's right to have due care taken of his or her interests and so presumably it will not be read as going further. In an occupiers' liability case, presumably it is still open to D to argue a notice was all that was required to warn P of the danger. In a negligent misstatement case, D can argue that, in the light of the notice and its prominence, it was unreasonable for P to rely on D's statement. But the *Eric S Bush* case gives little encouragement to this argument, emphasising that exemption clauses are caught by the Act *whatever* form they take (s 13) (**5.24**). Section 2(3) may have been meant to preserve the defence of consent in cases of obvious risk. However, it is very obscurely worded and there is no consensus on its meaning: 'Where a contract term or notice purports to exclude or restrict liability for negligence a person's agreement to or awareness of it is not of itself to be taken as indicating his voluntary acceptance of any risk'.

Other statutory controls

11.15 The Unfair Contract Terms Act 1977 put other statutory controls somewhat in the shade, but did not abolish them. Of particular interest to tort lawyers is Road Traffic Act 1988, s 149, which applies to liabilities caught by compulsory third-party insurance. The section provides that agreements by passengers not to invoke this liability are void, and '[t]he fact that a person so carried has willingly accepted as his the risk of negligence on the part of the user shall not be treated as negating any such liability of the user' (s 149(3)). This broad wording seems to catch not merely contractual exclusions, but any variety of the consent defence (*Pitts v Hunt* (1990)). In general, liabilities stricter than the negligence duty may be excluded; though see Consumer Protection Act 1987, s 7 (absolute duty in respect of defective products is not excludable).

The limits of consent

11.16   There are certain situations where the criminal law does not permit a defence of consent; most famously in recent years in *R v Brown* (1993), where a group of sado-masochists were convicted of assaults upon one another. However, the criminal law and civil law pursue rather different objects, and it by no means follows that consent would be no defence in a civil action on the same facts. The practical answer is probably that any likely action would fail for illegality (**11.26**) and so the consent point would not arise.

Contributory negligence

Introduction

11.17   Under the defence of contributory negligence, D argues that P was also to some extent to blame for the loss P suffered. At common law, this was a complete defence to P's action. The old doctrine generated a complex jurisprudence around it, and in particular around the idea that whichever of P and D had the 'last opportunity' to avoid the harm should bear the loss himself. The 'all or nothing' quality of the defence ensured that there were plenty of cases, but came to be seen as its principal disadvantage.

Under the modern law, statute provides for a *reduction* in damages if the defence is established, the judge having a discretion in the matter. While the sophistications of the old law were never expressly abolished, they have quietly withered and can now be forgotten. In some ways, the existence of the defence is a curiosity, for it enables the courts to do something which they staunchly decline to do in other areas: namely, to reduce the liability of an admittedly guilty defendant on the ground that someone else is also responsible (see **9.26**). It is not entirely clear whether, on balance, the legislation has made matters better for plaintiffs or not. Certainly it means that a finding of contributory negligence has less drastic consequences than it would have done before. It is also probably true that the change has made it harder to dismiss P's claim outright on the ground of neglect of obvious risk and therefore contributed to the decline of the defence of consent. On the other hand, the existence of the defence is a good general weapon in D's hand for the reduction of damages which before the Act D would have had to pay in full.

In which torts does the defence apply?

11.18   Most of the case law concerns D's liability in negligence, where it is well settled that the defence applies. It is not absolutely clear which other torts are caught:

- There is a conflict of authority on whether the defence can apply to assault or battery (*Lane v Holloway* (1968) says that it does not; *Murphy v Culhane* (1977) says that that it does).

- It has recently been held that the defence is not available in cases of fraud (*Alliance and Leicester Building Society v Edgestop Ltd* (1994)) or conspiracy to bribe P's employees (*Corporacion Nacional del Cobre de Chile v Sogemin Metals Ltd* (1997)). This is obviously fair in cases where P is suing a fraudster. It seems unreasonable to allow a defendant who has exploited P's gullibility to reduce the damages on the ground that P should not have been so gullible. But it is not so obvious where, as in *Edgestop* itself, D's liability is vicarious only.

- In the tort of negligent misstatement, it is a pre-requisite of liability that P's reliance on D's statement be reasonable. Accordingly, pleas of contributory negligence can be expected to be rare, possibly being confined to cases where P's reliance was initially reasonable but ought reasonably to have stopped before it did. It has occasionally been assumed that the defence applies, without any consideration of the point (eg *Edwards v Lee* (1991); *Platform Home Loans v Oyston Shipways Ltd* (1998)).

- It is clear that the defence applies to breach of statutory duty (*Caswell v Powell Duffryn Associated Collieries Ltd* (1940)). This was not obvious, as much liability in breach of statutory duty exists precisely to save workers from the consequences of their own neglect of their safety. It is the careless workers, not the careful, who need the protection of the legislation. This problem is resolved by findings that the worker's share of the responsibility is relatively low.

- The defence applies to nuisance (*Trevett v Lee* [1955] 1 WLR 113, 121, Evershed MR), and to liability for animals (Animals Act 1971, ss 5(1) and 10).

The Law Reform (Contributory Negligence) Act 1945

11.19 In cases where the Act applies, '[w]here any person suffers damage as the result partly of his own fault and partly of the fault of any other person or persons, a claim in respect of that damage shall not be defeated by reason of the fault of the person suffering the damage, but the damages recoverable in respect thereof shall be reduced to such extent as the court thinks just and equitable having regard to the claimant's share in the responsibility for the damage' (s 1(1)). It seems clear that the Act applies in any tort action where the defence of contributory negligence is available. It is much disputed whether or when the Act may be invoked where D has been found liable only in breach of contract. The Act implies that D must be guilty of 'negligence, breach of statutory duty or other act or omission which gives rise to liability in tort ...' (s 4). In *Forsikringsaktieselskapet Vesta v Butcher* [1988] 2 All ER 43, 53, O'Connor LJ was prepared to agree that the Act applied in a contract action where the contractual duty was the same as the tort duty that would exist independently of the contract. But the point is controversial and it seems strange if P, having established that D is liable in contract, is required to discuss whether or not a claim could also have been brought in tort.

Contributory 'negligence' and causation

11.20 It is not strictly correct to describe carelessness by P as contributory 'negligence', for 'negligence' strictly implies breach of a duty of care (**1.22**). It is simply a well-established phrase meaning that P is insufficiently careful in respect of his or her own safety. It is irrelevant that P was careless at the incident at which P's injuries resulted, if there is no causal link between the carelessness and the damage. The defence is not meant as a punishment for carelessness, but as a finding that P as well as D was responsible for the loss P suffered. P will escape a reduction of damages if there was no causal link. So if D runs down a drunken pedestrian, the pedestrian will recover in full if it is clear that the incident would not have gone differently had the pedestrian been sober. Nonetheless, partly as a reaction to the tangled pre-1945 law, the courts are reluctant to involve themselves in any very precise analysis of causation here.

> *Jones v Livox Quarries Ltd* (1952) In defiance of work safety instructions, Jones accepted a lift on the back of a company quarrying machine as it drove along. He was crushed when another vehicle went into the back of it. Jones argued that the purpose of the safety instructions was to guard against workers being thrown off the machine as it drove, and his breach was therefore irrelevant to the accident which happened. Held: Jones was contributorily negligent and his damage should be reduced by 20%.

It appears that the burden of proof on causation is on D.

> *Owens v Brimmell* (1977) P was injured in a car accident. He had not been wearing a seat belt. It was unclear whether P had been injured through being thrown forward, or through part of the car being forced back on him. Held: there would be no reduction for contributory negligence on this ground, though there would be reduction of 20% for driving with a drunk driver.

P's characteristics

11.21 P's 'negligence' or lack of it will be judged by the standard of the reasonable person of P's characteristics in P's situation. Where P is under 18, P is entitled to be judged by the standard of a reasonable person of that age (*Gough v Thorne* (1966), which concerned a 13½-year old). There are *dicta* that there are ages below which young children can never be found guilty of contributory negligence at all – though there are *dicta* to the contrary as well. A 12-year old, who ran out into the road without looking, was held 75% responsible for his injuries in *Morales v Eccleston* (1991). One Scots case, *McKinnell v White* (1971), considered a 5-year old contributorily negligent for running out into the road; it is doubtful whether this would be followed south of the border. As a rule of thumb, we can say that the law usually makes allowance for P's physical infirmities, though not P's mental ones.

Examples

11.22 *Motoring and road use* The duties required of drivers and other road users are very diverse. It sometimes happens that the court considers that the reasonable traveller would not have set out on the journey which P did, so that the entire drive is one long example of contributory negligence.

> *Gregory v Kelly* (1978) A passenger accepted a lift in a car. Both the passenger and the driver knew that the foot brake was not working. Neither wore a seat belt. When an accident resulted, the passenger sued the driver. Held: the passenger could recover damages, but with a reduction of 40%.

The courts have not only been reluctant to lay down many general rules here, but have positively stated that it will usually be wrong to do so. To see why, consider the suggestion made in *Bailey v Geddes* (1938) that if a car collides with a pedestrian, then this cannot be contributory negligence if the collision took place on a pedestrian crossing. As rules go, this is not a bad one, but almost immediately exceptions began to be made. So *Bailey* was distinguished in cases where the pedestrian stepped in front of the car unexpectedly (*Knight v Sampson* (1938)). Case law began to tackle such questions as precisely when P was required to be 'on the crossing' for this purpose, and what counted as the 'crossing'. For example, was a traffic island in the middle of the road part of the 'crossing'? (Held: No; *Wilkinson v Chetham-Strode* (1940).) Later cases found it necessary to emphasise that the reasonable driver must be prepared for ill-advised acts by pedestrians, while not blaming them for anything truly unforeseeable (eg *Hurt v Murphy* (1971)). Clearly, any hope for a clear rule dividing responsibility between P and D was almost hopeless before the 1945 Act, and entirely hopeless after it. The point is not that the behaviour of the courts is random and unpredictable, but merely that it cannot be reduced to a clear set of rules. Indeed, any judge who tries to extract *rules* from past authorities, as distinct from using them as examples for comparison to the instant case, is likely to be making a mistake.

Having said that, some straightforward situations recur with regularity. So without denying that each case is to be judged on the basis of its own peculiar facts, nonetheless it is possible to generalise about what the court will say. One such area is that of accidents caused by D where P was (if a car driver) not wearing a seat-belt or (if a motorcycle rider) not wearing a crash helmet. *Froom v Butcher* (1976) established that contributory negligence in such cases will be somewhere in a band running from 0% to 25%, the precise point on the band being established by reference to a number of factors:

- *Causation is the major factor*   If P's injuries would have been wholly avoided if P had been wearing a belt, a 25% deduction will be appropriate. If wearing a belt would have made no difference, or if it would have meant that P would have suffered different but equally serious injuries, then no deduction should be made. 15% would be a typical reduction, where P's injuries would have been considerably less severe if P had been wearing a seat belt.

- *Unreasonableness of wearing a belt*   Certain plaintiffs will be able to escape a reduction if they have particular reasons why it would have been pointless, unsafe or otherwise for them to wear a belt. Possible examples are if P is heavily pregnant, or is unusually fat, or has a phobia about constraint (*Condon v Condon* (1978)).

- *Other factors*   If there are other heads of contributory negligence by P, this may push the total reduction up beyond 50%, as where P fails to wear a belt in the knowledge that the ride is likely to be a little rough.

It seems to make relatively little difference whether the case against D is an unusually strong one, or whether it is just an ordinary example of negligence. Since the time of *Froom v Butcher*, legislation has provided that it is a criminal offence, in most situations, not to wear a belt (Road Traffic Act 1988, s 14, consolidating a provision in force 31 January 1983). However, this does not seem to have altered the seriousness with which the courts view failure to wear a belt. This is no great surprise, as *Froom v Butcher* was happy to amalgamate the law on failure to wear a belt (not then illegal) with the law on failure to wear a motorcycle helmet (already at that time illegal).

It remains to be seen whether the courts will in time rule that cyclists injured in road accidents will have their damages reduced for failure to wear a cycle helmet. As with seat belts, there are arguments both ways. How much safer do the helmets make cyclists? Is the gain in safety really so significant that a decision not to wear one is comparable to life-threatening negligence on the road? Do the helmets in fact make cyclists *less* safe, by bestowing a feeling of security and therefore encouraging more risk-taking?

11.23 *Employment* The duties of employers are extremely diverse, whether under the tort of negligence or through the many statutory duties applicable to the employment relationship. It appears that in such cases the courts pay some attention to the seriousness of D's breach, and so will attribute a lesser share of the responsibility to the employee in cases where D's breach was a relatively serious one (*Quintas v National Smelting Co Ltd* (1961)). While the exercise is in essence one of comparing P's fault and D's fault, however, there is no pretence that P and D are to be judged by the same standards:

- *Burden of proof* It is for D, not P, to establish the defence, and accordingly there will not be a finding of contributory negligence merely because this is one possibility and P has not established precisely how the accident occurred (*Smithwick v National Coal Board* (1950)).

- *Allowances made for P's situation* Not too much will be expected of P. Attention must be paid 'to the long hours and the fatigue, to the slackening of attention which naturally comes from constant repetition of the same operation, to the noise and confusion ... to his pre-occupation in what he is actually doing at the cost perhaps of some inattention to his own safety' (*Caswell v Powell Duffryn Associated Collieries Ltd* [1940] AC 152, 178-179, Lord Wright). Much of the point of industrial safety legislation is lost if a momentary lapse of concentration deprives P of a claim – no matter how foolish this lapse can be made to appear in the calm of a later court hearing. Indeed, in one case it was said that industrial safety legislation is not merely for the protection of the careful, 'but, human nature being what it is, also the careless, the indolent, the inadvertent, the weary, and even perhaps in some cases, the disobedient' (*Carr v Mercantile Produce Co Ltd* [1949] 2 KB 601, 608, Stable J).

- *Care by employer* P is entitled to assume that the employer has been careful and has complied with all relevant statutory duties. The courts will be unsympathetic to an argument that P ought to have realised that this was unrealistic (*Westwood v Post Office* (1974)).

- *P's 'fault' does not occur in a vacuum* The employer's duties may include a duty to warn P of poor work practices, and accordingly any argument that an accident is 'wholly' P's fault will receive close and suspicious scrutiny (eg *General Cleaning Contractors Ltd v Christmas* (1953)).

One example of the lack of symmetry between P's fault and D's fault is where the 'fault' attributed to D consists wholly of some default by P. In *Stapley v Gypsum Mines Ltd* (1953) the plaintiffs were instructed by their foreman to bring down the roof of a certain section of mine before they began work there. This proved more difficult than they had anticipated. In defiance of their orders, they began work there anyway. The roof collapsed on its own. Their widows sued the company: for the men to be working with the roof in that condition put the employers in breach of their statutory responsibilities. Even though the Lords considered that there was no failure of supervision – the employees were responsible and had considerable experience – they nonetheless held that their widows could recover, subject to a deduction of 80% for contributory negligence. There are occasionally cases where damages are altogether refused, either on the ground that the employee's carelessness breaks any causal connection between D's default and P's injuries (eg *Norris v W Moss and Sons Ltd* (1954), where P's 'fantastically wrong' initiative resulted in injury), or where the court feels that P's responsibility for the accident must be assessed at 100% (*Jayes v IMI (Kynock) Ltd* (1985)).

It should now be apparent why the decision in *McWilliams v Sir William Arrol & Co Ltd* (1962) is regarded as so anomalous (**10.25**). Where D is bound to provide safety equipment and to take reasonable steps to persuade the site workers to use it, and then P is injured through failure to use the equipment, then evidence that P would have refused to use it is a ground of contributory negligence. But it is curious to find a court putting *all* of the blame on the worker, by a ruling that the employers' behaviour did not 'cause' the accident. It seems a classic case of joint responsibility. If a culture had grown up in the firm in which the use of safety equipment was neglected, then the employer's duty was not satisfied by simply accepting this situation. But it is in any event hard to reconcile all these cases in this difficult area.

100% contributory negligence: a problem

11.24 The Act of 1945 appears to have been drafted so as to give the court a free hand in apportioning liability between P and D. Nonetheless, it was suggested in *Pitts v Hunt* (1990) that the court cannot use it to apportion 100% of the blame to P. The reasoning appears to be that the Act only applies where P suffers damage 'as the result partly of his own fault and partly of the fault of any other person' (s 1(1)), whereas a 100% reduction implies that it is wholly P's fault. This seems dubious, however. There does not seem to be any logical inconsistency in saying *both* that P and D are at fault *and* that it is 'just and equitable' to reduce P's damages to zero. In any event, the Court of Appeal's logic seems to stop short of its proper end: if the Act does not apply, then presumably the old common law rule, defeating P's claim entirely, applies, with the effect that the claim is defeated. So it should make no difference whether the Act applies or not. *Pitts v Hunt* did not refer to earlier cases which allowed a 100% reduction (eg *Jayes v IMI (Kynock) Ltd*) (**11.23**), and is therefore a weak authority.

'Proportionate fault'

11.25 The contributory negligence rule only reduces P's damages for P's own fault. It is anomalous. Generally speaking, where D has been found responsible for P's damage, it is no defence for D to show that others too were responsible, and the risk of not being able to make out a case against any of them is on D, not P (**9.26**). Various critics have recently suggested that D should be entitled to a reduction in damages for 'proportionate fault'. That is, that while D was responsible for P's loss, nonetheless the fault was by no means as grave as that of others, and accordingly D should be entitled to a reduction, regardless of whether those others can be caught. This has been pleaded especially in cases where D's fault was in not warning P of the activities of criminals who go on to harm P: D's fault is not to be equated with that of the criminals, and so D's liability ought not to be as great (**1.29**). This view has however found little sympathy in the courts so far.

Illegality

Introduction and definition

11.26   It is sometimes open to D to argue that P's claim should 'shock the conscience of the court', or that it is so undesirable that it should not be permitted. The principle is well established, but its application is vague, as are the goals the courts are attempting to pursue here. The doctrine has been summed up as being that 'bad people get less' (Weir, *Casebook on Tort* (7th edn, 1992), 256). But this gives a misleadingly broad impression of the doctrine. It is certainly true that bad people get less in tort. For example, those who already have bad reputations will have a hard time convincing a court that any defamatory utterances made their reputations worse (**8.22**). But P can be as bad as you like, yet still be entitled not to be run over by D's car – no matter how saintly D might be as a rule.

The rule is that there must be something so shocking about *the claim P is now making* that it cannot be permitted. The Latin tag is *ex turpi causa non oritur actio*: 'No action arises from a disgraceful cause'. The defence is not an opportunity for D to sling mud at random, but rather to show that P's activities *in the case before the court* were so thoroughly tied up with serious illegality that the two cannot fairly be separated. The connection must be a close one. It has been said that if two burglars are on their way to a house they mean to steal from and one picks the other's pocket, there is no defence to an action in tort. The tort is quite distinct from the illegal plan (*National Coal Board v England* [1954] AC 403, 429, Lord Asquith). There is no necessary connection with 'illegality' in any normal sense. Workers who are guilty of offences against industrial safety legislation do not seem to be in any danger of being met by a defence of illegality if they sue for injuries suffered. Perfectly legal conduct may in some circumstances sufficiently affront the public conscience as to make recovery impossible (*Kirkham v Chief Constable of the Greater Manchester Police* [1990] 3 All ER 246, 251, Lloyd LJ).

Serious crime

11.27   Where P and D are jointly engaged in a serious criminal escapade, such as a robbery, then an action in consequence of injuries sustained will fail. So the classic example given is where one burglar blows the lock off a safe so carelessly that it injures the other (*National Coal*

Board v England [1954] AC 403, 429, Lord Asquith). Some judges prefer to put this on the ground that it is impossible to set an appropriate standard of care in such cases. But it is not *meaningless* to say that the careless burglar did the job badly; it is another question whether it provides a good ground for his colleague to recover damages. Examples are hard to come by, however. In *Ashton v Turner* (1980) one participant in a drunken attempt at burglary sued the other for injuries sustained as they attempted a high-speed getaway. Illegality was one ground given for rejecting this claim, but consent to run the risk was another, and quite sufficient in itself. Where the action is against those who were the victims of the crime, or were trying to prevent it, there is little sign that the defence is available. Rather, an artificially low, but nonetheless real, standard of care is applied, so that P can recover, but only after producing a great deal more evidence of lack of care by D than is usually required.

> *Marshall v Osmond* (1983)   Marshall was attempting to drive off with a stolen car, but was followed by a police constable. Marshall then stopped and attempted to run away, but was knocked down by the police constable's car. Held: no defence of consent was applicable, but the duty owed by road-users was relative to the circumstances in which they were placed, and by that standard the police constable was not negligent.

It was at one time suggested that if a householder shot a burglar then the burglar has no cause of action, even if the householder's use of force was subsequently found to be excessive, or indeed if manslaughter were established (*Murphy v Culhane* [1977] QB 94, 98, Lord Denning MR). However, it appears that this is not the law. In *Revill v Newbery* (1996) burglars attempted to break into a garden shed. Unknown to them, the owner was hiding inside to forestall theft, and in a panic fired his 12-bore shotgun through the keyhole, causing one of the burglars serious injuries. The civil court rejected the owner's defence of self-defence, which had been accepted by a jury on a criminal charge of wounding. Contributory negligence was assessed at 66.66%; the defence of illegality was rejected entirely. The decision is a controversial one, but in line with earlier cases. So for example in *Farrell v Secretary of State for Defence* (1980), where would-be robbers were shot dead by soldiers who thought they were terrorists, the issue was whether the use of deadly force was justified in the circumstances, and if it was not there was no additional defence of illegality.

At the root of criticism of *Revill v Newbery* (1996) seems to be dissatisfaction with the law on self-defence and the defence of property. If the current law is accepted as good, so that those who use deadly force where it cannot be justified are themselves guilty of serious criminal offences (a big *if*!), then there does not seem to be anything wrong with *Revill*. Both P and D are criminals, and the most that P is entitled to is a division of responsibility between them.

Fights

11.28 It appears to be the law that where P and D fight and D injures P, it is a defence if it can be shown that P provoked the fight. This is sometimes put on the ground of illegality and sometimes, confusingly, on the ground of consent. So if P sets out to beat up D but meets with a fiercer response than he bargained for, P has no action whether or not D exceeded the limits of permissible self-defence (*Murphy v Culhane* (1977)). However, this may not be so if P's attack on D, while unjustified, was nonetheless relatively trifling when compared to D's response (*Lane v Holloway* (1968)). In a case of that sort, consideration needs to be given to a reduction for P's contributory negligence, though the Court of Appeal in *Lane v Holloway* declined to make one.

Tax evasion

11.29 In *Saunders v Edwards* (1987), which concerned deceit over the sale of a flat, it appeared that both parties had engaged in a fraud on the revenue, grossly overstating the value of fixtures in the flat to reduce liability to stamp duty. This was not regarded as providing a defence to action in deceit. The case can be viewed as one where the illegality was rather peripheral to the cause of action. It was also one where the court regarded D's fraud as rather more deserving of condemnation than P's tax evasion. 'The moral culpability of the defendant greatly outweighs any on the part of the plaintiffs. He cannot be allowed to keep the fruits of his fraud' ([1987] 2 All ER 660, Kerr LJ).

Reckless driving

11.30 In *Pitts v Hunt* (1990) P (aged 18) and D (aged 16) spent the evening getting drunk at a disco. They then set off home on D's motor-cycle, with P riding pillion. With encouragement from P, D drove in a reckless manner, doing his best to startle other road users. They collided with an on-coming car; at the inquest, D was found to have double the legal blood-alcohol level. P survived and sued. Liability was refused on the ground of illegality. The result is not surprising, but it does not sit happily with the other material on illegality. The activity of the defendants was undoubtedly criminal in several respects, especially given that D was neither licensed nor insured to drive the motorcycle and might have led to serious injury to other road users (though it didn't). But the criminality in the case is hardly in the same league as bank robbery. The real complaint against P and D's conduct is not so much that it was illegal as that it was crazy. The case is indeed a teenage re-run of *Morris v Murray*, where P and D were older and had access to a more impressive vehicle, but showed a similar level of concern for their own and others' safety (**11.8**). The court doubted whether it was possible to reduce damages for contributory negligence by 100% (**11.24**); in any event, they said, when P and D were both engaged in an unlawful and dangerous exercise, the appropriate reduction would be 50%. The case is best categorised as an application of the defence of consent, with the court being unwilling to acknowledge that it applied in the face of Road Traffic Act 1988, s 149(3), which excludes the defence in cases involving compulsory third-party road insurance (**11.15**). Certainly *Pitts* is very unsatisfactory guide to liability outside its own immediate facts.

The mentally ill plaintiff

11.31 Controversially, the Court of Appeal has recently held that where P commits a serious criminal act, P cannot sue a health authority for failing to treat his mental illness, even if reasonably good treatment would have avoided P's later act (*Clunis v Camden and Islington Health Authority* (1997)). The criminality in the case was of the very highest sort. P, who had a long history of mental illness, had stabbed another man to death, three months after his release from hospital, and was convicted of manslaughter. *Clunis* in effect contradicts earlier, similar cases where no illegality point was raised, and P was allowed to succeed (eg *Meah v McCreamer* (**10.38**)). The Court of Appeal stressed that P's plea of insanity at his trial for murder had been rejected, and so P had to be treated as an independent agent, responsible for his actions. However, his plea of diminished responsibility had been accepted (thus reducing what would otherwise have been murder to manslaughter), so this point seems doubtful. This is plainly a rapidly developing area of the law.

Limitation

Introduction

11.32   For a number of reasons, it is considered to be unfair to leave D at risk of a legal action for too long. Accordingly, action for a tort must be brought within a certain period of time of the tort's commission. If D raises the issue, it is for P to prove that the action has been brought within the period. The basic period is six years (Limitation Act 1980, s 2), but there are a number of exceptions:

- actions for *defamation* must be commenced within one year, though there is a discretion to waive this period where it would cause unfairness to P (Limitation Act 1980, ss 4A and 32A, as amended by Defamation Act 1996, s 5);

- actions in *negligence for personal injury* must usually be commenced within three years, though there are wide exceptions to this (**11.36**);

- special provision is made for *latent damage* by statute (**11.41**);

- a claim for *contribution* against a fellow tortfeasor must be brought within two years of the judgment or settlement which creates the claim (Limitation Act 1980, s 10);

- actions under the *Consumer Protection Act 1987* are subject to the normal time limits for the type of injury suffered, but also to an absolute ten-year longstop from the date on which D supplied the product to someone else (Limitation Act 1980, s 11A). This longstop is absolute, with no exception for disability (**11.33**) or concealment (**11.34**).

There is much case law on when the period first begins to run. The usual rule is that it begins to run from the first instant when P could have served a writ, whether or not P knew this. It will therefore sometimes be necessary to distinguish between torts, such as negligence, which are only actionable on proof of special damage, and torts which are actionable without it (see above, **10.9**). The former situation is by far the most common in practice. The basic time-limit in contract is also six years, but nonetheless tort is more favourable, as in contract time usually runs from the date of the breach of contract, whereas in tort it is usually from the date of the damage, which will be later. A special situation is the 'continuing tort', such as a 'continuing trespass' by leaving something unwelcome on P's land, or 'continuing nuisance' by allowing a state of affairs constituting a nuisance to continue for a period. A fresh tort is committed for every day that the tort is allowed to continue. Accordingly, a writ issued too late to complain of the commencement of the tort may nonetheless complain of the portion of the tort which fell within the limitation period.

Infancy and other disabilities

11.33 If, when time would ordinarily start to run against P, P is under 18 or suffering from unsoundness of mind, or both, then time does not run. It begins to run when P is both of age and of sound mind, or alternatively when P dies (Limitation Act 1980, s 28(1)). P suffers from unsoundness of mind if P is incapable of managing and administering his or her affairs by reason of a mental disorder under the Mental Health Act 1983. Disability delays the start of the period, but cannot stop the clock running once it has started. So if P suffered mental illness before his or her 18th birthday, it will stop the clock from ever starting. But a mental illness which was absent on P's 18th birthday will not stop the clock on any cause of action arising before it.

Concealment

11.34 Where D has deliberately concealed the commission of the tort or some material fact, or the action was itself based on D's fraud, then time does not begin to run until P could, with reasonable diligence, have been expected to discover the cause of action (Limitation Act 1980, s 32(1)). 'Deliberate concealment' is widely defined: 'deliberate commission of a breach of duty in circumstances in which it is unlikely to be discovered for some time amounts to deliberate concealment of the facts involved in that breach of duty' (s 32(2)). There is no test of moral turpitude beyond the fact that the concealment must be deliberate.

Kitchen v Royal Air Force Association (1958) Solicitors negligently failed to advise a widow of her possible claim for her husband's death. Subsequently, after the period of limitation had run on that claim, the solicitors deliberately failed to pass on an offer of £100 from those responsible for the death, in case their earlier negligence was revealed. Held: their original failure to give good advice did not constitute 'concealment', but their suppression of the offer letter did.

The effect of the section is only to prevent time running in the first place. If time has already started to run, subsequent concealment by D will not affect it (*Tito v Waddell (No 2)* [1977] 3 All ER 129, 245, Megarry V-C).

Personal injuries

11.35 *Assault and battery*   After some controversy, it has now been settled that the period for deliberate injuries is six years from their infliction, and that the special provision for personal injury caused by negligence (**11.36**) does not apply.

> *Stubbings v Webb* (1993)   Stubbings, over 30 at the time she issued the writ, sued Webb for assaults committed between her second and fourteenth birthdays, including rape when she was aged eleven. She claimed that she had not appreciated that she might have a cause of action until she realised that there might be a link between her early experiences and her later psychiatric problems. Held: the period was six years from the end of her minority, and so she could not issue a writ after her 24th birthday.

It is irrelevant whether Stubbings' action was framed as one in battery or in negligence. The question is whether it is P's case that D committed the tort negligently or intentionally.

11.36 *Negligence: The primary period*   Before 1963, the period in respect of personal injuries caused by negligence began to run as soon as the damage was suffered by P. The House of Lords held that this applied even where the damage was initially undiscoverable and only became unmistakable outside the period (*Cartledge v E Jopling & Sons Ltd* (1963)). Dissatisfaction at this result lead to a change in the law, so that time will now run only from the first point when P could reasonably have been expected to consider legal action. There is also a general discretion to waive the limitation period if justice would be served thereby (**11.37**).

Under the modern law, time will therefore begin to run only from 'the date of knowledge' (Limitation Act 1980, s 11(4)); that is, the first date on which P knew or ought reasonably to have known *all four* of the following:

- *That the injury was significant*   An injury is significant if a reasonable person in P's position would think it worthwhile suing someone liable for it, if they admitted liability and had funds to meet the claim (Limitation Act 1980, s 14(2)).

- *That the injury was attributable to the act or omission constituting the tort*   It is sufficient if in general terms P can be said to have this knowledge, whether or not P has precise knowledge of the acts or omissions concerned (*Wilkinson v Ancliff (BLT) Ltd* (1986)). It is not enough, however, if P knew the injury resulted from a surgical operation unless P also knew that the operation was negligently performed (*Bentley v Bristol and Weston Health Authority* (1991)).

- *D's identity*   It sometimes happens that P is initially ignorant of the identity of the appropriate defendant, as where P is the victim of a hit-and-run driver. Or again, P may initially have a false idea of the defendant's identity. For example, P might mean to sue his employer, which is part of a group of companies, the wrong company being specified on P's written contract of employment (*Simpson v Norwest Holst Southern Ltd* (1980)).

- *(Where D is allegedly liable for the fault of another) the identity of the other, and the additional facts showing that D is liable.*

P's 'knowledge' for this purpose includes everything that a person 'of the plaintiff's age, with his background, his intelligence, and his disabilities' would reasonably have known (*Davis v City & Hackney Health Authority* (1991)). It also includes things discoverable with the help of expert advice which it would have been reasonable to seek; though if P does in fact act reasonably in taking professional advice, P is only responsible for what P *in fact* finds out (Limitation Act 1980, s 14(3)). It is unclear precisely when P can be said to 'know' things of which P has only a strong suspicion. The courts seem reluctant to equate knowledge with belief. Certainly in cases where there was plainly something wrong, but P's beliefs fluctuated over a period, the courts seem reluctant to put the 'date of knowledge' too early, particularly as the statute does not allow the clock to be stopped once it has started. The mere fact that P's solicitor has issued a writ against D does not prove that P 'knew' D was liable; the solicitor may simply have been safeguarding P's position, in case D turned out to be liable (*Stephen v Riverside Health Authority* (1990)). It has even been held that a plaintiff who is certain in his or her own mind that D is responsible does not have 'knowledge' in a case where it is reasonable to ask for expert confirmation. The clock does not start until an expert has confirmed P's suspicions (*Nash v Eli Lilly & Co* (1993)). P's knowledge of the relevant law is absolutely irrelevant (Limitation Act 1980, s 14(1)).

11.37 *Negligence: discretion to waive the period* Even if this primary period has run, it is still open to P to argue that it would be equitable for the period of limitation to be waived (Limitation Act 1980, s 33). Various factors are taken into account under the section:

- Why did P delay so long? Did P act promptly and reasonably once P knew there might be a legal action?

- Will the evidence, on either side, still be coherent?

- How did D behave after the cause of action arose? In particular, how helpful or otherwise was D when responding to P's reasonable requests for information?

- Was P under any disability while time ran and, if so, for how long did it last?

- What steps did P take to get advice, and what was that advice?

All relevant circumstances are to be taken into account, whether or not they are specifically mentioned in the Act (s 33(3)). Any delay which can be attributed to P's own solicitors counts against P's case, partly because it is unfair that D should be prejudiced by such errors, but also because P might have a remedy against the solicitors themselves. The power to waive the primary period was originally meant only for exceptional cases, but it appears that the court's discretion is in no way fettered, and P does not have to demonstrate that the case is an unusual one (*Firman v Ellis* (1978)).

The section does not apply when P issued a writ within the primary period but then failed to serve it (*Walkley v Precision Forgings Ltd* (1979)). This rule may perhaps be justified on the ground that it will usually be P's own solicitor who is at fault in such a case. However, the rule applies whether or not there was a good reason for the failure to serve the writ (*Chappell v Cooper* (1980)); though if the failure was in some sense D's fault, D may be estopped from saying that the writ was too late for service (*Forward v Hendricks* (1997)).

11.38 *Negligence: the effect of P's death* Where P dies, there are two types of claim which might be brought: a claim by P's estate on the surviving cause of action, and (where the death was the result of the tort) a claim by P's relatives for loss of their dependency (**10.66**). The limitation rules are the same for both claims. Assuming that the death occurs while the primary period is still running, then the claim on death arises automatically, with its own three-year period which runs from the death or of the claimants' 'date of knowledge', whichever is the later (Limitation Act 1980, ss 11(5) and 12(2)). The discretion to waive the primary period applies to this claim.

Property damage

11.39 *Negligence: the primary period* The unfairness of holding P to a six-year period, regardless of whether P could possibly have discovered the damage within that period, much exercised a number of judges in the 1970s and 1980s. Indeed, the Court of Appeal was at one point prepared to say that P's cause of action only really arose when the injury was reasonably discoverable by P, so that time only began to run at that date (*Sparham-Souter v Town and Country Developments (Essex) Ltd* (1976)). The Lords soon overruled this, saying that the relevant date was the date of the damage, not the date when P could reasonably have discovered it (*Pirelli General Cable Works Ltd v Oscar Faber and Partners* (1983)). However, what the courts took away with one hand they gave back with the other. If the foundations of a house are damaged, this may have no immediate effect on the main structure of the building, let alone the safety of the inhabitants. So damage to a particular part of a building is suffered only when *that part* is damaged, even if the problem can be traced to structural damage committed at an earlier date (*Nitrigin Eireann Teoranta v Inco Alloys Ltd* (1992)). Confusingly, the Lords in *Pirelli* suggested that the matter might be different if the building was 'doomed from the start', in which case it would not be realistic to divide it up in this way. Most of the difficulties in this area have been avoided only by the *Murphy* decision, which effectively ruled out most of these claims as being claims for purely economic loss (**5.4**).

11.40 *Negligent misstatement: the primary period* Where P acts on D's poor professional advice and P comes to harm as a result, when does P's claim accrue? Some cases hold that it is when P first acts on the advice, others when P in fact suffers harm. The cases are not easy to reconcile, but an obvious date is the last date at which P (if well informed) could possibly have avoided the loss. When P enters into a disadvantageous transaction, the terms of which cannot later be corrected, the loss is suffered at that time, even if the loss only becomes apparent at a later date.

> *Forster v Outred and Co* (1982) After poor advice from her solicitors, Forster mortgaged her house to cover her son's debts. Subsequently her son went bankrupt and the mortgage company enforced its security. Held: Forster's action against her solicitors ran from the date of the mortgage.

However, no such general rule is stated in the cases, and it is impossible to reconcile it with some of them.

> *Bell v Peter Browne and Co* (1990) On their divorce, the Bells agreed that the house should be put into the name of the wife and that the husband's interest should be protected by registration. The husband's solicitors negligently failed to take this elementary precaution, and eight years later the former wife sold the property, extinguishing her former husband's interest. Held: the damage occurred at the date a competent solicitor should have effected a registration, even though this could have been done at any time before the former wife sold.

11.41 *Negligence: extended period* Where the primary period has expired, there is another extended period of three years from the date on which P could, with reasonable care, have discovered the loss (Limitation Act 1980, ss 14A and 14B). This is defined in similar terms to the 'primary period' for personal injury actions (**11.36**): time begins to run from the 'date of knowledge', at which P ought reasonably to have realised that D was liable and worth suing. The period is, however, subject to a longstop of fifteen years from the time D broke his or her duty, unless D is guilty of fraud or deliberate concealment. The extended period does not apply to actions which were already time-barred before this period became part of the law (18 September 1986).

Necessity

General

11.42 In very rare circumstances, D can defeat P's claim by arguing that commission of the tort against P was the lesser of two evils. For a number of reasons, the courts are very reluctant to allow this plea to succeed, even in cases where the public interest was plainly served by D's acting as he or she did. For one thing, defendants are not to be encouraged to take the law into their own hands in this way. For another, the question whether the community benefits from D's actions is quite different from whether P ought to receive compensation. So the defence may be raised to cover action taken to avoid an imminent disaster, as where D destroys P's property to create a fire break (*Cope v Sharpe (No 2)* (1912)). But the courts have always refused to allow hunger as a defence to taking food belonging to P, or homelessness as a defence to trespassing in P's empty house. To allow the plea in those circumstances, it has been argued, 'would open a door which no man could shut' (*Southwark London Borough Council v Williams* [1971] Ch 734, 744, Lord Denning MR).

The defence is narrowly confined. Any negligence by D, either in letting the emergency arise or in dealing with it, will prevent reliance on the defence. So even if the police are entitled to take extreme measures to deal with serious public disturbances, and so to that extent have a defence of necessity, that does not excuse negligence on their part.

> *Rigby v Chief Constable of Northamptonshire* (1985) The police fired a canister of CS gas into P's shop, as part of a plan to flush out a dangerous psychopath. P's shop burnt out in consequence. Held: P's action in trespass to land could be defeated by a plea of necessity, but action in negligence succeeded, as the police had not taken reasonable precautions to stop the spread of fire.

Indeed, some writers deny that necessity can ever be a defence to an action for negligence, as nothing can excuse carelessness in this context. But this seems to go too far, as necessity could surely in some cases justify D's running a risk of injury to P, which would normally count as negligence.

Medical treatment

11.43 In cases where P is unconscious, or for some other reason temporarily incapable of considering whether consent is appropriate, justifiable medical interventions will not be treated as batteries. This doctrine has also been applied in cases of mentally incapable plaintiffs. In that context it has also been used to justify intervention which seems to be in their best interests and not strictly 'necessary' (*Re F* (1990)). But this decision has attracted criticism, especially insofar as it relied on the *Bolam* rule, that the courts will not question doctors' views of what is reasonable (**4.46**). In some cases, statute authorises intervention against P's will (eg Mental Health Act 1983, s 63).

Outside those cases, it is occasionally suggested that necessity can be a defence, even where P is entirely capable and has made it absolutely clear that the intervention is not being consented to. A particularly topical area is where a hospital insists on delivering a child by Caesarean section, the mother insisting that she would rather run the risks of a natural birth. Is this a battery against the mother? In *Re MB (Caesarean section)* (1997), the Court of Appeal held that if the mother is legally competent, she is absolutely entitled to refuse her consent. The court rejected the argument that the hospital could intervene in the interests of the child, arguing that the mother's interests could not in that situation sensibly be separated from the interests of the child. Yet, on the facts, it denied the claim. The mother agreed with the doctors that the intervention was necessary, but had refused out of a phobia of needles. The court therefore considered her temporarily incompetent to take a rational decision on the matter. *Re MB* cannot be the last word on this issue; for what it is worth, the case suggests that the result may depend on the reason for the mother's refusal: phobia, religious objections, a considered weighing-up of the risks, or some other reason.

Further Reading

Relevant sections of tort reference books may be supplemented with:

Tan '*Volenti non fit injuria*: An alternative framework' (1995) 3 *Tort Law Rev* 208.

Gravells 'Three heads of contributory negligence' (1977) 93 LQR 581.

Plomer 'Judicially enforced Caesareans and the sanctity of life' (1997) 28 *Anglo-American LR* 235.

Self-test questions

1. What factors are relevant when, in a personal injury action, P invites the court to waive the primary limitation period (**11.37**)? In what circumstances is there a similar jurisdiction to waive the period for property damage (**11.41**)?

2. Can P sue P's employer for risks which were obviously inherent in the job when P took it (**11.9**)?

3. P and D set out to rob a house. Before they reach their intended target, they argue over the division of any goods they steal, and D assaults P. Can P sue (**11.27**)?

4. If P accepts a lift from D and is then injured by D's drunk driving, does D have any defence to P's action for negligence (**11.7**, **11.22**)?

5. To which torts is contributory negligence a defence (**11.18**)?

Index

347

355

357